Resisting Redevelopment

The politics of urban development is one of the most enduring, central themes of urban politics. In *Resisting Redevelopment*, Eleonora Pasotti explores the forces that enable residents of "aspiring global cities," or economically competitive cities, to mobilize against gentrification and other forms of displacement, as well as what makes mobilizations successful. Scholars and activists alike will benefit from this one-of-a-kind comparative study. Impressive in its scope, this book examines twenty-nine protest campaigns over a decade in ten major cities across five continents, from Santiago to Seoul to Los Angeles. Pasotti sheds light on an approach that is both understudied and remarkably effective: the practice of successful organizers deploying "experiential tools," or events, social archives, neighborhood tours, and performances designed to attract participants and transform the protest site into the place to be. With this book, Pasotti promises to provide a creative and novel contribution to the literature of contentious politics.

ELEONORA PASOTTI is Associate Professor of Politics at the University of California Santa Cruz. She is the author of *Political Branding in Global Cities*, published by Cambridge Studies in Comparative Politics.

Cambridge Studies in Contentious Politics

Rina Agarwala, *Informal Labor, Formal Politics, and Dignified Discontent in India*
Ronald Aminzade, *Race, Nation, and Citizenship in Post-Colonial Africa: The Case of Tanzania*
Ronald Aminzade et al., *Silence and Voice in the Study of Contentious Politics*
Javier Auyero, *Routine Politics and Violence in Argentina: The Gray Zone of State Power*
Phillip M. Ayoub, *When States Come Out: Europe's Sexual Minorities and the Politics of Visibility*
Amrita Basu, *Violent Conjunctures in Democratic India*
W. Lance Bennett and Alexandra Segerberg, *The Logic of Connective Action: Digital Media and the Personalization of Contentious Politics*
Nancy Bermeo and Deborah J. Yashar, editors, *Parties, Movements, and Democracy in the Developing World*
Clifford Bob, *The Global Right Wing and the Clash of World Politics*
Clifford Bob, *The Marketing of Rebellion: Insurgents, Media, and International Activism*
Robert Braun, *Protectors of Pluralism: Religious Minorities and the Rescue of Jews in the Low Countries during the Holocaust*
Charles Brockett, *Political Movements and Violence in Central America*
Marisa von Bülow, *Building Transnational Networks: Civil Society and the Politics of Trade in the Americas*
Valerie Bunce and Sharon Wolchik, *Defeating Authoritarian Leaders in Postcommunist Countries*
Teri L. Caraway and Michele Ford, *Labor and Politics in Indonesia*

(*continued after index*)

Resisting Redevelopment

Protest in Aspiring Global Cities

ELEONORA PASOTTI

University of California, Santa Cruz

CAMBRIDGE UNIVERSITY PRESS

CAMBRIDGE
UNIVERSITY PRESS

University Printing House, Cambridge CB2 8BS, United Kingdom

One Liberty Plaza, 20th Floor, New York, NY 10006, USA

477 Williamstown Road, Port Melbourne, VIC 3207, Australia

314–321, 3rd Floor, Plot 3, Splendor Forum, Jasola District Centre,
New Delhi – 110025, India

79 Anson Road, #06–04/06, Singapore 079906

Cambridge University Press is part of the University of Cambridge.

It furthers the University's mission by disseminating knowledge in the pursuit of education, learning, and research at the highest international levels of excellence.

www.cambridge.org
Information on this title: www.cambridge.org/9781108478021
DOI: 10.1017/9781108775700

First published 2020

A catalogue record for this publication is available from the British Library.

Library of Congress Cataloging-in-Publication Data
NAMES: Pasotti, Eleonara, 1972– author.
TITLE: Resisting redevelopment : protest in aspiring global cities / Eleonara Pasotti.
DESCRIPTION: New York : Cambridge University Press, 2020. | Series: Cambridge studies in contentious politics | Includes bibliographical references and index.
IDENTIFIERS: LCCN 2019038897 (print) | LCCN 2019038898 (ebook) | ISBN 9781108478021 (hardback) | ISBN 9781108745444 (paperback) | ISBN 9781108775700 (epub)
SUBJECTS: LCSH: City planning–Chile–Santiago. | City planning districts–Chile–Santiago.
CLASSIFICATION: LCC HT169.C52 P37 2020 (print) | LCC HT169.C52 (ebook) | DDC 307.1/2160983315–dc23
LC record available at https://lccn.loc.gov/2019038897
LC ebook record available at https://lccn.loc.gov/2019038898

ISBN 978-1-108-47802-1 Hardback
ISBN 978-1-108-74544-4 Paperback

To those affected by displacement, and those who fight to preserve a home

Contents

Illustrations

Figures

Tables

Acknowledgments

In their remarkable ability to stunt criticism with catchall branding campaigns, the powerful mayors of my first book left me with significant anxiety. How does opposition reframe, once traditional cleavages of contention have been veiled over or even invalidated by mayoral messaging? How do critics garner support, when public opinion is distracted by flashy mega-projects and the festivalization of politics? Not quite knowing how to tackle this issue, I embarked on a long trip across South American capitals searching for clues. When, along a leafy street in Santiago I noticed a kiosk selling a glossy magazine titled *Bello Barrio*, I knew I found what I had been searching for. The unlikely mobilization and impact of the neighborhood group that had issued the magazine provided the impetus for this book.

The scope of the project grew, and so did the list of individuals without whom it could not have come to light. For inspiring this project, I feel indebted to my adviser, Chuck Tilly – and on many occasions wished he was still with us, ready to provide his characteristically crystal-clear recommendations.

The power of comparison allowed me to uncover trends and variations in resistance, but I would be lying if I didn't state that I often regretted the scale of this endeavor. This was particularly the case because I did not have prior knowledge of the complex and multilayered urban contexts described in this book. Many experts, with wise theoretical insights and vital empirical advice, generously lent their knowledge and helped me better understand and research the cases. I cannot emphasize enough my gratitude to these individuals. The complete list would take several pages, but for essential help at various stages and in the different sites of this long project, I am especially grateful to: David Amaral, Chad Anderson, Sandra Annunziata, Fernando Arias, Camilo Arriagada, Leonardo Arriola, Kaydeen Banks, Emmanuelle Barozet, Eva Bernat, Elizabeth Blaney, Shauna Brail, Irene Bude, Özlem Caliskan, Rosario Carvajal, Erbatur Çavuşoğlu, Myung Rae Cho, Natalia Cosacov, Ranko Cosic, Justine Davis, Becky Dennison, Steve Diaz, Jan Dohnke, Jamie Doucette, Denise Earle, Esra Eksibalci, Muge Akkar Ercan, Abigail Friendly, Miriam Greenberg, Osvaldo Guerrica Echevarría, Mai Gredilla, İbrahim Gundogdu, Alberto Gurovich, Suzy Halajian, Kisa Hamilton, Tolga Islam, Kurt Iveson, Paola Jiron, Miguel Kanai, Christian Karl, Jeeyeop Kim, Jieun Kim, Soochul Kim, Arzu Kocabas, Gillian Kranias, Blaz Križnik, Beomchul Kwon, Jakob Lederman, Jong Youl Lee, Sergio F. León Balza, Gonzalo Maestro, Marcelo Magadan, Nat Marom, Mary MacDonald, Sandra McNeill, Georg Moeller, Pablo Monje Reyes, Paul Neill, Alicia Novick, Derya Nuket Ozer, Bae-Gyoon Park, Eusan Park, In Kwon Park, Andrea Peroni, Eliana Persky, Alison Post, Cuz Potter, Maria Carla Rodríguez, Fiona Ross, Federico Rossi, Tony Roshan Samara, Christoph Schäfer, Vera Schattan Coelho, Jefferey Sellers, Jong Gyun Seo, Michael Shalev, Kate Shaw, Susanne Sippel, Carmen Smith, Yifat Solel, Jun Won Sonn, Mario Torres, Hade Turkmen, Leonardo Vilchis, Carlos Vidania, Nicole Vrenegor, Pete White, Murat Cemal Yalçıntan, and Hani Zubida.

Further, this project could not have been completed without the superb, enthusiastic, and valiant help of these research assistants: María Elena Acevedo, Daniel Beluardo, Emily Caramelli, Andrew Zhani Cohen, Angela Erpel, Felipe Ghersa, June Hur, Dickran Jebejian, In Seon Jeong, Jaeyeon Jeong, Edward Kim, Antonio Montañés, Martin Ordoñez, Anika Riley, Alexia Sánchez, and Valentin Tazare. I am thankful for the financial support received from the University of California, Santa Cruz, which facilitated various stages of fieldwork. Last but not least, I consider myself blessed to work with the best group of colleagues and friends anyone could wish for at the UCSC Politics Department. In particular, I thank Kent Eaton, Ben Read, and Roger Schoenman for their repeated and generous help and support at various stages of this project.

Given the scope of the book, it is unsurprising that the first revised version amounted to a tome of unpublishable proportions. The loss of historical detail in the cases pained me but was a necessary compromise for readability, and I am indebted to Pamela Haag for her merciless but skilled cutting of hundreds of pages, and to Michelle Niemann for her additional editing. Thanks to Herwig Scherabon for letting me use one of the mesmerizing elaborations of gentrification data from his *Landscapes of Inequality* collection as the cover of this book. I am also grateful to Senior Editor Robert Dreesen and the entire production team at Cambridge University Press for their continued and extremely competent support. I thank three anonymous reviewers for the extensive, encouraging, and detailed feedback on the first version of this book. An author could not wish for better reviewers: Your insights were critical to making the book what it is today.

Over the decade that it took to complete this project, my family has shown more patience than I can express during the many, many months in which I was literally tied to the screen. Roger, Oscar, and Stella, you are the main reason why I am glad this project is finished. Thank you for your love and support – I look forward to lots of precious and carefree adventures together.

As an uninvited guest to these sites, my principal debt is to the activists and communities that hosted me. The work that they do requires more courage than I can describe. I have struggled deeply with how my role in these places might contribute to dynamics of displacement by making sites and practices more legible to outsiders. Notwithstanding this risk, I hope this book contributes to sharing lessons that can help us move closer to housing justice. This work is accountable to the groups and individuals who generously shared their stories and recognizes them as the primary experts whose experience I try to interpret and translate. What follows, I have learned from them, and it is to them and their fearless and vital quest that I dedicate this book.

PART I

SETTING THE COMPARISON

1

Introduction

In 2006, a group of residents in Yungay, a working-class neighborhood of low-rises in the center of Santiago, attended a public hearing organized by city officials. The neighbors had expected a perfunctory event, and attended somewhat by chance. Instead, to their surprise, officials informed participants of a plan to change zoning laws that would have dramatically augmented the construction of high-rises in their neighborhood. Residents knew that the threat was real. They had already observed waves of high-rises being built throughout the city, as the mayor pursued flagship projects and infrastructure modernization to position Santiago as a competitive center for international investment. This was taking place in the heart of a country considered the historical hotbed of neoliberalism: unions were weak, and the fiscal, planning, and taxation environments had traditionally and strongly favored developers.

Defying the odds, these neighbors, organized as Vecinos por la Defensa del Barrio Yungay (Neighbors for the Defense of the Barrio Yungay), mobilized a broad and diverse set of residents in protest. Their organization pursued a complex and multipronged strategy that relied on extensive citywide networking and lobbying. But, above all, it relied on experiential tools: it offered transformative experiences designed to attract supporters. The organization generated a full calendar of cultural activities to convene residents from different ages, economic statuses, and sexual orientations. These activities were not explicitly framed as political mobilization, and even less as protest. Residents joined tours of their neighborhood that elicited their pride in living in a unique place and alerted them to the risks of losing their quiet, tree-lined village-within-the-metropolis. The organization also led "memory workshops" and a "heritage registry" to construct the history of the barrio and elaborate its cultural significance.

This indefatigable effort to bring together diverse residents resulted in an extraordinary mobilization, and the accumulation of significant political clout. The group was able to halt new high-rises in the neighborhood through the achievement of landmark status in 2009 for 113 hectares, at the time by far the largest heritage area ever registered in Chile. The organization also achieved several institutional victories. It gained seats on the municipal council and the national civil-society council. It even managed to change the decision-making process itself by advocating for popular elections for a key municipal institution. It then began to scale up: It instituted a national league of neighborhood associations and deployed its strategies to other areas, which reshaped barrio policy at the national level. The group has continued with the same leadership, and in 2018 it extended the original heritage area by an additional 117 hectares, for a total of 230 hectares.

How was it possible that a group of residents with no prior background in activism, in a city with unsympathetic political institutions and leadership, organized and achieved such remarkable and sustained policy impact, in such a short time? Experiential tools were critical to this outcome. The group has grown in influence, and has institutionalized, yet it still relies on the original strategy of cross-cleavage mobilization, with a calendar of experiences that help construct and remind resident-participants of their ties to the neighborhood. Careful political messaging is communicated amid joyful dances, communal meals, movie screenings, and storytelling. Vecinos por la Defensa del Barrio Yungay primed neighbors for action by making the protection of their neighborhood a defining personal moment.

This book seeks to answer two key questions, implicit in the unlikely story of Yungay: How have citizens adapted resistance against urban redevelopment to profound political, social, and technological changes? And under what conditions do they reach their goals? It analyses the kind of experiential tools evident in the Yungay campaign, and many others, and the conditions under which they have an impact against urban redevelopment. The central argument made in this book is that experiential tools contribute heavily to social mobilization, especially when combined with protest legacies and broad networks. However, protests drawing on experiential strategies are most likely to have strong impacts under certain conditions: When protesters possess political allies in city government, and there is a lack of right-wing partisan alignment between their mayors and executives at higher tiers of government.

* * *

Government-led redevelopment is an enduring feature of local politics. Yet scholarly consensus holds that over the past two decades, city governments worldwide have shifted from facilitators to initiators of systematic redevelopment (see, for example, N. Smith, 2002; Uitermark, Duyvendak, & Kleinhans, 2007), to the extent that much scholarship considers "contemporary urban policy to be a form of state-led gentrification" (Lees, 2003, p. 62).[1] Political-science scholars have also emphasized the role of urban redevelopment, arguing that urban politics is above all the politics of land use for cities that compete in order to maximize their economic standing (Logan & Molotch, 1987; Peterson, 1981; Stone, 1989). These policies have been consequential and controversial. They are tied not only to development and prosperity but also to displacement and social injustice.

The impetus behind urban redevelopment observed in the past twenty years can be explained as a strategic response to new political economic contexts at the local level. Governments embraced fiscal austerity (Blyth, 2013), the pursuit of global status (Pasotti, 2009), and neoliberal policies (Brenner & Theodore, 2002) following the Thatcher and Reagan administrations, thereafter consolidated by Third Way and Washington Consensus approaches. This wave of urban redevelopment started in high-income countries but took hold even more dramatically and consequentially in many middle- and lower-income countries, especially in the aftermath of currency and real-estate crises, the weakening of organized labor, the privatization of public goods, and the ideology of holding the poor accountable (Peck, 2011; Wacquant, 2010). Urban redevelopment has benefited city coffers in both advanced and developing economies. With a neighborhood upgrade, municipalities can receive funds from a variety of sources: permits, fees, and taxes from developers; increased real-estate taxes from the overall increase in property prices; tourism; direct and indirect taxes from new high-income residents; and from

[1] Gentrification involves at least four key elements: (1) reinvestment of capital; (2) local social upgrading by incoming high-income groups; (3) landscape change; and (4) direct or indirect displacement of low-income groups (Lees et al., 2008).

investors, more likely to target in cities where their mobile, highly skilled workforce would want to live.

Regime and growth-machine theories have identified political patterns that lead to displacement and dispossession for disadvantaged groups in this urban-development process. Regime theory (Stone, 1989) identifies four regime types. "Development" regimes focus on the expansion and development of the city. To secure resources to accomplish this goal, governments rely on the local business sector, endowed with systemic power that emerges from wealth and landownership. Growth-machine theorists (Logan & Molotch, 1987) argue that in these settings land-use officials and local executives use zoning and other land-use regulations so that development benefits elite coalitions. Logan and Molotch describe how urban politics and policy-making are dominated by a coalition of "place entrepreneurs" composed of business, cultural, and government elites united by their shared interest in economic growth. This coalition maximizes rents and land values to capture the benefits of growth, as government adapts to the pressures of international competition. As a result, local growth elites emerge as hegemonic figures in political, economic, and cultural institutions (Logan & Molotch, 1987). In these cities, there is little difference between regime theory and growth-machine theory as to who governs and why.

Stone's other three regime types are all rare and fragile. The first is "middle-class progressive regimes" (identified as "progressive regimes" by Dreier, Mollenkopf, & Swanstrom, 2001), which seek neighborhood and environmental protections, and favor investment in affordable housing and urban amenities. But these regimes require particularly effective leftist political actors and are limited to small and medium cities.[2] The next type, "lower-class opportunity expansion regimes," require such considerable mass mobilization that they are not only rare but even "largely hypothetical" (Stone, 1989, p. 20). The final type is "maintenance regimes," in which local-governance coalitions act as caretaker regimes, and such regimes are both rare and short-lived.

Among the possible regimes, development regimes emerge as empirically pervasive (Altshuler & Luberoff, 2004; Domhoff, 2006; Jeong & Feiock, 2006; Logan & Crowder, 2002), and nearly all of the cases

[2] The most notable exception in the literature is San Francisco, in the US context, and a few other cities such as Amsterdam, which Fainstein (2010) identifies as (historically) relatively equitable, thanks to the rare combination of centralized revenue provision and decentralized decision-making.

examined in this book take this form. As they pursue growth at all costs, development regimes emphasize their attractiveness as investment hubs – often exemplified by how close they come to achieving global city status.

In the early 1990s, Saskia Sassen popularized the concept of the global city, by which she meant primary nodes in the world's economic network and hubs of international financial services. But even before that time, urban governments were pursuing the status of global city. These "aspiring global cities" prioritized the attraction of business investment to pursue growth and to move up in globalization indices, which in turn would attract more international investment (Gotham, 2006; Harvey, 1989; Sassen, 1994; Sirmans & Worzala, 2003).[3] Yet pro-growth coalitions in local governing regimes have also deepened inequalities and thwarted alternative governing regimes (Logan, Whaley, & Crowder, 1997). These factors invite conflict over growth. Often, however, communities facing redevelopment are too disadvantaged to mount much protest and opt instead to attract investors and align themselves with business interests, hoping thereby to obtain desperately needed infrastructural investments.

This book describes cases, in contrast, where residents threatened with displacement have engaged in resistance against redevelopment. These cases of resistance are important to study because their success is both rare and unexpected under dominant regimes and pro-growth coalitions.

While most cities continue to operate as growth machines, over recent decades urban redevelopment has tilted toward cultural-economic and consumption-based strategies. Governments shifted their focus from suburban to downtown recreation as the core of urban growth and pursued this new vision with megaprojects that included stadiums (Altshuler & Luberoff, 2004) but also extensive cultural facilities. Sharon Zukin, one of the first scholars to identify the trend, writes of the "artistic mode of production." This approach seeks economic growth by revalorizing the built environment for cultural consumption and historic preservation; promoting cultural industries to address youth unemployment; and deploying cultural meanings that value urban space and labor for their aesthetic rather than productive contributions (Zukin, 1987, p. 260; see also Hutton, 2015). Taking this a step further, the shift to cultural industries embeds a new concept of "productivity." Indeed, the activists interviewed for this project see the city as "the new factory": a site of

[3] Scholars have also referred to them as "wannabe" world cities (Lehrer 2017; Short et al., 2000).

production no longer of industrial goods but of desire, which is materialized through consumption and lifestyle (Schäfer, 2010). The shift reaffirms Castell's seminal argument that the arena of history has moved from the factory floor to the neighborhood, where people seek control not of the means of production but of collective consumption (Castells, 1983). In this "factory without walls," the entire urban fabric is the terrain of capitalist accumulation but at the same time also a stage for resistance (Negri, 1989, p. 97). The cultural consumption approach to the city sets up both an urban growth strategy and the experiential tools deployed by those who resist it.

The debate over cultural-economic urban redevelopment was sensitive to consumption-side theories that explained gentrification and redevelopment as answers to middle-class demands for downtown amenities (see, for example, Ley, 1997). But the conversation was deeply reframed by Richard Florida's intervention. According to Florida, the knowledge economy has become the main site of competition for global cities, and governments' priority should move from simply attracting investment to focusing on attracting and retaining a mobile population of highly skilled knowledge workers with amenities that this "creative class" prizes (Florida, 2002; see also Landry, 2012). This prescription puts social diversity, artistic production, and creativity at the forefront of mayors' growth agendas.

But who exactly belongs to the creative class that cities must lure by all means possible? According to Florida, the creative class includes those involved with traditional cultural management (museums, libraries, festivals, crafts, and so on), contemporary cultural art management (arts and entertainment activities, exhibition spaces, and production), media (audiovisual products, books, magazines), and design (software, digital content, advertising, architecture, and so on), as well as scientific research. Florida was criticized for his overly broad definition of creatives, and I therefore follow other scholars' preference for "cultural producers," i.e. contributors to the cultural industries who "combine cultural expression and creativity with material production, tradable goods and, to a greater or lesser extent, market-based consumption" (Montgomery, 2005, p. 340; see also Krätke, 2010; Novy & Colomb, 2012).

However the creatives are defined, governments of aspiring global cities around the world quickly embraced Florida's revolutionary growth prescription. This changed urban capitalism and, with it, urban redevelopment. It catalyzed urban redevelopment because the promotion of creative industries required a specific kind of infrastructure and to fully embrace Florida's recipe, city governments in the early 2000s vigorously appealed to creatives' consumer and cultural demands.

In this way, contemporary capitalism forges links between consumption, culture, and urban redevelopment. Socio-spatial transformations provide experiences and leisure facilities that a city can market as hip, culturally vibrant, and socially diverse. These links are so strong that the study of urban redevelopment protests yields important insights about aspects of contemporary capitalism.

* * *

The present emphasis on culture-led regeneration and redevelopment in cities also has redistributive political consequences that extend well beyond the development of physical infrastructure (Porter & Shaw, 2013).

Through redevelopment, city governments shift resources to new sectors (such as biotech, high-tech, and design) but also privilege the marketing of specific neighborhoods and the creation of cultural content for tourists (Judd & Fainstein, 1999). Municipal policies have territorial impact, not least on a neighborhood's residents (Colomb & Novy, 2016; Chetty & Hendren, 2018; Sampson, 2012). For example, creative city agendas tend to shift resources to "marketable" diversity (Boudreau, Keil, & Young, 2009), which entrenches racial and class inequalities (Atkinson & Easthope, 2009; Catungal, Leslie, & Hii, 2009; Grundy & Boudreau, 2008; Parker, 2008; Peck, 2011). Often, marketable diversity means the fetishization of ethnic diversity through the "spectacular commodification of difference" (Goonewardena & Kipfer, 2005, p. 672), primarily with events and spaces that appeal to middle-class professional tastes and their perceptions of diversity in a way that privileges some immigrant groups over others depending on their marketability (Ahmadi, 2016; Hackworth & Rekers, 2005; Kipfer & Keil, 2002). This dynamic builds on a notion that the creative class seeks out urban locations that are "authentic" and "diverse" (Peck, 2005, p. 745).

Such culture-led regenerations and redevelopment tend to promote or accompany gentrification and produce spatial inequalities; in other words, inequalities in access to urban space (Brenner, 2014). Gentrification can have positive effects, such as enhancing city centers, promoting urban densification, diluting poverty, addressing disinvestment, and increasing the local tax base. For this reason, some scholars and policymakers in the 1990s, especially, promoted gentrification as a "rising tide that lifts all boats" (Duany, 2001, p. 36; see also Musterd, De Vos, Das, & Latten, 2012). But evidence for the lifting effect of that rising tide has been thin. Instead, the overwhelming majority of scholars assess gentrification as harmful, largely because of household displacement and community conflict (Betancur, 2002). Gentrification-induced displacement can take several forms. The signal work by Peter Marcuse identified four manifestations. The two most visible types are "direct chain displacement," which refers to dislocation due to deterioration of a building or rent increase, and "direct last-resident displacement," which refers to dislocation due to physical or economic actions by landlords (such as harassment or rent increase). Important but harder to detect are two additional types of gentrification-induced displacement: "exclusionary displacement," which occurs when households lose previously available housing because it has been gentrified or abandoned, and "displacement pressure," which afflicts current residents during the gentrification of their own neighborhood and takes a few forms, including harassment, decline in access to services, and alienation (Marcuse, 1985; Zhang & He, 2018). Increased rents can lead to involuntary immobility (Newman & Wyly, 2006), when residents who want to stay put in the neighborhood are forced into overcrowded or substandard living conditions. This displacement typology applies both to residential and commercial sites (Zukin, 2008; Zukin et al., 2009).

It is difficult to quantify displacement as a consequence of gentrification, or even to define displacement consistently across scholarship (Zuk et al., 2015, p. 46; to illustrate the controversy, see, for example, Atkinson, 2002; Freeman, 2005; Newman & Wyly, 2006; Vigdor, Massey, & Rivlin, 2002). Scholars increasingly recommend a more fine-tuned understanding of mobility that considers *types* of mobility rather than simply mobility rates – that is, why people move rather than simply how much they move – to capture gentrification-led displacement (Ding, Hwang, & Divringi, 2016).

Despite these definitional and quantification challenges, most studies agree that gentrification at a minimum leads to exclusionary displacement because of a reduced pool of affordable housing, and that it can also include the direct displacement of renters (see, for example, Atkinson, 2002; Bridge, Butler, & Lees, 2012; Chaskin & Joseph, 2013; Lees, 2008; Shaw & Hagemans, 2015; Slater, 2006; Zuk et al., 2015). And, across time and space, local governments have often aided, and even led, in the systematic and institutionalized racist and classist management of housing values, as Trounstine has shown in the US case. Such government interventions can promote enduring segregation or displacement, depending on interest configurations (Trounstine, 2018). When state-led or state-facilitated gentrification takes place, low-income neighborhoods with strategic locations, usually close to downtown, are targeted to satisfy the growing middle-class demand for urban living because they offer the highest rent gap, i.e. the greatest disparity between actual value and potential value in real estate (N. Smith, 2002). They are especially vulnerable to redevelopment by pro-growth coalitions because these poor residents have little political clout and occupy land that could be put to higher-value uses (Logan & Molotch, 1987).

When a neighborhood is identified as a good candidate for redevelopment, prospective investors and municipalities can further depress actual real-estate values (Lees, Shin, & López-Morales, 2015). In a practice called blockbusting, investors attract residents viewed by existing owners as "undesirable" (because of their race or income) and then persuade existing owners to sell their property cheaply in fear that the new arrivals will start a downward price spiral. In a second common practice, redlining, municipalities label the neighborhood as "blighted," which discourages banks from funding mortgages and housing renovations, thereby making blight a self-fulfilling prophecy.

Such territorial stigmatization – through both "urban degradation and symbolic devaluation" – crucially promotes public support for redevelopment (Wacquant, 2010, p. 218). Once investors gauge that property values have hit bottom, they can buy property *en masse* directly or through agreements with the municipality, and proceed with redevelopment. This pattern, where the opportunity for profit comes through the displacement of previous residents, has been labeled "accumulation by dispossession" (Harvey, 1978). Notwithstanding important variations, the overall effect is often what Smith defines as third-wave gentrification: "retaking the city for the middle classes" to turn areas "into landscaped complexes ... based on recreation, consumption, production and pleasure as well as residence" (N. Smith, 2002, p. 443). Lefebvre's "right to the city" is rearticulated as the "right to consume the city," and "quality of life" is conflated with "quality of lifestyle" (Kern, 2010, p. 170; Rae, 2015).

Janoschka and Sequera (2016) identify four distinct sources for gentrification-related displacement, which apply also to the cases in this book. They are: (1) displacement following heritage promotion of historical city centers (e.g., Tel Aviv); (2) displacement by cultural dispossession (e.g., the appropriation of tango culture for tourism in Buenos Aires); (3)

displacement by anti-criminality campaigns (for example, Madrid); and (4) displacement by ground-rent dispossession, when capital returns to previously downgraded inner-city neighborhoods to exploit the gap between existing and potential returns on real estate (for example, Santiago, Hamburg, and Seoul). Ground-rent dispossession is the most common factor, but multiple factors can coexist. (For example, in Los Angeles, I find displacement by ground-rent dispossession exacerbated by heritage promotion and anti-criminality campaigns in downtown areas.)

The loss of housing has been identified as a critical (and the most understudied) cause for persistent and systematic urban poverty (Desmond, 2016). But actual displacement is not the most relevant variable for this study. This book is about what moves residents to protest. Therefore, residents' *perception* of displacement is a more important variable than actual displacement. As these chapters will show, different kinds of perceived displacements move residents to protest, ranging from the material loss of physical shelter, to the symbolic and emotional loss of neighborhood meaning.

Although the always-challenging task of measuring the actual extent of physical displacement is not central to my argument, I do not mean thereby to collapse all forms of displacement and argue that they have the same effects. They do not. Many Marxist scholars do not distinguish the defense of neighborhood-use values from class struggles over exploitation and surplus value. For example, Harvey argues: "Conflicts in the living space are, we can conclude, mere reflections of the underlying tension between capital and labor" (1978, p. 289). In contrast, this book recognizes the key differences between, for example, exploitation (direct, physical displacement) and symbolic dispossession (conflicts over use value). It confirms that the loss of place can be inequitable and disorienting even for residents who manage to remain, as it alienates them from the experience of their lived space and daily practices; and that the ability to stay put often comes at the cost of overcrowding or poor housing quality (Davidson, 2008; Fainstein, 2010; Freeman, 2011; Marcuse, 1985; Shaw & Hagemans, 2015; Zukin, 2010). This book invites readers to consider displacement in all of these manifestations, to achieve a richer perspective on what drives resistance.

* * *

Struggles against urban redevelopment distill many of the economic and social transformations that have inspired new perspectives on contentious politics. Scholars have examined how contemporary capitalism, and specifically austerity and neoliberalism, motivates and transforms protest (see, for example, Bennett et al., 2004; Della Porta, 2015; Della Porta & Tarrow, 2005). Yet the context of urban redevelopment is especially useful to examine protest under current capitalism, because centers of economic growth are overwhelmingly in large cities, and urban redevelopment has become a widespread primary growth strategy for cities worldwide (see, for example, Glaeser, 2000; Harvey, 1978; Sassen, 1994).

To understand protest in contemporary capitalism, we have to understand how this shift has reshaped resistance strategies available to urban residents. To that end, this book contributes to the cross-fertilization of the social movement literature – largely housed within sociology – and the cross-disciplinary urban-movement literature. Some definitions of "urban movements" prioritize a spatial community (Castells, 1983), while others focus on specific targets of action, and political contexts (Fainstein & Fainstein, 1985). Some scholars privilege informal groups over associations and NGOs (Mayer, 2003); others consider a variety of urban movements, "from counter-cultural squatters to middle-class neighborhood associations and shanty town defense groups" (Castells, 1983, p. 328), with varied strategies, including lobbying, protesting, rent strikes, squatting, and subversive forms of reclaiming.

Interest in urban movements has resurged in recent years. Translations of *The Right to the City* (Lefebvre, 1996, 2003) launched a new wave of scholarly work on social justice in the neoliberal context (Brenner, Marcuse, & Mayer, 2011; Harvey, 2008, 2010, 2012; Leitner, Peck, & Sheppard, 2007; Marcuse, 2009; Mitchell, 2003; Purcell, 2008, 2013; Soja, 2010). More recently, scholars have revisited the *Right to the City* and argued that it betrays an urban and intellectual bias (Uitermark, Nicholls, & Loopmans, 2012) and that its endorsement by institutions depoliticizes and de-radicalizes the message (Belda-Miquel, Peris Blanes, & Frediani, 2016). Indeed, as we will see in this book, claims made in the name of the Right to the City sometimes defend the particular interests of middle-class urbanites (Brenner et al., 2011) and can actually weaken and fragment broader movements (Blokland, Hentschel, Holm, Lebuhn, & Margalit, 2015).

Notwithstanding this body of work, there is still a notable lack of mutual engagement between urban-movement and social-movement scholarship (as noted by Lees & Ferreri, 2016; Lees, Slater, & Wyly, 2008; Pickvance, 2003). Recently, scholars have begun bridging the gap

(Belda-Miquel et al., 2016; Mayer, Thörn, & Thörn, 2016; Miller & Nicholls, 2013), and this book contributes to that effort, with a focus on mobilization in the context of contemporary urban political economy.

Cities are absolutely critical sites of protest. As Miller and Nichols remind us, urban institutions make many decisions affecting people's everyday lives, and city officials "enjoy wide discretion over how actual rights are distributed and regulated" (Miller & Nicholls, 2013, p. 457). For example, a constitution might grant a freedom of religion, but city officials might limit the exercise of that right by restricting the construction of worship sites with zoning regulations. Or, local zoning regulations for housing or transportation can be designed to sidestep equal-rights provisions devised by national government. Local policing choices might limit the right of public assembly. In this way, countless "governance practices make cities key arenas of struggle shaping how rights are distributed, implemented, and violated" (Miller & Nicholls, 2013, p. 458). Cities can make controversial policies, and they can also incubate networks and alliances across ideological boundaries.

Therefore, struggles over urban redevelopment are opportunities to study contention following the deep and widespread political, social, and technological changes of recent decades. Mobilizing structures that supported social movements in the 1960s and 1970s no longer offer the same ideological, material, and organizational resources. Unions have declined in membership and influence (Baccaro & Howell, 2011; Burgess, 2004; M. L. Cook, 2010; Murillo, 2001; M. Wallerstein & Western, 2000). Programmatic mass parties of the left and far left have entered a protracted phase of deep crisis (Huber & Stephens, 2001; Van Biezen, Mair, & Poguntke, 2012). In some countries, social movements spurred by austerity policies have given rise to new protest parties, often on the left (Della Porta, Fernández, Kouki, & Mosca, 2017). However, these parties have not uniformly facilitated local protest. (In some cases discussed here, they actually delegitimized it.)

These dynamics introduced significant obstacles to mobilization. Tarrow (2013) shows how the decline in references to class and labor by parties of the left, in conjunction with diminished subjective perceptions of class in popular culture, is connected to the emergence of a new, more individualized language in protests in line with fluid and atomized participation. This atomization of participation has in fact been shown to extend well beyond protest to include a wide range of forms of popular engagement (Collier & Handlin, 2009). As a result, while distinct populations may suffer common grievances, their membership is highly fragmented because members lack and sometimes even reject memberships in "integrative structures" such as unions, parties, churches, or political groups that traditionally offer collective identities, resources, and organizational structures (Bennett and Segerberg, 2012).

As traditional structures of mobilization weakened, the Internet fundamentally changed how mobilization occurs and how contentious politics unfold. Social-media communication increases protesters' efficiency and effectiveness in gathering information and resources, immensely facilitating coordination, innovation, and diffusion. Further, the Internet itself is a new arena for contention and a new public sphere. While television, radio, and the press connected one to many, and telephones connected one to one, the Internet is a platform that connects many to many and thus shatters the traditional barrier between information producers and consumers. And with all media now digital, the Internet combines information provision with social coordination, allowing viewers to react individually and collectively to new content (Shirky, 2008). A new form of mobilization has resulted, where "movements ignored political parties, distrusted the media, did not recognize [almost] any leadership and rejected all formal organization, relying on the Internet and local assemblies for collective debate and decision-making" (Castells, 2015, p. 4). Fragmented populations can find in social media a type of communication that allows them to channel their personal stories into protest movements.

Urban redevelopment is an especially fruitful context to explore contentious politics in this transformed, neoliberal context, for several reasons. Not only is redevelopment probably the most common and influential policy expression of large city governments, its planning explicitly involves public and private actors. In most other policy areas, private-sector roles and interests vary and are less transparent than those of real-estate developers and commercial entrepreneurs. Urban planning is largely under municipal (as opposed to regional or national) jurisdiction; therefore, planning choices are likely to reflect municipal priorities more reliably across the world than many other policy areas (for example, transportation, social policy or education, which often reflect political preferences of higher levels of government). Finally, urban planning is relatively more amenable to international comparison. Even when important differences exist between cities, they are more commensurate than is typically true in other policy areas, where different arrangements with national authorities make international comparisons extremely challenging. In contrast, the land-use plans, challenges, and debates of cities on opposite sides of the world often bear remarkable resemblances.

Urban redevelopment struggles give us new and vital perspectives on contentious politics. It is here that essential elements of contemporary capitalism, such as conflicts over consumption, cultural production, and spatial access and inequality, are revealed; it is in the urban context that tectonic shifts in partisan politics, the decline of unions, and the rise of digital communication are most visible.

OVERVIEW

This book starts by examining the degree to which neighborhood-level protest groups are able to organize residents and identifies factors that drive mobilization, as measured by the number of participants in a campaign's largest events. On that basis, it then analyzes factors behind variation in protest impact. To gain a more refined understanding of impact, case analysis distinguishes between various degrees of success.

What emerges from the analysis is that changes in urban governance have increasingly been matched by changes in resistance. In the cases that follow, governments seek support and legitimacy to pursue redevelopment plans, while protesters seek support and legitimacy to resist them. Governments and dissenters alike have reacted to the decline of traditional means of consensus building and mobilization by engaging in forms of persuasion that target the individual citizen and are less mediated by political institutions. Both use communication strategies that include post-political images and slogans and exclude conventional political messaging. Although these strategies have deep redistributive consequences, in rhetoric at least they often transcend previous cleavages of contention.

Instead of relying on traditional political divisions, both city governments and protesters increasingly build their connection with citizens by providing them with narratives and values that satisfy psychological needs for belonging, self-worth, or legitimacy. Notwithstanding variations, protesters and city governments are remarkably similar in how they compete to shape citizens' subjectivity, with the goal of acquiring their support.

To this aim, city governments deploy branding as a key tool for both political competition and governance, as I showed in *Political Branding in Cities* (Pasotti, 2009). This book focuses on the other side: how protesters have adapted to political changes and shifts. It finds that they increasingly deploy a set of instruments that I call "experiential tools." This addition to the repertoire of contention (Tilly, 1976) includes a wide range of activities designed to attract supporters by offering events that their targeted participants will experience as defining and transformative. Participants are attracted to action by the psychic benefits of participation, often unrelated to the political goals of the protest; and persuasion happens not through speeches but rather through experiences and self-discovery, in which emotions play a key role. Experiential tools can take many forms, but they are all instruments by which organizers seek to define and shape a community of participants. So they often take the shape of neighborhood festivals or similar communal events with hedonistic elements. They are sometimes combined with protest squatting or encampments.

This approach to mobilization is a substantial departure from the militantism historically associated with social movements, to the point that in some of the cases discussed in this book critics viewed experiential tools as "too easy" to constitute genuine protest. Far from facing significant costs or risks, participants often seemed to do little more than show up for a party.

This criticism misses the point. In the cases described here, the planning of experiential tools is among the very first steps taken by protest organizers, who see these activities as critical to snowball and sustain mobilization, and who rely on large and diverse audiences, which they attract with experiential tools, to display their clout and legitimacy to opponents and allies alike.

Experiential tools are not entirely new to social mobilization, but they are understudied, increasingly prominent, and remarkably effective at providing residents with political influence in resisting or shaping redevelopment (especially when protesters lack the support of powerful unions). What sets experiential tools apart from conventional moments of celebration in protest campaigns is that these usually hedonistic activities are not the *result* of campaigns, as scholars have observed in the past, but rather the first *tools* of mobilization, deployed to grow and shape the base of support.

The analysis that follows of twenty-nine protest cases in ten cities reveals that experiential tools are essential components for significant mobilization but need to be combined with protest legacies and/or broad networks, two well-documented factors in the contentious politics literature. Further, mobilizations based on experiential strategies are most likely to have significant impact under certain conditions: when protesters acquire *both* allies in the local council (typically, the municipal council) *and* support by a progressive mayor and/or higher tiers of government.

In addition to the novel treatment of experiential tools, this argument contributes two important results. First, it identifies a local council ally as a *necessary* condition for impact that has been previously overlooked. Second, protesters *can* circumvent mayors, specifically by exploiting partisan dealignments between local and higher-level executives; this finding alerts us to how higher government tiers can block municipal policies and thereby affect local protest outcomes, even over a policy (zoning) conventionally considered as preeminent domain of local authorities.

The remaining chapters in Part I of this book consider the theoretical contribution of the argument, explain the research design, present an overview of the results, and provide background on the ten aspiring global cities and their theoretical and empirical comparability.

Part II examines factors associated with successful mobilization. Chapter 5 analyzes cases featuring a combination of experiential tools and networks. It examines Santiago, where despite an especially adverse institutional context, protesters were able to succeed thanks to an extensive deployment of experiential tools and networks. The chapter briefly reviews two cases of weak mobilization in Istanbul, and then homes in on cases in which the deployment of experiential tools and networks led to mass mobilizations in Istanbul and Tel Aviv. Chapter 6 examines the complex role of protest legacy in squats in Seoul, Hamburg, Toronto, and Madrid. The analysis illustrates that prior protest is helpful in gaining the squat, but an enduring outcome depends heavily on organizational features and varieties of capitalism. Chapter 7 focuses on cases in which protest relied on complex judicial tools. The cases examined are Madrid's PAH Centro, as well as Los Angeles' LA CAN and TRUST South LA. In this type of protest, expertise is absolutely central. However, none of these campaigns is waged solely in the courts. Therefore, even in these cases, experiential tools play important roles, including sustaining resident engagement, publicizing concerns, and displaying clout to allies and opponents. Chapter 8 examines mobilization in three cases in Buenos Aires, where union support is strong. It shows that when unions failed to support a neighborhood organization, residents shifted their strategy to experiential tools instead.

Part III focuses on impact. Chapter 9 begins by illustrating the role of partisan dealignment, with a discussion of Buenos Aires and Santiago. Cases in these cities followed different paths to mobilization, yet in both sites protest had high impact because organizers found allies at the national level. It then illustrates the pivotal role of the councillor in single-member districts with two divergent cases in Toronto. These cases also illustrate the co-optation of the creative class by real-estate developers – an important lesson because signs indicate that co-optation will become more common. The chapter then examines impact under right-wing partisan alignment by considering cases in Istanbul and Seoul.

The empirical analysis concludes by presenting cases of protest against redevelopment that display unlikely characteristics. Chapter 10 zooms in on resistance in public housing estates, a most unlikely setting because residents are transient and vulnerable. The chapter presents two pairs of cases, in Toronto and Melbourne, each city displaying a success and a failure in both mobilization and impact. The Toronto cases show how cultural producers engaged in boosterish programming that distracted public opinion from ongoing displacement in one site, while in the other experiential tools and preexisting networks combined to foster a strong residents' voice in revitalization plans and prevented displacement. The analysis of Melbourne's estates confirms the powerful role of union support and shows how a councillor's ideology gains salience in the context of multi-member districts. Chapter 11 examines a group in the Boyle Heights neighborhood of Los Angeles that deployed a radical approach to fighting displacement: it directed its militant protest at art galleries, identified as the key culprits of gentrification. While the group had some success, it is too early to assess the overall impact of the strategy. The approach merits examination because it is an innovative, ambitious, and analytically coherent response to the threat of displacement.

The conclusion elaborates on the implications of the use of experiential tools in violent or confrontational tactics. It then examines lessons derived from the case studies that can be useful in limiting displacement, summarizing and expanding on various resistance strategies toward prevention, mitigation, and provision of alternatives to residential displacement in the face of gentrification and urban redevelopment.

2

Explaining Protest against Urban Redevelopment

Resistance against redevelopment in the neoliberal context has ranged from traditional strategies of protest to more novel forms focused on experience. My research builds on earlier works that identify civic events as overlooked but critical elements of collective efficacy. In a groundbreaking article, Sampson et al. proposed a novel paradigm to understand changes in collective action over recent decades. They argued that "collective civic engagement appears to have changed rather than declined, with sources that are organizational rather than interpersonal in nature" (Sampson, McAdam, MacIndoe, & Weffer-Elizondo, 2005, p. 675). In a monumental shift from an emphasis on individual traits in earlier social-movement studies, these scholars proposed that we focus on the density of civic organizations and what they termed "blended social action." By blended action, they meant "hybrid events that combine public claims making with civic forms of behavior" (Sampson et al., 2005, p. 673). These civic events were collective. They brought together members of the community in ways that paralleled protest events, because participants sought resources. Yet they differed from protest events because rather than expressing collective interests in a way that challenged the existing system they celebrated community (p. 676).

In a survey of 4,000 collective civic-action events in Chicago from 1970 to 2000, Sampson et al. found that such "blended social action" substituted for what they termed "sixties-style" protest. Notwithstanding their fundamental empirical and theoretical contribution, their analysis did not explain this observed shift. Even more importantly, the article invited a contextualization of how exactly "blended social action" worked, under what conditions, and when it was selected.

Independently of Sampson et al., I identified a similar trend in my own research, and wanted to explain it. I have found that what Sampson et al. call blended social action, and I call *experiential tools*, can and often do constitute protest, even if, as they observed, the events usually do not explicitly target political opponents. Experiential tools cut across the usual bifurcation of civic and protest events and, for this reason, reveal new perspectives on social movements. Events that *seem* civic actually constitute protest, for example, because they defy the use of space prescribed by the establishment and therefore enact a spatial appropriation with political ramifications. This is the case even if no protest messaging occurs at the event, or if messaging is limited to the interpretation of the event on social media by participants rather than organizers. In the most interesting deployments, the events seem civic because they are art installations (e.g., in Gängeviertel and Mullae, described in Chapters 6 and 9). But these ostensibly community-sponsored vernissages end up instead supporting the goals of a protest campaign by sheer bodily presence and the mere act of attendance. Organizers create events through the experiential approach that appear civic but that constitute protest – a protest that is protected against repression or even controversy by its very appearance as a civic event. The event becomes a moment of individual *and* collective expression.[1]

Therefore, my analysis emphatically supports Sampson et al.'s finding that the most visible function of these events is a community celebration. But even though individual membership or relational bonds are no longer the main predictors of participation, as Sampson et al. argue, it is nevertheless impossible to understand experiential tools without taking into account participants' individual traits. Indeed, experiential tools emphasize an individual participant's experience in the event rather than an explicit campaign goal. Participants primarily seek to develop and assert narratives of identity (and connect with like-minded people) rather than pursue a campaign goal, which my interviews often reveal to be secondary or even unclear to the participant. Collective efficacy is built not only from group goals but also from individual incentives that *happen* to support collective goals.

[1] In this study, I refer to collective identity as a property of individual participants, who acquire a sense of membership in or affinity toward a community or cause. A collective identity thus requires that group members develop "shared views of the social environment, shared goals and shared opinions about the possibilities and limits of collective action" (Klandermans, 1992, p. 81).

But this does not mean that the events lack political significance or valence. Government and protesters, facing similar challenges in the mobilization of support, both try to shape subjective notions of identity, belonging, and space among potential supporters. Thus, we must examine contemporary politics of redevelopment with an eye to discourses of persuasion. On an intricate landscape of winners, losers, enablers and bystanders, physical and symbolic urban makeovers are carefully managed to persuade both public opinion and players with veto power. In most cases, governments and developers engage in sophisticated marketing campaigns that stigmatize areas facing renovation and entice with dreamlike, futuristic renditions of serene, productive, and sustainable spaces and sites for the middle class and elites.

In this environment, then, the definition of what constitutes the "legitimate" and "authentic" urban experience itself has turned into a crucial terrain of struggle. The party capable of shaping and delivering the most persuasive narrative of "legitimacy" and "authenticity" (Brown-Saracino, 2010; Lakoff, 2008; Silver, Clark, & Navarro Yanez, 2010; Zukin, 2010) gains political clout. This in turn can facilitate the mobilization of the support needed to claim city space, its use, and its meaning. Far from politically immaterial, as Sampson et al. might argue, civic events and their production of the urban experience and subjectivity – while rooted in symbols, discourses, or everyday practices – significantly affect how different actors are able to influence redevelopment and, consequently, the redistribution of quite tangible resources and space.

My emphasis on the interaction between material and immaterial dimensions of displacement builds on current protest research that sees both dimensions at work in the struggle over subsistence, such as shelter security: "when people perceive that markets have put relationships with subsistence goods at risk, material and symbolic worlds are both at stake; citizens take to the streets to defend not only their pocketbooks but also their perceptions of community" (Simmons, 2016, p. 3). This book seeks to uncover tools that organizers use to articulate and invigorate that perception of community and neighborhood identity – the immaterial dimensions of material struggles and protest.

Branding is important, certainly. Branding is an approach to persuasion that goes beyond language to encompass the design of experiences for the target participant (whether customer or voter) that augment brand loyalty. Transliterated from marketing to politics, the commitment is to a politician and their plans (Pasotti, 2009). Yet, as this book shows, groups fighting displacement *also* pay close attention to branding, a shift that gives cultural producers a special advantage in protest struggles. As Hamburg artist and activist Christoph Schäfer argued, "If subjectivity is the new front of capitalism, then artistic practices get, potentially, more power" in protest (Schäfer, 2010). The new context puts artistic practices and cultural agents in a privileged position to shape protest and political participation.

Experiential tools can be understood as a kind of branding. As in branding, the sharing of experiences that takes place with experiential tools facilitates sharing cognitive frames that in turn inform beliefs and values and motivate action. Thus, experiential tools heighten participants' enthusiasm and commitment by providing experiences that help them define their identity, give them a sense of self-worth, and embody the values that they want to project. Donatella Della Porta (2011, p. 273) discusses protest camps and occupations, for example, which can be designed as experiential tools, and finds that these events constitute "free spaces" that encourage participants to socialize, "allowing feelings of solidarity to grow with the awareness [of the struggle]." Participation in these events has a fundamentally social and hedonistic dimension, as people visit the encampments for morning coffee, for an alternative dinner or to enjoy a concert. Participation is thus "seen as gratifying in itself, as it becomes part of everyday life" (Della Porta, 2011, p. 273). She also highlights the creative aspect of protest, where participants find efficacy and meaning in their contribution of a new slogan or banner, leading them to see these as essential moments of personal growth that introduces "a different kind of life" (p. 274). We will see similar language in case studies here, including Tel Aviv, Istanbul's Gezi Park, and Seoul. As Della Porta concludes, these activities and events – by creating alternative and creative spaces – constitute protest but also create resources for different forms of protest.

Indeed, experiential tools generally do serve a variety of purposes. Their first and primary goal is recruitment of participants and allies. Successful experiential events and activities are targeted to suit broad tastes and transmit catchall values and messages. In the cases that follow, experiential tools are deployed both effectively (when they inspire participation among different groups of residents, stakeholders, and veto players) and ineffectively (when they fail to elicit cross-cleavage participation). Thus, the mere adoption of experiential tools – no matter how creative – is far from a guarantee of substantive mobilization.

A second goal is to promote solidarity among participants, a sense of neighborhood or movement membership that sometimes takes place before the more explicitly political phase of protest. Third, experiential tools promote loyalty and commitment to the cause. Fourth, experiential tools can be the occasion to present specific initiatives by organizers (for example the restoration of a monument that is important to the identity of the neighborhood; or activities that support the group's vision of the neighborhood; or the presentation of alternatives to government-supported redevelopment). Finally, they can be the occasion where core activists coalesce around a challenge and get energized by its success. One or two events can be selected as emblematic and become persistently linked with the protest group.

WHEN EXPERIENTIAL TOOLS AID MOBILIZATION

Experiential tools do not always succeed. My research finds that they tend to be successful in mobilization under certain conditions and when used in particular ways.

They are successful when protesters use as many types of experiential tools as possible, from among the four major categories. These categories are *events*, which range from festivals with family activities (as illustrated in Santiago and Hamburg) to encampments (the protest in Tel Aviv and Gezi Park); *archives* (such as in Toronto's Lawrence Heights, as well as Santiago and Hamburg); *tours* (such as in Santiago); and *performances* (such as games in Hamburg, or street theater in Los Angeles).

Experiential events are usually the first deployed, and the most common. They often take the form of communal dinners, block festivals, barter markets, or concerts. They require organizational skills and benefit from creative input. These tools bring together residents in a joyful and hopeful atmosphere. They lay the foundation for political efficacy because they display the size of the community potentially ready for political action. This is an important message internally and externally to a variety of actors, both allies and opponents.

The second most effective and common tool is the archive: a collection of residents' stories assembled in a variety of possible formats. The archive moves participants from the hedonistic or consumerist phase of the event to an activity that more consciously offers and demands resident participation. Storytelling is a powerful political catalyst for action because it helps orient the individual story (here, typically of a resident's "threatened place in the neighborhood" through displacement) in the context of systemic analysis, thereby overcoming a fundamental obstacle to political participation.

The other two experiential tools are ancillary and are often present in cases that rely most elaborately and extensively on experiential tools. They usually involve the most support from cultural producers because of the skills they require. The third most common type, neighborhood tours, usually requires didactical skills and a substantial knowledge of the history of the neighborhood. Often led by teachers, tours can provide more detailed information to prospective participants (as well as the media, allies, and potential political supporters) about the neighborhood and ongoing processes of displacement.

Performances, the fourth type, are relatively rare because they are more complex and require notable artistic skills. They involve the highest levels of irony and defamiliarization, and most intensively utilize cultural producers. Performances can range from local versions of games such as Monopoly, to street theater, or other playful expressions of the concept and costs of displacement. These stir participants' attention, and commitment. They also effectively encapsulate the issues of concern in a format that is attractive to the mass media and general public. While they are the hardest to deliver, performances can be very helpful in promoting an issue.

In a few case studies discussed here, the types overlap. For example, in Gängeviertel, the key experiential tool was an occupation set up as an art exhibit in the buildings that protesters sought to gain. This was both an experiential event, because it attracted potential participants to come together and enjoy the art exhibit, and also a performance that used irony to attract media attention. The fact that the "occupiers" were pieces of art rather than people was meant to shock the public and authorities into reflection on the implications of displacement for artists. It achieved that goal, stirring a wave of mass-media coverage and public discussion.

The most successful cases use a variety of experiential approaches, across all four types. Organizers typically start with events, then move on to archives, and eventually to tours and performances. The four types aid protesters by building visibility, networks, legitimacy, and political clout. My cases do not clearly indicate whether the relationship between different types of tools is additive or more complex. However, a positive relation does emerge between the sheer number of tools utilized and the likelihood of success. The four types are not mutually exclusive but mutually reinforcing, and the choice does not depend on political context.

* * *

A successful deployment of experiential tools resonates with target participants. It echoes neighborhood values and narratives. In deploying the concept of resonance, I build on theories related to framing (Benford & Snow, 2000; Chong & Druckman, 2007; Hajer, 1995; Steinberg, 1998). As we learn from Snow and Benford (1988), to be resonant, frames must fit with existing beliefs of potential recruits, involve empirically credible claims, be compatible with their life experiences, and fit with narratives they tell about their lives. These same concerns apply neatly to experiential tools.

In addition, the emotional dimension of resonance is critical: to succeed, the message and content of the collective identity must stimulate feelings of pride, hope, and even joy in the target population. Outrage is the rare negative emotion associated with experiential tools, but successful mobilization cases couple outrage with the positive portrayal of alternatives.

Resonance is typically pursued through an appeal to historical heritage, which can be based on architectural patrimony, or on the legacy of a particular economic activity (e.g., the neighborhood of the port, or of metalworkers). It might rely on the area's historical role in the city (e.g., the first settlement, the first destination for immigrants, or the ancient ghetto), or of a particular cultural or civic tradition (e.g., the reference site for tango). These interpretations of neighborhood heritage by protesters often clash – sometimes openly and blatantly – with the branding operations of governments and real-estate developers, who build legitimacy for their redevelopment plans by persuading the public of enticing new (or revisionist) visions for the area.

In especially interesting cases, the narrative of historical pride is based on traits that were earlier considered stigmas. In these cases, organizers engage in a form of storytelling meant to reappropriate the trait and turn it from a flaw into an object of pride and honor, to stimulate feelings of worth, respect, and confidence. This is what Norton (1988, pp. 89–90) calls "trait-stripping." Norton discusses "liminars," groups seen to be living on the margins of society. These groups formally belong to the polity yet are not thought to embody that polity's core norms. Mainstream voices tend to threaten, ostracize, and stigmatize them. Through trait-stripping, the stigmatized group reappropriates in its label, language, and visual expression the trait at the core of the stigma and turns it into a statement of pride (as illustrated by the reappropriation of the n-word by African-American communities).

For example, some organizers put forth the core trait of their neighborhood as *picante* ("naughty"), or highlight its tradition as a red-light district. These appropriations turn the sites from places of marginality into places of experimentation, possibility, openness, intense life experiences, and antiestablishment adventure. This rhetorical approach is typical of neighborhoods that I identify as especially resilient because of their marked vulnerability to gentrification due to enduring stigmatization. Here, organizers exploit neighborhood stigma and even foster perceptions of disorder because such perceptions deter gentrification (Herzer, Di Virgilio, & Rodríguez, 2015; Hwang & Sampson, 2014).

* * *

Successful experiential tools target residents of all social profiles, in a variety of ways. The archives use individual storytelling that fuses anecdotal and personal experiences with the systemic dynamics of displacement. Individual stories are assembled into a collective expression that ranges from a wall decoration, to a virtual repository with online stories and interviews, to a museum filled with items that neighborhood residents have volunteered. When the archives' items are produced or provided only by intellectual elites, in the form, for example, of an exhibition, the tool does not provide the same psychological effects of awareness, self-identification, commitment, and, ultimately, mobilization.

The perception of grassroots participation matters in other experiential tools as well. With events, for example, residents' perceptions of collaborative and inclusive approaches to decision-making, management, and even provision of the events are associated with broader mobilization. Tours are not typically grassroots in their delivery, as they are devised by protest organizers. But when successful, they include grassroots components in their content, message, and itinerary (for example, linking narratives to individual residents).

With experiential tools, the process of place-making is infused with emotional content that, to succeed, must be perceived as emanating from the contributions of residents across many different cleavages. The breadth of representation translates into legitimacy and political clout for the protest group. Organizers are aware of the beneficial impact of diversity and inclusiveness on both motivating their internal membership and supporting their claims to legitimate representation outside the neighborhood.

At the same time, the management of successful experiential tools is not participatory. In a wide range of settings and types of protests, experiential tools are managed hierarchically, with clearly identifiable protest leaders. While at times groups strive to present an aura of horizontal decision-making, this is not associated with strong and sustained experiential programming or, for that matter, successful impact and mobilization. Even with anarchic occupations – the main setting where decision-making is horizontal – the process is far from spontaneous and relies instead on participants' internalization of strict procedures, usually derived from prior protest experiences.

* * *

Finally, successful experiential tools are carefully documented and avoid immediate political references. There are many venues for documentation. Successful experiential tools invite representation on traditional media. Yet social media introduces new forms of grassroots participation by allowing fragmented populations to channel their personalized stories into sustained protest movements. This phenomenon, which Bennett and Segerberg call "connective action," emerges when dense, complex, and even redundant social networks construct physical and virtual associations and determine their scale, speed, endurance, and impact (Bennett & Segerberg, 2012). For Bennett and Segerberg, connective action therefore emerges as an alternative to collective action and is based on digitally personalized action frames – meaning the micro transactions of participants who tweet, message, tag, and thereby share their stories and encourage others to participate.

Bennett and Segerberg identify three ideal types to explain how organizations and social networks interact. The cases discussed in this book largely fall into their first and second categories – organizationally brokered collective action and organizationally enabled connective action – because there are always *leaders* who initiate and sometimes tightly control communication. (Only cases in Istanbul and Tel Aviv resemble their third type, where social-networking technology platforms directly take the role of political organizations of mass protest.)

Groups that organize the campaigns described in this book usually rely on Facebook pages, moderated by leaders and often closed in membership, as well as websites and blogs whose content is carefully managed, and even other more traditional mass-communication outlets such as a streaming video channel, a radio program, or a local newspaper. With these tools groups could document experiential tools on a variety of mass media that they actually controlled and display logos and visual or content cues to reinforce membership with the group.

Yet the pace of technological change over the decade of research conducted for this book profoundly affected protest: Digital media evolved from broadcast instruments for neighborhood groups to sites of multiple and complex functions. The evolution in technology allowed media management to go from top-down (controlled and administered by protest organizers) to participatory. This shift toward grassroots production of communication can be problematic because successful experiential tools are managed closely by organizers who exercise message control.

Close attention is dedicated to the style and presentation of these media, so critical to the group's own branding. Experiential tools are initially presented as primarily social and only secondarily as political moments. The emphasis is on the activity, which elicits positive feelings such as joy, hope, belonging, and hipness. Participants, we know from neuropsychology, are attracted to and seek association with coolness because they anticipate the social reward they can get in their respective milieu. They embrace effective campaign brandings as extensions of themselves (Quartz & Asp, 2015).

Political goals are not imposed from above but rather emerge out of the self-discovery that comes from experience. Participants' perception of coming to a political stance through self-discovery as opposed to instruction significantly elevates their level of commitment (Aronson, 1999), which is further heightened if the experience involves self-sacrifice (Grant, Dutton, & Rosso, 2008). Rather than putting participants in a passive, listening position, a successful experiential tool actively engages them, and even requires some kind of contribution. This indirect persuasion often deliberately uses irony. As Bertolt Brecht understood, such forms of defamiliarization intrigue the audience and shock it into questioning and critically observing underlying conditions.

Although a core of participants with a keen understanding of the political issues is essential for recruitment into protest-management positions, many more participants in experiential events are not fully aware of the goals or strategies of the protest. They are attracted to the events for their own individual psychic benefit, which is related to building self-worth, affiliating with social groups or broadly defined missions, creating a self-narrative, or connecting with peers and potential peers.

Organizers often argue that more participants are attracted to entertainment events than to political rallies and thus avoid overt politicization. Several of them specifically state their concerns about co-optation by political parties and therefore bar elected officials from any involvement with mobilization and membership. Instead they deploy experiential tools to publicize grievances and allow participants to come together to challenge the government and find energy and sustenance in the experience of community and solidarity. Archives are interesting instances in this respect because while the content of biographical storytelling is usually apolitical, participants draw connections in the process between their experiences and the systemic factors that motivate the protest. Yet even at this stage there are plenty of participants who contribute stories that bear no obvious connection to the ongoing resistance against displacement.

In contrast, performances and tours tend to come later in the mobilization strategy and are more explicitly connected to the protest. Tours usually tell stories about evictees, buildings, or blocks that are undergoing demolition. Performances utilize irony and defamiliarization (e.g., with games) or direct impersonation (e.g., with street or popular theater), and thus the novelty of the presentation attracts participants or media and elite attention as much as the message.

* * *

In combination, and when deployed successfully to mobilize participants, experiential tools construct or reconstruct neighborhood identity to fit with organizers' goals and strategies.

Following the wave of urban uprisings in the 2000s (Mayer, Thörn, & Thörn, 2016), scholars have renewed their focus on the collective experience in iconic urban locations as spaces of contention, chosen for their symbolic dimension (Tahrir Square, Zuccotti Park, etc.). I build on this scholarship, although my work focuses distinctively on the neighborhood. The emphasis on place-as-rhetoric connects the location of protest to strategic communication. Endres and Senda-Cook persuasively explain how place becomes an inherent component of the protest message. According to their account, protesters can build on preexisting meanings associated with a site, or challenge (and temporarily reconstruct) a dominant meaning, or repeatedly build a new meaning by continuous reference to a specific place (Endres & Senda-Cook, 2011). Confirming their argument, several of these approaches appear in the case studies here.

Neighborhood and neighbor, of course, are both social constructs. Organizers construct places often in the spirit of Hobsbawm and Ranger's *Invention of Tradition* (Hobsbawm & Ranger, 1983), to the point that observers have sometimes criticized organizers for the lack of "authenticity" and historical accuracy. The point of experiential tools is not historical accuracy but, rather, to motivate attendance and pride in the neighborhood, which primes political efficacy.

Political scientists have examined how the social construction of neighborhood often defies official borders (e.g., Sampson, 2012; Wong, 2010). In geography and sociology, scholars have developed the concept of "scene" (Leach & Haunss, 2009; Silver et al., 2010). Scenes have a distinct culture and fluid boundaries, and they emphasize the role of physical space in social movement action. This makes the concept useful in this book's analysis. While Leach and Haunss present scenes as more likely to emerge among left-radical groups, the cases below show that they can emerge out of a variety of ideological settings. Most important here is that scenes rely on community-specific cultural consumption that makes them especially effective at mobilizing participation. As Leach and Haunss (2009, p. 270) argue, "movement scenes serve as a gateway to active engagement in the movement – a low-pressure context in which people are exposed to movement norms and then feel drawn to make greater commitment due to consistency pressures." Experiential tools thus curate scenes that integrate political action with personal life, blending everyday living with political expression. For example, participating in a protest is also a moment of self-definition, and participating in a campaign can reveal to the attendee alternative social options.

Further, in both experiential events and scenes, identity construction is centered in the symbolic, physical, and social space. In both approaches what is essential is not the everyday per se but, rather, the focus on *practice* of a lifestyle that expresses a specific neighborhood identity, political belonging, and dissent. My emphasis on experience (with experiential tools) highlights precisely this aspect.

The term "neighbor" itself invites scrutiny and suggests exclusions almost intrinsically. In cases in this book, activists appropriate the term to define their own version of the legitimate and engaged resident. As Hernández points out in the case of Buenos Aires (but it holds in other cases as well), the neighbor connotes a resident who is politically relevant. These actors exercise decisive leverage, and the discourse of neighbor lets them "appear as apolitical" and with a "first-hand knowledge about the reality of the city," which legitimizes them as claimants before the government (Hernández, 2013, p. 51). The notion of neighbor should therefore be treated critically because precisely in its powerful cross-cleavage valence it can obscure important tensions and differences among stakeholders.

The prominence of the (ostensibly) apolitical voices of neighbors is unsurprising in the current mobilization environment. The effect of unions in popular mobilization is widely acknowledged (Castells, 1983; Collier & Handlin, 2009; J. Smith, 2001). Yet, today, mobilization increasingly takes place without connections to unions, political parties, or traditional media. The present project contributes to scholarship on alternative approaches to popular organizing (Silva, 2009) and reveals that experiential tools are especially likely to be deployed in contexts where traditional mobilization structures are weak or unwilling to provide support for the struggle. Therefore, while experiential tools might not be entirely new, their role has gained prominence in the many sites where union membership and influence has waned.

Experiential tools do more than fill the gap left by union organizing, however. The shift from an industrial to service economy has important repercussions for contentious politics because potential protest participants are more likely to be service providers. This means that they are inherently involved in the creation of experiences, whether for businesses (e.g., in financial services or infrastructural support) or for consumers (e.g., in entertainment or education). By the very nature of their jobs, service-sector workers share a deep understanding of experience provision and therefore constitute an especially well-predisposed audience to be persuaded by experiential tools. Service-sector workers and the creators of experiential tools, in one sense, speak the same language.

In constructing and reconstructing neighborhood identity, cultural producers emerge as important and understudied political actors. Because of their educational and professional background, creative producers are especially endowed with the skills suited to the creation and deployment of experiential tools (Novy & Colomb, 2012). In most successful instances of mobilization, creatives are part of the original group of organizers. They are residents (and therefore have local networks and ties), often underemployed (and therefore are available for protest), and have relevant technical expertise.

Many cultural producers are also eager to participate because culture-led growth, paradoxically, often negatively redounds on cultural producers themselves, threatening them with spatial exclusion and economic marginalization. In addition to rising real-estate costs, artists and art organizations face funding challenges wherever neoliberal cultural policies slash resources for grassroots organizations and shift them toward competitive grants that pressure artists to form boosterish partnerships with businesses (McLean, 2014). Participants in "indie" subcultures need central and cheap locations and thus must choose between displacement or fighting for their space in the city (Boudreau, Keil, & Young, 2009; Shaw, 2013a).

Hence the focus here is not on the economic contribution of cultural producers to urban growth (Grodach, 2013; Silver & Miller, 2013) but rather on their impact as political actors, which comes from their status in a culture-led growth paradigm. In this context, of course, cultural producers do not behave as a monolith (Bain & McLean, 2012; Leslie & Catungal, 2012). Reactions range from leadership in radical protest, to co-optation by real-estate developers at the expense of lower-income residents left behind by culture-led growth. In most cases, within the same protest campaign, some cultural producers at least implicitly support redevelopment plans, while others oppose them. At times cultural producers are squarely in the leadership of protest (Hamburg and Seoul); at other times they are important partners and supporters (Santiago and Los Angeles). Cultural producers who support redevelopment plans are often also eager to publicly distance themselves from those policies, while in fact their marketing promotes the legibility of previously off-limit neighborhoods, thereby enabling access by outside elites (Buenos Aires). At times, cultural producers risk displacement and yet witness protest from the sidelines (Melbourne). Some lucky few are co-opted beneficiaries of gentrification (Toronto). At other times, artists who are deeply critical of redevelopment policies find the best strategy for resistance in place-branding and institutional infiltration (Seoul's Mullae). Experiential tools deployed against displacement also risk attracting an audience of outsiders that could undermine the long-term goal of keeping the area affordable; and both activists and artists face the conundrum concerning what audience their experiential tools actually targets and benefits. Among the cases in this book, nowhere are cultural producers more divided on this issue than in the case of Los Angeles' Boyle Heights, where some are key partners in a protest through social practice art, while others run the galleries that are the protest's main targets.

* * *

With its analysis of experiential tools, this book makes multiple contributions to our understanding of mobilization. First, its interpretation of experiential tools in mobilization turns some social-movement theory on its head: collective entertainment, in the form of festivals, games, or other ludic activities, is no longer the *result* of successful urban movements (Castells, 1983) but rather a key *tool* of movements, for mobilization and protest action.

I do not mean to say that experiential tools were never deployed in earlier cases. Yet the rise to prominence – and the observed effectiveness – of this approach in recent years is remarkable. Moreover, interviewees who were involved in experiential campaigns emphasized that this approach to protest was new to them and to their cities, and consistently described it as a radical departure rather than a modification or adaptation of earlier strategies. These opinions find confirmation in the literature, where Hamburg, Santiago, and Seoul see the most dramatic shifts from militancy to experiential protest. (On militancy legacy in these cities, see, for example, Birke, 2014; Davis, 2011; Espinoza, 1998; Garcés, 2002; Herrmann, Lenger, Reemtsma, & Roth, 1987; J. Y. Lee, 1990; Lehne, 1994.)

The approach of experiential tools builds on Snow et al.'s crucial contribution of "frame alignment processes" (Snow, Rochford, Worden, & Benford, 1986, p. 464), by which they mean the processes that social-movement organizations use to align their interpretations with those of their target audiences, to increase mobilization or support. In both approaches, tools are successful when they "resonate" – when they offer "believable and compelling" (Snow et al., 1986, p. 477) renditions of a given concern. Yet, unlike frames, which focus on verbal, written, or visual communication, experiential tools produce lived experiences. They thus combine frames with the bottom-up tools of personal storytelling (Polletta, 2006) and the political action rooted in the physical and emotional interactions of the neighborhood (Auyero, 2003).

This book also fills gaps in the existing scholarship, which explores how a movement grows and scales up, but does not sufficiently explain *why* participants are actually moved to join protests (Beissinger, 2007; Kuran, 1995; Lohmann, 1994). I show how cultural producers help to mobilize participants with the attraction of memorable experiences.

This contribution is even more relevant in the age of social media. Bennett and Segerberg explain the fragmented, individualized, and fluid nature of participation in social media based on personal action frames. However, they go too far in arguing that this connective logic "does not require strong organizational control or the symbolic construction of a we" (Bennett & Segerberg, 2012, p. 748). Gerbaudo provides an important corrective in explaining how influential Facebook and Twitter admins and activists set the scene for "a process of symbolic construction of public space which facilitates and guides the physical assembling of a highly dispersed and individualized constituency" (Gerbaudo, 2012, p. 5), thereby offering an account of how Bennett and Segerberg's atomized crowd is actually able to coalesce into a coherent identity.

In this important debate between the atomized notion of participation advanced by Bennett and Segerberg, and the emphasis on collective identity advanced by Gerbaudo, this book returns back to questions of instrumentality and materiality. Scholars in this debate tend to consider expressive and instrumental communication as opposites, but with experiential tools, expressive communication *is* instrumental communication, at every step of the way. It is instrumental to supporters, who seek participation for the psychological benefits of belonging and expression; and it is instrumental to organizers, who craft and share specific visions of collective identity for a neighborhood to build legitimacy and clout.

Further, while the virtual sphere has undeniably grown into a critical space of action and identity formation, we ought to keep in mind that physical space is equally important, as are the material practices and objects that constitute experience. With experiential tools, organizers express a material dimension of belonging, whether in everyday routines or exceptional events; whether in the form of shared food and music in a festival, or artifacts and objects, such as documents, archives, games, and even the act of walking as a group on a neighborhood tour. The personalization of participation that Bennett and Segerberg describe through digitally personalized action frames also takes place in actual neighborhoods, outside of social-media networks. In the cases that follow, organizers facilitate participants' contribution of their individual stories through local archives. The personalization of participation, in these cases, happens in the tangible, hands-on contribution of physical documents such as letters, diaries, photographs, or other storytelling objects. Technological advances, no matter how transformative, should not cause us to forget the relevance of material artifacts to social coordination (Hutchins, 1995).

THE ROLE OF NETWORKS AND PRIOR PROTEST

The struggles examined in this book unfold within the context of wider institutional, geographical, and social controversies. A discussion of these wider struggles for each case is beyond the scope of the book. I will comment on these related struggles when it is especially germane to the case at hand, but readers should be aware generally that none of the campaigns I discuss, even the ones that seem most limited in scope, are only about residential displacement in a specific neighborhood. The best way to manage this complexity has been to focus on the *relational structure* of the groups I examine.

Networks play a pivotal role in coordinating important activities and tasks in social movements (Castells, 2015; Diani & McAdam, 2003; McAdam, 1999; Routledge, 2003; J. Smith, 2001; Tarrow, 1998; Tarrow & McAdam, 2005; Tilly & Wood, 2015). In my cases, social networks perform a variety of functions. They allow organizers to build legitimacy, recognition, and clout. They help mobilize and allocate resources, especially organizational resources such as infrastructure or contacts across groups. They circulate information about campaigns or threats, and current responses. Networks also promote the sharing of competences and strategies for protest, including experiential strategies. Indeed, some groups, such as the one in Santiago, make strategy diffusion a critical goal. Further, and this was visible across all successful mobilization cases, dense networks promote the development of shared collective identities, expand recruitment, and solidify long-term commitment from both individuals and organizations.

Of course, networks have these benefits when they develop from and are motivated by shared goals, worldviews, and sometimes even collective identities (Mische, 2008). That in itself is a great challenge for groups. In some cases (e.g., Los Angeles), groups initiate campaigns already embedded in preexisting and dense organizational networks. In others, groups start in relative isolation, or with just a couple of organizational connections. In the most interesting cases (e.g., Santiago), groups are responsible not only for the campaigns but also for the activation of networks.

Some networks link individuals, and others link organizations. At the individual level, scholars agree that dense social relationships facilitate participation in social movements, that prior social ties are critical to recruitment, and that social settings are critical to the emergence of movements (Diani & McAdam, 2003; McAdam, 1999). In resistance against urban growth, links between organizations are even more relevant. Opposition is most often associated with existing organizations (Logan & Molotch, 1987, pp. 134–139) that can train resistance leaders, identified in scholarly literature as "anti-growth entrepreneurs" (Dreier 1996; Henig, 1982; Meltzer & Schuetz, 2010; M. Schneider & Teske, 1993; Shaw, 2013b).

In the present analysis, I consider both aspects of social networks. The networks that I observe vary in the degree of their formal organization, ranging from explicit coalitions (in several cities, such as Los Angeles or Madrid) to social milieus (in Seoul), or both (in Hamburg, where both the artists' milieu and the Right to the City coalition play key roles). Individuals may also be linked by social networks based on indirect ties that are generated by their joint involvement in specific events, prior to any face-to-face interaction (in Tel Aviv).

Due to the variety of cases, this book does not differentiate when it comes to network cohesion. Scholars distinguish between social movements (characterized by densely connected networks of organizations that share both interests and strong feelings of collective identity) and coalitional processes. In coalitional processes, groups collaborate in the context of a specific goal, sharing material and symbolic resources. However, such collaboration is driven by instrumental logic rather than identity, and it does not necessarily continue after the campaign is concluded (Diani, 2005).

For my purposes, *network breadth* is the most important variable. Often, campaign goals are specific and bound by both time and space. Typically, neighbors simply seek to stop or alter the zoning in their neighborhood, or to stop a wave of new construction, or to secure just compensation for their displacement. In such issue-based campaigns, whether networks manifest as coalitional processes or as social movements does not make a visible, systematic difference in either mobilization or impact – but breadth does, primarily because it communicates the political clout of the group.

Therefore, this project contributes to recent work that emphasizes local collective action rather than the more prevalent scholarly emphasis on the macro-dimensions of social movements. While much is to be learned from broad societal perspectives, this book embraces McAdam and Boudet's (2012) exhortation to think about actors as engaged in (often isolated) *instances of collective action*, rather than social-movements industries (McCarthy & Zald, 1977).

Groups may become part of movements through the important avenue of institutionalization, which happens when groups develop a social base and bureaucracy that will survive beyond the leadership of its founding members. Such institutionalization is rare in the cases I discuss, because most of the campaigns have limited scope and time horizons. However, some groups do achieve institutionalization. In so doing, sometimes they change legal status, for example registering as a foundation in order to better compete for government funding. They also institutionalize by establishing regular sites for outreach, recruitment, education, and advertisement of grievances, often in collaboration with centers of academic scholarship. In these cases they organize conferences, workshops, and even schools that offer meeting venues to pursue the group's goals and turn the group into a regular voice in the debate over neighborhood policy and displacement. Such institutionalization is an important prerequisite for moving the group from isolated and specific campaigns to a broader, policy-oriented approach. It is also critical to expanding and solidifying networks with sister organizations and is associated with the growth of alliances into sustained coalitional processes and movements.

However, the potential for upscaling is limited. Specifically, organizers in these groups are not necessarily the "rooted cosmopolitans" of Tarrow's transnational movements, who are active in domestic civil society and politics (Tarrow, 2005; Wood, 2012). I find that transnational activism has limited effect on both mobilization and impact because neither international coalitions nor validation by international bodies translate into local political clout, and zoning is largely ruled at the local level.

* * *

Within organizational networks, it is important to consider the variation among neighborhood groups. Several associational types are discussed in the chapters that follow, and three are especially important. First, of course, are the neighborhood associations that are the topic of this book. While they vary considerably, these groups always (with the one exception of Melbourne) begin without input from a political party. When recruiting, these groups steer away from party affiliation to maintain grassroots credibility and avoid alienating any potential participant.

A second type of neighborhood organization is the preexisting tenant, owner, and/or business association. These organizations vary in partisan alignments and privilege quality-of-life issues. In Madrid and Buenos Aires, national governments promoted forms of these associations during democratic transitions. In Madrid, these organizations became the conduit for specific political parties. Often, the preexisting association and groups resisting displacement have a tense relationship, as they challenge each other for leadership in neighborhood representation. Preexisting associations are generally more favorable to redevelopment and to ongoing changes in the neighborhood (above all, to gentrification). In fact, the resident groups that I discuss often arise precisely in light of the perceived inaction of these preexisting associations. The older associations, however, play interesting roles on the neighborhood political landscape because they enjoy better access to funding. Their funding makes them attractive allies for newcomers such as the groups I describe – thereby initiating a conflicted relation based on both co-optation and competition (see, especially, Madrid).

A third type is formed by the government or developers in response to neighborhood groups that advance resistance. These shadow organizations have similar names and allege similar motivations – to act in support and aid of residents – while in fact these organizations' primary goal is to promote redevelopment. These organizations are often involved in negotiating individual compensation claims, which contribute to a divide-and-conquer strategy by the government or developers: targeted compensation sows divisions and mistrust among affected residents. This approach was apparent in Istanbul, and in Buenos Aires, where gentrifying commercial interests formed a neighborhood group.

A wide range of submunicipal arrangements also deserve mention as neighborhood associations. In contrast with residents associations, submunicipal units are clearly political and administrative government institutions, and usually reflect political majorities in city council. These institutions are important because they are often protest organizers' first institutional sites of contact. In several cases, organizers use these arenas to obtain information, learn about political allies or opponents, and call their issues to the attention of institutions (Parque Lezama in Buenos Aires, for example). The institutional power of these subunits is typically very limited, but a staunch opposition in these arenas often closes some opportunities for protesters (in Toronto's Mimico or in Seoul's Myeongdong neighborhoods). Protesters can gain influence over the executives in these units (in Boyle Heights' neighborhood council), or instead maintain a distance from these institutions, which they see as co-opted by the agenda of real-estate developers (in downtown Los Angeles).

* * *

Networks in the social-movement literature are largely considered in their relational dimension. But geographers remind us of the need to consider also their territorial dimension if we want to understand how they affect outcomes. Social networks merge with physical space in neighborhoods – space that is appropriated with events or outright occupations, "connecting cyberspace and urban space in relentless interaction" (Castells, 2015, p. 11). Nicholls insightfully argues that "understanding social movements requires us to account for the particular geographical constitution of the complex networks that underlie them" and specifically distinguish between distant allies, which facilitate the flow of information and political backing, and strong ties, which provide emotional, material and symbolic resources essential for mobilization (Nicholls, 2009, p. 79). Further, physical proximity helps generate and sustain social networks (Martin, 2003; Tilly, 2005), while neighborhood solidarities can strengthen trust (Nicholls, 2003) and play a more important role than class in motivating people to engage in protest (Gould, 1995).

Nicholls (2009) identifies three distinct mechanisms by which place-based social networks strengthen collective action: by translating general sociological attributes into political attitudes; by providing relational and cognitive attributes that strengthen the cohesiveness of collective actors; and by promoting a local solidarity that enables collective action. All three hypotheses find validation in the cases here. First, organizers emphasize the connection of social attributes (ethnic, class, professional background) with neighborhood identity when they prime residents for resistance. When organizers craft cultural representations of the neighborhood (primarily through experiential tools), they provide frames and meanings (a "sense of place") that guide how residents and groups make sense of the struggles they face. Third, the construction of relations as neighborly, and therefore spatially centered, is essential to promote solidarity among residents from different social backgrounds. In addition, I find that proximity lowers the cost of contact and collaboration for groups and individuals. And dense group networks at the neighborhood level usually transform into dense organizational networks at the city level.

Scholars of urban movements have identified as the main structural limitation of place-based networks their "militant particularism" (Castells, 1983; Harvey & Williams, 1995; Nicholls, 2009), which undermines the possibility of moving from local to broader issues of contention. Instead, in the cases here, several successful organizers *are* able to use locally based solidarity to expand organizational networks and mobilization. As illustrated in Santiago, but also in cases from Madrid, Los Angeles, Tel Aviv, and Hamburg, organizers are able to connect neighborhood identity and challenges with systemic struggles at the city level and beyond. In these cases, and contrary to scholarly expectations, place-identity does not promote NIMBYism or undermine progressive politics. Rather, particular defensive struggles are combined with and justified by universal claims against global dynamics of dispossession. Therefore, place-bound contentious episodes in some cases become incubators or platforms for broader social movements, offering both locations and goals for growth.

* * *

In addition to experiential tools and broad networks, this book considers the role of prior protest involvement as the third factor that explains mobilization. Several signal interventions in the social-movement literature identify prior protest involvement as an important predictor of protest participation (Ancelovici, 2002; Bennett et al., 2004; Hirsch, 1990; Jasper & Poulsen, 1995; McAdam, 1999; Tarrow, 1998; Whittier, 2010). Also, the literature on urban antigrowth movements identifies the presence of previously existing organizations as a facilitator of resistance (Burbank, Heying, & Andranovich, 2000).

I apply these insights to my cases, where I observe great variation in protest organizers' backgrounds. In Los Angeles, Madrid, Hamburg, and in some of the Istanbul cases, organizers were activists with very extensive (even professional) prior experience in similar struggles. However, in most cases, organizers had no prior experience in protest related to redevelopment. Surprisingly, the initial core of organizers often declared no prior protest activity at all. (This is dramatically the case in Tel Aviv, but also in Santiago, which are both successful cases of mobilization.) In other cases, organizers had some form of protest experience, but in different fields. (In Seoul, organizers were active in the democratization movement.)

So the role of prior protest experience emerges as far less influential than the existing scholarship would predict. When prior strategies differ dramatically from strategies that are more suited to the current environment, this cultural baggage is irrelevant or even counterproductive because it leads organizers in the wrong direction (Yongsan in Seoul, for example). That said, prior protest experience does play a positive role in the vast majority of cases. Yet the reasons why this is true vary depending on the protest contexts. I identify two contexts of special interest in urban contention: (1) anarchic occupations and (2) protest based on judicial strategies. Anarchic occupations require significant organizational know-how for their day-to-day operations, as well as the management of conflicts internally and externally, with police, neighbors, and government representatives. Fieldwork made clear that leaders' extensive prior experience was critical to success in these cases.

Protests based on judicial strategies were even more dependent on prior experience in similar forms of protest because of the technical expertise required to implement such strategies, to the point that protest actors who successfully pursued this strategy had not only extensive experience and organizational memory but also important connections with think tanks and other organizations specifically dedicated to this expertise. In other words, the legal approach to protest creates high barriers to entry.

EXPLAINING IMPACT

Scholars of social movements have long argued that the impact of mobilization is mediated by political context. Mobilization in the cases here largely takes place apart from political parties, but those parties become salient in explaining the impact of protest groups. In particular, allies in city council and the exploitation of partisan divisions between different levels of government emerge in my research as the two critical factors that account for protesters' impact on redevelopment.

In identifying structural factors that affect impact, I follow McAdam et al.'s list of four widely agreed-upon elements of opportunity structures: (1) the degree of openness of the institutional political system; (2) the presence of elite alignments; (3) the presence of elite allies; and (4) the state capacity and propensity for repression (McAdam, McCarthy, Zald, & Mayer, 1996, p. 27). Although these factors are still open to different interpretations (Jasper & Goodwin, 2011), I adopt McAdam's framework because it facilitates a disciplinary conversation.[2]

[2] Some scholars highlight the omission of discourse from McAdam et al.'s list of structural opportunities. The critique has special salience here because of the prominence of the discourse of culture-led growth in aspiring global cities (as discussed in Chapters 1 and 4). To explain, discourses are patterns in language use that enable or constrain political action, by legitimizing certain concerns and forms of engagement (Koopmans, 2004; Laclau & Mouffe, 1985; Wetherell, Taylor, & Yates, 2001). The discourses themselves provide opportunities and limitations to be seized (Bröer & Duyvendak, 2009) and can

I focus on two of the four factors: the presence of elite alignments and elite allies. I do not focus on the remaining two factors – repression and the degree of openness of the political system – because my research strategy limits cases to democratic settings. In these cases, policy change is possible, and political offices depend on the outcomes of free and regular elections. Similarly, limiting the scope of research to democratic settings confines protest cases to those where organizers and protesters are relatively free from fear for their safety, liberty, or property. As fieldwork revealed, however, "relatively" needs to be underlined because even in the most advanced democratic settings, such as Los Angeles and Hamburg, organizers had serious concerns about police repression, confirming the international trend observed by other social-movement scholars away from passive protest policing toward the militarization of police tactics (Tarrow, 2005).

* * *

The main factor affecting impact is institutional support within the local council (nearly always at the municipal level). This confirms other scholars' findings; for example, McAdam's (1999) study of Black insurgency in which elite support followed rather than preceded mobilization.

Under what conditions do city councillors depart from their usual stances to support protesters? The cases indicate that three factors are important: (1) the perception that the campaigns' demands are restricted to select issues and that they will not constrain the councillor's subsequent decisions; (2) sustained, intense, and public pressure by protesters; and (3) the perception of protesters as a necessary, long-term political constituency in the neighborhood.

The electoral system for local institutions has profound effects. Above all, single versus multimember districts for council elections explain the different strategies protesters can pursue as they seek councillor support. Councillors elected in wards pay close attention to their constituency because they have fewer options to chase different pools of supporters than councillors in larger districts (Clingermayer, 1993). However, to have a voice, protest groups have to be highly concentrated in the ward

explain the emergence of contexts favorable to protest. The turn to cultural industries legitimized cultural producers, giving them augmented status and political voice. The discourse that was associated with cultural industries often proved a formidable weapon that protesters consciously deployed (nowhere more evidently and successfully than in Hamburg).

and compose a substantial portion of its population (Trounstine & Valdini, 2008).

I find confirmation for these findings, originally derived from the US context. In councils elected through single-member districts, the support of the relevant councillor is absolutely critical to the group's success. The territorial dimension of representation in these settings overwhelms the representative's partisan or ideological characteristics. A centrist and even generally pro-development councillor can be persuaded by individual campaigns to deviate from their usual line and play a pivotal role in support of protesters. (Los Angeles is an especially powerful illustration of this dynamic.) On the other hand, where the single-member-district representative is not supportive, protesters have little hope of impact.

In contrast to territorial representation, in cities where councillors are elected in a single citywide district or in multiple multimember districts, council support for protesters materializes almost exclusively when far-left parties (left-socialist or communist) have a significant presence (as in the Yarra council in Greater Melbourne). In these settings, partisan factors are influential and shift protesters' strategy from targeting their territorial representative to pursuing a variety of councillors whom they consider potential supporters, based on ideological affinity. The combined effects of territoriality and ideology (with multiple multimember districts) can mitigate the most adverse settings, where the mayor and higher levels of government are strongly aligned in favor of development, and offer unexpected space for protest impact (e.g., as observed in Duriban, Seoul).

In addition to lobbying for support in the local council, sometimes organizers seek to directly infiltrate municipal institutions. Political opportunity is not just a fixed external environment that insurgents confront but also something activists can alter (Tarrow, 1998). Thus, in addition to seeking council allies, of the seventeen campaigns successful in reaching their main goals, ten also gained institutional representation in the process (e.g., on a local council). This did not happen when the goals were very limited in scope because organizers lacked the motivation or capacity to pursue the issue at an institutional or systemic level (e.g., Duriban and Colina).

* * *

Partisan dealignment across different levels of government is the second element of structural opportunity. In the common cases of pro-growth mayors, partisan alignment between mayor and higher levels of government advantages real-estate interests almost insurmountably. Even mass mobilization fails to achieve significant policy impact (although protest can still have ancillary discourse-building and network-building effects). On the other hand, partisan dealignment can offer protesters a powerful ally against a pro-growth mayor as they seek institutional support for their cause at higher levels of government.

The idea that fractures in elite alignment create possibilities for contention is supported by many scholars. Meyer and Staggenborg (1996) find that conflicts are most likely to emerge and endure in states with divided governmental authority, and governments in unitary states are better able to fulfill their policy goals without veto players. At the urban level, tensions between municipal and higher levels of government (regional or national) imply that even in unitary states movement leaders can exploit tensions between different levels of government.

Political scientists have joined social-movement scholars in further articulating this dynamic and emphasizing the role of partisanship. Gibson's contribution is especially relevant. In both Gibson's (2005) and in my case studies, local opponents find support at higher levels of government in their quest to undermine local executives. While opponents in Gibson's analysis include both civil-society organizations and local party rivals, however, the current analysis focuses only on the former. More importantly, his argument explains changes in local executive influence based on the degree to which local executives can isolate local politics from the attention of national level actors. This is only possible because Gibson examines cases situated in peripheral regions. In contrast, the cases here are located in the most important cities in each nation, often the capitals, where the opposition has easy access to the higher level of government. Thus, the issue of concern for protesters in this book is not isolation but rather the availability of powerful allies in higher levels of government – and their availability depends on partisan alignment between local and higher levels of government.

As illustrated in this book, organizers operate across different types of jurisdictions with remarkable fluidity and efficacy. The observed interaction exploits partisan tensions but is also transversal, as understood by Hooghe and Marks (2003). Their model identifies two types of multilevel governance: the first type includes jurisdictions that are at specific institutional levels and general in purpose; the second type includes jurisdictions that operate at numerous territorial scales and are task-specific. Organizers here operate smoothly in both types, as they are able to identify and connect with the national level policy arena that can provide them with the maximum leverage on their specific local struggle. Target institutions are often government ministries but sometimes include the national legislature, police, judiciary, and more. Therefore, while the power over zoning (and especially residential zoning) generally rests firmly at the municipal level, higher-level government institutions can influence the local outcomes by interfering transversally.

While scholars have emphasized how opportunities trigger political action, in the cases discussed here protesters typically cannot wait out the most propitious institutional opening to launch into action. Rather, they respond to the often-sudden emergency of threatened displacement. Over time, scholars have observed a dialectical dimension in the interaction between windows of opportunities and movement capacity. They underscore how, as movements grow in experience and expertise, they might reach results even in the face of diminished opportunities. However, I find that when groups enter a phase of adverse partisan alignment, they are more likely to go into abeyance (Taylor, 1989) and wait for the return of more propitious conditions to reinvigorate action. (For example, in Santiago, protesters took advantage of partisan dealignment in the first campaign, then waited out a period of partisan dealignment, only to pick up the first strategy again and lock in important victories as soon as a subsequent period of partisan dealignment presented itself.)

* * *

These two factors – allies and partisan alignments – create dynamic opportunities for protest. There are also static structural features that affect organizers' and cultural producers' strategic choices, and their impact.[3] I build on critical insights in the literatures of varieties of capitalism (following Soskice & Hall, 2001) and legal-origins theory (building on La Porta, López-de-Silanes, Shleifer, & Vishny, 1998). Both literatures draw a key distinction between Anglo-Saxon countries (liberal market economies with English legal origins) and other countries

[3] Other scholars emphasize permanent features of political opportunity structures, such as the openness of the regime and state capacity (Kitschelt, 1986); social cleavages (Kriesi, Koopmans, Duyvendak, & Giugni, 1995); or electoral rules (Amenta, 2006). Recent contributions specifically identifying the structural features that determine protest regimes in regard to housing (Dufour & Ancelovici, 2018) are important contributions, and those findings can be accounted for by the approach developed in this section.

(coordinated and hierarchical market economies, whether with French or German legal origins). The low formalism of Anglo-Saxon legal systems, and their emphasis on contract enforcement and market-based solutions to economic conflicts, diverge sharply from the other systems, in which governments are more likely to play interventionist and regulatory roles, and where economic conflicts are more likely to be addressed through corporatist negotiation or institutional authority.

These deep and systematic differences in political economy shape the regulatory landscapes and available institutional avenues. They also influence the culture and expectations around conflict resolution and the role that private agents or the government might play therein. The distinction provides insights into several secondary questions connected to my analysis. For example, the staunch enforcement of private contracts and especially property rights helps explain why protesters are less likely to pursue squats in liberal market economies, and even less likely to succeed in establishing long-term occupations, while their counterparts in coordinated market economies and some hierarchical market economies are more likely to have squats tolerated and even turned into officially sanctioned arrangements (this takes place despite a tremendous variation in squatting logics and methods, as discussed by Prujit, 2013). Likewise, in liberal market economies, cultural producers are more apt to abandon contention and be co-opted by developers through the assignment of live-work spaces in new high-rises. This is unsurprising, as these economies privilege a culture of market-based solutions and compensation for grievances. On the other hand, in coordinated and hierarchical market economies (as long as governments are not openly hostile to protesters), organizers are more likely to seek government intervention and regulatory outcomes.

* * *

My research design is intended to avoid theorizing starting from the North, but nevertheless it is helpful to address how this book contributes to enduring exchanges in urban studies that largely derive from North America. Here, leading theories in urban economics (Glaeser, 2000), in neo-Marxist-inspired critical urban studies (Brenner & Theodore, 2002; N. Smith, 2002), and in urban power relations (Logan & Molotch, 1987; Peterson, 1981; Stone, 1989) hold that gentrification is driven by irresistible political and economic forces wherever there is a profit to be made from land rents. Different theories about the mechanisms thus converge on a remarkably similar conclusion.

In contrast, the cases in this book reveal the roles of strategy and political context in driving variation. They show parallel processes of contention in aspiring global cities, regardless of the level of national development and the global region. But they also illustrate structural parameters and choices that enable or limit mobilization, and its effects. Thus, beyond the lessons about how anti-gentrification movements succeed, this analysis provides a counterpoint to dominant perspectives and shows that politics does matter, under the right circumstances.[4]

The successful campaigns that I describe range from piecemeal resistance, simply aiming to mitigate the negative consequences of a particular development project, to full-fledged coalitional processes or even social movements, whose participants and leaders aim to shift development policy away from exchange value toward use value (Burbank et al., 2000). These findings support recent studies, which identify the possibility for sustained and influential antigrowth sectors against real-estate interests, even in the unlikely setting of global cities (Been, Madar, & McDonnell, 2014). However, Been et al. identify such resistance among a high social-status group (property-owners), supporting conventional wisdom that connects socioeconomic status and participation – both in general (Brady, Verba, & Schlozman, 1995) and in the specific context of resistance against urban growth (Dubin, Kiewiet, & Noussair, 1992). This book adds to that research by demonstrating the possibility for such movements beyond high-social-status groups.

With a focus on especially vulnerable populations, the book explores two connected but separate outcomes of interest: (1) the *degree of mobilization* achieved by a given resident group in a given campaign, and (2) its *degree of impact*. The analysis of mobilization centers on strategic factors – the crafting of collective identity and commitment through experiential tools – but also considers structural factors such as the strength of supporting networks and prior protest. The examination of impact emphasizes the institutional environment and focuses on the presence of allies in city council and on the degree of partisan alignment (or conflict) between executives at the local level and at higher levels of government.

[4] I am grateful to an anonymous reviewer for the suggestion that this aspect of the study be highlighted.

3

Research Design and Overview of Results

This work joins the literature that aims to develop "knowledge, understanding, and generalization at a level between what is true of all cities and what is true of one city at a given point in time" (Nijman, 2007, p. 1). Notwithstanding obvious differences among cities, I focus on lessons we can draw from similarities across cases. Some scholars discourage what they see as "quasi-scientific" approaches to comparative urban studies as "inappropriate to the multi-dimensional, contextual, interconnected, and endogenous nature of urban processes" (McFarlane & Robinson, 2012, p. 767; Robinson, 2011). This book takes a different approach. It isolates a set of cities and cases as comparable sites for inquiry, and argues that we can learn from both their similarities and differences. The intention is to produce hypotheses that can be tested and applied analytically to other sites under similar conditions as recommended by Scott and Storper (2015).

This project's context was delimited by a focus on recent, neighborhood-centered protest in aspiring global cities that have regular and competitive elections. There are theoretical and empirical reasons to focus on "aspiring global cities" (see Chapter 4), and not just any cities, since the politics of urban redevelopment and its associated displacement are *most acutely* expressed here. Leaders in these cities are integrated into circuits of international competition, ambitious to raise their global status, and under pressure to identify and pursue high rent-gap areas for redevelopment. These factors establish comparability, even with extreme cross-regional variation.

Aspiring global cities share an approach to urban political economy that is widespread but not universal, and characterized by urban governments that prioritize economic competitiveness. Competitiveness involves a complex array of policies largely oriented toward attracting investment and high-skilled labor on international markets. No single or even handful of measures can entirely capture the phenomenon, but several existing indexes can be used to identify aspiring global cities. Two prominent indexes were especially helpful:

1 The Globalization and World Cities (GaWC) Index, which innovatively measures globalization not through the internal structures of discrete cities, but with measures of relations between cities. It ranks over 230 cities worldwide based on network analysis of the office locations for 175 advanced producer service firms (Globalization and World Cities Research Network, 2012).
2 The Economist Intelligence Unit Global City Competitiveness Index, which ranks 120 cities on the extent to which they are able to attract capital, businesses, talent, and visitors (EUI, 2012). It assigns higher relative weight than other indexes to a city's ability to attract capital and business, with greater focus on economic, institutional, financial, and infrastructural strength.[1]

These and other indexes of global cities overlap considerably. These two indexes are the most useful for the current project because they rank a relatively large number of cities. Usefully, the GaWC Index relies entirely on objective data (the network of firm offices), as opposed to expert evaluations. However, its reliance on a single variable limits its usefulness for the current study. The EIU (Economist Intelligence Unit) Global City Competitiveness Index emerges as the most useful index to establish the scope of research here because of its specific and richly

[1] Three additional indexes were analyzed for the study but do not directly determine the population selection. First, I examined the Anholt-GfK Roper City Brands Index, which is based on the idea that cities compete for limited resources such as investors, tourists, and consumers; and that brand promotion is the key element of their "competitive identity" (Anholt, 2007). This index uses online surveys to rank about fifty cities worldwide based on respondents' perceptions of economic, political, and cultural influence of given cities. Second, I examined the Global Power City Index, in which eminent scholars rank cities building on the concept of "global city" (Sassen, 1994). It ranks thirty-five cities based on six main functions representing city strength (such as economy, research, culture, and livability) and the degree to which cities attract the five groups identified as key to city strength (managers, researchers, artists, visitors, and residents). Third, I examined the A. T. Kearney Global City Index, in which expert assessment ranks about sixty-six cities based on market influence, ability to attract high-skill labor, media and internet penetration, cultural experience, and political influence (Hales & Pena, 2012).

developed focus on economic competitiveness, and its lower weighting of cultural and political influence compared to other indexes. The EIU's emphasis on competitiveness is captured with thirty-one indicators that rank cities by assigning a weight of 30 percent to economic strength; 15 percent each to human capital and institutional effectiveness; 10 percent each to financial maturity, global appeal, and physical capital; and (in contrast with other indexes) only 5 percent each to social and cultural capital, and to environmental hazards. With its attention to economic strength, financial maturity, and global appeal, the EIU Index captures complex elements tied to globalization. Rather than investigating *de novo* the various components of globalization, the present study uses the Index to understand the components that make these cities beacons of contemporary capitalism. The Index provides independent justification for the comparability of these cities, such that various dimensions of international competitiveness and global status do not need to be disaggregated.

However, not all cities in the Index are suitable for a direct comparison. First of all, the current study focuses on politics in *aspiring* global cities and not established global cities, as discussed, for example, in Sassen (1994). To differentiate established from aspiring global cities, the GaWC Index breaks down the rankings into several intervals. Structurally established global cities belong to the two top groups (Alpha++ and Alpha+ cities), while aspiring global cities belong to the Beta groups and below. The EIU Index does not introduce such discrete intervals. Therefore, I used the GaWC list to identify the ranked position of Alpha cities in the EIU Index, and to deduce the associated categorical thresholds. The comparison indicated that in order to eliminate Alpha cities from the population, I should exclude from the analysis all cities that rank above 64 points in globalization in the 120-strong EIU list. Consequently, I eliminated the cities that in fact top nearly all globality indexes: New York, London, Tokyo, Paris, Zurich, Frankfurt, Washington, DC, Chicago, Boston, Singapore, and Hong Kong.

This project takes "cities" to mean political jurisdictions with legal powers and responsibilities distinct from other levels of government, rather than dense agglomerations of urban populations (Post, 2018). The project also focuses on politics in democratic contexts. Across several political regimes, including authoritarian regimes, governments use land to regulate the economy (managing the land supply to stimulate growth or cool overheating). In several settings, local governments rely on land-related fees and revenues to finance budgetary expenditures, in the context of dwindling transfers from central governments. These dynamics are nearly always associated with dispossession and displacement across a variety of regime types (see, for example, Rithmire, 2017). However, the present focus is on explaining protest, where instruments and dynamics differ fundamentally in authoritarian and democratic regimes. While some of the findings here might apply to authoritarian regimes, the much higher costs of protest in those settings do not make those cases directly comparable.

Therefore, I eliminated cities in countries that were not democratic according to Polity IV scores for regime type over the period from 2010 to 2013. (In the Polity scale, 8 is the lowest and 10 is the highest value for a democracy. I selected cities in countries that averaged at least 8 over the time period.) The alternative – considering the degree of democracy at the city as opposed to national level – is not suitable for this research project. The level of local democracy, expressed for example through the degree of partisan turnover or electoral competitiveness in local elections (Gibson, 2005), hinders rather than helps in the current analysis because my interest in the degree of democracy is not related to the likelihood of a change in local government. Instead, it focuses on the degree to which we can expect residents to engage in protest without fear for their lives and freedom. The Polity scores as employed here are a superior indicator because I am interested in identifying settings with adequate political associational space for popular organizing.

Further, to facilitate comparison, I restricted the population to cities that are relatively large (at least 1.5 million residents) and relatively rich (at least $23,000 in city gross domestic product at purchasing power parity prices per capita in 2014. Finally, since this book examines variation in mobilization and impact, and not the presence of relevant protest, I further limited the population to cities in which neighborhood-centered protest against urban redevelopment was: (1) sustained (at least six months of activity); (2) significant (at least two public protest events reported in the local press); and (3) occurred between 2002 and 2016 (although a given protest group might have begun activities before 2002, or continued them after 2016). The period is chosen because social-media technologies became widespread in the first years of the new millennium. Unsurprisingly, almost no cases needed to be excluded because they lacked contention over redevelopment. (The most prominent exclusion was Vienna.)

SELECTION OF THE SITES

Among the large remaining set from the EIU Index I proceeded to select ten cities for investigation. I sought to maximize geographical diversity. The regions that emerge as most prominent from the indexes are: North America, Europe, Pacific Asia, South America, and the Middle East (in that order). Therefore, out of the qualified set of ranked cities in the EIU Index, I selected *the two top-ranked cities from each of these regions*. To maximize not only geographic but also institutional variation, I selected only one city per country. When two cities from the country were adjacent in ranking, I selected the one where protest provided the most helpful variation in the underlying features of interest. (This criterion applied, for example, to Berlin versus Hamburg and Sydney versus Melbourne.) The cities thus selected from the EIU Index for further analysis are: Toronto and Los Angeles for North America; Melbourne and Seoul for Pacific Asia; Santiago and Buenos Aires for South America; Tel Aviv and Istanbul for the Middle East; and Madrid and Hamburg for Europe.[2]

Through its selection process, this book engages with the debate in comparative urban politics around global and "non-global" cities. Sassen's (1994) early focus on a few urban centers generated an artificial dichotomy between cities viewed as integral to globalization and cities considered relatively immune to it. In response, another body of scholarship has argued to the contrary that developing-world cities follow in the footsteps of their advanced industrial counterparts on a path of urban internationalization (McCann, 2002; Robinson, 2002). Yet a third perspective ascribes to cities in the so-called Global South specific political challenges and opportunities as local elites seek to integrate into the global economy (Moncada, 2013).

In parallel, scholars have also debated the degree to which gentrification processes were first seen as applicable across a wide range of

[2] In Europe, in order to further expand regional variation, a previous version of this book additionally included Vilnius, the city from the former USSR which best fit the selection criteria (presenting the highest combination of values for Polity IV score; population size; GDP/capita, PPP; and GaWC Index ranking in the former USSR). The protest case of ProTest Lab in Vilnius displayed highly creative experiential tools, but lacked extensive support networks and prior protest experience, thereby confirming the overall argument presented here regarding the dynamics of mobilization.

settings globally (Atkinson & Bridge, 2005; Lees, Slater, & Wyly, 2008; Porter & Shaw, 2013; N. Smith, 2002) or, later, deemed specific to location or cultural affinity (Janoschka, Sequera, & Salinas, 2014; Lees, Shin, & López-Morales, 2015). The more fine-grained understanding of variation by location is an absolutely fundamental contribution, yet these critiques lack the theoretical grounding to explain differences across cities and regions.

The research design of the current project helps address lacunae in both debates. It helps assess the role of North and South bifurcations for theoretical purposes with a medium-n design that leaves the outcome open to empirical assessment. It also allows theoretical considerations rather than specific regional expertise to drive the explanation for the observed variation in gentrification and associated resistance. The sequence of research in my ten selected cities was designed with these debates in mind and intended precisely to test (and disprove) the notion that location (rather than variation in systemic structures) drives the observed outcome. The first fieldwork site was a city located in the South, so as to limit undue theoretical influence from the North. Specifically, hypotheses formulation started on the first observation of a critical and puzzling case: the emergence of strong resistance in Santiago, the historical hotbed of neoliberalism. However, hypotheses were immediately put in conversation with cases in the North, and the study subsequently alternated North and South cities.

Thus, while scholars have recognized that different locations have different patterns of urban redevelopment, gentrification, and displacement, the current approach helps find deep, enduring, and systemic sources of such variation in political, economic, and legal structures. In so doing, it connects to earlier scholarship that identified different paths to urban development along liberal, Keynesian, and neoliberal economic models (Harvey, 2010; N. Smith, 2002), or interpreted different tracks of gentrification vis-à-vis political economy (Betancur, 2014; Lees, Shin, & López-Morales, 2016). It proposes an innovative interpretation based on institutional factors as well as contributions by the varieties of capitalism and legal origin theories.

SELECTION OF THE CASES

"Cities" are not "cases" in this book. Cities are the environment within which I investigate cases. The units of analysis in this book are campaigns against redevelopment and/or gentrification led by groups that consider themselves related to a specific territorially defined community, usually a neighborhood.[3] For ease of comparison, the project mostly focuses on conflicts over the redevelopment of formally defined areas in central lower- and lower-middle class neighborhoods rather than the suburban outskirts or informal settlements.

A variety of phenomena are linked to neighborhood resistance against redevelopment, such as:

1 conflict over redevelopment of formal housing or surrounding public spaces;
2 resistance against gentrification in formal neighborhoods;
3 resistance against evictions of legal renters in formal neighborhoods;
4 resistance against evictions of occupiers in formal neighborhoods;
5 resistance against evictions of owners or renters in informal neighborhoods;
6 calls to formalize or improve infrastructure in informal neighborhoods;
7 homeless services.

Comparative work within this complex environment demands criteria for case selection. First, while I cover temporary protest encampments, I do not focus on permanent or semipermanent informal settlements (also known as slums, *gecekondular*, *villas miserias*, *villas de emergencia*, and *asentamientos*), despite the fact that they are often in the center of the city, and in areas of extremely high rent gap. The logic and demands of informal settlements are different from formal settlements (Auerbach, 2016; Auerbach, LeBas, Post, & Weitz-Shapiro, 2017; LeBas, 2013), and thus informal settlements are not treated in this book because their inclusion would impair comparability. Cases in the book focus on categories 1 through 4, above. This set includes housing that, while formal in the sense of having land titles, is decrepit enough that it is not sanctioned for residence, and thus is squatted. It is not viable to exclude this housing from the analysis, because owners or the state often deploy safety concerns as administrative tools to justify displacement.

In sum, cases are defined by a specific protest group, engaged in a specific campaign, in one of the ten selected cities. Case selection of

[3] Following Sampson, a neighborhood is defined "in theoretical terms as a geographic section of a larger community or region (e.g., city) that usually contains residents or institutions and has socially distinctive characteristics" (Sampson, 2012, p. 56).

protest groups and campaigns follows an "at-risk population" approach. Anecdotal evidence makes clear that it is exceedingly rare for neighbors in aspiring global cities to be able to significantly organize, and even rarer to succeed in modifying redevelopment plans. Therefore, the investigation had to focus efficiently on cases most *likely* to display the two traits of interest: success in mobilization, and success in policy impact. This is not equivalent to selection on the dependent variable, however. I do not select cases based on their observed success – and in fact the dataset includes several cases of failed mobilization or policy impact. Rather, I select cases within each of the ten cities by focusing on the most prominent neighborhood-level protests against redevelopment and displacement during the period of interest, because groups that have not even achieved recognition in a given campaign are least likely to teach us about what explains success. I identify "prominence" through internet and archival research, press analysis, and expert consultation. With this approach, for example, I chose a protest group active in a campaign in the Istanbul neighborhood of Fener and Balat instead of Süleymaniye, because the latter, despite even more dramatic displacement, did not exhibit significant collective resistance.

One downside to this selection strategy is some loss of variation in the tools and coping mechanisms that residents utilize against displacement: Millions of people fight displacement every day, and my focus on prominence eclipses the "weapons of the weak" (J. C. Scott, 1985) approaches through which people resist silently and with support networks that do not coalesce into outright protest groups. Notwithstanding this limitation (Annunziata & Rivas, 2018), the present selection strategy makes sense because it identifies both mobilization approaches and structural conditions most associated with policy change.

I regularly followed up on all the cases, as long as the cities remained within the scope of the investigation. (In the 2016 Polity update, Istanbul was no longer considered a democracy and its cases were no longer updated.) This book highlights the period in which each case is most theoretically relevant.

As a result, within each city, I study between two and five protest groups engaged in specific campaigns, for a total of twenty-nine cases. This approach addresses concerns over incommensurability across cities and regions, and facilitates comparative analysis of the factors that are specifically strategic, rather than structural.

Most neighborhoods discussed in this book share a remarkably consistent set of features, despite their dazzling geographic variety, and resemble what urbanist Jane Jacobs saw in New York City's Greenwich Village in 1960 and described in *Life and Death of Great American Cities* (Jacobs, 1961). They are relatively low-rise, with plenty of sidewalks, a combination of retail and residential spaces, small blocks, historical buildings, and more trees and public spaces than is usual for the city. These spatial characteristics are especially true of the neighborhoods that host successful mobilization cases, further corroborating the importance of spatial factors for civic engagement that Jacobs identified and that has been subsequently confirmed (Knudsen & Clark, 2013). In addition, some of these neighborhoods are within a few hundred meters of their cities' institutional power centers. Protest organizers (above all in Santiago, Buenos Aires, Madrid, Tel Aviv, and Los Angeles) stated that these spatial features facilitated protest organizing in their neighborhoods. However, it was precisely this centrality that simultaneously helped to make these places high rent-gap destinations for investment. These neighborhoods usually see high rates of redevelopment in their vicinities, which makes clear to residents the implications of redevelopment for symbolic or material displacement. However, as will be shown, this is not sufficient for mobilization *per se*.

Socially, these neighborhoods are more diverse (in the rates of foreign-borns, minorities, or marginal populations), and have higher population densities than the city average. Residents are a mix of renters and homeowners, with a largely lower-middle-class profile, but (especially in successful mobilization cases) often with higher social capital. These features confirm earlier research that found antigrowth coalitions more likely in neighborhoods with highly educated residents and with high rates of workers in professional and high-tech sectors (Clark & Goetz, 1994).[4] Clark and Goetz connect these factors to identify a *new political culture*, one characterized by social and cultural rather than fiscal issues, that favors lifestyle and the neighborhood's use value over exchange value and economic growth. They identified this political landscape in the US context, but several of the neighborhoods discussed here confirm it. Often these neighborhoods are known artist hubs or destinations for work, play, and/or residence, which confers on them the status of "scenes"

[4] Clark and Goetz also identify high income as a factor facilitating organizing, and surely this is a positive factor for political participation, but richer neighborhoods are not typically facing the extreme high rent gaps that attract investment and therefore are not discussed in this book. (Mimico in Toronto provides the highest income neighborhood among the cases.)

(Silver, Clark, & Navarro Yanez, 2010). This greatly facilitates the emergence of collective identities and the associated recruitment of participants in political struggles.

Public-housing settings do not conform to these spatial characteristics as they are often (but not always) marred by topographies of isolation. Nor do they fit the same social profiles, as they display especially low socioeconomic levels combined with short tenures and diversity rates so high that they hinder political organizing. For all of these reasons, they are especially unlikely settings for successful mobilization. Scholars should play close attention to the circumstances in which we do observe mobilization in these settings, and for that reason they are treated in Chapter 9.

VARIABLE SELECTION AND OPERATIONALIZATION

This book explores two outcomes of interest: (1) group effect on mobilization; and (2) group effect on policy and institutional change. Tables 3.1 and 3.2 present the operationalizations of the two outcomes of interest and the respective contributing factors. There are challenges to selecting and operationalizing explanatory factors in such disparate cities. Despite the qualitative approach of this project, I strived to identify factors that could be easily coded, to facilitate future extensions and testing by other scholars.

Mobilization is operationalized based on the number of participants in the largest events organized by the protest group (as indicated by interviews and corroborated by photographs, press reports, or other archival tools). The factors deployed to explain paths to mobilization build on the theoretical analysis discussed in Chapters 1 and 2. They are: (1) the deployment of experiential tools; (2) the deployment of city-level networks of supporting groups and organizations; (3) the organizers' prior involvement in protest against redevelopment; and (4) the degree of union support for the campaign. The social-movement literature provides much support for the role of the last three factors in mobilization. The analysis assesses the impact of experiential tools and their interaction with the other factors to explain mobilization.

City income per capita was added as a commonly considered underlying factor. Both case-study analysis and qualitative comparative analysis indicated that city income was not consequential in explaining protesters' strategies, and it was therefore dropped from the narrative that follows. In addition to city income per capita, there are other aspects

TABLE 3.1 *Operationalization of the factors related to mobilization*

	Codings			
Factors	0	0.25	0.75	1
Union support	No support	Minimal turnout support without official coordination or endorsement	Significant logistical & turnout support	Union leaders publicly involved with the campaign
Experiential tools	No experiential tools	Minimal & ineffective use (e.g. a small event over the course of a campaign)	Significant use (e.g. multiple community events or one landmark event)	Extreme use of sustained, innovative, creative events to attract participants
Within-city networks	Fewer than five groups are involved in the campaign	Few groups involved (between six and ten)	Several groups involved (between eleven and fifteen)	More than fifteen groups involved
Prior protest	No prior experience in protest against displacement among organizers or in the neighborhood	Moderate prior experience in protest against displacement among organizers or in the neighborhood	Prior experience in protest against displacement among organizers or in the neighborhood that reached significant local press coverage for its impact in traditional media	Prior experience in protest against displacement among organizers or in the neighborhood that reached national coverage in traditional media and/or academic coverage for its impact
Mobilization	<50 participants in major events	50-150	150-300	Over 300

TABLE 3.2 *Operationalization of the factors related to impact*

	Codings			
Factors	0	0.25	0.75	1
Mobilization	<50 participants in major events	50-150	150-300	Over 300
Ally in city council	Councillor is against protesters	Councillor supports protesters at rally but not in council	Councillor provides support in council	Protesters place their own representative in council, or state that result would not be achieved without councillor support
Leftist local executive	Local executive is affiliated (or independent in coalition) with a party on the right	N/A	N/A	Local executive is affiliated (or independent in coalition) with a party on the left
Leftist higher-level executive	Higher-level executive is affiliated with a party on the right	N/A	N/A	Higher-level executive is affiliated with a party on the left
Impact	The protest group gains neither acceptance nor advantages	The protest group gains acceptance without advantages; at the most marginal demands are met	The protest group gains full acceptance as well as some advantages	The protest group gains full acceptance as well as key demands & even institutional changes

of market dynamics that were considered for examination but dismissed for lack of variation. For example, in nearly all cases, informal economies played a role, especially in the livelihood of at-risk residents, making them especially vulnerable to uprooting and displacement.

The distinction between renters and homeowners is discussed in specific cases but not treated as an independent control variable. In addition to the absence of comparable data on this variable at the neighborhood level, recent scholarship indicates that the distinction lacks significant explanatory power when discussing attitudes toward market-rate housing redevelopment in high-rent cities. Relative to their respective national contexts, all cities in this book can be considered high-rent, in the sense that renters displaced by redevelopment lack nearby neighborhoods with equally affordable rents. In high-rent cities, recent research indicates that renters mirror homeowners in opposing new market-rate housing construction in their neighborhood, though for different reasons: homeowners primarily seek to preserve home value and quality of life, while renters fear gentrification (Hankinson, 2018). This argument emerges from the US context but supports the evidence and narratives in this book across a wide variety of settings.

Further, I offer no measure for the strength of the real-estate sector. Measuring comparatively the strength of the real-estate sector and the pro-growth coalition is beyond the scope of this book and is remarkably challenging (Logan, Whaley, & Crowder, 1997, p. 609). Available evidence already indicates limited variation in the (very high) degree to which pro-growth coalitions dominate localities in development regime contexts (Logan et al., 1997, p. 610). This mitigates the absence of a measure. In keeping with the scholarship's predictions of pervasiveness (Altshuler & Luberoff, 2004; Jeong & Feiock, 2006; Logan & Crowder, 2002), the cases discussed here are nearly all clear-cut examples of development regimes with strong pro-growth coalitions (the only exception being in Mullae, Seoul, under Mayor Park, the closest that I found to a progressive regime). Thus, while I cannot offer quantitative comparative measures, it is clear that in each of the aspiring global cities discussed in these chapters, the real-estate sector constitutes an extremely influential lobby, as documented by secondary literature.

We can therefore capture the factors associated with high mobilization, the first outcome of interest in this book, as follows:

Outcome of interest 1:

- Deployment of experiential tools
- City-level organizational support network
- Local prior protest against redevelopment
- Union support

To assess group impact, the second outcome of interest, I adopt Gamson's (1995) focus on the degree to which groups achieve recognition and advantages. However, I change Gamson's taxonomy because there is no case of "preemption," where the protest group does not gain acceptance but does gain advantages. Instead, I pursue a more fine-grained assessment of policy impact. I distinguish between no impact, minimal impact (when only marginal demands are met; e.g., protesters were fighting a new high-rise, but all they achieved was the elimination of a couple of floors), partial impact (when some key demands are met), and full impact (when most key demands are met, sometimes accompanied by institutional changes). Among many possible outcomes, scholars of social movements often emphasize the degree to which collective action prompts cultural effects, or gives voice to participants (Jasper, 2008). This is surely essential to the analysis that follows, but it is discussed as a possible gateway to mobilization rather than as one of the two outcomes of interest.

Yet another approach in the literature on antigrowth protest is to sort impact into two types: piecemeal campaigns and antigrowth movements (Burbank, Heying, & Andranovich, 2000). Piecemeal campaigns try to mitigate the negative consequences of a particular development project, while antigrowth movements coalesce and express a common commitment to shifting development policy away from exchange value toward use value. Burbank et al. argue that piecemeal resistance is characterized by its narrow scope. It focuses on negotiation for individual concessions, as well as various types of protests and advocacy. Antigrowth movements, in contrast, have broader scope and move conflict from the zoning bureaucracy to the larger political arena through ballot initiatives and support for municipal candidates.

Burbank et al.'s approach is useful as a compilation of different factors involved in the overall assessment of a group's impact, yet it is not the best approach for coding impact in the present inquiry, for two reasons. First, several of the groups discussed here do not aspire to become movements, and if their piecemeal motivations are met, then this inquiry requires coding their impact as high. Second, it is hard to draw the line between piecemeal resistance and antigrowth movement in empirical analysis, because both dimensions can coexist within organizations. I even observe lack of agreement on common goals within successful antigrowth coalitions – which is unsurprising in settings known for their dense but fragmented civic networks, such as Los Angeles (Stone et al., 2015). Disagreement and ambiguity pertaining to goals were noted, whenever observed.

Mobilization, the first outcome of interest, becomes a contributing factor in the analysis of impact. Thus, building on the theory in Chapter 2, the factors examined to explain impact are: (1) the degree of mobilization, (2) the degree of support by councillors (because they can provide access to crucial institutions), and (3) the degree of support by a progressive mayor and/or a leftist higher-level executive (because partisan alignment can strengthen the hand of municipal governments against protesters, while dealignment can provide protesters with means to counter local executives). To summarize:

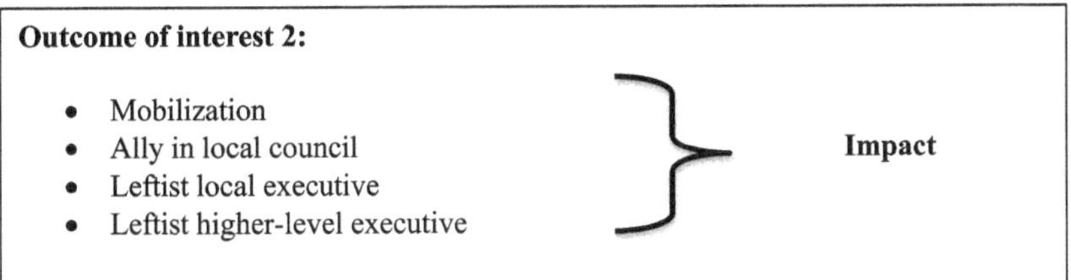

DATA COLLECTION

This project relies on several methods used for the study of protest (Della Porta, 2014). Drawing on multiple methods and triangulating varied forms of data helped reveal parallels and contrasts as the comparison proceeded. Fieldwork was conducted between 2009 and 2016 in all cities except the English-speaking sites of Toronto, Los Angeles, and Melbourne, where interviews were conducted remotely. During fieldwork, I combined participant observation in neighborhood life and associational meetings with in-depth and follow-up interviews with academics, activists, and members of civil society, identified through a snowball approach. The frequency with which an individual was named suggested their influence in the organization or relevance to the research question. Interviews for each resistance case continued until reaching "saturation" (Small, 2009), i.e. when additional interviews did not lead to further significant explanation in the empirical analysis. Nearly all interviews lasted between one and two hours. The number of interviews ranged from five to twenty-five per city. (Fewer interviews were needed where archival data were especially rich.) Interviews' recordings and transcripts are available upon request. I was not directly involved in any of the protest cases described in this book.

In addition, I relied on archival research, press analysis, and a thorough examination of activists' internet-based sources. This included videos and photos of protests, which I used to triangulate, verify, and confirm reported attendance at protest events and the degree of demographic inclusiveness (providing an approximate estimate of participants' age, gender, and ethnic background). Interviews provided a static perspective on the cases because they largely consisted of ex-post reflections, but several online sources such as social-networking sites, blogs, chat spaces, photos, videos, and listservs, typically date their entries and allowed me to reconstruct protest strategies and events as they unfolded. Similarly, fieldwork provided a snapshot of neighborhoods after the culmination of protest events. I integrated my spatial analysis with historical Google Street View data from different periods to trace the different stages of spatial contestation.

The book has the benefits and weaknesses of a single-author project. While I strived for coherence and consistency that is hard to achieve in multi-authored projects, in order to set the context of the cases and improve the depth of the analysis I relied on secondary literature and on the generous help and advice of many area specialists. This was necessary given the number of sites and the fact that I conducted all interviews and fieldwork myself.

ANALYSIS AND RESULTS

Cases were examined with fuzzy set qualitative comparative analysis (fsQCA) based on the variable codings presented in Tables 3.1 and 3.2. Two independent coders used case descriptions that I provided to code all the variables.

Qualitative comparative analysis isolates cross-case patterns, while appreciating the heterogeneity of the cases with regard to their different causally relevant conditions. It thus allows for complex causal patterns, which involve different combinations of causal conditions that might generate the outcome of interest (see Ragin, 2013). Cress and Snow (1996) and McAdam and Boudet (2012) have applied this approach to the study of local protest and mobilization, although the method has been criticized in recent years (Hug, 2013; Lucas & Szatrowski, 2014). The fsQCA analysis indicates that three paths explain cases with high mobilization: the intersection of experiential tools and activated networks; or the intersection of experiential tools and legacy; or the intersection of union support and activated networks. fsQCA also confirms that high impact is associated with the intersection of mobilization, allies in city council, and a leftist mayor; or the intersection of mobilization, allies in city council, and a leftist higher-level executive, thereby confirming the helpful role of partisan dealignment. (See Appendix 1 for detailed results.)

In addition, a reduction of the variables to binary codings informed flowcharts. Flowcharts are highly revealing of the dominant patterns in mobilization and impact. In presenting the results, I start by dividing the analysis into cases with and without union support. The reason for this separation is the idea, widely acknowledged in the social movement and participation literatures, that the context of protest has been changed in fundamental ways by the decline of unions (and associated far-left parties). Unions offered critical infrastructure, resources, and frames for mobilization, and their decline brought about the atomization of potential participants, who are no longer connected to protest activities through the institutional networks of the union but rather choose to attend protest based on concerns and motivations elaborated at the individual level. This documented change in dynamics of popular participation sets the stage for the shift in the repertoire of contention that is at the heart of this book with the analysis of experiential tools – tools that can be successfully deployed in the absence of union support.

These theoretical insights find confirmation in the empirical analysis, which, with the aid of qualitative comparative analysis, separates the path with the deployment of union support from the remaining two paths that include deployment of experiential tools. Thus, based on these theoretical and empirical considerations, the cases can be separated into two groups: cases with low and high union support. The variables and cases are then represented in the flow charts Figures 3.1 and 3.2.

Figure 3.1 displays the cases that share low union support. In bold are cases of successful mobilization. The main outcome is that *all – and only – the cases of successful mobilization shared the deployment of experiential*

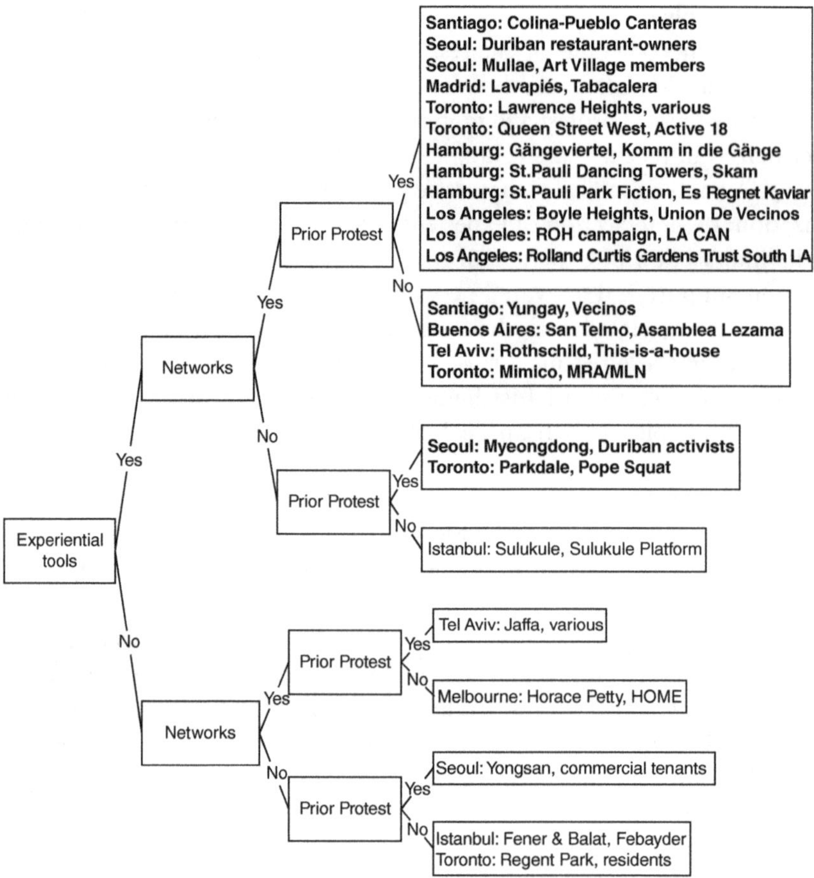

FIGURE 3.1 Mobilization under low union support (high mobilization cases in bold).

tools in combination with either protest legacy or broad networks. Thus, in the population under consideration, the combination of experiential tools and either networks or protest legacy emerges as necessary and sufficient for successful mobilization, even absent union support.

As shown in Figure 3.1, in the cases that display all three factors, mobilization is overdetermined, and the case studies that follow trace which factors played a more decisive role. In contrast, four cases of successful mobilization are explained by the combination of experiential tools and networks (without a legacy in prior protest), while two cases are explained by the combination of experiential tools and protest legacy (but

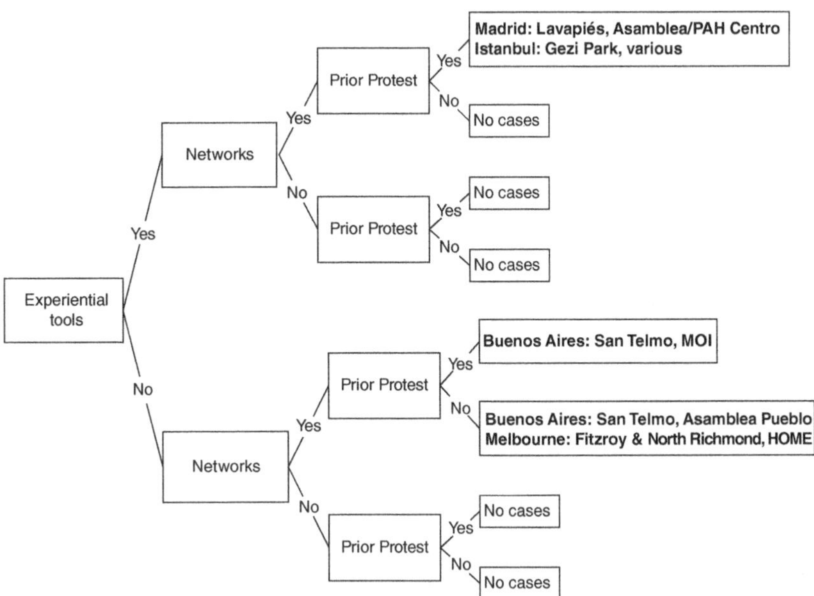

FIGURE 3.2 Mobilization under high union support (high mobilization cases in bold).

not networks). This suggests that experiential tools facilitate mobilization even in settings that have no prior history of mobilizations, which is an important finding that gives hope to residents of such areas.

In the absence of union support, experiential tools are necessary to mobilization. One case indicates that the deployment of experiential tools alone is insufficient for mobilization. Similarly, other cases indicate that neither legacy nor network activations are sufficient on their own: No cases that rested on either element alone succeeded in mobilizing for protest.

Most of the campaigns that successfully mobilized relied on extensive and broadly targeted experiential tools. To illustrate, organizers in Yungay, Santiago, relied on all four types of experiential tools, including a packed calendar of events, memory workshops, and a heritage registry, all based on pride in the neighborhood. In Buenos Aires, the Asamblea fighting against the enclosure of Parque Lezama organized several events, culminating in a "mass embrace" that brought together over 1,400 participants. The campaign of Park Fiction in Hamburg featured celebratory events, such as concerts, documentary screenings, and puppet shows, intended to declare the appropriation of space by neighbors against the use intended by city government. It also explicitly drew on archives, with the Archive of Desire Ballot Boxes. In Toronto, organizers at the public housing estate of Lawrence Heights set up a "memory wall" as part of the Heritage Plan, which was meant to identify and communicate key historic, cultural, and social references in order to integrate them in the redevelopment of the estate.

The findings also confirm the important mobilizing role of networks, as indicated by the literature. In successful cases, multiple cross-sectorial groups within the neighborhood and/or sectorial groups across the city supported resistance campaigns. Support of broad local networks lent legitimacy and indicated that protesters enjoyed committed political clout. Protesters especially pursued alliances with groups with a history of successful struggles because they signaled to authorities their determination and capacity to sustain protest.

Assessing the role of legacy is more complex. In some cases, legacy is present, yet not influential, or even counterproductive (as in Yongsan, Seoul). In others, legacy was clearly essential – for example, in three squats (Hamburg's Gängeviertel, Toronto's Pope Squat, and Madrid's Tabacalera), where mobilization strategies relied on long-standing anarchist groups. In another set of cases, legacy was critical because protest focused on judicial tools, an institutionally complex approach that required long-standing expertise (as illustrated by the cases of PAH in Madrid, as well as LA CAN and TRUST South LA in Los Angeles).

In contrast to numerous cases that display a strong reliance on experiential tools and weak union support, the cases that displayed significant union support are distinctly uncommon, as shown in Figure 3.2. This is unsurprising, given the protracted weakening of unions. According to the Organisation for Economic Co-operation and Development and the International Labour Organization, union density data for the regions and period under examination range from 6 percent in Istanbul to 40 percent in Buenos Aires. In countries with liberal market economies, density ranges between 14 and 25 percent. Even where they are influential, unions tend to have pro-growth agendas in tension with protesters – with the well-documented exception of Melbourne (Burgmann & Burgmann, 1998; Haskell, 1977; Iveson, 2014). These tensions are especially evident when the cause is housing preservation, and are alleviated when the protesters' goal is the construction of affordable housing.

The main finding displayed in Figure 3.2 is that *all available cases with high union support are successful at mobilization*, which indicates that union support remains very effective, although rarely available. In fact, *when union support is present, the only other necessary factor to achieve mobilization is broad network activation. Neither experiential tools nor protest legacy is necessary*. Cases from two cities are especially instructive here: Melbourne, where union support was critical to the mobilization that saved public space; and Buenos Aires, where two of the anti-displacement groups examined actually constitute official chapters in the national union, Central de Trabajadores de la Argentina. That link provided renters and squatters with exceptional organizational and mobilization resources.

As the case studies in this book illustrate, cultural producers tend to be less involved in protests when campaigns are supported by unions (as in Melbourne and Buenos Aires) or when they rely on judicial strategies and bureaucratic engagement (as in Los Angeles and Toronto). Instead, they play an influential role in protests that rely on gaining public opinion clout and therefore must create a buzz (cases in Seoul, Tel Aviv, and Hamburg illustrate this point).[5]

The flowchart in Figure 3.3 illustrates the path to impact. Mobilization is nearly always necessary for a protest to impact policy, but the outcome ultimately depends on the political context. These findings confirm the theory presented in Chapter 2. The main factor that facilitates impact is institutional support within the local council (nearly always at the municipal level). The electoral system for local institutions affects the strategy deployed by organizers in seeking council support. In councils elected through districts, the support of the ward councillor is absolutely critical to the outcome. The territorial dimension of representation in these settings trumps partisan affiliations. In contrast, ideology matters in a single multimember district, and in multiple multimember districts. In

[5] The cases presented in this book offer instances of grievance connected to contentious politics in the welfare state since they involve the curtailment of important housing benefits in a variety of ways, from gentrification to the reduction of public housing. Yet the degree of grievance is not directly related to the size of the resistance (Gurr, 1970). The type of displacement, whether symbolic (manifested through use value conflicts) or direct (loss of shelter), had surprisingly little effect on features of the observed struggle. Given the medium n, the effect of the type of struggle could only be tentatively explored. No strong relation emerged from an analysis of the data. While the degree of successful mobilization was similar, struggles over direct displacement relied more on unions and prior protest, while struggles on use value displayed higher average network engagement. The use of experiential tools was similar across cases. Struggles over direct displacement were slightly less impactful on average, a result not driven by income because the cases of direct displacement and use value struggles were similarly distributed across income groups.

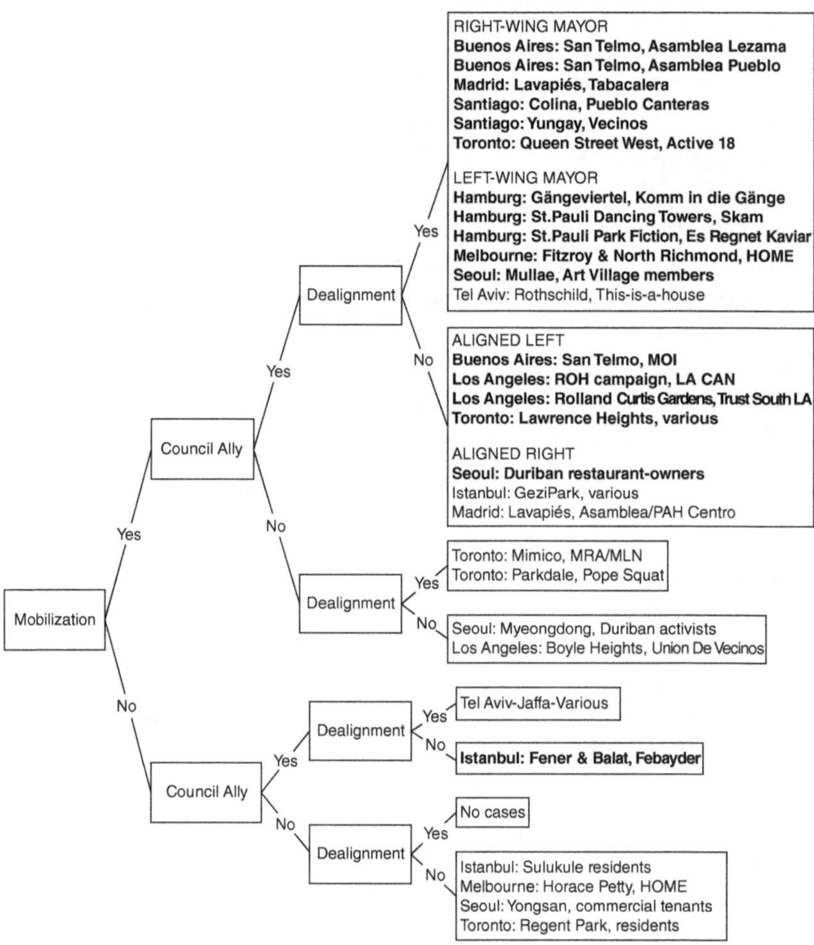

FIGURE 3.3 Impact (high mobilization cases in bold).

these settings, protesters shift from targeting their territorial representative as a necessary step to impact, to pursuing a variety of councillors whom they consider potential supporters based on their ideological stance. However, these differences in approach do not translate into differences in impact. The role of councillor support is vital regardless of the institutional context especially to explain cases of protest impact in the most adverse settings: those of right-wing partisan alignment, in which local and national political elites share the same favorable vision of urban redevelopment. There, in both a single multimember district (e.g., Istanbul) and multiple multimember districts (e.g., Seoul), it is sometimes possible for protesters to succeed, but the outcome is heavily driven by the degree of council support.

Building on this observation, the second institutional variable to influence protest impact is the degree of mutual support or competition between the local level executive and the relevant higher-level executive. The intuition for partisan alignment is that when the local government enjoys the backing of the relevant higher-level executive over redevelopment projects, it is unlikely that local resistance will have any impact on policy outcome. If the higher-level and municipal executives are political rivals, however, protesters can exploit the rivalry to find allies, pitting actors at different institutional levels against each other. The relation between municipal and national executives is expected to be salient in unitary states, especially those with a high degree of centralization (such as Israel, South Korea, Turkey, and Chile). But the role of higher-level governments can also apply in federal states; specifically, where the city in question is the country's capital, the relevant higher political level is usually the national (rather than regional) level. This is due to the special visibility and sometimes legislative status of the capital city. (A good example is Buenos Aires.) In federal systems where the city under observation is not the capital of the country, partisan alignment applies to the relation between municipality and state or provincial authority. (Among the cases covered in this book, Australia stands out as a system in which state governments are especially influential relative to municipalities.)

Figure 3.3 indicates the different modalities for groups to obtain impact. High mobilization and council support are common to nearly all positive outcomes. Four scenarios are possible, depending on partisan alignment. *Two scenarios always deliver positive outcomes for protesters in the reviewed cases.* The first is when both local and higher-level executives are aligned on the ideological left. This sort of left alignment is, unsurprisingly, a favorable setting for protesters. More theoretically interesting is the second scenario, of partisan dealignment with a leftist higher-level executive. In these cases, protesters nearly always seek support at the higher level to circumvent local opposition. The third scenario also contradicts conventional expectations: The presence of a left-wing mayor, in the absence of a left alignment across levels of government, is *not* sufficient to explain positive outcomes, even with high mobilization and council support. This outcome is explained by the fact that development regimes with strong pro-growth coalitions can coexist with leftist mayors, as is true in Tel Aviv. In other words, it takes a progressive coalition (led by a mayor on the decisive rather then moderate left) to protect residents from displacement, as was the case of Mullae in Seoul. The Hamburg and Melbourne cases in this third group offer a somewhat specific setting due to their particular institutions. The local councils in those cases lack the power over zoning that is typical of municipal authorities but are influential because they are very sternly and historically aligned on the far left. Finally, the presence of partisan alignment on the right creates the most adverse scenario to protesters. Failure in such cases is unsurprising, and yet we observe a success in Duriban and Fener and Balat, thanks to support from the local council.

In sum, these results confirm but also challenge conventional wisdom. Left- and right-wing alignment between local and higher-level executives have the expected impact in support for and opposition to protesters, respectively. However, when only one level is supportive, protesters find more promising the ideological affinity with higher-level rather than local executives. This result unsettles predominant views because we think of zoning as driven by local executives and because we think of aspiring global cities as powerful, influential, and increasingly autonomous centers of political power and governance. And yet, even in aspiring global cities, and even on issues that concern the local provision of affordable housing and nearly always affect very circumscribed areas (rather than, say, megaprojects), higher levels of government are extremely influential.

* * *

Beyond the core interest in mobilization and impact, the insights from the literatures on varieties of capitalism and legal system origin help address additional questions that emerge from the analysis and permit us to identify how enduring institutional structures and traditions affect the choices of strategies. The empirical data suggests some trends, depending on whether the city was set in a coordinated market economy (which includes the European cases, and by extension Israel [Knell & Srholec, 2007] and South Korea [Hall & Gingerich, 2009; B. R. Schneider, 2013]), a liberal market economy (the Anglo-Saxon cases), or a hierarchical market economy (which according to Schneider, 2013, includes the South American cases, although Argentina is somewhat of an outlier, and Turkey).[6]

[6] Knell and Srholec do not consider the possibility of hierarchical market coordination and identify Turkey as a mildly coordinated market economy, with values close to Israel (Knell & Srholec, 2007, table 2.4, pp. 60–61).

Structural features influence the selection of protest targets. In cities set in liberal market economies, private actors (typically land or property-owners, or real-estate developers) are the main targets of protest, while protesters are likely to see government as a competitive arena for interest representation through lobbying. (This was especially clear in Toronto and Los Angeles.) In non-liberal market economies, government is more often included as a target because protesters are more likely to identify government as complicit and co-responsible for an adverse outcome or a displacement threat. This is because protesters are more likely to expect solutions through government-led negotiations as governments play more active roles in these settings. The argument, of course, does not hold for public housing redevelopment, where the government is the target of resistance, regardless of the type of economy.

As hypothesized in Chapter 2, coordinated and hierarchical market economies, which more weakly rely on and enforce contract law, displayed more tolerance toward squatters and evictions (Djankov, La Porta, López-de-Silanes, & Shleifer, 2003). Long-term squats were tolerated and even regularized in Hamburg, Buenos Aires, and Madrid, but not in Toronto (nor in Los Angeles, or Melbourne, in squats associated with cases below but not directly discussed). In coordinated and hierarchical market economies there is a rich tradition of self-managed occupation, in contrast to a more intolerant stance in liberal market economies. As the cases attest, systemic differences in political economy undermine protesters' ability to utilize occupation – a tool that is of practical use against displacement but is also critical to raising consciousness of and support among mainstream voters for alternative social and political worldviews.

The type of economy also helps explain where developers offer incentives to co-opt artists. Co-optation is most clearly displayed in Toronto and Los Angeles. In contrast, in at least three out of four coordinated market economy cases, as well as the hierarchical market economy setting of Buenos Aires, the government (rather than private developers) is the central node in the relationship between redevelopment and cultural producers because as part of culture-led growth policies, it offers them spaces to live and work. Thus, as expected, in coordinated market economies the government has programmatic functions beyond short-term rent-maximization. We can expect increasingly widespread efforts by developers to co-opt cultural producers with the offer of space, especially where creative presence fits with their neighborhood branding. However, these arrangements will continue to be more common in liberal market economies because participants there are more primed to market-based solutions.

Protesters' use of judiciary tools is especially complex. As can be expected, in liberal market economies protesters rely extensively on judicial avenues and long-standing collaboration with legal aid organizations for the expertise required to navigate this complex strategy. Cases in Istanbul (hierarchical market economy) and Seoul (coordinated market economy) also display some attempts at judicial initiatives, only rarely with positive outcomes.

In fact, the cases in these two countries allow us to evaluate the explanatory role of national level differences. National differences do not translate systematically into explanations of the observed outcomes; and this is somewhat surprising and unexpected in a comparative analysis. However, it does not mean that national factors have no influence in the specific case but rather that no overall pattern of influence emerges.

Seeking out expected variation at the national level still proves instructive because it reveals understudied sites of difference. Istanbul and Seoul, for example, are in countries that rank on the lower end of the democracy measure used to select research settings. By conventional wisdom, this factor should translate into higher rates of repression. Instead, national differences play out more idiosyncratically. For example, in both countries, protesters face significant and specific institutional obstacles in the judicial realm: In Seoul, the compensation for commercial business is not adequately covered by the legal system, leaving commercial evictees vulnerable. Residents in Istanbul contend with a convoluted legal system strongly tilted toward real-estate interests, and the obstacle that only registered professional bodies such as the Chambers of Architects and of Planners, and not organizations or individuals, can bring lawsuits.

Buenos Aires, meanwhile, stands out as a place where resistance often, and successfully, builds on legal battles. This seems to contradict theoretical expectations, given that Argentina is a hierarchical market economy and rooted in the French legal tradition, two factors that are more associated with negotiation and regulation than judicial strategies to resolve disputes. But specifically in the city Buenos Aires, protesters rely on the *recurso de amparo*, an active and influential citizen ombudsman statute of North American inspiration (Lazzarini, 2000). While *amparo* exists also in Madrid and Santiago, special provisions make it far more helpful to protesters in Buenos Aires because there, and not elsewhere, the statute covers constitutional rights and rights derived from international treaties, national law, and the city's progressive 1994 constitution.

Protection in Buenos Aires can thus be initiated by any inhabitant and legal person, as well as users or consumers, defending against any form of discrimination, or in cases where collective rights or interests are affected, such as the protection of the environment, work and social security, or the cultural and historical heritage of the city (Maraniello, 2011).

The impact of liberal, coordinated, and hierarchical economies will be further explored in the following chapters, yet this summary illustrates the multiple ways in which political institutions influence protest strategies. The remaining chapters will develop a more fine-grained argument through a narrative of the case studies, which is designed with the dual goal of developing the argument thematically and of facilitating the exposition by keeping within-city comparisons together.

4

Aspiring Global Cities

Despite important variations, the cities examined in this book share these core features:

1. They are key national and regional nodes of business and politics.
2. They experienced major and controversial redevelopment, which has caused different forms of displacement.
3. They have intensified the use of branding and cultural policies as engines of economic growth, often thereby promoting the "creative class."

SHARED PROMINENCE DESPITE INSTITUTIONAL VARIATION

The cities' status as national and regional nodes of business and politics in their countries and regions is indicated by their high ranking in the EIU globalization index. Globalization indicators were useful for case selection, but they reflect much more than globalization alone. Their constituent indicators, items like air traffic and corporate offices, also depend on the role of these cities in national economies and societies (Fainstein, 2002). As illustrated in Table 4.1, these cities are engines of national or regional development and economic growth in contemporary capitalism and globalization, regardless of region, or the level of national development.

Let me briefly highlight a few economic features from representative cities. Seoul nicely illustrates the centralization that is common among aspiring global cities. In addition to containing nearly half of the entire Korean population, the Seoul metropolitan area contains over 40 percent of the universities, nearly 90 percent of information-technology

TABLE 4.1 *Cities' population and income overview data.*

Metropolitan Area	Metro Share of National Population 2014 (%)	Metro GDP, 2014 (US$ bn at PPP)	Metro GDP per capita, 2014 (US$, PPP)	National GDP, 2014 (US$ bn at PPP)	Metro Share of National GDP, 2014, PPP
Buenos Aires	31.1	316	23,606	851	37.1
Hamburg	4.0	161	49,757	3,814	4.2
Istanbul	18.1	349	24,867	1,524	22.9
Los Angeles	4.1	860	65,082	17,393	4.9
Madrid	14.4	262	39,288	1,566	16.8
Melbourne	18.9	178	40,244	1,086	16.4
Santiago	40.3	171	23,929	407	42.1
Seoul	48.8	846	34,355	1,707	49.5
Tel Aviv	43.8	153	42,614	287	53.4
Toronto	17.0	276	45,771	1,604	17.2

Source: Metro GDP, PPP and population from Metropolitan Policy Program at Brookings "Global Metro Monitor 2014." National GDP, PPP and population from the World Bank.

manufacturing, and is responsible for nearly half of the national GDP (K.-H. Shin & Timberlake, 2006). Thanks to its increasing prominence in both industrial production and international capital coordination, Seoul has become a key urban center in East Asia (S.-H. Yim & Lee, 2002).

Similarly, the metropolitan region of Santiago has over 40 percent of Chile's population; it is the industrial and financial center of Chile; and it generates 42 percent of the country's GDP. With a population ten times greater than Chile's second-largest city, the province of Santiago is often referred to as the "epitome of the centralized Latin American capital city" (Siavelis, Valenzuela Van Treek, & Martelli, 2002).

Istanbul is not only the largest city in Turkey but is also one of the fastest-growing: half a million immigrants arrive each year, and 63 percent of residents were born elsewhere. It has not been the capital since 1923, but the Istanbul metropolitan municipality hosts the headquarters of 242 of the 500 largest industrial companies of Turkey, contributes 23 percent of Turkey's GDP, and accounts for more than 40 percent of taxes collected nationally.

The city-state of Hamburg is the second-largest city in the Germany and has by far the highest GDP per capita and the country's largest number of millionaires. Due to the structure of the German economy, the city contributes only about 4 percent of the country's overall GDP, but the city is highly influential, thanks not just to its ports and shipyards but also its national prominence in the civil aerospace, insurance, and media industries.

Despite being part of a much smaller economy, Tel Aviv also is regionally prominent: it comprises 7 percent of the land in Israel yet contributes 44 percent of the population and 54 percent of the labor force. The metropolitan area accounts for over half of national GDP (Felsenstein, Schamp, & Shachar, 2013).

In most of the cities analyzed, the state or provincial governments are involved in strategic planning, and sometimes also in final approval. However, the municipal and/or the metropolitan level are responsible for urban planning and management, including changes in zoning, as well as the implementation of most development projects. Yet, despite their global similarities, these cities vary remarkably in institutional features, as Table 4.2 illustrates.

Santiago, Tel Aviv, as well as municipalities in Melbourne and Istanbul, do not have submunicipal administrative units – but other cities do. Officials in these submunicipal bodies are sometimes selected with elections that parallel elections for city mayor and city council (as in Seoul, Hamburg, and, starting in 2011, Buenos Aires). In Los Angeles, neighborhood councils are not mandated by law but, where they exist, representatives are selected by direct popular election. In other cities, submunicipal councils are populated by different mechanisms, such as mayoral appointment or an overlap in function between city and submunicipal councillor (Toronto and Madrid). These submunicipal bodies largely channel citizen participation, and, even more so, top-down directives. They have limited functions and funding. If they are aligned with protesters, they can offer an institutional voice for dissent. In most cases, they align with the municipality. Table 4.2 lists districts (rather than municipalities) as the relevant lower level institution in Seoul and Hamburg because in both cities districts are relatively more influential political and administrative sites, and campaigns found essential allies there.

Table 4.2 also indicates the presence of metropolitan governments. The strength of these governments varies widely. In Istanbul and Seoul, the metropolitan government is the effective government of the city, and the place for most policy directions and decisions about zoning and planning. In other cities (for example, Los Angeles, Buenos Aires, and Melbourne), the absence or weakness of metropolitan governments substantially fragments policy-making, which can benefit real-estate developers (regarding Los Angeles, see Stone et al., 2015).

TABLE 4.2 *Institutional variation.*

Relevant local level jurisdiction	Relevant lower level institution and its selection mechanism		Local executive selection	Most relevant higher level institution
Toronto	Municipal council	SMD	Direct	State
Los Angeles	Municipal council	SMD	Direct	State
Yongsan-gu, Mapo-gu, Jung-gu, Yeongdeungpo-gu in Seoul	(Submetropolitan) District council	MMMD	Direct	Metropolitan and National
Yarra and Stonnington in Melbourne	Municipal council	MMMD	Indirect	State
Santiago Centro	(Submetropolitan) Municipal council	SMMD	Direct	National
Buenos Aires	Municipal council	SMMD	Direct	National
Madrid	Municipal council	SMMD	Indirect	National and Regional
Tel Aviv	Municipal council	SMMD	Direct	National
Fatih, Istanbul	(Submetropolitan) Municipal council	SMMD	Direct	National and Metropolitan
Hamburg-Mitte	District council	SMMD, mixed-member PR	Indirect	State

Key: SMD: single-member districts; MMMD: multiple-multimember districts; SMMD: single-multimember districts; PR: proportional representation.

A key hypothesis in this book is that support within local councils is critical to protesters' impact, so Table 4.2 also shows the selection mechanisms for both councils and executives. Members of the relevant local councils are elected: In single-member districts (SMD); in multiple-multimember districts (MMMD); and in a single-multimember district (SMMD).[1] Protesters adjust their strategies as they seek council support depending on the electoral system for local councils. When district size is small, and representatives have thus strong territorial linkage, protesters necessarily need the support of their representative if they are to have any impact. In these settings, ideological overlap with protesters helps but is not necessary: sometimes protesters can find in their representative a temporary ally despite different ideological outlook overall. With SMMDs, however, ideology becomes more salient, because protesters can seek out the representative who is ideologically closest and thus most likely to support their cause.

The neighborhoods examined in this book are often in the largest cities in the country, and higher levels of governments – regional or national – almost invariably influence redevelopment. Five cities in this study are in federal states, and five are in unitary states. In highly centralized systems, the most politically influential level of government in the campaigns examined below, after the city or metropolitan level, tends to be the national government. This is the case in Madrid, Santiago, Seoul, Tel Aviv, and Istanbul. In federal systems where the city under consideration is not the country's capital, the state (and not the federal) government emerges as the most influential higher level. This is the case for Toronto, Melbourne, Los Angeles, and Hamburg. In Buenos Aires, being the capital, the national government is most salient. The power balance between cities and states varies, as will be examined with each of the cases that follow.

[1] Hamburg had closed-list SMMD elections for both district and state legislatures until 2004, and has since progressively moved to the more personalized system of mixed-member personalized proportional representation with cumulation and *panachage*. Cases center over the period 2002–2009, when parties were formally still very influential despite the vibrant civic movement to increase voter influence and candidate accountability.

Istanbul's metropolitan municipality implements state-sponsored plans across local district levels, with neither coordination with nor approval of the respective local districts. Fatih district, which is the district of interest in the cases below, is also relevant because districts can propose developments within their own borders without coordination and approval from the metropolitan municipality.

Institutional variation is reflected also in the fact that Toronto and Los Angeles have non-partisan city-council elections.

The role of higher levels of government is especially pronounced in cases of right-wing partisan alignment (as in Seoul and Istanbul) or dealignment with a right-wing mayor (as in Buenos Aires and Santiago). Overall, the degree to which higher levels of government interact with municipalities over redevelopment policies depends on institutional designs, political histories, and, above all, the ideological position of the parties governing each level at a given point in time.

REDEVELOPMENT UNDER NEOLIBERALISM

In aspiring global cities, governments launch grand projects to raise their globalization status, but there is significant variation in how markets and governments combine to pursue international competitiveness policies and the often-associated urban redevelopment. In developmental states, urban redevelopment in the capital is a critical instrument for nation-building. An essential feature of this process is urban upgrading and the elimination of informal settlements, with the consequent massive and brutal displacement of the poor. Despite tactical differences, these goals are vigorously pursued across different continents, as briefly illustrated with reference to Seoul, Istanbul, and Buenos Aires.

In Seoul, urban redevelopment has been an instrument of nation-building throughout recent decades, and the government has scrupulously managed the housing supply, especially through credit and land control (H. Cho, Kim, & Shilling, 2012; Kyung & Kim, 2011; C. Lee, Lee, & Yim, 2003; B.-G. Park, 1998; Xiao & Park, 2010).

The key tool that accelerated extensive redevelopment and the reduction of informal settlements was the 1983 Joint Redevelopment Program (JRP). This innovative legislation limited the role of government in development to a supervisory function. Under the JRP, a commercial developer led redevelopment together with an association of property-owners, both pursuing a maximization of returns. The JRP transformed low-rise substandard or unplanned settlements into high-rise commercial housing estates, greatly increasing the housing stock. However, it displaced residents (Lee et al., 2003) due to owners' realization of a dramatic rent gap (Shin, 2009). The New Town Initiative, introduced by mayor Lee Myung-bak in 2002, accelerated the trend when it designated for redevelopment nearly 2,400 hectares, containing 97,000 privately owned households and 194,000 tenant households (S. Kim, 2010). Following the 2008 crisis, the cooling of the real-estate market slowed the pace of construction, but it did not slow residential displacement and the razing of lots in preparation for better economic tides. As the cases below testify, especially where displacement was controversial, developers swiftly proceeded to raze the lots in order to wipe off traces of opposition.

Throughout this history, squatters and low-income families have suffered significant human-rights and social-justice violations. This is especially the case for renters (Ha, 1999, 2015; Kwaak, 2015; Kyung & Kim, 2011; Lee et al., 2003). Moreover, forced evictions were (and continue to be) extremely violent, spurring national and international condemnation by international organizations, including the UN Commission on Human Rights (Asian Coalition for Housing Rights, 1988; S. Kim, 2010).

In the early 1980s, squatter tenants organized a powerful anti-eviction and housing-rights movement, in conjunction with the democratization movement (H.-S. Kim, 2010; J. Y. Lee, 1990) and the massive redevelopment for the 1986 Asian Games and the 1988 Olympic Games (Davis, 2011; Shin, 2018). In response, the Roh Tae-Woo administration announced the first construction plan for public rental housing units (S. Kim, 2010). Such initiatives placated the evictees' movement, although demolition records suggest that evictions have increased in the 1990s and 2000s (Davis, 2011; Ha, 1999). Short-term renters are now the main residential category that is not meaningfully protected, but they are also the least likely to protest because they lack networks and a sense of belonging in their neighborhood (Ha, 2010). For this reason, the cases here focus on displacement of commercial rather than residential tenants. This category is extremely vulnerable because of a lack of regulation for compensation in evictions caused by redevelopment, and the sector has seen the most prominent cases of protest against displacement over the past decade (Shin, 2018).

Similarly, since the 1980s, Istanbul's executives – liberal, social democratic, Islamic, and conservative – have all pursued the modern city (Lelandais, 2016). In the 1980s, Bedrettin Dalan sought to "transform Istanbul from a tired city, whose glory resided in past history, into a metropolis full of promise for the twenty-first century" (Aksoy, 2012, p. 97). Among other ambitious projects, he encouraged skyscrapers, famously wanting to recreate Manhattan in Istanbul. The Erdoğan government and mayor Kadir Topbaş (2004 to present), both from the conservative Justice and Development Party (AKP), joined forces to reach profound and systemic changes. When campaigning for reelection in 2008, Topbaş stated that he would remove informal slum housing within the city. Topbaş funneled resources to redevelopment and launched a branding campaign that culminated in the 2010 European Capital of Culture, arguing that regeneration was key "to rise up and shed [Istanbul's] deformed and twisted image and become a world city" (Aksoy, 2010, p. 3).

Planning in Istanbul is challenging because of conflicts and overlaps between national, provincial, metropolitan, and district (municipal) authorities. When tensions emerge, the national government devises new regulations to suit its goals. At the same time, the lack of funds induces municipalities to grant negotiating power to private parties, typically close to the national government, and allow to them to define location, function, and conditions of large-scale projects (Tasan-Kok, 2004, p. 145). Thus, governance in Istanbul often relies on informal networks; public–private partnerships are poorly regulated and monitored, and, due to extremely cumbersome regulation, "oral agreements, friendships, and informal networking seem to become the most important elements of procedure" (Tasan-Kok, 2004, p. 147). This approach to governance has major implications for planning, which often fails to keeps up with changes on the ground. For example, the master plans in 1995 and 2006 featured none of the regeneration areas and the infrastructural investments that actually took place (including major projects such as the third bridge over the Bosporus, two new ports and a tunnel project).[2]

Since 2000 especially, redevelopment is concentrated in areas that are central, enjoy beautiful landscapes, are earthquake-resistant, and offer the highest rent gaps (Dinçer, 2010). In addition to industrial conversions, the land slated for redevelopment therefore comes from inner-city slums and informal settlements. There are vast reservoirs of such land: At the turn of the millennium, 70 percent of the housing stock in Istanbul was illegal, but with redevelopment governments are also eliminating that informality. TOKİ (the Housing Development Authority of Turkey, responsible for the provision of public housing) together with KİPTAŞ (the metropolitan housing agency) undertook a massive construction program in collaboration with private developers (Çavuşoğlu & Yalçintan, 2010) and built a staggering 623,000 units between 2003 and 2014 (Bilgic, 2014). By 2012, only 6.51 percent of projects managed by TOKİ was in public housing, while 72.25 percent was in for-profit housing (Lelandais, 2014, 2016).

[2] Other striking changes unaccounted for by master plans are the increase in bed capacity in five-star hotels, which rose from 2,000 in 1980 to 6,786 in 1990 and 10,199 in 2007, and the explosion of shopping malls: Out of a total of forty-four as of 2010, thirty-four were constructed after 2000 (Çavuşoğlu & Yalçintan, 2010).

As in Seoul, the shift from piecemeal interventions in the 1980s and 1990s to the systematic redevelopment since 2002 owes much to specially designed legislation. Laws in 2003, 2004, and 2005, respectively, transferred public land to TOKİ and gave it the right to expropriate areas of urban renewal and to undertake renewal projects not only in blighted areas but also in historic districts (Dinçer, Enlil, & Islam, 2008; Gulersoy-Zeren, Tezer, Yigiter, Koramaz, & Gunay, 2008; Lelandais, 2016). The 2005 law (No. 5,366) allowed large private developers to turn whole blocks of historic areas over to new uses and to demolish listed buildings and replace them with replicas. The law also granted authority to municipalities to turn developers into co-owning partners without consulting the property-owners (Aksoy, 2010, p. 10). The Urgency Compulsory Purchase Act in 2006 further strengthened municipalities by allowing them to expropriate inner-city areas and resell them to corporate developers. In 2012, Law No. 6,306 delivered even more sweeping powers by extending TOKİ's rights to expropriate property on the basis of earthquake risk, even mandating that owners pay for demolition. This extensive legal infrastructure to legitimize extensive redevelopment and displacement shows that in weak institutional settings, "when the growth coalition cannot obtain the desired outcomes with existing institutions, it simply invents new ones" (interview with Murat Cemal Yalçintan, Professor of City Regional Planning, Mimar Sinan University, Istanbul, December 17, 2010).

In Buenos Aires, the human cost of redevelopment was similarly dramatic. The pursuit of global city status was connected with a shift from industrial to service sector associated with a raise of the informal economy and social polarization (Carbajal, 2003; Ciccolella, 1999; Pírez, 2002; Silvestri & Gorelik, 2000; H. A. Torres, 2001). To generate growth and revenues, the national government promoted real-estate development with favorable legal and material conditions (Crot, 2006; Guevara, 2014), and the branding of Buenos Aires (Carman, 2006).

Buenos Aires illustrates, as do Seoul and Istanbul, the displacement that follows when governments aim to turn informal settlements into areas fully integrated with formal markets, in line with global city aspirations. In 2009, the Advisory Group on Forced Evictions reported 170,000 people living in shantytowns and 200,000 squatters occupying formal buildings (Advisory Group on Forced Evictions, 2009). Between 2000 and 2014, over 20,000 people were evicted in the city of Buenos Aires (M. C. Rodríguez & Di Virgilio, 2016). Following changes in the legal code over the period from 1995 to 2008, city government policies toward squatting shifted from an emphasis on negotiation to usurpation (Verón, 2014). By 2011, over 5 percent of households lived in precarious homes. Overcrowding (defined as the number of households with two or more people per room) stood at 10.4 percent of households in 2011. In District 1 (home to the San Telmo neighborhood that I examine below), overcrowded homes reached nearly 18 percent, far exceeding the city average (Dirección de Estadística y Censos, 2012).

Over the same period, residential segregation deepened. Some sections of the middle and upper middle classes, especially in the affluent north and west of Buenos Aires, moved to a specific form of gated community, the walled towers (*torres jardín*), with amenities and security (Carbajal, 2003). Elite consumption was catered for with redevelopments such as the traditional Abasto market, an iconic Art Deco building from the 1930s located in the city's core. Residential segregation and the pursuit of global city status were exemplified with Puerto Madero, where land and docklands adjacent the central business district were transformed into one of the most expensive real-estate areas in the country (Cuenya, 2003).

* * *

Santiago, Chile differs from the other cities described thus far because it had far fewer informal settlements (dwellers had gained land tenure in the 1970s and 1980s), and the country is a highly institutionalized developmental state. However, even in this context, laws were written to dramatically favor developers at the expense of poor households. Santiago offers an interesting illustration of how fiscal, taxation, and planning regulation facilitate displacement in a state recognized as the vanguard of neoliberalism.

The Chilean government's tax regime heavily favors real-estate developers. The central government collects 95 percent of all taxes. After transfers, property tax is the single largest source of local revenues and is levied at a rate of 1.5 percent of cadastral evaluations, but with very outdated assessments (M. Torres, 2006). A decree from 1959, designed originally to promote middle-class real-estate investment, exempts dwellings of less than 140 square meters from property tax – which translates into an exemption for 70 percent of residential properties – and also from tax on rental income (Sabatini, 2000).

Real-estate developers are also favored by revenue sources. In addition to property taxes, building permits constitute an important source of funding for municipalities and promote the construction of multistory buildings. Business licenses (*patente comerciales*) are also issued and collected locally and incentivize municipalities to offer business-friendly conditions. Vehicle-registration fees constitute a third revenue source that is closely related to urban redevelopment. These fees range from 1 to 4.5 percent of the value of the vehicle and foster intense competition among municipalities because vehicles do not have to be registered in the municipality of residence of the owner. In the richest municipalities, vehicle registrations constitute about 20 percent of municipal revenue.[3]

Urban planning also facilitates redevelopment. Chile lacks a tradition of urban planning legislation and has historically favored the rights of property-owners and developers. Since the 1979 elimination of the law on "urban limits" and other market-oriented reforms, the urban area of Greater Santiago (which includes Santiago Province) has quadrupled. The major instrument to regulate land use, among a few, is the 1994 Metropolitan Regulatory Plan for Santiago (Plan Regulador Metropolitano de Santiago [PRMS]), subsequently modified and broadened in 1997, 2003, and 2014. However, scholars have lamented the lack of integrated territorial development and noted how land liberalization has fed speculation (Sabatini, 2000; Trivelli, 2006).

The extension of Santiago's urban boundary opened the way for private developers to take over lots of more than 300 hectares for the development of high-density sub-centers, called ZODUCs (Zonas de Desarrollo Urbano Condicionado; conditional urban development zones). In this context, private developers play a key role in urban planning and often – in exchange for surface rights – take over the task of providing amenities such as playgrounds or parks; infrastructure such as schools, shopping and healthcare facilities; and even major infrastructure such as underground parking areas, public transportation facilities, and subway extensions.

A lack of territorial coordination led to weak overall logic or to what local residents refer to as *cosismo*. Mayors compete with each other and shape their own zoning plans (*planos reguladores comunales*) to attract investments with "signature projects to enhance their status" (Siavelis et al., 2002, p. 290) such as the tallest building, the most dramatic bridge, the most important embassy. Thus, construction is rampant in Santiago:

[3] It should be noted that only 40 percent of the local proceeds of property tax goes to the municipality, while 60 percent is contributed to the FCM (Fondo Común Municipal, or Joint Municipal Fund), a national body that redistributes resources across municipalities. In the rich communes of Santiago Centro, Providencia, Vitacura and Las Condes, these proportions are 35 and 65 percent, respectively (Razmilic, 2015, p. 61).

Among hundreds of high-rise office and residential buildings, especially prominent is the Costanera Center, a mega-project in the financial district that includes a 280,000-square-meter mall and three towers, including the tallest building in Latin America.

* * *

While in developmental states, redevelopment translated primarily into the elimination of informal settlements, in more advanced economies a key dynamic was the deep erosion of public-sector housing through lack of maintenance and the privatization not only of the existing stock but also of public housing agencies, as we see in Hamburg, Madrid, Los Angeles, and Melbourne. A common and widely documented approach in liberal market economies was, and is, mixed-income redevelopment. In these schemes, governments enter into partnership with private developers and fund the renovation of ailing public housing estates by building and selling private units on the estates, thereby reducing the stock or size of the public units. This process has occurred even in European cities in recent years, and, rather than herald social integration, it amounts often to state-led gentrification (Bridge, Butler, & Lees, 2012; Häußermann, Läpple, & Siebel, 2008, p. 355).

Hamburg, to illustrate the point, is one of the richest cities in Europe yet is marred by social polarization. In 2010, 230,000 residents were on social welfare – their rent was covered by the state – and about 10,000 residents were considered homeless (Buchholz, 2016). The municipal housing company SAGA (an acronym based on its original neighborhood-based version Siedlungs-Aktiengesellschaft Altona) was founded in 1922 and tasked to "ensure the supply of safe and socially responsible housing for broad layers of the population at appropriate prices" (as stated on SAGA's website). But in the early twenty-first century SAGA shifted direction. It acquired the municipal company that deals with real-estate construction (GWG; Gesellschaft für Wohnen und Bauen mbH). While SAGA policies used to privilege redistribution through the provision of rental housing to low-income residents, it now shifted to maximizing land returns and promoting gentrification. The agency abandoned a tradition of bargaining to extract social benefits such as price ceilings for the sale or rental of new units. A number of rental developments were allowed to move to ownership. The rent index (*Mietenspiegel*) – set by SAGA to regulate rent increases outside of re-letting – accelerated because it was biased upwards by rentals in new developments and upgraded buildings.

As a result, average rents increased at a steadily rising rate since 2000, from an increase of 2.1 percent in rent between 2003 and 2005 to an increase of 6.1 percent between 2013 and 2015.[4] These patterns affected a large portion of residents, as 76 percent of households in Hamburg rented rather than owned (Vogelpohl & Buchholz, 2017). They especially affected vulnerable populations, which also found less shelter in social housing. Social housing in Hamburg consisted of rented housing in privately owned properties for which the municipality covered the gap between the portion that tenants were required to pay and market rent, for a predefined period, called the lock-in period. The lock-in period was cut from thirty to fifteen years by the conservative government in 2003, which directly eroded housing stock. For example, nearly 30 percent of units with social-housing status were set to expire in 2017 (Vogelpohl & Buchholz, 2017).

From the mid 1990s to the mid 2000s, the number of social-housing units dropped from 250,000 to less than 150,000, and by 2014 the number stood at under 100,000 (Birke, 2016, p. 212). City governments changed hands from center-left to center-right, but they all shared these strategies until the housing crisis became a major electoral issue in the municipal elections of 2011, which gradually led to some policy changes to alleviate displacement.

Toronto also suffered from a well-documented long-term trend of gentrification and displacement (Skaburskis, 2012). Instead of addressing the need for affordable housing, starting with the new millennium, high-rise development largely aimed for middle- and higher-income sectors surged, justified by demographic projections. By the early 2010s, Toronto was the city in the Western Hemisphere with most high-rise development (Gillad Rosen & Walks, 2015). In October 2012, the city had 147 high-rises under construction, twice as many as New York. By 2015, the city had forty-four skyscrapers 150 or more meters tall, triple the number (thirteen) it had in 2005 (Melanson, 2013).

Like other cities in this book, planning in Toronto was driven by a political agenda focused on international competition "with other so-called global cities for investments, an educated work force (the so-called creative workers) and tourist dollars," in a sharp departure from the city's working-class history (Lehrer, Keil, & Kipfer, 2010, p. 83; Todd, 1995). The pressure of competition imposed leaner and faster planning

[4] See www.mieterverein-hamburg.de/de/aktuelles/statistiken-wohnen-hamburg/index.html (accessed June 15, 2017).

approval procedures, and looser zoning regulations (Lehrer & Laidley, 2008), while culture and branding figured prominently with an intensified focus on museums and heritage (Jenkins, 2005).

Nearly half of Toronto residents were renters, yet the condo boom was geared to young professionals, first-time homebuyers, empty nesters, and affluent immigrants (Lehrer et al., 2010), providing the urban experience that would attract and retain "creatives" and high-value workers. The effect was a well-documented boom in new-build gentrification (Davidson & Lees, 2010; Kipfer & Keil, 2002; Kipfer & Petrunia, 2009; Lehrer et al., 2010; Lehrer & Wieditz, 2009).

Through mixed-income redevelopment, densification especially affected public housing estates. After the bulk of public-housing construction between 1964 and 1984, budgetary concerns curtailed expenditures and progressively moved public housing policy from non-market to market-conforming approaches, which encouraged ownership and introduced cash transfers (Hulchanski, 2004). Cash transfers shifted subsidies to landlords, rather than financing long-term infrastructure. In addition, since the mid 1990s, the federal government devolved the responsibility of public housing to the provinces. Cash-strapped provinces sought to promote the involvement of the private sector in affordable housing provision through tax incentives. Toronto turned to the private sector for funding partnerships in a variety of urban interventions, including public housing. The result was a turn from public housing to mixed-income estates and the connected privatization of public housing. Under pressure to cut costs, the Toronto Community Housing Corporation also sold a significant share of public housing (over 700 single-family homes in 2012 alone). The removal of rent caps, and the increased demand for affordable housing due to demographic changes, further contributed to lengthening Toronto public-housing waiting lists to nearly 90,000 applicants by 2010 (Sweetman, 2011).

CITY BRANDS AND CULTURAL INDUSTRIES

In the aspiring global cities discussed here, redevelopment policies were often supported by city branding and legitimized by connections to cultural industries as new engines for economic growth. Mayors also branded to compete with other cities (Anholt, 2007), attract investment (Greenberg, 2008), and increase political clout and legitimacy (Pasotti, 2009). By the twenty-first century, significant investment in city branding was all but ubiquitous.

Among different kinds of branding, each urban government in this book promoted its city's historical heritage, and typically to great political effect. This is not surprising: We know that heritage management – the present's instrumental use of the past – can be an extraordinary tool to build legitimacy and political support (Ashworth, 2017; Ashworth, Graham, & Tunbridge, 2007; Graham & Howard, 2008; Littler & Naidoo, 2005; N. Moore & Whelan, 2007; Tunbridge, 2004; Tunbridge & Ashworth, 1996). The "revaluation" or "conservation" of a neighborhood's cultural heritage (always reflecting a specific view of its history) thus becomes contested territory. Tel Aviv is a terrific illustration of how governments can deploy heritage conservation and branding in support of redevelopment.

For most cities, branding is a relatively recent phenomenon, but not for Tel Aviv. Official policies have aimed to present the city as a compelling place not only to tourists and investors but also to its own citizens since its very founding. Azaryahu (2008) identifies four stages of cultural positioning in the city's history. The first stage (1909–1950s) presented Tel Aviv as the "First Hebrew City" and thus as the beacon of Zionism. The city was the site of historical redemption, where Jews could truly prove their abilities. The second stage (1960s–1970s) promoted Tel Aviv as a modern cosmopolitan city and the regional window to the West, a message delivered with references to European cafés and commercial sophistication centered along Dizengoff Street. In the third phase (1980s–1990s), the city was officially branded the "Nonstop City," moving the emphasis to a vibrant lifestyle, with special emulation of New York and its nightlife, epitomized in the rebirth of Sheinkin Street as the new bohemian center of Tel Aviv, a local version of Greenwich Village.

Of particular relevance to this book, as elaborated Chapter 5, the fourth stage launched the "White City," which promoted Tel Aviv's international (or Bauhaus) architecture (LeVine, 2004; Nitzan-Shiftan, 1996, 2000). This approach departed significantly from the earlier three. It shifted from lifestyle to physical heritage in the city core, and thus privileged the elites residing in these areas as exemplars of the authentic urban experience. Politically, the discourse of the "White City" dislodged the bohemians and "creatives" who had been at the core of the city brand since the 1960s (Alfasi & Fabian, 2008). From a fiscal perspective, the White City brand drove perceptions of value, and thus land prices, opening new opportunities for investors and city government (Margalit, 2009). The political benefits of the brand were similarly notable. After the ideological crisis spurred by the kibbutzim decline, the rise of the religious right, and the immigration waves of the 1990s, politicians needed new narratives about Tel Aviv's place in Israel, and the world. Determined branding efforts culminated in 2003 when UNESCO announced the "White City of Tel Aviv" as a World Heritage Site (Amit-Cohen, 2005; Fenster & Yacobi, 2005; Margalit, 2013). In the process, as Rotbard shows in his wonderful account, the historical city of Jaffa was constructed as an "inverted reflection" of Tel Aviv, not shining and white but nocturnal, criminal, dirty, a "black city" (Rotbard, 2015; see also LeVine, 2004; Margalit & Alfasi, 2016).

* * *

Redevelopment was legitimized in many of these cities through the promotion of cultural industries. In Seoul and Buenos Aires, for example, governments promoted cultural-industry hubs to justify development, illustrating that this convergence of branding and cultural industries occurs in developmental states as well as advanced economies.

For decades, downtown Seoul had been in crisis. From 1975 to 1995, Seoul's population increased by 44 percent, yet the downtown population decreased by 52 percent. By 1995, the proportion of households with an education level lower than middle school in the downtown area was 40 percent, compared to 25 percent in the city of Seoul as a whole. These social features were reflected in housing quality, as substandard housing types (mostly rentals or squatters) accounted for 35 percent of downtown housing – 2.5 times the average in Seoul (Amirtahmasebi, Orloff, Wahba, & Altman, 2016).

To turn around downtown, the Seoul metropolitan government founded the first city marketing department in preparation for the 2002 FIFA (Fédération Internationale de Football Association) World Cup, and expanded it under the Lee mayoralty. In his last year as mayor, Lee moved city branding from an ad-hoc approach to a longer-term strategy (C. Kim & Kim, 2010). Lee's branding emphasized Seoul's natural and cultural heritage and presented Seoul with the slogan "a clean and attractive global city," making it the fifth city in the world for convention tourism (Křižnik, 2011). The brand built on Lee's several environmental interventions, such as the Seoul Forest Park along the Han River and the construction of a grassy field in front of Seoul City Hall, which now hosts nearly daily cultural events. His signature project was the restoration of the Cheonggyecheon stream, whose success catapulted him to the presidency in 2008.

In 2007, the mayoralty passed to another conservative, Oh Se-hoon. The tight alliance between city and national governments from 2006 to 2011 meant that branding involved unprecedented efforts and investments (H. Lee, 2015). Oh focused on cultural industries; for example, design, fashion, performing arts, and digital media (Y.-S. Lee & Hwang, 2012). He took stock of the tremendous expansion of Korean popular culture in films, TV series, and contemporary music and dance – a global phenomenon nicknamed the "Korean wave" (S. Kim, 2009) – and combined economic arguments with popular ones about the "creative class" (Florida, 2002), the "creative city" (Landry, 2012) and "creative economies" (Howkins, 2002).

Embracing these approaches, cultureconomics, as Koreans named this approach, posits that growth depends on the ability to attract high skilled labor, which is mobile and moves to areas dense with amenities. Creativity and the presence of artists came to be considered key amenities, and cultureconomics became a buzzword for local and national governments (H. Lee, 2015).

Despite some criticism (Ra, 2008; Yi, 2009), government institutions, such as the influential Seoul Institute (Byeon & Park, 2008; Ra, 2010; Ra, Park, Oh, & Woo, 2008), and civil-society actors prominent in the planning discourse, such as the Architectural Institute of Korea (I. Kim, Kim, Seo, & Choi, 2010), embraced the creative-industry idea. But they actually referred to radically different sites and phenomena: The government and some scholars focused on megaprojects such as the futuristic Dongdaeumum Design Center (Križnik, 2013) or the R&D cluster of the Digital City (D. E. Cohen, 2014); civil-society actors and some other scholars focused on grassroots cultural sites such as Mullae Art Village, discussed in Chapter 9 (H. Lee & Lee, 2013).

The Seoul metropolitan government identified several cultural hot spots, largely in low-income areas, and built structures in these locations to promote artistic production and consumption. The Seoul Foundation for Arts and Culture was officially in charge of the program, which ambitiously opened ten new Seoul Art Space facilities throughout the city.

Oh also set up institutions to promote the role of design, such as the Seoul Design Foundation, the Global Design Cities Organization, and the Seoul Design Olympiad. In 2010, these efforts gained Seoul the designation of UNESCO City of Design and World Capital of Design, which contributed to the city's brand value, its competitiveness in the design industry, and its tourist appeal. Different indexes indicated a rising profile for Seoul, with the city breaking into the top 10 on the A. T. Kearney

Global Cities Index and moving up on the global and world cities index between 2000 and 2010 (Globalization and World Cities Research Network, 2012; Hales & Pena, 2012). However, the branding was also heavily criticized by citizens for lacking popular participation and being excessively grandiose (H. Lee, 2015).

Buenos Aires pursued a strategy parallel to Seoul's, as projects to accommodate the urban professional elite were accompanied by a new emphasis on the rehabilitation of heritage areas and a significant investment in cultural industries. In the 2000s, devaluation produced unprecedented international affordability. The city government capitalized on this to increase global status and reshape the local economy by fostering a tourism boom. The new brand emphasized cultural dimensions (Kanai, 2014).

Mayor Mauricio Macri (2007–2015) embraced neoliberal policies (Rodríguez, Arqueros Mejica, Rodríguez, Gomez Schettini, & Zapata, 2011) and was especially keen on branding, since before he became chief of government for Buenos Aires he had been the chairman for Boca Juniors, an internationally recognized football team. Under Macri, the brand invoked Buenos Aires as the cultural capital of Latin America (Dinardi, 2015). Through professionalized and coherent urban branding, city and government overlapped with the slogan "Making Buenos Aires" ("Haciendo Buenos Aires") (Méndez & Tyrone, 2014). The communication was highly polished: in yellow, Macri's signature color, the same fonts and logos appeared not only on all city websites but also on all government buildings, vehicles, and venues. During his tenure, tourism in Buenos Aires grew dramatically, reaching an all-time high in 2010 when the city hosted approximately 10 million visitors, 30 percent of whom were international tourists (Kanai, 2014).

Artists strongly contested Macri's approach to cultural industries. His focus on tourist-oriented cultural entrepreneurialism departed dramatically from previous administrations, which had promoted social inclusion and supported grassroots neighborhood development (Kanai & Ortega-Alcázar, 2009). Instead, the Macri administration cut initiatives such as the Neighborhood Cultural Program (Programa Cultural en Barrios), in place since 1983, and closed several independent, nonprofit cultural centers. Two opposing views of the city thus emerged:

> On the one hand, a modern cultural city whose sophistication and openness were rooted in the development of cultural festivals and events, a city of spectacles and business, leading Latin America by virtue of its creativity and diversity of spaces for cultural consumption. On the other hand, a city of artistic

> expressions, a place in which culture seems to be not entirely commodified, citizens' identities not simply forged by consumption, and a place where collective and inclusive projects can come into being.
>
> (Dinardi, 2017, p. 95)

Buenos Aires' brand as Latin America's cultural capital involved a variety of initiatives, both discursive and budgetary, with a focus on tango (the Argentine tango was declared part of intangible cultural heritage by UNESCO in 2009); on the editorial sector (Buenos Aires was proclaimed World Book Capital by UNESCO in 2011); on design (based on the UNESCO 2005 declaration); and on hospitality, as the city presented itself as the regional hub for conferences. Buenos Aires added international festivals, such as the Tango World Cup and the Book Fair. The city started to host a dozen additional festivals focused on jazz, Shakespearean theater, independent films, alternative music, and contemporary dance, with significant impact. To illustrate, the Tango Buenos Aires Festival and World Cup in 2013 attracted 550,000 participants, with 80,000 out-of-town visitors, mostly from beyond Argentina (Kanai, 2014). The marketization of culture was confirmed by Macri's 2010 description of tango as equivalent to a cash crop for Porteños, a comment criticized by artists and representative members of the tango community.

As in Seoul, city branding was accompanied by investment in cultural infrastructure and cultural industries (Kanai, 2011). Despite political fluctuations and changes in funding in the early 2000s, administrators overall who were interviewed for this project noted a high degree of continuity in the emphasis on cultural infrastructure and industries (interview with Fernando Arias, coordinator for the Observatorio de Industrias Creativas [Creative Industries Observatory], Buenos Aires, November 26, 2015). This was confirmed by budgetary analysis: between 2001 and 2004, budgetary allocations for the secretary of culture increased steadily, reaching 170 million pesos ($60 million) or the equivalent of 4.5 percent of the total city budget in 2004. Between 2002 and 2011, public investment in culture as a percentage of budgeted expenses for the city of Buenos Aires remained between 3.43 and 3.85 percent (CABA Observatorio de Industrias Creativas, 2012). Creative industries contributed between 8 and 9.2 percent of domestic product in Buenos Aires between 2005 and 2010. Moreover, the sector contributed to 9.6 percent of employment in the city, compared to 5 percent in Argentina overall (CABA Observatorio de Industrias Creativas, 2012; García Pérez & Sequera Fernández, 2014).

The investment in city branding and cultural promotion stimulated extensive urban redevelopment in both heritage management and infrastructure for cultural industries. Given the city's extraordinary architectonic stock, the focus on heritage was not new. For example, San Telmo, the downtown neighborhood where my research is located, was the first area to gain heritage status in 1979, a status that was modified in the 1990s and in the 2000s to accommodate redevelopment in line with globalization and tourism promotion. Thus, cultural industry infrastructure served the dual function of fostering economic growth and "regenerating" areas deemed decayed (economically, physically, or socially) but with valuable cultural assets. Characteristic of growing redevelopment trends, this approach combined progressive discourses of urban regeneration with elite and real-estate interests (Herzog, 2006; Scarpaci, 2005).

Creative industries were typically located in or close to the city center. Therefore, the historical core, with San Telmo, was the first and most prominent object of this kind of intervention, marked by public space improvements, rehabilitation of the housing stock, and social and educational programs.

In neighborhoods farther from the center, where the productive potential of tourism was more challenging, the city government of Buenos Aires introduced clusters of cultural industry, beginning in 2001. La Boca, San Telmo, and a portion of Barracas were designated as art districts. The city built Usina del Arte, a center for music and dance performance and training in La Boca. Barracas was chosen to host the design district, and there the city built the Centro Metropolitano de Diseño, created starting in 2001 from the renovation of a long closed fish market. The area of Parque Patricio hosts the technology district, where the city built the Instituto Tecnológico de Buenos Aires. The area west of Palermo was designated as the district for audiovisual arts, with a major infrastructure to promote video and music production called Dorrego.

These creative industries' clusters were to promote entrepreneurialism and attract outsiders and tourists through the agglomeration of products and services, while reinforcing (or outright creating, in the case of Parque Patricio and Barracas) local neighborhood brands. With a permanent staff of about thirty, the Centro Metropolitano de Diseño provided technical and financial support and improved competitiveness for small firms, independent professionals, and micro-entrepreneurs through extensive training and about twenty office and production spaces. In addition to the business incubator program, the center hosts the Observatory of Cultural Industries, which promotes sectorial research and training with conferences and seminars; and the City Cultural Fund, which awards funding and recognition to emerging talented creatives. Its grand hall is often buzzing with outreach activities, such as during my visit in November 2015, when a full-day fair was held to promote the center with food, music, prizes and about 500 invitees.

Although the two cities share similarities, the Buenos Aires program was more ambitious than Seoul's because in addition to infrastructural development, the city promoted the districts to private investors. Buenos Aires artists who risked being priced out contested the developments, building on a long history of local activism (Dinardi, 2015; Herzer, Rodríguez, Redondo, Di Virgilio, & Ostuni, 2005), but were sidestepped when the city government adapted a discourse with values of inclusion, growth, and diversity. This approach is typical of brand mayors (Pasotti, 2009) and difficult to counter, because as Lederman (2015, p. 47) argues, the branding reflected market-oriented goals that increased inequality, but the policy was justified with the idea that "a creative city is an integrated, sustainable, and socially equitable city" – a framing that undermined possibilities for contestation.

* * *

As a third aspect of branding, many cities focused on culture as an economic resource, to be consumed. To some extent, this strategy was pursued in all the cities examined here, but Los Angeles aptly illustrates the approach.

Downtown Los Angeles is composed of several districts, focused on industry, fashion, arts, entertainment, civic institutions, finance, and the historic downtown. However, the main brand of this area in recent decades has been tied to cultural consumption. The opening of the Staples Center in 1999 brought a new wave of consumers to downtown, and an adaptive reuse ordinance passed by the City of Los Angeles in that same year granted the conversion of commercially zoned buildings into residential structures (Beacon Economics, 2015). The ordinance was supported by property-owners eager to accommodate artists and vanguard gentrifiers, after noticing that area squatters had started a lively underground arts scene. Soon these artists organized an "Art Walk" to promote their work and the area as an artistic hub. The monthly event combined open studios and galleries with drinks and music "at a time when most Angelenos still avoided this downtown area because of its reputation for being dangerous and dilapidated" and transformed the area "into a vibrant corridor of cultural activity and public life" (Collins & Loukaitou-Sideris, 2016, p. 406). In the wake of this success, the local neighborhood council formed a Gallery Row committee, and the city council approved the designation of the area as the Art Walk District. Investors were attracted by tax-relief and business incentives related to the Federal Empowerment Zone. Public–private initiatives were set up by city officials, property-owners, business organizations, and actors linked to the Art Walk to foster entrepreneurship in cultural industries and high-tech. Consequently, employment in what became known as Gallery Row nearly doubled in less than a decade, largely driven by top salary earners. The Art Walk, with over 20,000 visitors by 2008, was an essential component of the gentrification process. Real-estate agents saw peaks of interest in the week after Art Walk, and rents soared 382 percent between 2000 and 2010 (Collins & Loukaitou-Sideris, 2016).

But the boom in cultural consumption extended well beyond Gallery Row. Since 1999, iconic entertainment and cultural megaprojects in all of downtown Los Angeles (rebranded as DTLA) have grown dramatically. DTLA was heavily promoted as the creative hub of Los Angeles, due to the hosting of the Museum of Contemporary Art, the Staples Center, LA Live, the Broad, the Music Center, and its arts district and gallery scene, of which the Art Walk was an important feature. The Business Improvement District (BID) launched a program designed to encourage leasing of office space by "educating" brokers and prospective tenants on the advantages of a DTLA location (Downtown Center Business Improvement District, 2015b). The branding campaign pointed to over a hundred live-music venues, sixty art galleries, fifteen farmers markets, grocers and coffee roasters, the 5-hectare Grand Park, the improved public transit and bike lanes, and the acclaimed restaurant scene. BID curated a website and social media as well, and augmented their efforts with several campaigns (Downtown Center Business Improvement District, 2015a). Also, to capitalize on social-network marketing, BID launched a social-media influencer campaign. The goal was to promote the area and specific venues by assigning to influential social-media personalities curated and themed itineraries in which they would share their experience with their social-network audiences. The campaign alone generated over 2 million "impressions" on social media. A "team" of downtown guides also distributed materials, directions, and welcome bags.

Over the years, this kind of branding effort attracted both investment and the target workforce: as of 2015, 75 percent of DTLA's 54,000 residents were between the ages of twenty-three and forty-four, and

320,000 workers with at least a bachelor's degree lived within 16 kilometers of DTLA. From 2006 to 2013, employment in DTLA outpaced citywide growth, with much of it concentrated in leisure and hospitality, which since 2008 grew by more than 20 percent. The overall economic impact of this strategy was remarkable. From 2006 to 2015, the total gross receipts in DTLA increased by 25.7 percent compared to just 3.3 percent in the City of Los Angeles overall. Further, from 2008 to 2013, gross receipts in retail increased by 33.1 percent, and accommodation and food receipts grew by 68 percent (Beacon Economics, 2015).

Unsurprisingly, property prices soared dramatically: From 1999 to 2015, the average price per square foot for a condo in DTLA increased from $169 to $605; the number of residential units climbed from 11,626 to 35,449. Over 800 new restaurants, bars, retail, and nightlife businesses served these customers. Between 1999 and 2015, residential property values grew from 4.8 billion to $13.6 billion; over the same period, real-estate investment in arts and entertainment was $1.49 billion, in civic and institutional buildings $4.01 billion, in commercial venues $1.22 billion, and toward mixed-use $6.76 billion (all data from Downtown Center BID, 2015a).

* * *

The remainder of this book will examine how opposition to these cultural-growth strategies motivated neighborhood struggles and sometimes policy changes. Comparative analysis of the twenty-nine cases identified three paths to mobilization, examined in Part II: (1) Protesters deploy experiential tools and activate citywide networks of like-minded organizations; (2) protesters deploy experiential tools and rely on substantial previous legacy in resistance against redevelopment; (3) protesters activate citywide networks of like-minded organizations and rely on the substantial support of unions. Part III will then examine the impact of these mobilizations on redevelopment zoning outcomes.

We begin with cases from Santiago, Istanbul, Tel Aviv, and Jaffa that illustrate varying degrees of success in mobilization when the use of experiential tools is joined by dense and broad support networks.

PART II

EXPLAINING MOBILIZATION

5

Experiential Tools and Networks

THE KEY ROLE OF EXPERIENTIAL TOOLS: SANTIAGO

In many respects, Santiago, Chile, is the core puzzle of this book. The municipality of Santiago Centro was governed in the 2000s by stanchly pro-business mayors. Further, Santiago is the political and economic center of the country that launched neoliberalism, and the regime is heavily tilted toward real-estate interests. Multi-country surveys find in Santiago the lowest level of popular trust in associations (Collier & Handlin, 2009). Surely, this was an adverse setting for residents to organize against an invasion of high-rise construction in their quaint, quiet, and attractive neighborhood. Yet residents mobilized, and succeeded. They even turned their organization into an influential political actor. And, as we will see, experiential tools and strong networks were key to their accomplishments.

The barrio Yungay lies at the heart of Santiago Centro, one of the thirty-two municipalities that form the Province of Santiago (largely overlapping with the metropolitan area). The municipality derives its influence from the large population coupled with a traditional role as center of cultural and political life. Data from the 2002 Census provides the background conditions for the events described below. Santiago Centro had a population of about 200,792, of which barrio Yungay was only 12,962. The barrio had a population density of 13,893 people per square kilometer, much higher than the Santiago Centro average of 8,964. The rate of foreign-born residents was 14.05 percent (against an average for Santiago Centro of 9.61), while the rate of education was in line with the city average at 10.67 years of schooling (against an average of city average of 10.94). The rate of renters was 54 percent (against a city average of 47 percent).

Until 1835, the area belonged to José Santiago Portales Larraín, father of the minister Diego Portales. The family subsequently subdivided and sold the 350 hectares. In 1839, at the end of the war against the Peru–Bolivian confederation, the president signed a decree to give the barrio the name of the battle that sealed the victory: Yungay. That same year, José Zapiola composed the "Hymn to the Victory of Yungay," which was used as the Chilean national anthem. The barrio has been characterized since the mid 1800s as an area of the middle classes and public employees. Several important buildings and churches were constructed during the demographic growth at the end of the 1800s, but the symbol of Yungay became the Monument of the Common Chilean, sculpted by Virginio Arias in 1888, which sealed Yungay as the barrio that carried national identity.

Starting in the 1930s middle- and upper-middle-income residents emigrated from the barrio to new, affluent municipalities in the east (like Providencia, Nunoa, and Las Condes). The barrio slowly deteriorated, but, like several other working-class neighborhoods in Santiago, it maintained a vital community and rich everyday life. Thanks to its many low-rise buildings and quiet streets, it enjoyed a provincial air and close neighborhood relations. Residents kept alive traditions such as a famous carnival. The neighborhood had a great social mix, ranging from high middle classes to low-income immigrants (Contreras, 2011), and was a place that residents valued for the intimacy, the personal contact, and peaceful pace encouraged by its low-rise architecture and multiple meeting points, such as the five food markets held in various locations at different days of the week. The barrio is also considered a cultural magnet, and houses Santiago's most important theaters and museums: the Contemporary Art Museum, the Natural History Museum, Artequín, the Mirador Interactive Museum, the Novedades Theater (founded in 1920), the Matucana 100 Cultural Center, the American Popular Art Museum, the Library of Santiago, and the Museum of Memory, as well as several cultural centers, such as the Víctor Jara Foundation and Galpón, the Manuel Rojas Cultural Center, and the Spiral Dance Center (Bulnes, 2012).

The barrio deteriorated further after the 1985 earthquake, and gentrification began. The Ley de Renovación Urbana 18.595 aimed to rehabilitate housing and guided the 1987 declaration of Yungay as an urban renewal area (*zona de renovación urbana*). The central government granted subsidies to promote the renovation of deteriorated and affordable housing in the city center. The Corporation for the Development of Santiago (Corporación para el Desarrollo de Santiago, a.k.a. Cordesan) provided innovative municipal management of these programs. Starting in 1985, Cordesan established a strong link between the municipality, the local community, and the real-estate sector. The corporation halted the abandonment of the city center with the removal of undesirable structures (a prison and a derelict transportation infrastructure), improvements in public spaces, the rehabilitation of heritage buildings, and the construction of cultural facilities and parks (Greene & Rojas, 2010). By bridging government programs and real-estate developers through the Repopulation Program (Programa de Repoblamiento) (enacted from 1990 to 1994), Cordesan was able to attract public school teachers by offering them new subsidized housing, and when this successful program was extended to other aspiring residents, it fed gentrification (Trivelli, 2011). At the same time, in some neighborhoods, gentrification was also fed by an opposite mechanism – redlining – whereby financial institutions declared an area not viable, thereby depriving owners of maintenance and repair funds. Abandonments followed, and buildings could be bought cheaply, which fed a boom in new construction (López-Morales, 2010). In fact, between 2002 and 2012, the population of the municipality of Santiago increased by 55 percent while the housing stock almost doubled (Amirtahmasebi, Orloff, Wahba, & Altman, 2016).

In other words, different levels of government did not act in unison: "while the national state decisively promote[d] a model of inner city social housing upgrading [...], other national- and local-level branches of the state prioritize[d] the high-rise construction" (López-Morales, 2010, p. 163). Municipal regulation undermined small-scale redevelopment and therefore prevented small owners from realizing their homes' rent potential. Following this highly entrepreneurial and contradictory role of the state, real-estate developers turned eagerly to the historical center of Santiago. Many old buildings were replaced with high-rises, displacing previous residents (Navarro Ayala, 2006). Over the 2000s, Yungay thus turned into a hot spot of real-estate production (Paulsen, 2014, p. 77) that fragmented the landscape and threatened preexisting social relations.

In the municipality of Santiago, the construction of new apartments increased tenfold, from 1.1 percent of units and 1.16 percent of square meters offered in 1989, to 13.8 percent of units and 11 percent of square meters offered in 2001 (Rojas, Rodríguez, & Wegelin, 2004). Special regulations benefited very large construction companies, as can be deduced from the average size of new buildings, which increased from eleven floors in 1996 to eighteen floors in 2006. The number of apartments built per condominium also soared from 78.5 in 1991 to 207.5 in 2005 (López-Morales, 2010). Appreciation per square meter was four times higher in the Santiago municipality than in the whole of Greater Santiago during the 1990s (Trivelli, 2006), and significant displacement occurred (López-Morales, 2016).

Of the 1,070 new construction permits issued for the municipality of Santiago between 1989 and 1999, 715 (equivalent to nearly 67 percent) were issued in the western sector and concentrated in the area that contains Yungay and its adjacent neighborhood of Brasil. A desire to safeguard architectural heritage followed. Buildings listed for historical conservation in the municipality increased from 43 to 1,342 in 1997; of those, 25.4 percent were concentrated in Yungay (Paulsen, 2014). This extension was followed in 2003 by legislation mandating density limits in the area adjacent to listed buildings, which significantly limited the scope of new construction.

Heritage revaluation, the associated public investment in beautification of urban space, and the development of commercial and recreational activities, together fostered gentrification in the neighborhood, documented with changes in the housing supply (G. Mardones, 2016, 2017). It can also be captured by observed increases in average income and in the rate of education among its residents. The 2011 census showed a nearly 15 percent increase in the top income quintile in this area, and decreases in the lowest three quintiles. Yungay was now the area with the highest education level in the entire municipality. Thirty-one percent of residents had high-school diplomas, and nearly 29 percent had college degrees (Paulsen, 2014, p. 87).

In this context, the association Vecinos por la Defensa del Barrio Yungay wanted an alternative to the common socioeconomic and development dynamics of heritage sites, by which authorities largely respond to tourism and elite economic interests and push out long-standing residents (A. Rodríguez & Rodríguez, 2014). It also wanted a more autonomous role in the management of its living space. Decidedly grassroots, it promoted heritage preservation along with a sustainable, inclusive development model that championed citizen participation and fought the dislocation and displacement of lower income residents (Bulnes, 2012; Paulsen, 2014). Participants spanned low and middle classes and educational and professional backgrounds. Organizers had no significant background in protest. However, over the course of a few years, amateur leaders of the group turned into savvy political operators, to the point that a decade later they were sometimes referred to as professional politicians, and the group was successfully institutionalized: it came to be seen as a political lobby for heritage preservation at the national level.

At the start, however, organizers generated political clout through successful neighborhood mobilization. It all started with a quality-of-life concern: Vecinos por la Defensa del Barrio Yungay was formed in the fall of 2005 when neighbors met and organized over the poor quality of their garbage collection. They collected over 2,000 signatures and sent them to the municipality, the regional executive, the general secretary of government, and the metropolitan health office. And they organized over twenty-five demonstrations in the fall and winter against mayor Raúl Alcaíno.

In May 2006, the founders of Vecinos por la Defensa del Barrio Yungay attended a public hearing and were surprised to learn of a plan to modify the Plan Regulador Comunal de Santiago, Sector Parque Portales (the sector that includes Barrio Yungay). With the extension of Parque Portales, the municipality planned to raise the allowable building height to twenty floors and remove several buildings from the heritage protection list (Departamento de Urbanismo de la Dirección de Obras de la Municipalidad de Santiago, 2006). The association reacted swiftly because "once more the authorities expected to impose on us a model of city in which the community has no role in decision-making" (Carvajal, Pascual, Arancibia Rodríguez, & Osorio, 2007) based on a "misguided modernistic approach to development" (from the website of Vecinos por la Defensa del Barrio Yungay). Quickly the narrative became one of protecting the barrio from real-estate speculation (Calcagni González & Migone Widoycovich, 2013, p. 7).

The leader of the association was Rosario Carvajal, an energetic historian who was born and still lived in the neighborhood. She fits the profile of the "antigrowth entrepreneur" identified by Schneider and Teske (1993). Under her guidance, a handful of professionals and academics in the field of architecture and law began to organize. Therefore, the original group included creatives who were long-term residents, often underemployed, and equipped with relevant technical expertise. Because they were long-term residents, they could connect with working-class inhabitants.

Several studies and surveys have examined this neighborhood's unusually intense sense of belonging and pride, which is expressed in a variety of ways but above all through street-level personal interaction and consumption patterns that privilege local markets and mom-and-pop stores. The most extensive study emphasizes the role of Vecinos por la Defensa del Barrio Yungay in promoting belonging, participation, and a shared barrio identity (Calcagni González & Migone Widoycovich, 2013).

The group mobilized low-income residents around the idea that the neighborhood's identity was constituted by its architectural as well as its social heritage and that the proposed redevelopment threatened this identity and had to be opposed by alternatives devised through participatory self-management. Therefore, the group emerged in response to a threat, and, although it was not explicitly against gentrification, it was firmly against displacement. Ingeniously, their platform linked architectural preservation – the group's original priority – with the preservation of its existing population. Heritage preservation was a more promising route to gain institutional support than an anti-gentrification discourse, but by successfully protecting old buildings, the group also fought displacement of low-income tenants.

The concept of joining architectural and social heritage became both the glue and the catalyst for mobilization, and helped to negotiate class, age, and employment differences among participants. The group was consciously transversal, and ranged from hotel and restaurant owners to artists and unemployed, unskilled workers. Several interviews reveal that organizers were deeply aware of the power that came from being a diverse group of claimants (Bulnes, 2012).

To deliver its ideas, Vecinos por la Defensa del Barrio Yungay built on and expanded far beyond the traditional protest repertoire. The association started mobilization and protest with traditional tools: signature collections, street protests, sit-ins, and teach-ins. It quickly established links with traditional media (the press, radio, and television). However, it also developed media outlets that it could directly control, such as a website, a listserv, a glossy monthly magazine distributed in municipal kiosks (*Bello Barrio*), radio programs, and even an internet television channel (TV Patrimonio). The motto of the association was "to disseminate, to disseminate, to disseminate" ("difundir, difundir y difundir"). Over time, the group migrated from a strong reliance on its carefully edited webpage and blog to more participatory platforms such as Facebook and Twitter. This reflects large technological shifts but also changes in the use of media for mobilization.

In addition to these conventional instruments, the group relied heavily on the successful deployment of experiential tools, utilizing all four types (see Chapter 2). Experiential tools were essential to display and invigorate a sense of belonging in the neighborhood and to bring together residents from across class and age cleavages who would not normally have crossed paths. They helped recruit both participants and allies among other groups, supporters among politicians, and connections with institutions. Their sustained deployment over time in a variety of forms, including schools and workshops, signaled the enduring commitment to protect the neighborhood from real-estate development. These experiential tools constructed a cross-cleavage narrative about the identity of the neighborhood while at the same time freezing that identity in its state of early gentrification. The role of resident creative producers was essential, as a local organizer explained: "I think we were quite pioneers in the use of creativity ... The cultural axis was important with commemorations of the neighborhood ... things like neighborhood dances, concerts, meetings, events with craftsmen, fairs" (Gloria Konig, 2011, cited in Bulnes, 2012, p. 52). The group quickly turned to revamping, and even in some cases creating, neighborhood events. Some criticized the events for their lack of "authenticity" and historical accuracy, but this criticism missed the point. The goal of the events was not to represent "typical" examples of common life; rather, the events were inviting spaces of participation and self-expression. They were superb instances of experiential tools. Through these initiatives, Vecinos por la Defensa del Barrio Yungay was recognized as a new form of grassroots organization in Santiago and a catalyst for a new "strong identity" (Bulnes, 2012, p. 28). In turn, this identity allowed social and political groups to converge into grassroots collective action to defend a shared heritage and fight displacement.

Participants were engaged and mobilized through events that avoided explicit political valences. These occasions presented specific association initiatives; for example, a restored monument, or a newly founded group of artisans. They offered the opportunity for core activists to coalesce around a challenge and be energized by its success. They mobilized previously latent residents, as well as outsiders – including municipal institutions, other levels of government, and sectors of civil society and business.

Major events every few months succeeded because they resonated, avoided partisanship, appealed to residents broadly, deepened loyalties, and were carefully documented. In January, the Festival of the Common Chilean (the Festival del Roto Chileno) commemorated the Battle of Yungay on January 20, 1839, between the Peru–Bolivian Confederation and the Peru–Chilean United Restoration Army. The victory by poor and untrained soldiers (the "Common Chilean") ended the Peru–Bolivian

Confederation. The organization revitalized and renewed this traditional event, and in January 2010 its attendance reached 13,000. In May, the association started a tradition of the Day of Yungay Heritage (Día del Patrimonio en Yungay). In June, the association organized a council called Cabildo de Santiago, which attracted increasingly influential participants and hundreds of residents (in June 2009, attendees included the ministry general secretariat of government, members of parliament, regional councillors, and municipal councillors). Council organizers asked participants to bring photos of the neighborhood, describe their desired changes, and select committees on which to volunteer.

And, starting in 2007, the association organized a grand celebration each September of the barrio's founding. Its 170th anniversary was celebrated with a communal open-air dinner for hundreds of residents and an artistic gala. Finally, each November since 2007, the barrio has celebrated the Festival del Barrio Yungay, in which more than 200 artists participate across several locations, with a myriad of activities and attractions, ranging from dozens of bands and musicians to baby football games and other sport events; to theater plays, art walks, carnival parades, and children's activities. Several lectures, public readings, photo exhibitions, and arts workshops dealt with representations of the barrio, ranging from historical depictions to the latest graffiti.

Experiential tools also included a photo and audiovisual archive assembled with residents' contributions and "memory workshops" in which residents came together to construct the history of the barrio. The "heritage registry" was an especially strategic invention. As an archive of local family histories, it drew on cultural and *emotional* heritage to legitimize and anchor residents and small businesses in the neighborhood. The registry communicated the imperative idea that the barrio's identity was based on not only architectural but also social heritage. The strategy culminated in the opening of a community museum of Barrio Yungay in 2014.

In addition to their exceptional and extensive deployment of innovative experiential tools, Vecinos por la Defensa del Barrio Yungay engaged dense networks and in fact became a broker and coordinator for action in heritage defense and struggles against displacement. The association pursued an ever-larger network of sister movements. First, it built a coalition based on sectorial interests with a variety of cultural agents in Yungay (foundations, museums, artisan and artists' groups, heterogeneous cultural centers and movements). Subsequently, the network was extended to areas outside the neighborhood, producing *hermaniamentos* (brotherhoods) with neighborhood associations (*juntas de vecinos*) and like-minded groups around metropolitan Santiago, among them Bellavista, Vitacura, Qilicura, Matta Sur, Lo Espejo, and Colina. Further, after expanding the outreach to the regional level, they established international links. Throughout 2009, they forged links with groups in Argentina (and in particular the Buenos Aires neighborhood of San Telmo discussed below), Montevideo, Uruguay, and Colombia. With growing visibility, the association was invited to the Seventh Conference of Historical Centers in Cartagena, Colombia, organized by the Heritage Program of the Spanish government in July 2009. On that occasion, the association was recognized as pioneering and unique in Latin America because it managed to build a model of local development from a heritage perspective that reserved an important role for popular participation.

Interestingly, a national network was established last (perhaps because Santiago's exceptional size and influence made it hard to translate and replicate its experiences elsewhere). In July 2009, the Chilean Association of Neighbors and Barrio Organizations and Heritage Areas (Asociación Chilena de Vecinos y Organizaciones de Barrios y Zonas Patrimoniales) was founded with an initial membership of twenty like-minded groups. Those participants all came from within a 15-kilometer radius of central Santiago, but their goal was to promote a national movement – connecting urban and rural heritage – and by April 2010 the association already had members from seven of Chile's thirteen regions.

Experiential tools continued to be deployed, especially to sustain recruitment and to reinforce the group's frame of neighborhood identity. The activities of the national association were celebrated with the first Citizen Council for Heritage in January 2010. In this context, one should note the hierarchical nature of the organization, where the leadership core remained the same after well over a decade, and expanded its role in the upscaling of the organization. Rosario Carvajal, founding president of Vecinos por la Defensa del Barrio Yungay, also founded and presided over the Asociación Chilena de Vecinos y Organizaciones de Barrios y Zonas Patrimoniales.

Experiential tools and this extensive networking together led to extensive and sustained mobilization and engendered a new type of contention, best understood as brand-oriented struggles. A conflict between the group and the mayor over the use of a popular art center and concert hall aptly illustrates the brand struggle. A rising star in the center–right coalition, mayor Pablo Zalaquett was elected in 2008. Due to his reliance on mass media and his telegenic style, he was quickly dubbed the "media mayor" (*alcalde mediático*). The confrontation between the mayor and the association therefore featured two media-savvy opponents. Zalaquett argued that redevelopment in a neighborhood with such prominent architectonic heritage was financially advantageous: "We have several private projects that increase the attractiveness for tourists, promise vitality and generate a more interesting space as municipality" (F. Mardones, 2009). The association retorted that the aim instead was to replicate the intense gentrification that had already taken place in other neighborhoods (such as Lastarrias and Bellavista), and proposed measures to protect squatters as well as long-term renters and owners. Theirs was a cross-cleavage mobilization and support strategy.

The struggle balanced on conflicting meanings of neighborhood identity, as both the mayor and the association based their arguments on heritage. In his battle over the definition of heritage, Zalaquett shut down the space occupied by the Foundation Victor Jara (a close ally of Vecinos por la Defensa del Barrio Yungay) and the connected cultural center, Galpón. At stake was the definition of "folk art." According to the mayor, the center was being used for events that were not "true" to the folk art of the city, and was therefore abusing its license. In defining an "authentic" barrio identity, the mayor relied on a nostalgic, highbrow, and elitist notion of the neighborhood. The association, instead, enjoyed the political advantage of a broad definition of local heritage, which united residents who listened to traditional music with those who skated to hip-hop during barrio festivals. The association had the upper hand in the branding contest, given its previous work and mobilization. In the battle that followed, media and public opinion sided with the organization, and the mayor abandoned his struggle.

In this context, and with its experiential arsenal and compelling account of neighborhood identity, the association pursued its primary goal: the establishment of a *zona típica* (heritage area), according to Law 17.288, which governs national monuments. The association mobilized institutional support in opposition to the mayor by lobbying local politicians, such as municipal and regional councillors, but above all by seeking supporters in the national government, and especially in the ministry of culture. This strategy was successful, judging from the fact that increasingly prominent politicians were recorded as attending events sponsored by the association. On these occasions, officials were interviewed, and both videos and transcripts were posted on websites of the association and the foundation, thereby contributing to the careful documentation of experiential tools.

In this case we also observe a powerful instance of institutional infiltration – the pursuit of goals from within government. Association members participated successfully in elections. In October 2008, an ally of the association gained a seat on the municipal council of Santiago. The association continued to have close supporters in the municipal council, and in 2016 Rosario Carvajal, the association's founding president, herself won one of the ten seats. Further, the association fought to introduce popular elections for the Consejo Económico Social Comunal, an influential municipal consultative body with thereto appointed representatives from the leading civic organizations. Having achieved that goal, in September 2009 Carvajal won a seat on the first election. Finally, in November 2009, Rosario Carvajal was offered one of twenty-three seats on the Consejo de la Sociedad Civil, a consultative body recently established under the Ministerio Secretaría General de Gobierno to foster the influence and participation of civic actors and organizations in national policy-making.

In the end, the struggle between the association and the mayor was solved at the national level. The association took advantage of partisan dealignment at the time under the center–left Bachelet administration. The Vecinos por la Defensa del Barrio Yungay could pursue its claims of heritage protection at the national level, and specifically through the Consejo de Monumentos Nacionales. The national level was also instrumental because several sources from the national government – primarily the National Fund for Cultural Development and the Arts (Fondo Nacional para el Desarrollo Cultural y las Artes [FONDART]) – funded the study conducted by neighbors to prepare the application for heritage protection and subsequent initiatives.

In 2009, 113 hectares of Yungay barrio obtained the status of *Zona Típica*. Next they pursued the enlargement of the Zona Típica to the entire north and west of the municipality of Santiago. At the same time, several petitions applied to extend protection also to individual buildings with the status of national monument (*monumento nacional*). Following the return of Bachelet, an additional 117 hectares were included in the heritage area in January 2018, just weeks before the installation of the second Piñera presidency.[1]

[1] While the Piñera administration initially blocked the extension, the organization's political clout allowed it to obtain the Act's ratification in April 2019. The association celebrated the signing in the context of the 180th anniversary of the barrio with a special public

The declaration of Zona Típica in Yungay was a turning point: After this moment, heritage declaration was no longer conducted at the behest of the state but only at the behest of citizens. Before the Yungay campaign of 2009, of a total twenty-three initiatives for area heritage protection initiated in the metropolitan Santiago, fifteen were initiated by the state and only eight by residents. Further, the largest resident-initiated heritage area prior to the Yungay campaign was only 10 hectares, in comparison to the Yungay scope of 113 hectares (Rojas Morales, 2014).

The organization became a key supporter of similar struggles in other areas. By 2014, Santiago had over twenty neighborhood groups specifically dedicated to the preservation of socio-architectural heritage through the process of Zona Típica (Rojas Morales, 2014). Colina is a municipality north of Santiago, within 20 minutes driving distance from the center of the city. There, the association brought its expertise to mobilize a petition for Zona Típica for an area that included its historical quarries. The area had become of great interest to real-estate developers during the 1990s, and especially after the 1997 modification of the metropolitan master plan (Plano Regulador Metropolitano de Santiago). This plan extended the urban growth boundary to the province of Chacabuco, to create subcenters around the city. Despite several years of economic recession, over the 1990s land value in the municipality of Colina increased by 18.6 percent annually (by comparison, areas in southern Santiago, the second in growth, increased only 10 percent). Speculation was rampant, driven by the fact that with the construction of shopping malls and urban facilities land could be reclassified from rural to urban, which would raise prices (Trivelli, 2006, 2011). The Colina municipality was strongly motivated to encourage development, which would bring millions in building permits as well as new driving licenses and vehicle registrations, and supported two Conditional Urban Development Zone projects, El Chamisero and Pan de Azúcar, around the local historical quarries.

With the help and guidance of the association Vecinos por la Defensa del Barrio Yungay, 500 families from the Pueblo de Las Canteras de Colina (People from the Quarries of Colina) succeeded in obtaining the status of Zona Típica in January 2010. The new status protected the quarries of Pan de Azúcar from redevelopment, which prevented the displacement of hundreds of masons. Vecinos por la Defensa del Barrio

event – this time even with the official support of the newly elected mayor, eager to promote the area's heritage brand for tourism.

Yungay assisted in preparing the application, participated in demonstrations, and lobbied city councillors and members of the National Monuments Council. They developed the argument that for over a century quarry workers had contributed to the construction of Santiago and especially its cobblestone (*adoquín*) streets. To build the case for cultural heritage, experiential events always included several artists and stonecutters who demonstrated how the cobblestones were made. The Zona Típica act was not signed by the minister, and developers made gains in the Piñera presidency, which was a phase of partisan alignment and thus adverse to protesters. Once again displaying how partisan dealignment creates opportunities for protesters, the act was finally signed into law (albeit with a reduction of the protected area) in the last month of the second Bachelet administration.

Vecinos por la Defensa del Barrio Yungay was becoming institutionalized. These campaigns, the association's various committees, and the coordination of the numerous festivals required more volunteers. The leadership mobilized and educated continuously. Starting in 2009, the association started an elaborate education program of workshops, seminars, conferences, and schools to incorporate neighbors into the movement. Conferences covered topics such as community heritage defense, public policies for the heritage development, and proposals for community heritage management. Courses held in various municipalities in and around Santiago (Matta Sur, Talagante, Valparaiso, Coquimbo) covered community organizing, community and cultural management, identity development as immaterial heritage, heritage media, and mass communication.

The most significant school was inspired by the 2009 visit to Colombia mentioned above. Invited to Cartagena to present strategies and results, association leaders observed a masonry school that helped teenagers at risk by teaching them to repair local historical buildings and to contribute to the local arts-and-craft tradition. This workshop school, the Escuela Taller de Cartagena de Indias, was founded in 1992 and trained about 100 youths from disadvantaged backgrounds for 18 months in the restoration of real estate in the city center. The approach innovatively addressed both unemployment and heritage conservation. Vecinos por la Defensa del Barrio de Yungay campaigned to open a similar school, the Escuela Taller de Artes y Oficios Fermin Vivaceta, and lobbied authorities for funding.

Within a few hours after the earthquake on February 27, 2010, and despite the fear and chaos that always accompany such shocking events, the association was in motion, strengthened by its extensive networks and committed followers. The media presented an image of Yungay as heavily damaged, which was interpreted as a veiled form of redlining – fraudulently giving the impression of neighborhood deterioration so as to induce owners to sell at a loss – the classic antecedent to gentrification. The association criticized the mayoral message to the media, which "gives public opinion the impression our neighborhood is in ruin and that it shall be demolished tomorrow … following the interests of real-estate developers to destroy our heritage barrio" (from the website of Vecinos por la Defensa del Barrio Yungay). Not losing a minute in the counter-offensive, the association mobilized 1,000 volunteers on the day of the quake to register 1,500 buildings and inspect 350. Within a few days it had established a fund for reconstruction and repair, the Fondo de Restauración Patrimonial del Barrio Yungay. Problem-solving teams walked the neighborhood to address residents' emergencies. A program "godfathered" damaged buildings, preparing them for repair and protecting them from demolition. And the local heritage masonry school, in the works since the association's visit to Cartagena the previous August, now seemed more timely and urgent, and opened less than two months later.

To further prevent displacement, the group also founded the Office of Community Heritage Management, designed to support individual needs for housing repairs and upgradings; and the Housing Committee for Latin American Integration, which specifically supported the housing needs of recent immigrants, one of the most vulnerable groups in the barrio. In these ways the group continued to promote the goals of heritage-driven repopulation (working toward affordable housing) and an eco-heritage neighborhood (which combined concerns for environmental sustainability with protected historic districts) (Rojas Morales, 2014). To support and further strengthen cross-class and interethnic collaboration and barrio identity, the group founded a very active sporting club, the Club Deportivo El Gran Yungay, and extensive art programming for school-age children with particular outreach to immigrant families.

As part of institutionalization, the group changed its legal status to facilitate fund-raising and kindred goals of network expansion and legitimation. Because foundations have better access to public funding than associations, both nationally and internationally, the association established a sister foundation, Our Heritage Foundation (Fundación Patrimonio Nuestro).

Vecinos por la Defensa del Barrio Yungay pursued an effective, multi-pronged strategy, for which it had no preexisting model. In only a few years, this strategy achieved important and tangible results. It was able to stop new-build gentrification and the associated displacement with a heritage area declaration. In 2014, the municipality turned to promoting Yungay for tourism, with an aggressive branding campaign and beautification proposals for some sites. Yet, a few years later, "except for isolated and minor interventions, it is not yet possible to see the effects in the neighborhood" (G. Mardones, 2017, p. 68). The resistance put up by Vecinos por la Defensa del Barrio Yungay catapulted the association to the forefront of Chilean civil society in the field of culture and heritage. To achieve these goals, the organization deployed formidable experiential tools, paired with an increasingly extensive network of like-minded organizations.

WHEN LOCAL NETWORKS ARE WEAK: ISTANBUL

In contrast, two cases against redevelopment in Fatih, a district in the core of Istanbul, illustrate protest where networks are weak. Protest in the Sulukule neighborhood utilized experiential tools but was unable to mobilize a substantial number of residents. Resident organizers lacked prior protest experience and relied on outside experts. Further, instead of a broad, diverse set of supporting groups within the neighborhood, their network was largely composed of intellectual elites, fragmented and unable to coalesce into a substantial political force. In the neighborhood of Fener and Balat, organizers also lacked prior protest experience (though they learned from observing Sulukule and other displacement cases), made only minimal and ineffective use of experiential tools, and had networks limited to intellectual elites, and even sparser than in Sulukule. Consequently, mobilization was minimal. In response to the inability of these campaigns to mobilize large crowds, activists subsequently focused on tightening network connections across the entire city and deploying experiential tools in the protest against the redevelopment of Gezi Park. The result of that campaign was a mass mobilization of absolutely historical magnitude.

Since the early 2000s, urban renewal in Istanbul has intensified, with fifty neighborhoods slated for regeneration. The process was coordinated by the housing development authority, TOKİ; its metropolitan counterpart KİPTAŞ; the Istanbul metropolitan municipality, and district municipalities. Plans privileged the Ottoman heritage and era, which had great symbolic significance for the Islamic and conservative AKP. Instead of being renovated, Ottoman-period dwellings were demolished and rebuilt in faux-old style to make space for commercial use and upscale residences. Housing authorities typically sold new housing units on the periphery at subsidized prices to owners of dwellings slated for regeneration, while the regeneration areas were sold to developers, often without the original owners' consent or even knowledge.

Overall, 20 percent of Fatih municipality was slated for renewal by the early 2000s, for a total of 230 hectares. In the Süleymaniye neighborhood, the core of the UNESCO area with Aghia Sophia and the Blue Mosque, regeneration covered 10 hectares with 333 historic buildings, of which KİPTAŞ planned to demolish 200, to make space for 400 concrete replicas of old houses. Residents were largely renters, who had recently migrated from Anatolia, and they offered little resistance to the project (Turkmen, 2014).

In contrast, two conflictual interventions in the Fatih municipality took place in the neighborhoods of Sulukule and Fener and Balat. Sulukule lies in a strategic location at the beginning of the highway that connects downtown to the airport. The area was a centuries-old documented Roma settlement in grave disrepair, with a population that survived in the informal economy, traditionally employed in tourist facilities and "entertainment houses" (establishments with dancers and live music). The city closed these houses around 1992, which exacerbated the area's economic decline. According to a 2006 survey, 30 percent of residents were illiterate (against a city average of 3.8 percent), and only 4 percent had completed high school (against a city average of 18 percent). Unemployment was 77 percent (against a city average of 14 percent), and 13 percent relied only on income supplied by children (Karaman, 2014, p. 295).

The neighborhood was about 8,000 square meters, with a population that over the 1990s fell from 10,000 to 3,500 (Uysal, 2012, p. 14). It was slated for "regeneration," and, despite the fact that most of the 5,000 residents had property deeds, plans called for the immediate expropriation and demolition of all existing 690 dwellings, to make space for new deluxe housing, commercial services, and tourist facilities. This was one of the first cases of displacement for regeneration in the city's core, so it would shape behavior expectations and norms thereafter, for both resistance and the government. Stakes were especially high for the government because if the resistance succeeded then all regeneration projects would come into question.

The struggle in Sulukule culminated between 2006 and 2008, by which time demolitions were well under way and had already displaced residents. The mayor of Fatih led the way in stigmatizing residents and labeling them as undesirable as a rationale for demolition. He called for the "clearing of the depressed and deformed settlement areas, and their transformation into a contemporary and livable city" (cited in Aksoy, 2010, p. 10). Prime Minister Erdoğan referred to the neighborhood as a "monstrosity" (Karaman & Islam, 2012).

As opposed to the Yungay case in Santiago, resistance in Sulukule did not involve dense neighborhood participation but came instead from outside actors such as the Chamber of Architects and Engineers. Another important player was Solidarity Studio, a small cluster of architects and planners, which had organized resistance in two *gecekondular* (informal settlement) areas slated for regeneration on the Asian side of the city, starting in 2005 (Lelandais, 2014). Primarily, these intellectual activists wanted to protect the Roma culture in the neighborhood (Dinçer, Enlil, & Islam, 2008). A handful of middle-class professionals (a journalist, a lawyer, and an NGO worker, none of them from the neighborhood) organized the resistance alliance Sulukule Platform, joined by academics, professional chambers, and groups from outside the neighborhood (e.g., Imece, or the Popular Urbanism Movement; Direnistanbul, or Resist Istanbul; and SOS Istanbul). These groups, uncoordinated, struggled to mobilize residents in protest (Karaman, 2014).

Sulukule Platform events emphasized the cultural contribution of the Roma community and deployed experiential tools such as workshops, classes, concerts, and children's activities that "emphasized – and to a large extent actively constructed representations around – common neighborhood life and moral community" (Karaman, 2014, p. 304). For example, the Forty Days and Forty Nights Festival, organized in 2007, forty days prior to the first demolitions, included performances, exhibitions, workshops, conferences, and community meetings (Uysal, 2012). It also included grassroots archives, as some residents involved in the struggle encouraged the documentation of their individual stories (Uysal, 2012).

However, these initiatives with experiential tools lacked effectiveness because they were set in the context of weak and fragmented networks. Mobilization within the neighborhood was limited to a few residents, who formed the Romany Culture and Solidarity Association (also known as the Association for the Development of Romany Culture). These isolated activists were undermined because in response to local organizing, the Fatih municipality funded its own association to divide residents and entice them with the prospect of nicer homes and financial compensation. Thus, the "culture-centered mobilization strategy alone proved inadequate" (Uysal, 2012, p. 15) as Sulukule Platform leaders were challenged by those residents who did not self-identify as Roma and those who preferred to negotiate compensations over outright struggle and thereby fed galloping land speculation (Uysal, 2012, p. 17).

Realizing that support for the Roma community would not reach beyond leftist intellectual circles, activists deemed as infeasible any widespread mobilization against regeneration. So they sought political clout by mobilizing extraordinary international pressure. They organized conferences around the world and started programs in Turkey and abroad (e.g., University College London had a specific planning unit dedicated to the issue). International artists campaigned and visited Sulukule. Internationally sponsored petitions traveled the web and garnered tens of thousands of signatures. The Turkish mass media and the highest echelons of diplomacy at the European Union, UN-Habitat, and the UN Human Rights Council took notice, which resulted in a strongly worded recommendation by the United Nations in the context of the UNESCO World Heritage Centre/ICOMOS Joint Mission to the Historic Areas of Istanbul World Heritage Site (UNESCO, 2008). As a result of this international pressure, Solidarity Studio and other academics – organized under the label STOP (Autonomous Planners Without Borders) – were allowed to submit an alternative plan to prevent displacement of the Roma community.

Yet the alternative plan had to contend with resolute political will behind the original proposal, and it failed to even enter the agenda for the government's mandated renewal committee. Under these circumstances, international linkages proved ineffective. In the absence of both substantial resident mobilization *and* lack of support in the municipal council (Uysal, 2012), Prime Minister Erdoğan intervened and pressured for the continuation of the plan – a striking display of the power of partisan alignment. By September 2009, all the buildings in Sulukule were demolished, and residents were displaced, mostly to Taşoluk, an isolated development 35 kilometers away. Informal workers depended on location for access to work and support services, and of the approximately 500 families displaced, nearly all returned to live (many in shacks) around Sulukule within a few years (Cin & Egercioğlu, 2016; Karaman, 2014; Uysal, 2012).

* * *

The second Fatih case displays not only a lack of broad support networks and prior protest experience but also the near absence of experiential tools. The most visible resistance in 2010 to regeneration was in two adjacent neighborhoods, commonly referred to together as Fener and Balat. In 2010, Fener and Balat had a population of 13,802 over 0.4 square kilometers. As most in this book, this was a very dense neighborhood, with 34,086 residents per square kilometer, much higher than Istanbul's 2,523 and higher even than the surrounding Fatih municipality, which had 32,787 residents per square kilometer (TUIK, 2006).

Historically, these were Greek and Jewish neighborhoods and had been inhabited thereafter by immigrants from the Black Sea region who arrived in several waves, as well as a more recent, small group of gentrifiers. (The 2006 census of the neighborhood reported only one-quarter of residents as born in Istanbul.) The neighborhood suffered from several economic, social, and urban problems, such as high unemployment, poor urban services, high crime rates, and low education. Less than 1 percent of the population had a university degree, while 48 percent had completed only elementary school, and 33 percent only middle school. Sixty percent of residents were tenants. Income profile changed significantly in recent years: While in 2000, 46 percent of households were below the poverty line (Ercan, 2011, p. 299), due to gentrification, income levels were more evenly distributed by 2014, with 17 percent of the population in the lowest quartile, 32 percent in the second lowest, 28 percent in the third, and 22 percent in the top quartile. In terms of political orientation, the neighborhood was known for its conservative and nationalist profile, and gave the AKP 71 percent of valid votes in the 2011 general elections, and 68 percent in the 2014 local elections.

The area had received a major European Union grant at the turn of the millennium to experiment with a model of urban upgrading compatible with social cohesion and participation. Although it was the object of hopeful academic studies, the renovation of dozens of houses did not have an impact because even renovated units were slated for demolition in regeneration plans. The Fatih municipality simply did not support this socially grounded approach to redevelopment (Ercan, 2011; UNESCO, 2006). Instead, the municipality finalized plans to redevelop 28 hectares of the shoreline, including the ancient Jewish market, the influential Greek Orthodox Patriarchy headquarters, and the neighborhood's distinguished and highly cohesive architectural heritage.

Earlier in the decade, the neighborhood had been beyond the purview of redevelopment because the ownership structure discouraged investors:

In Fener and Balat, one building could often have as many as a dozen owners, some of whom lived outside Istanbul, or even abroad (Bezmez, 2008, p. 835). But Law No. 5,366 in 2005 solved this problem because it granted draconian eminent domain powers that opened the neighborhood to investors. Throughout the inner city, "renewal" projects replaced earlier "rehabilitation" projects on the basis of the newly implemented law. Real-estate prices rose dramatically in the area slated for renewal – according to sources, almost tenfold between 2009 and 2011. This paved the way for the displacement of 900 resident households (Gulersoy-Zeren, Tezer, Yigiter, Koramaz, & Gunay, 2008; Gunay & Dokmeci, 2012; Limoncu & Çelebioglu, 2012; Mutman & Turgut, 2011, 2018).

There was no project office or website where residents could view plans, models, and renderings of the new development (Schwegmann, 2013). Members of the local neighborhood association became aware of the project in July 2009, when they received notices informing them that Law 5,366 gave the municipal government the authority to grant private investors 58 percent of shares in the redeveloped properties, with existing owners left with only 42 percent of their properties. (In other words, the existing structures were to be demolished and rebuilt, and existing owners would own only minority shares in the new dwellings.) In August 2009, a full two years after an original contract had been signed, and just a month after the plan was made public, owners hastily founded a neighborhood association called FEBAYDER, short for Fener-Balat-Ayvansaray Property Owners and Tenants Association for Rights Protection and Social Assistance. While tenants were part of the association's name, they were not mobilized (interview with Çiğdem Şahin, general secretary of FEBAYDER, Istanbul, December 18, 2010).

The group was founded by two academics who had resided in the neighborhood since about 2000, and eleven other long-term white-collar or self-employed owners. Members had no prior experience with urban resistance. Further, FEBAYDER's networks were as fragmented as in Sulukule. In fact, instead of attempting to overcome sparse local networks by extending internationally, FEBAYDER's networks were so limited that the organization failed even to engage *adjacent* neighborhoods facing the same displacement threat (Turkmen, 2014).

Protest actions fell into the traditional repertoire of marches, petitions, letters, and billboards, under the slogan "Don't touch my house." Traditional media, including CNN Turkey, reported on the campaign. Yet the only actions with any resemblance to experiential tools were a sparsely attended event for children and tours in collaboration with SOS Istanbul, which organized visits to endangered areas. During a tour that I observed, participants took a break in the association's offices to discuss regeneration plans, and the overall tone was one of resignation. Participants were overwhelmingly students from outside the neighborhood. The tour did not qualify as an effective experiential tool: It focused on the architecture without linking it to emotional elements of everyday life for current residents; it did not target a variety of participants; and it was not documented in the press. Moreover, the tour did not build on significant prior deployment of experiential events and archives, which are much more effective as recruitment mechanisms.

The absence of events and archives helps explain the group's inability to forge a *collective* identity and *cross-cleavage* solidarity within the neighborhood, as opposed to the Yungay case. The association's participants were overwhelmingly elderly conservative men, yet some interviewees characterized it as "unrepresentative of the neighborhood" simply because of the presence of a couple of socialist residents (interview with Erbatur Çavuşoğlu, Professor of City Regional Planning, Mimar Sinan University, December 15, 2010). These tensions were symptomatic of how neighborhood cleavages remained – between Halevi and Sunni Muslims, between renters and owners, and between conservative and leftist voters. The lack of a proud collective identity – and indeed the mistrust – within the organization and across the neighborhood undermined broad mobilization and involvement in the protest (Turkmen, 2014).

Another significant factor was the high percentage of Kurdish immigrants who had arrived in the 1990s. The majority of residents, conservative and nationalist, viewed the Kurdish population suspiciously. Mostly renters, the Kurds were more likely to be dependent on the municipality for food and heating material, locked into clientelistic relations, and eager to avoid conflict (Schwegmann, 2013). Further, Kurdish owners who had only recently arrived were more likely to be willing to sell and relocate (interview with Erbatur Çavuşoğlu, December 15, 2010). For these reasons, this population was especially unlikely to mobilize and further deepened splits within the neighborhood.

After the Fatih council approved the project in 2010, FEBAYDER, represented by the Chamber of Architects, initiated a long court case for heritage protection, which it won in 2012 as judges recognized the need for heritage and social conservation and the good condition of the dwellings that had been restored through the European Union project. Before the victory, organizers were careful to avoid partisan claims and focused on a generic discourse of residents' rights to property. However, political divisions within the group that had been veiled as residents united in opposition to the plans came to the fore just as soon as this temporary legal victory sidelined the displacement emergency. Only a few dozen members attended a rally organized on the eve of the legal success, and the organization's board split in 2013 over partisan dissent. Şahin led the progressive wing and formed a separate organization called Fener-Balat Kultur Miraslarini Koruma Dernegi (Association for Protecting the Cultural Heritage of Fener-Balat).

While they differed in the deployment of experiential tools, Sulukule as well as Fener and Balat illustrate the obstacles facing organizers who are unable to overcome preexisting social cleavages within the neighborhood and who lack diverse and dense neighborhood and citywide support networks.

Although they did not achieve broad mobilization, campaigns such as these did lay the foundation for a broader movement. Activists throughout Istanbul recognized their fragmentary networks as highly problematic. In interviews, a leading activist explained:

> Unless neighborhoods share their struggles and experiences with the other struggling areas, the resistance will be incomplete ... I think we should be able to reunite all the opposition groups in the city. ... The struggle will be about not only the right to housing, but also the right to the city, not only for the working class, but also for the middle class. Unless we unite all the actors in a city, victims and their foes, the struggle for the right to the city won't be complete.
>
> (Erdoğan Yildiz in an interview conducted by Adanalı, Korkmaz, & Yücesoy, 2009)

After all, the activists' opponents were indeed united, as evidenced by the fact that Çalık Holding, a redeveloper with close family ties to Erdoğan, was awarded the majority of the regeneration contracts in Istanbul.

EXPERIENTIAL TOOLS, NETWORKS, AND MASS MOBILIZATION: ISTANBUL AND TEL AVIV

The protest of Gezi Park has received much scholarly attention, which will only be selectively summarized here. Primarily, this case shows the close connection between symbolic and material displacement theorized in Chapter 2. Even with extensive and brutal displacement happening throughout Istanbul under the auspices of regeneration, the case that first triggered mass protest was the defense of a green space. It started with a small demonstration of activists tied to the Right to the City movement.

They were protesting plans to build a mall and a large mosque in Gezi Park, the only green area in Taksim and a highly symbolic space in the city. It was not only a tourist and economic hub but also, more importantly, the site of many historical rallies. The planned mall was to replicate Ottoman-era military barracks, which alarmed the opposition for its Islamist connotation, and the plan would have outlawed future rallies on the site.

This symbolic displacement motivated a rapid and vast mobilization, perhaps precisely because it presented the issue of loss of place as something larger and more abstract than the direct loss of shelter.

The protest was remarkable for its growth and magnitude, and the breadth of its participants. The action started when twenty activists camped out overnight to stop the eradication of trees (Abbas & Yigit, 2015). After the police reacted with harsh repression, the protest grew, and over a few days it reached 235 protests in 67 Turkish cities, leading to 1,730 arrests, 5 deaths and over 10,000 injured. Over half of the protesters were workers (mostly in the service sector), 37 percent were students, and 6 percent were unemployed. The participants' average age was twenty-eight.

Given the close connections between real-estate developers and the government, the protest also became an anti-government campaign (Gül, Dee, & Nur Cünük, 2014). However, even in this politically tense context (a coup against the government would be attempted only three years later), participants in the protest did not identify along party lines. This observation supports this book's argument that mobilization – and especially mobilization that deploys experiential tools – does not display specific partisan linkages, and, even if they are present, it does not emphasize them. Thus, in Gezi, protesters attended mostly as individuals, with no specific partisan or associational identity. In surveys taken in the most intense phase of mobilization, 79 percent of respondents stated that they did not belong to any party, political organization, or NGO, and over half of them were either undecided about their vote, or planned not to vote (Farro & Demirhisar, 2014) – "leftists, rightists, Kurdish, ultranational, green, conservatives and liberals" came together, despite ideological differences (Abbas & Yigit, 2015, p. 70).

In addition to overcoming previous network fragmentation, organizers in Gezi Park deployed several experiential tools from each of the four types. They planned events. In addition to the experience of the encampment itself, and several concerts, there was a grassroots library and a garden. They developed archives, both backward- and forward-oriented, in the form of an open-source protest museum and a wishing post. They staged games, with mimes and dancing. There were also iconic destinations for a local "tour": the Ataturk center, slated for demolition and appropriated with banners, and the "graffiti bus," a landmark created by protesters and a popular backdrop for snapshots. These experiential tools actively involved participants in the creation of the protest, which was experienced as a key moment in their existence, as respondents reported marking their lives in terms of "before" and "after" the Gezi protest (Farro & Demirhisar, 2014, p. 181).

These experiential tools had all the hallmarks of success: All four were deployed, and they targeted a heterogeneous population with highly emotional and grassroots-oriented content, aimed at building a sense of collective identity and solidarity among participants. The tools were heavily documented and, given the circumstances, relatively light on political connotation (and above all free of any messaging connected to specific parties).

* * *

These mobilization tactics in Gezi Park – the participants' focus on self-expression and life narrative, and their weak partisan allegiances – recur in the 2011 mass protest in Tel Aviv. The analysis of Tel Aviv shows how cultural producers effectively appropriated discourses activated by a highly successful city branding campaign and turned them into formidable mobilization tools. The resulting protests in the summer of 2011 were the largest in Israeli history. Yet the protests failed to produce notable policy results because organizers privileged maximizing mobilization by enabling participants' self-expression rather than building and delivering an explicit and coherent policy program. Subsequently, the protest message was co-opted by a rival political entrepreneur, landing him a historical victory with a new political party, *Yesh Atid*, which for the first time displaced security as the central issue in Israeli national elections.

The "White City" branding (see Chapter 4) led to dramatic increases in real-estate prices and gentrification in Tel Aviv. Residents responded by mobilizing for their right to the neighborhood. The most mobilized group was composed of Ashkenazi urbanites, yuppies, and dinkies who had moved back to the city core in the 1980s to follow new jobs in finance and services (Schnell & Graicer, 1993). Protest groups formed around the mid 2000s and first coalesced in a large event in June 2007 at Cinematique, a prominent White City location, to denounce the rise in rent and the dislocation of 1980s and early 1990s in-migrants (and their offspring) by more recent and affluent residents.

The organization that emerged mounted a surprising challenge against the incumbent mayor Ron Huldai (2003–present) in the 2008 election. It was led by Dov Khenin, a member of the Knesset for the communist party Hadash. Khenin was a lawyer, an activist for socioeconomic equality, and an environmentalist. His Ir Lekhulanu (City for All) list received the most votes, largely from the White City area. The slogan "City for All" signaled opposition to mayor-supported development and gentrification. In a dramatic display of counter-branding, Ir Lekhulanu linked gentrification to the loss of diversity in the city – implicitly questioning what Tel Aviv was to be about, whether beautiful architecture for the upper classes or the vibrant lifestyle that emerged from its diverse population. At stake was the "authentic" Tel Aviv experience. Khenin stated:

> Over the years the city has become home to all kinds of people, becoming a symbol of sane and dynamic living, bubbling with freedom and creativity. Sadly, this unique human and cultural fabric is under real threat. In recent years, troubling developments have affected the city. In many ways, it is becoming a city for the rich alone. Growing numbers of its citizens sense they no longer have any place here.
>
> (http://city4all.org.il/dovkhenin)

Khenin's alternative was a turn to diversity as the essence of the city and called for shifting the brand from heritage preservation to lifestyle:

> A "city for all" intends to restore the city to its residents. It is the people of this city – not the skyscrapers – that make it so enthralling. ... Together we shall restore the city to its residents and make it into a place that is good, healthy and fun to live. A city for us all.
>
> (http://city4all.org.il)

The campaign thus captured the frustration of citizens who felt left out of the recent growth and redevelopment, and the Ir Lekhulanu coalition grew, both spatially and ideologically. While the coalition's support was centered in the White City, it broadened its appeal with an inclusive vision of city planning. For example, Khenin denounced evacuations of Jaffa's Ajami neighborhood. Problems of housing costs and displacement transcended traditional ideological lines. Because in Israel security dominates political cleavages and defines concepts of "left" and "right," Khenin's focus on housing and planning brought together groups usually on opposite sides of the aisle. It included religious traditionalists and secular individuals; residents of affluent northern neighborhoods alongside those living in the south; Jews and Arabs, as well as a broad representation across generations and genders.

The 2008 campaign came to fruition in July 2011, when Daphne Leef, a newly evicted freelance filmmaker, launched an event on Facebook to set up tents in the city center in protest against rent increases. Despite a tradition of urban social movements in Israel (Hasson, 1993), Leef and most other organizers were not activists, and this was the first Facebook event to reach outside of her network of friends. This case illustrates how individuals may be linked by social networks based on indirect ties generated by their joint involvement in a specific event, even before any face-to-face interaction.

The Ir Lekhulanu network quickly mobilized to join Leef's initiative. The protest spoke directly to young Israeli adults who were observing pessimistically how cuts in housing and employment policies undermined the reproduction of the middle class (Rosenhek & Shalev, 2014). Within a week, an inner core of ten organizers emerged, most of whom Leef had never met (interview with Daphne Leef, protest initiator and leader, Tel Aviv, December 18, 2011). They were overwhelmingly Ashkenazim, and from the media sector, with middle-class backgrounds, yet deeply disappointed – even alienated – by both politics and the economy, and largely facing precarious employment (Grinberg, 2013). The oldest was thirty-four years old, with most in their mid-twenties. Leef's professional background activated media workers, including the top bloggers in the country, and this brought the protest to the forefront of the news, creating both exceptional attention and expectations.

Organizers capitalized on the media attention by staging a highly engaging event, with all the characteristics of a successful experiential tool. Participants, organizers, and observers interviewed for this study consistently explained the success of the 2011 mobilization with reference to its hipness: the tent camp was the *cool place* to be in Israel. In the words of one organizer: "It had to be cool and hip for our generation to come. Only protesting and demonstrating is boring. We must think of our *customers* – the civilians are our customers of the protest, of the demonstration. We need to sell it in the right way" (interview Yigal Rambam, organizer responsible for security in the Rothschild encampment, Tel Aviv, December 16, 2011). Other protest leaders highlighted the key role played by the "fun factor." Stav Shaffir, a leading organizer and spokesperson, explained in an interview: "Happiness was the key. Journalists asked, 'Is it really serious? Because I see a lot of people smiling.' I said that's what makes it serious. People have hope again" (Vick, 2011).

Protest organizers were keenly aware of the value of sophisticated branding in contemporary mobilization. Inspired by the Arab Spring, Madrid's Indignados, and Hooverville encampments in Central Park during the 1929 recession, the action initially lacked a polished brand (the title of Leef's Facebook event was a clunky "Emergency: Bring a Tent and Take a Stand"). But quickly, designers and marketing experts were brought on board, and the brand was polished into something seductive, and powerful. The slogan became "Bet-ze-Ohel," a word play difficult to translate because it refers to a well-known children's alphabet song in which the letter A stands for "tent," and the letter B for "house." Moreover, "Bet" phonetically means "house" in Arabic. The slogan translates into English as "H [the first letter for 'house'] like Tent" and communicates that "a house is a tent and a tent is a house."

The graphic was simple, since the slogan referred to a children's song, and presented the letter Bet (for house) inside a tent. Other words from the same children's alphabet song inspired most of the subsequent rallies and protest themes, with logos designed in the same style (for example, "E like Education"). Sometimes a different letter would be used to create dissonance. The simplicity contributed to the logo's success, and it soon appeared on windows, in stores, on clothing, on cell phones, and on computer screens. The logo was also used in numerous songs, videos, and poems created by supporters. Leef explained:

> The brand is naive, childish, simple, in a way. It's straightforward. It says that you can be in a tent and it would be your home. It's very Jewish; it's connected with traveling and being a Bedouin. I said: "I can't believe that by giving up my apartment I would find my home" and that's the essence: it's not real estate; it's a place for yourself to blossom. It stands for community.
>
> (interview with Daphne Leef, December 18, 2011)

As had happened in Gezi Park, the mass mobilization took organizers and observers by surprise. Ten days after the first tent, there were 20,000 to 40,000 protesters; the following week there were 150,000; a week later, 300,000. Tent camps mushroomed to twelve around Tel Aviv, and 110 throughout the country. By mid-August, there were about 2,350 tents nationwide, with an estimated 800 on Rothschild Boulevard. The camp on 2.5 kilometers of Rothschild Boulevard was the point of reference for media and much of the public. This was the base for the culmination of the protest: ten weekly rallies, each focused on a different social concern.

What started as protest over housing prices, on Facebook, grew into a largely middle-class revolt against the rising cost of living, on the streets. The rallies brought to the streets the largest crowds in Israeli history, with a peak on September 3 of 400,000 participants (300,000 in Tel Aviv, and 100,000 in the rest of the country), according to cell-phone signals alone. (Israel's total population is 7.6 million.) The rallies also elicited the support and collaboration of several organizations and lobbying groups – most importantly, the national union of students (Rosenhek & Shalev, 2014).

The focus of this analysis is not on the rallies, however, but the genesis and dynamics of the encampments. Various factors contributed to their success. The protest had a propitious face: that someone such as Daphne Leef would camp out on the street was highly unusual and thus appealed to the media. She had a privileged background as an educated, green-eyed Ashkenazi woman from the middle class, who belonged to the intellectual elite (interview with Hani Zubida, leading Israeli blogger, activist and academic, Tel Aviv, December 16, 2011). In fact, although the tent protests appeared to include participants across all cleavages and sectors in society, subsequent analysis reveals that core supporters were drawn mostly from the middle class (Rosenhek & Shalev, 2014).

The timing of the tent protest was also key. First, the mayor had made incendiary remarks that belittled the problem of Tel Aviv's affordability. Second, the middle class was feeling the pinch of welfare benefits cuts, exacerbated by the 2008 recession. Third, because the protest took place in the summer, it could attract large numbers of students on vacation. In addition, the protests took place during a quiet window in foreign relations, as the debate over the UN recognition of a Palestinian state was on pause in the summer of 2011. So this was a rare opportunity to shift the focus away from the "existential threat" (Grinberg, 2013).

The location was also critical. Authorities moved the event permit from the initial request of the lavishly renovated, huge expanse of Habima Square to the tree-lined Rothschild Boulevard, and this turned out to be ideal for protesters. Participants felt less monitored at the elongated Boulevard location than they would have felt in the centralized square with its inhuman proportions. Moreover, the Boulevard sees enormous vehicle and foot traffic: Ordinary citizens as well as participants could walk and explore many perspectives in an exciting succession of happenings, forums, concerts, discussions, teach-ins, and plain fun activities, heightening the impact of these experiential tools. The landscape facilitated multiple centers and communicated a horizontal and decentralized governance (interview with Yifat Solel, activist and lawyer, Tel Aviv, December 14, 2011). The serpentine line of tents made the protest novel and innovative, which was vital to sustain media attention. Organizers identified tents with numbers as addresses, to mimic a city-within-the-city, and decorated them with ironic and patriotic artifacts. To heighten what was already an extraordinary experiential event, organizers closely managed entertainment to ensure daily concerts and interventions and thereby further sustain hipness, media attention, and mobilization.

The Boulevard was sited perfectly to challenge the municipal version of the White City brand, as it sat in the core of the heritage area, graced on all sides with dozens of newly renovated glamorous buildings that testified to the ongoing redevelopment and gentrification (Hatuka & Forsyth, 2005). The symbolic location had "always been the most exclusive address in Tel Aviv since the city's establishment in 1909, signifying both economic capital and social-cum-spatial distinction" and connected "Tel Aviv's 'global' CBD [Central Business District], with bank headquarters and financial institutions and more recently also high-tech 'start-ups,' on its south side, with the apogee of refined culture on its north side – a 15-minute walk along lively kiosks and cafés, trendy restaurants, galleries and public art installations" (Marom, 2013, p. 2829). In short, the location nicely encapsulated the conflict over the legitimate meaning of urban experience in the center of Tel Aviv. A tent camp on Rothschild Boulevard amounted to an outspoken reappropriation of gentrifying space by a bohemian middle class intent on "redefining its access, appearance and representation, and reinterpreting its dominant cultural purpose" (Hatuka, 2011, p. 2).

Most important, protesters identified an especially effective messaging strategy to challenge the White City brand. The White City encapsulated the Zionist dream and linked citizenship and the urban experience with the European ancestry of early settlers. It hearkened back to a time of challenge, optimism, pioneering, and hope. Therefore, the White City, as the specific physical and symbolic location of the protest, activated the sense of betrayal experienced by Jewish middle classes, because it embodied nostalgia for the Zionist promise of welfare and solidarity right where the impact of gentrification was especially evident. The protest strategy effectively built on Zionist nostalgia for frontier life with its tent encampments. By choosing the tent as a symbol, the protest also connected to antiquity, the heritage of nomadic life, and "authenticity." The symbol of the tent exuded youth, defiance, and empowerment. This further connected the protest experience to the myth of the founding of Israel. According to organizers, the encampments succeeded because participants could find utopia and a space for self-realization, a context unimaginable in daily life, which permitted discussion of a better, more equitable future. Participating meant making history. It was an adventure that emphasized not only community but also individualism through its kaleidoscopic celebration of otherness, horizontality, and diversity. The emphasis on exploration and self-discovery fed a more intense commitment to the cause than being passively persuaded by others (Aronson, 1999). Thus, the experience was described in the media as transformative, not only for participants but also for the country, and was presented as a pilgrimage of mythical significance. This understanding, which is drawn from interviews with organizers, mirrors the larger survey data from Gezi Park in exemplifying the identity-defining power of successful experiential events.

The protest's messages and images traveled far and wide across mass media, thanks to the skills, social networks, and broad sectorial sympathy that organizers enjoyed as professional cultural producers. Finally, in this context of myth reappropriation, it is important to recognize the protest's generational dimension. For many, it presented the occasion to "fight" with vision and honor, and thereby debunk the popular image of downtown Jewish youth as soft, directionless, and hedonistic (Schnell, 2007). Organizers utilized abundant war images when they described the protest. Daphne Leef, who did not serve in the army, even received a medal of honor from a soldier, exemplifying generational redemption through a new, now social, reading of the "existential threat."

These factors together explain the extraordinary success in mobilization of the 2011 protest. However, the protest failed to deliver significant policy outcomes to alleviate the cost of living concerns that had motivated it. This is because throughout protest events, and especially in tent camps, the emphasis remained on participation rather than outcome: press reviews and interviews indicate that participants were drawn by self-expressive purpose more than specific policy goals.

Media communication compounded this shortcoming. Given their professional background, organizers were well versed in shaping how they were portrayed and did so to sustain the flow of participants. Their anti-institutional and anti-party stance supported a broad mobilization of outrage but undermined programmatic coherence. Yigal Rambam, a leading organizer responsible for security on the Rothschild camp, explained:

> It was like a family, then it became too big a family. It was a freak show: every person in Israel who had an ideology, a solution, came to Rothschild – Orthodox

Jews, secular people, right- and left-wingers, youth parties, anarchists, punks, artists, Holocaust survivors, reserve army soldiers and officers, dairy workers – everyone came to Rothschild.

(interview with Yigal Rambam, December 16, 2011)

The articulation of a specific program was further undermined by the refusal to engage in formal institutional linkages. Isolated collaboration with the workers' union and communist party Hadash provided the expertise and resources to produce the rallies. However, mistrust toward formal political institutions ran high and increased after the union refused to call a general strike in support of the protest. Protesters viewed as a tactical mistake an early stint of formal discussion of the yearly budget and staunchly refused any further formal talks. They not only lacked a coherent solution to address the crisis they were denouncing, they also strategically refused to provide one, in order to maximize mobilization. The insistence on a vague message marred policy discussions (Alfasi & Fenster, 2014).

Organizers thus reacted skeptically to the Trajtenberg Committee, which had been established by the national government to shape possible policy solutions. In truth, the skepticism was well placed, as the committee largely endorsed Netanyahu's call for streamlining and liberalizing housing regulation, thereby increasing rather than limiting the role of the market in housing. This approach did not counter the erosion of public housing or remedy the unaffordability of the private rental market – the dominant housing form in Tel Aviv – that remained exceptionally unregulated throughout Israel. (On the scant impact of the protest, see Alimi, 2012; Marom, 2011; Schipper, 2015.)

The combination of strong mobilization and inadequate policy proposals reveals an important weakness in protest built on the creation of spectacles. Between the fall of 2011 and the fall of 2012, the protest splintered into several uncoordinated and often rival groups. But new and unanticipated political entrepreneurs were able to reactivate the protest discourse to great electoral gains in 2013. Two parties put social issues at the forefront of their campaigns, with a focus on closing the income gap and curbing the cost of living. The first was the Labor Party, which also declared it would not enter a Netanyahu-led coalition. This stance persuaded protest organizers, who considered joining Netanyahu a betrayal of the movement's anti-neoliberal spirit. Thus, Itzik Shmuli, the chairman of the national student union, and Stav Shaffir, a prominent spokesperson for the protest, agreed to run with the Labor Party and won seats in the 2013 parliamentary elections, although many criticized their choice as co-optation (Grinberg, 2013).

Labor was not alone in harnessing the protest's values to attract voters. Charismatic journalist Yair Lapid formed a new populist party called Yesh Atid (There Is a Future), and made outright reference to the protest's call for change. Yesh Atid centered its platform on social rather than security issues, with a focus on improving living conditions for the middle class. Strategically, Yesh Atid was willing to enter a coalition with Netanyahu, who led the polls, which gave it an advantage over Labor. The election results took observers and commentators by surprise. Labor suffered a serious blow, and newly formed Yesh Atid was the surprise winner, entering government as the second-largest coalition party. The new party succeeded with a platform that was leftist on social issues and right-wing on foreign policy, and it won elections by co-opting the protest's values and calls for change.

This result – from the Trajtenberg Committee's lack of impact to the loss of message to Yesh Atid – is a cautionary tale about the limits of institutionalization when a protest movement relies too heavily on mobilization based on experiential tools at the expense of engagement with formal institutions. The case contrasts starkly with Vecinos por la Defensa del Barrio Yungay, which started as a neighborhood group with far less mobilization than in Tel Aviv but chose both to mobilize with experiential tools and also to engage in intense lobbying and institution-building, thereby developing a multipronged approach that turned it into an enduring actor on the national level.

DIVISIONS UNDERMINE EXPERIENTIAL TOOLS AND MOBILIZATION: JAFFA

The multiplicity of encampments throughout Israel increased the diversity and prominence of the protest, turning it into a national phenomenon and emphasizing the inequities between center and periphery (Allweil, 2013; Grinberg, 2013). This was especially visible in the predominantly Arab district of Jaffa, the oldest part of the Tel Aviv–Jaffa municipality, where segregation, discrimination, and cultural obstacles prevented the formation of shared collective identities among various groups left behind economically. Specifically, entrenched ethnic and political divisions undermined experiential tools, which to be effective must be broadly targeted and cross-cleavage. This case thus highlights the key role played by experiential tools in mobilization: Despite both prior protest against displacement *and* enduring organizational networks, in recent years the absence of experiential tools undermined effective mobilization against displacement.

With post-industrial restructuring, Ashkenazim fared far better than other groups. Even controlling for educational attainment, income gaps (measuring Tel Aviv and the rest of Israel) severely worsened between this dominant group and both Mizrahim, immigrants from the Soviet Union, and Arab Israelis (Goldhaber & Schnell, 2007; Menahem, 2000). Yet, these disadvantaged groups were unable to form sustained coalitions, partly owing to a profound lack of mutual trust, as documented across surveys (N. Cohen & Margalit, 2011; Raijman & Semyonov, 2004). Discursive obstacles revolved around "modernity, colonialism, capitalism, and nationalism, and the numerous binaries they create and sustain" (LeVine, 2007, p. 172). These cultural and ideological dimensions undermined and fragmented minorities (Yiftachel, 2006). Segregation was recognized as a key factor in these divisions, and was particularly acute in Ajami, the heart of Jaffa. North Jaffa, Lev Jaffa, and the eastern fringes were less segregated, due to both young Arabs entering formerly Jewish areas, and Jewish gentrification since the mid 1990s. A more mixed residential profile was explicitly pursued by the municipality in the 1990s with gentrification as a strategy to "rehabilitate" and "strengthen" Jaffa's physical and socioeconomic profile through the arrival of a wealthier population (Monterescu, 2009). However, the two groups failed to integrate, and declining residential segregation hid the exclusion of Arabs from the rehabilitated areas. Thus, even these more *residentially* mixed areas remained highly *socially* segregated.

Despite these structural obstacles, Jaffa had a notable legacy of protest and resistance. In the 1970s, the Jaffa Slope Plan (Plan No. 2,236) called for the demolition of most buildings, reclamation of a section of the shore, and the construction of hotels and amenities to transform the area into a luxury residence and tourist destination. Ajami residents were induced to leave through bureaucratic means. In particular, they were not allowed to repair or improve their houses, leading to a deterioration of the stock while public investments were halted, and the razing of thousands of dwellings. In the 1980s, Rabita, the leading Jaffa organization for collective claim-making around crime, housing, services, and education, protested against the Jaffa Slope Plan and scored a notable victory. On that occasion, Arabs and Jewish gentrifiers overcame ethnic divisions and organized 900 residents, and the plan was cancelled in 1984 (Menahem, 1994).

In 1987, Ajami was added to Project Renewal with the goal of renovating housing and social services, and in 1992 the municipality approved a new plan (TA 2,660), which focused on architectural preservation instead of demolition. Project Renewal augmented and formalized previous participatory practices among Ajami residents, organizing them into regular steering committees with assigned budgets. However, the successes of Project Renewal translated into accelerated gentrification by Jews and damaged the previous alliance between Jewish gentrifiers and Arab residents (Carmon & Hill, 1988), thereby undermining their ability to resist municipal and private redevelopments. Since about 2000, gentrification had split the wealthy northern area that attracted Jewish and foreign residents, and tourists, from the struggling south. While the municipality presented this residential trend as a sign of connection between Tel Aviv and Jaffa, it actually represented a further contraction of Arab Jaffa. Unsurprisingly, gentrifiers tended to generate antagonism among Arabs (LeVine, 2007). Resistance to the city's planning proposals was further undermined in the early 2000s, when the municipality-sponsored Jaffa Governance Unit engaged in selective and co-optive forms of resident engagement, meant to isolate the opposition (Leibovitz, 2007).

The eviction rate accelerated. Dislocation especially affected the 40 percent of the Palestinian population in Jaffa that lived under protected tenancy in absentee ownership properties; i.e. homes of Palestinians administered by the state since the 1948 war. In 1996, the Israeli lands administration decided to sell all absentee ownership properties. Although protected tenants were given first option, they were usually either unaware of or unable to meet the purchase and mortgage conditions. Amidar, the government-operated public-housing company contracted for the sales, was paid a flat fee for each sale and therefore avoided selling properties to protected tenants, because those transactions were more complicated. Consequently, most lots were sold on the market and tenants were forced to leave their homes. By 2009, of about 2,000 absentee-ownership homes, 497 faced eviction and demolition. Rabita provided legal aid for evictees, to little avail. Whereas in Jaffa protected tenants were unable to organize, and thus were not offered compensation or alternative housing, in Jewish villages under similar circumstances, residents organized and received both (S. Wallerstein & Silverman, 2009).

In response to these developments, in the early 2000s Jaffa Arabs pursued a variety of identity-building initiatives, such as the Yafa Café (a café, Arab bookstore, and cultural venue aimed to promote interethnic understanding) and the Arab Democratic School of Jaffa, which promoted cultural autonomy and provided Arabic, English, and Hebrew instruction that presented students with an alternative historical narrative.

However, documented mistrust and social fragmentation in the neighborhood made it difficult to build the kind of mobilization based on collective neighborhood identity observed in Yungay and elsewhere. Therefore, the main tool for resistance did not have an experiential protest component but rather focused on judicial activism. In this context, local NGOs, such as the Jaffa Association for Human Rights and Rabita, came together with national organizations – such as Bimkom (Planners for Planning Rights), the Human Rights Clinical-legal Programs at the Tel Aviv University Faculty of Law, the Association for Civil Rights in Israel, Shatil's Mixed Cities Project, Adalah (Legal Center for the Arab Minority Rights in Israel), and the Society for the Protection of Nature – to struggle over public access and urban rights (Gillad Rosen & Razin, 2009; Monterescu, 2009).

This approach won a few battles, such as the 2005 ruling to keep open the Arab Democratic School, and the 2007 ruling imposing public access through the luxurious Andromeda Hill gated community. However, in 2010, they lost their case against a housing project aimed exclusively at the Orthodox Jewish community.

The network emphasized NGOs and legal partners rather than protest-oriented coalitions, and this posed considerable limitations. First, judicial timelines were impractically long. Second, in the Israeli context, the courts were limited politically in their capacities to defend Palestinian rights. Third, court rulings were unpredictable: the very act of transposing a protest to the judicial arena meant that protest organizers lost control, which could have significant effects on protest legitimacy if the court failed to support resistance.

Another fundamental difference between protesters in the White City and in Jaffa was their brand control: While the former were able to appropriate the White City brand, the discourse over what constituted the "legitimate" and "authentic" Jaffa experience remained dominated by the municipality and investors, who crafted sophisticated messages to sell Jaffa to gentrifiers. While ethnic groups displayed mistrust and social fragmentation, which prevented the emergence of collective identities able to motivate broad mobilization, investors developed a powerful, unified message of the "Jaffa experience," imbued with ethnic exoticism and nostalgia, and a landscape meant to bring residents back to the "original" Mediterranean life, with exclusivity and privilege.

A stark illustration of this rewriting of the past in both physical and discursive spaces was the aggressive restoration of Old Jaffa, with a quaint and Disney-like effect (LeVine, 2004). Buildings were renovated to correspond to an "Oriental" past, while customizing them for modern commercial purposes and tastes. The earlier emphasis by government and media on Jaffa's blight, neglect, and danger was glossed over. The marketing goal was to provide a whiff of Jaffa from the safe seclusion of luxury balconies with resplendent views of the sea. Advertisements, often also in English and French, presented Jaffa as an extension of Tel Aviv – named "the jewel of Tel Aviv," in fact, in municipal brochures (Monterescu, 2009).

Jaffa was also made safe for investors and gentrifiers by being cast as a space for *a highly depoliticized* multicultural coexistence. In so doing, investors were able to build a consumerist version of multiculturalism, precisely while multicultural residents themselves were unable to overcome the distrust based on ethnic diversity to organize against investors. For example, the municipality turned an official discourse focused on incorporating cultural diversity into city policy with the 2005 "City Vision" initiative, which designated funding for cultural institutions contributing to the integration and the celebration of cultural diversity (theaters, museums, and community centers). In 2010, the TLV Global City initiative emphasized Tel Aviv's "multicultural lifestyle" as a critical advantage of the city's branding strategy, in which Jaffa was branded as "the center of Israel's fringe culture" (Marom & Yacobi, 2013). However, these efforts to strengthen cultural policy for Palestinian citizens of Israel residing in Jaffa (for example in the case of festivals, libraries, and the city's history museum), faced institutional limitations caused by entrenched discrimination and the unwillingness to accommodate opposing political perspectives: "Tel Aviv's cultural policies to promote diversity [could not] overrule the national, ideological and political context in which the city is embedded" (Marom & Yacobi, 2013, p. 75).

Another illustration of failed cultural integration was the headquarters of the Peres Center for Peace and the Jaffa port, whose fishing used to support 250 local families. The port was converted into alternative art galleries, chic cafés, and other commercial spaces. During my 2011 fieldwork, outrage by the local community manifested itself in graffiti in Hebrew calling for "Jaffa for Arabs Only!"; vandalized playgrounds along gentrified streets; or simply the request to refrain from photographing dilapidated Arab dwellings amid empty lots and shiny new residences. As Rotbard argued in a very influential book, the "White City" celebrated an early Zionist spirit, but also the marginalization of Arab Jaffa: white Tel Aviv existed in those places where black Jaffa did not, and vice versa (Rotbard, 2015). In the war of brands and frames,

Jaffa risked being "subsumed in its victorious neighbor as a tourist attraction" (Feige, 2008, p. 91).

During the summer of 2011, a tent city was set up in Jaffa as well, largely based on Ir Lekhulanu networks. This was part of the "periphery bloc," a coalition started by Mizrahim and Arab Israelis around the country to counter the centralizing and elitist perspective of Rothschild Boulevard protesters. The bloc wanted to promote interethnic solidarity. For example, it organized a rally with participants from Jaffa and the Jewish working-class neighborhood of Ha-Tikva. However, ethnic and nationalistic concerns overwhelmed social issues and undermined trust. To overcome these differences, organizers brought together members of the communities in cultural events that evoked their common roots:

> When they sit together ... they realize how they eat the same food, listen to the same music, drink the same coffee. All of the sudden, the walls they built around them are collapsing and they can't understand that. [Yet, there is still] the notion of Jews vs. Arabs: it is embedded in us because we were socialized into it.
>
> (interview with Hani Zubida, December 16, 2011; see also Allweil, 2013)

The 2011 protest also revealed tensions in the long-standing alliance between Arab Israelis and leftist Ashkenazim, leaving Mizrahim on an uncomfortable middle ground. In particular, in their commitment to mobilizing broad sectors of the population, White City protesters dissociated themselves from the Palestinian cause by refusing to take an official stance on the Arab–Israeli conflict, and banning Palestinian flags in rallies. Displacement and gentrification in Jaffa, which was highly visible in the Ir Lekhulanu movement, was subordinate in the Rothschild protests (Gordon, 2012).

Overall, residential and social segregation, institutional discrimination, and an adverse public discourse thwarted both experiential approaches to resistance that could produce cross-cleavages among different ethnic groups. As a result, mobilization in Jaffa was sporadic and failed to halt the neighborhood's dramatic gentrification and displacement.

* * *

Experiential tools have contributed to the cultural and ideational turn in social movements. In episodes as diverse as Yungay, Gezi Park, and Tel Aviv, protest organizers used experiential tools to mobilize participants. These tools promoted emotional associations with the core values of the protest, thereby heightening participants' commitment.

Experiential tools were most effective when they targeted participants across different cleavages – not only across socioeconomic status and generations, but also ethnic and religious divisions, and the systemic split between renters and owners. Heterogeneity – *when it could be managed* – turned into an asset, because it legitimized the group's claims.

The association Vecinos por la Defensa del Barrio Yungay, threatened by plans for extensive high-rise towers, mobilized with traditional tools; with extensive linkages with traditional media; and with internet media outlets on which it controlled the content. An impressive and absolutely crucial deployment of experiential tools augmented these efforts, with activities and events that defined a barrio identity in powerful and highly inclusive ways. This approach was not only successful at reaching the association's goals but also fully rearticulated the terms of the political conflict with the municipal government.

Cases in Istanbul illustrated attempts at mobilization with different degrees of experiential tools, yet marred by the inability of protesters to attract significant citywide networks beyond intellectuals. The case of Gezi Park showed how once these networks were activated, and with the support of experiential tools, dramatic mobilization followed.

Tel Aviv showed two contrasting experiences of protest and branding, with the Rothschild encampments and resistance in Jaffa. In Rothschild, mobilization was successful because organizers were able to make participation into an experience viewed by media and public as both cool and transformative. Protesters privileged broad mobilization over platform, and the protest fizzled out after a few months. However, the protest message was surprisingly resilient in national electoral debates, appropriated not only by protest organizers running for parliament but also by their political rivals. In Jaffa, despite a legacy of struggle against displacement, ethnic fragmentation undermined mobilization, and residents could not offset the challenge posed by real-estate institutional discrimination and branding campaigns – campaigns that ironically promised a stylized veneer of the "multicultural" experience even as the truly multicultural population could not overcome ethnic divisions adequately to combat the brand.

6

Squatting, Experiential Tools, and Protest Legacies

This chapter examines the path to mobilization characterized by the combination of legacy in prior protest and experiential tools, as applied to squats (understood here as the unlawful occupation of a vacant building). It begins with the case of Yongsan, Seoul, and then continues with Hamburg's Gängeviertel and its vital antecedent, Park Fiction, which relied on strong ties to artist communities. The chapter then discusses Pope Squat in Toronto, which was short-lived and ineffective despite significant citywide support, followed by La Tabacalera in Madrid, an iconic squat that strikingly illustrates the role of partisan dealignment in explaining its success. All cases of squatting in this book build on important legacies of networking and organizing, often spanning decades, yet their twenty-first-century success has varied. These cases indicate that networks are a more salient factor than prior protest in the first phase of mobilization and occupation. However, prior experience affects endurance: As emerges in the comparison of Gängeviertel and Tabacalera, when a squat is overwhelmed by new participants with no background in that movement, it is weaker and sometimes not even sustainable. These cases will also show that successful squats are rare and weak in liberal market economies, such as Toronto, in comparison to coordinated market economies.

BETRAYED BY A MILITANT LEGACY: SEOUL

The Yongsan squat in Seoul is arguably the most dramatic case of failure in this entire book. Here, legacy was prominent, and yet counterproductive, because it recommended a continuation of past tactics, even as the context for resistance had changed.

Widespread and violent protest in Seoul in the 1980s had brought about legislation to compensate residential tenants for displacement related to redevelopment (Oh, 2012). As a result, protest by residential tenants decreased dramatically. However, the same cannot be said for commercial tenants, who were still very inadequately compensated in evictions (Rim & Lee, 2011). The law governing compensation for commercial tenants was the law on land acquisition and compensation for public projects, which calculated compensation for businesses closed due to redevelopment with an appraisement of three months' income. Compensation did not therefore consider the actual costs of moving and restarting a business. Tenants could not contest the appraisals, which were assessed unilaterally and on a case-by-case basis by an evaluator assigned by the redevelopment association (composed only of property-owners).

Even more important was the neglect of the value of business rights, i.e. the cost entailed in the inability to conduct the existing business at the existing location, which encompassed existing infrastructure, supplies, equipment, and the loss of recognition value and the client base attached to that location. These costs were called *gwun li geum*, often translated as "key money" or, more accurately, the "right-to-business." Small businesspeople often consider right-to-business as by far the largest component of their business's value. While right-to-business was used widely in transactions, it was hard to find provisions for it in the civil code and related laws and regulations, and the Supreme Court of Korea many times unsuccessfully attempted to define it (E.-G. Lee, 2010; Y.-S. Yim, Lee, & Min, 2012). Thus, right-to-business evaluations and transactions were handled through unregulated and legally unsanctioned black-market exchanges whenever a business changed hands, whether sold or rented. The price was set informally and was extremely fluid, making business tenants "collectively and individually powerless in urban politics" (S.-Y. Lee, 2014, p. 299). Unsurprisingly, then, the most dramatic cases of protest against redevelopment in Seoul over the past decade have erupted over the lack of compensation for the right-to-business (E.-G. Lee, 2010).

Commercial tenants lacked any legal protection for a significant component of eviction-related costs, and they also faced especially brutal eviction practices. Developers hired demolition companies that had among their ranks large numbers of thugs, who were sent to intimidate, harass, and even beat tenants, and destroy property in cases of resistance.

In commercial redevelopments, violent evictions were much more common than in residential redevelopment because developers acquired direct property rights.

The four cases discussed in this book are the most prominent ones of commercial tenant resistance to redevelopment in Seoul from 2007 to 2013. (Three will be discussed in Chapter 9.) The discussion here explores the failed militancy in the case of Yongsan. Resistance against redevelopment in Yongsan became notorious because five protesters and one policeman died, and twenty-three were injured (J. Y. Lee & Anderson, 2012).

The Yongsan International Business District (IBD) was the crown of Mayor Oh's Han River Renaissance, an effort to transform a central but anonymous area along the north shore and next to Yongsan railway station into a spectacular global business hub. The Yongsan IBD was marketed as the "Dreamhub," with a budget of $28 billion for an area of 55 hectares that would include office towers, fairs, trade, and residential and cultural facilities. At the project's official launch in 2007, a consortium of thirty firms led by Korail invested nearly $193 million. The Yongsan IBD would occupy Korail's disused rail yard and a residential strip along the shore, but the plan also extended east of Yongsan station toward the US Yongsan garrison (then scheduled to be returned to Korea in 2014). The project envisioned a large green strip, surrounded by deluxe residential high-rises, to connect the Yongsan IBD with a park that would replace the US garrison. A New Town Initiative (NTI) plan approved in 2006 governed this latter section of Yongsan's redevelopment, with construction permits obtained in May 2007. Soon thereafter, Samsung, Daerim, and Posko, the three main construction companies, selected and hired contractors (Yeo & Choi, 2012).

Investors lost confidence in the Yongsan IBD after the 2008 crisis, with disagreements between Korail and Samsung over costs, opposition by resident owners along the shore, and weakened political support. Meanwhile, however, the clearing of the area east of Yongsan station led to the most dramatic eviction incident in recent Korean history.

The Yongsan district generally is home to the largest concentration of foreigners in Seoul, largely of Japanese descent. However, the neighborhood of the Yongsan tragedy was an ethnically homogenous enclave, built over decades around fish and wholesale markets and a bus terminal that for many was their arrival point into the capital. The area had a typical Korean commercial life, with dense social and business ties (Anderson, 2010). Largely covering the US garrison and the Yongsan railway station, the district of Yongsan-gu only contributed 2.9 percent of Seoul regional economic product in 2011. Within the district, the official neighborhood of Hangangno-dong, where the case takes place, had a population of about 16,500 over 2.9 square kilometers, though over half was occupied by the US garrison.

It is hard to overstate the hype around the Yongsan IBD, widely considered the country's largest single property redevelopment. Real-estate prices in Yongsan between 2007 and 2009 soared to become the most expensive commercial real estate in Seoul (Chosun.com, 2009). In July 2007, Horam Construction and HyunAm Construction were hired to conduct evictions, which started in July 2008 – although residents had been receiving eviction notices as early as December 2005, well before the project was approved (S.-H. Lee, 2013). The redevelopment east of the Yongsan station affected about 900 residents. Compensation was offered to 350 commercial and 430 residential tenants. Most residents left because they couldn't bear the brutality of the eviction thugs, and about 85 percent of proposed recipients agreed to the meager compensation.

In 2008, eighty-four commercial and twenty-six residential tenants formed the Eviction Alternative Council to contest the compensation scheme (Yeo & Choi, 2012). It was an isolated effort: They tried to connect to other groups in the city, but the issue did not attract much attention (interview with Won-ho Lee, an activist with the National Coalition for Victims of Forced Evictions, Seoul, September 14, 2012). The district office, city hall, and the police failed to intervene. Protesters sought help from the Democratic Labor Party (a far-left party founded in 2000), resulting in the Democratic Labor Party Evicted Tenant Committee for Yongsan District 4, but its role was limited to providing information and attempting legal recourse, and party officials admitted the inadequacy of the response (*The Hankyoreh*, 2009). The Yongsan-gu Office, demolition and redevelopment contractors, and the property-owners' redevelopment association shared the goal of rapid progress, and hence quick evictions: No one wanted to be seen as slowing the pace, or bear the financial consequences of that (Yeo & Choi, 2012). The conflict deepened, and disgruntled tenants staged rallies to call attention to their grievances.

The only civic actors to become involved were the Federation of Evicted People (Jun Chul Hyeob/Jeon Cheol Hyeop) and the Federation Against Housing Demolition (Jun Chul Yun/Jeoncheollyeon). Both groups provided residents with information based on experience acquired in earlier struggles. The Federation of Evicted People was more moderate and kept in the background, while the Federation against Housing Demolition took the lead in organizing. Established in 1994, it was known for its large occupations around the nation, its radical rhetoric, and its militant – even violent – tactics. The group's approach contributed to isolation because it further divided neighbors (*The Hankyoreh*, 2009), halving the number of protesters to about fifty families. The Democratic Labor Party Committee and the Federation against House Demolition organized sporadic protests on opposite ends of the large development lot, typically attracting no more than twenty to thirty participants. The two groups did not cooperate or share strategies. One focused on direct action and the other on legal struggle, which embodied the underlying split among residents (interview with Eun-jung Lee, tenant organizer from the Democratic Labor Party, Seoul, September 15, 2012).

Feeling increasingly isolated and powerless, protesters decided to build a fortified tower and to defend their occupation with an armed standoff. This strategy had proven relatively successful in recent struggles led by the Federation against Housing Demolition. In the capital area alone it had been deployed six times between 1995 and 2005. These standoffs were usually resolved with a negotiated settlement, after police had waited out protesters for weeks or months (Anderson, 2010). Activists embraced the tactic, and secretly planned its execution (interview with Won-ho Lee, September 14, 2012). On January 19, 2009, twenty-seven people, including evicted residents, members of the Federation against Housing Demolition, and the Federation of Evicted People, occupied the five-story Namildang building in Hangangno 2ga, demanding the abandonment of the NTI plan. They raised over $9,000 in advance of the occupation, built a fortified tower, stockpiled homemade weapons and supplies, and prepared for a standoff with police. Protesters allegedly launched projectiles at surrounding buildings and into traffic.

Against their expectations derived from earlier occupations, police commandoes reacted swiftly and forcefully. In the early morning hours of January 20, police forces were lowered onto the roof of the building in a cargo container. The forty protesters in the building reacted by spraying paint-thinner onto the container while bombarding it with Molotov cocktails and projectiles thrown by hand or shot from slingshots. This started a fire on the roof, which killed five protesters and one policeman, and injured twenty-three people. In Yongsan, then, the legacy of protest was counterproductive because it misguided protesters in their thinking about how events would unfold.

The tragedy shook the nation. Massive protests took place, starting at the hospitals where the injured and dead had been taken. Although denied permits, numerous marches took place (J. Y. Lee & Anderson, 2010). On January 21, 2009, about 100 civil, religious, and rights groups convened to form the Committee against the Brutal Repression of Yongsan Demolition Protest. They called for accountability and appropriate compensation (The Observatory for the Protection of Human Rights Defenders, 2010).

Yet the national reaction did not address, or redress, the protesters' root concerns. Debates over the next year focused on the tragedy rather than on the redevelopment compensation for commercial tenants. Leftists emphasized the disproportionate use of force by the police, while conservatives considered members of the Federation against Housing Demolition professional radical agitators and blamed their provocative tactics for the violence that followed. The prosecutor's office concluded that the police bore no responsibility and, instead, indicted nine protesters, as well as the leadership of the Federation against Housing Demolition.

Religious groups organized a protracted candlelight vigil and played a key role in negotiations between government and the families of the deceased over compensation (Yeo & Choi, 2012). The Seoul metropolitan government formed the Council for Measures Regarding the Yongsan Incident to find solutions to the crisis. The Seoul metropolitan government, the human-rights council, the redevelopment association, and the Committee against the Brutal Repression of Yongsan Demolition Protest only agreed on a settlement after lengthy negotiations. The tragedy dominated the news for the entire year, culminating with the prime minister's visit to a protester's mortuary on January 8, 2010, and a public funeral ceremony the next day, which turned into a national event.

The focus on the tragedy took the spotlight off tenants' original grievances, thereby undermining any reform over compensation for commercial tenants and prompting the demise of the Federation against Housing Demolition (interview with Eun-jung Lee, September 15, 2012). Despite the example of the Yongsan tragedy, redevelopment continued for a few years in the Yongsan area, with no significant resistance by commercial tenants (S.-Y. Lee, 2014). Yet, as of 2017, the cleared grounds in Yongsan were still barren.

Among lessons learned, activists and scholars identified timing as a key reason for the mobilization failure. By the time tenants were offered compensation, it was too late to organize, because redevelopment plans were already approved and contractors hired. By then, tenants lacked judicial avenues for resistance (S.-Y. Lee, 2014). Militant protesters recognized the lack of preemption and early networking as a major disadvantage. In their opinion, that left militancy – which they recognized as an inferior strategy – as the only option. My interviews with an activist with the National Coalition for Victims of Forced Evictions elaborated on this point:

> The evictees learn about their situation when it's too late and then also their efforts to inform others are too late. ... then the only option becomes militant fight. When all policies have been approved there is no political outlet to change the outcome. They can only physically try to stop it. At that point networking would not mean anything because if you are not in the tenants' shoes you will be limited in what you want to take on ... It is evident that the militant approach is meant to fail. So the only way to succeed is to make other people aware of these issues and get many others involved. [Protests] must reach out to the district, beyond the evictees. We need to form a network within the locality. But it's not going to develop as a form of volunteering, to help out.
>
> (interview with Won-ho Lee, Seoul, September 14, 2012)

The passage reveals the importance of forming a community beyond evictees to sustain protest. It also highlights that mobilization should not be based on aid or assistance but rather on a broader collective identity. The organization leaders interviewed for this project could not answer *how* such broad community support might be mobilized. Experiential tools offer such an instrument, yet they were too alien from the organization's repertoire of earlier experiences to be considered.

Yet the Yongsan tragedy inflected activism in Seoul toward experiential tools and vigorous network activation. Protests over the tragedy, while not directly helping evictees, strengthened activist networks and highlighted the brutality connected with redevelopment, thereby shaping a narrative of "no more Yongsan." Protests over the tragedy also consolidated new modes of mobilization. Candlelight vigils, previously used to commemorate the death of two girls hit by a car driven by US Army personnel, were appropriated to great effect. Artists also stepped in, and spoke to the drama of displacement in a variety of media. During the yearlong standoff with authorities, Jo-yak Gol, a well-known anarchist active in eviction struggles, started a Yongsan radio station and together with other musicians introduced a space for "alternative protest." Pop songs and two feature-length documentaries were released. As observed in previous cases, site tours shaped the memory and meaning of the tragedy.

The combination of activated networks and artistic input set the stage for a completely new approach to protest against redevelopment in Seoul. At the Yongsan public funeral in January 2010, anti-eviction activists learned through word of mouth that the struggle was not over and "a new Yongsan had just started" (interview with Jo-yak Gol, September 17, 2012). In Duriban, a small restaurant in west Seoul soon to become the epicenter of resistance against redevelopment, Yongsan survivors were invited to tell their story and urge a radically different approach to protest (Taewoo Park, 2012). The surprising success in Duriban will be discussed in Chapter 9. For now, we turn to cases set in Hamburg, a city well known for its important and very active squatting tradition. Here, cultural producers activated specifically against the city's campaign to "brand" the city creatively.

CREATIVES AT THE HELM OF PROTEST: HAMBURG

Hamburg is among the most dramatic cases of creative-industry branding. Long before Richard Florida's contribution, top German cities were competing with each other using cultural policy and cultural institutions. Frankfurt's leaders – eager to present their city as inviting, and something more than a banking hub – led the race. They built one museum every year from 1984 to the end of the 1980s, so that by the end of the decade the city had over thirty museums (Friedrichs & Dangschat, 1994). Meanwhile, Hamburg marketed itself as the center of insurance and media services and fared poorly by comparison in attracting tourists. Most scholars date Hamburg's city branding and neoliberal policies to social-democratic mayor Klaus von Dohnanyi, who presented his conception of "Hamburg the Enterprise" in an important 1983 speech to an exclusive circle at the Übersee Club (Birke, 2016). Dohnanyi's was the first intervention that explicitly aimed to attract wealthy residents and international investment. Cultural industries gained prominence when conservative mayor Ole von Beust (2001–2010) embraced Florida's ideas and hired him and Roland Berger Strategy Consultants to brand Hamburg as a global city (Overmeyer, 2010). Historically the city has largely been governed by social democrats (Sozialdemokratische Partei Deutschlands [SPD]), but from 2001 to 2011, Christian democrats (Christlich Demokratische Union [CDU]) held government, and spearheaded neoliberal policies.

As in other cities, cultural branding intertwined with extensive urban redevelopment plans. Von Beust's ambitious projects included deepening the Elbe, expanding the city southward, and converting the free port to commercial and residential use. The last project, named Hafencity, became the largest redevelopment in Europe, and when completed in 2025 it will host 12,000 inhabitants and 40,000 workers on nearly 162 hectares, with venues designed by top names in global architecture, such as Rem Koolhaas, Herzog & de Meuron, and Renzo Piano. Branding initiatives included Hamburg's candidacy as the cultural capital of Europe in 2010 and as host of the 2012 Olympic Games. (Another bid for Olympic Games 2024 was turned down by referendum in 2015.)

Yet Hamburg leaders were more sensitive than elsewhere to the idea that they had to protect indie culture to maintain vibrant creativity. The squat scene was lively, and government studies connected a healthy growth of creative industries to the activities of "radicals" (*Umbruchmilieu*). One government report identified radicals as "dedicated youth with high education, little financial resources, but high temporal and personal commitment and enthusiasm for and identification with their project" (Overmeyer, 2010, p. 45). It emphasized the vital importance of networks within this scene, thought to provide a "sense of belonging" and "personal ties," able to foster "an active exchange of views, know-how, but also material infrastructures" (Overmeyer, 2010, p. 45). Reports also referenced the need to protect "scenes," defined as trendy neighborhoods where indie culture thrived, and recognized the intense competition for space in central areas between developers and creatives. Nevertheless, creative city events usually privileged displays of diversity that appealed to the tastes and preconceptions of middle-class professionals and aligned with planning efforts to securitize neighborhoods.

Nowhere was this more true than in St. Pauli, identified as "the most important movement space in Hamburg" because of both the intense activism and the rampant gentrification (Birke, 2016, p. 225). I selected this neighborhood as a research site because it had characteristics similar to other resilient neighborhoods in the book: Historically it had hosted populations cast by authorities as "deviant" or "marginal," and redevelopment, gentrification, or displacement processes conjured a view of the neighborhood as "dangerous." This transversal comparison includes St. Pauli, Lavapiés, San Telmo, Parkdale, Yarra, and Skid Row. Authorities repeatedly cast these neighborhoods as "decayed" (and hence in need of "regeneration" or "sanitation") in part because of the resident population, comprised of groups perceived as outside of mainstream social order and norms, such as sex workers, undocumented immigrants, the homeless, the mentally ill, or criminals. What these neighborhoods actually do share is their centrality, their lower-than-average residential income, their experience of aggressive efforts to displace them, and their remarkable ability to resist. Residents in these communities were deeply rooted and fought gentrification and displacement because they had no alternatives for shelter and were particularly dependent on location. These neighborhoods also dramatically illustrate trait-stripping: the appropriation of an identity with negative connotations in the mainstream as a trait of collective belonging and pride (Norton, 1988).

St. Pauli has 21,100 residents and is located in the center of Hamburg. It is part of the district of Hamburg-Mitte and sits on the border with the district of Altona, two districts with about 300,000 residents each. Councils in both districts are traditionally on the political left. Hamburg-Mitte was led by a red–green coalition from 2004 to 2011. Following a citywide support wave, the CDU became the strongest party in the district for the first time in 2004, but the SPD regained the lead position in 2008. Between 2008 and 2011, Hamburg-Mitte was the only one of the seven districts of Hamburg in which the SPD was the strongest faction and administered with a red–green coalition. Because Hamburg is a city-state in a federal system, it is hard to compare it to other cases. For this reason, I have identified as the "local level" of government the local councils (Bezirk) and the "higher level" of government as the city-state government. Councils have limited political influence over zoning policy. Nevertheless, the staunch political orientation of Hamburg-Mitte and nearby Altona on the far left brings essential institutional access to protesters. For the period of analysis, protesters thus found allies in the district council but faced an adverse state legislature.[1]

At the beginning of the new millennium, St. Pauli was one of the poorest neighborhoods in Hamburg (with an unemployment rate at 10 percent against the city average of 6.5 percent) and one of the most diverse (with 21.8 percent of the population foreign, against a city

[1] Elections followed different rules during the period of analysis, but overall privileged parties over candidates. Until 2004, elections in both the state parliament (the unicameral legislature for the city state of Hamburg) and the district assembly in Hamburg-Mitte were by single multimember district with closed party list. In 2004, a measure that aimed to emphasize the role of candidates against party elites was passed in a referendum. However, in 2006, a senate law prevented the outcome of the referendum from being implemented and maintained much of the previous party influence. Following much controversy, changes were introduced in 2008, 2011, and 2015, with increases in personalization through the addition of small multimember districts to the preexisting single multimember district (all with open party list). Further, the voter can exercise cumulation and *panachage*. Elections in the district assembly of Hamburg-Mitte followed a similar structure.

average of 13.6 percent). It was a residential neighborhood with old multistory apartment buildings (population density was 9,173 residents per square kilometer against a city average of 2,295). Since it was a working-class neighborhood, many of its buildings were housing with publicly subsidized rents. Nineteen percent of apartments were social or public housing against a city average of 11.1 percent (Statistisches Amt für Hamburg und Schleswig-Holstein, 2013).

Close to the Elbe shore, St. Pauli borders some of the richest areas of the city. This privileged location, the nearby conversion of the port into Hafencity, the regeneration of the city center, and its historical buildings and artistic milieu made St. Pauli a prime area for redevelopment and gentrification. The erosion of public housing in Hamburg (see Chapter 4) strongly affected St. Pauli. In 1998, two-thirds of public housing in St. Pauli still lacked central heating and bathrooms. SAGA GWG allowed the housing to deteriorate to the irrevocable point when the housing would be uninhabitable. The subsequent massive program of renovation and construction priced out previous residents. In assigning flats in its St. Pauli buildings, SAGA privileges German renters over foreign-born renters, to the extent that the number of non-German citizen residents in the buildings fell from 40 percent in 1994–1997, to 30 percent in 1998–2003, and to 28 percent by 2006. The price of rentals also demonstrates gentrification. In 1994, newly let flats in St. Pauli cost €7.70 per square meter, and in 2008, €11.40 (against €9.75 for Hamburg overall). Displacement was confirmed by the fact that low-income residents were leaving the neighborhood: for example, social-support recipients fell from 18.5 percent in 1998 to 11.4 percent in 2003 (Bude, Sobczak, & Jörg, 2009). Rents for new contracts on the private market rose by 30 percent between 2004 and 2009 alone (Hohenstatt & Rinn, 2013). While poverty was reduced in absolute terms since the 1990s, income differences among the neighborhood's residents dramatically increased, which led scholars to identify the neighborhood as a place of small-scale polarization (Birke, 2016).

St. Pauli had a rich identity, enjoying the status of a quasi-village in the center of the city. Locals described it as cosmopolitan yet simultaneously communal, tolerant, tightly knit, provincial, and almost rural. In interviews, it emerges as a truly exceptional place within the city. Developers and SAGA, razing old apartment buildings to make space for steel-and-glass or faux-antique facades, deconstructed and reconstructed the neighborhood in complex ways, intended to maintain its "color" and "grittiness," yet make it acceptable and even intriguing to higher-class residents. The operation implied "cleaning," and in fact the German term for real-estate renovation, and much used in the context of gentrified real estate, is "sanitizing" (*Sanierung*).

Steffen Jörg's documentary about the demolition of the local historical and iconic St. Pauli brewery and the glass tower that replaced it shows the delicate balancing act in this gentrification project through poignant interviews (Bude et al., 2009). The developer portrayed the neighborhood as the blighted home to undesirable elements in order to legitimize intervention, and argued in favor of the reappropriation of the architectural heritage by the new high-income residents:

> Look across the roofs ... and see nice penthouse lofts develop on these old houses, fancy hotels in the old iron foundries ... Do you think that up to now only people have been living in St. Pauli who appreciated it when bottles were thrown against walls in the night, or that there is urinating and vomiting in the streets, or that women and children are being molested? I think you should not misrepresent things by saying that the new clientele that is moving here is destroying the ambiance in the area. I'm asking you whether you think these things are desirable.

As a result, far from becoming an integral part of residents' new lives in the neighborhood, local grittiness was kept at a safe distance and experienced in the havens of modern-minimalist café lounges that are fixtures of the aspiring global city and integral to the "pacification by cappuccino" approach so aptly captured by Sharon Zukin (1995, p. 28). The roughness (and consequent coolness) of the neighborhood was filtered through their panoramic windows, "with a clear message: we are inside and we are observing what is going on outside: we like it scruffy, but not under our very noses" (a resident interviewed in Bude et al., 2009).

At the same time, the city tourist board (Hamburg Tourismus Gmbh) wanted to maximize returns from the powerful neighborhood identity. The area of St. Pauli and in particular its famous vice street Reeperbahn were key to the city's economy and attracted the largest portion of tourists. Building on its image as a place of exception, starting in the 2000s the city tourist board concentrated in St. Pauli a variety of mass events that raised the number of visitors to 25 million annually. Rowdy parades to celebrate soccer victories, Harley Davidson yearly motorcades, or other events that attracted tens of thousands of loud and usually drunk participants disrupted ordinary life and created filth and noise, in a crass and sometimes even violent invasion of the space. Yet the tourist board saw the changes as an opportunity for growth, and it strived to position the area as "colorful, bold, and diversified" and develop it as "an amusement and event area, a 'Golden Mile' for everyone," as it stated in a promotional brochure.

Hamburg movements against these post-industrial challenges are now viewed as foundational to resistance in Germany and beyond, for the breadth of their networks, striking outcomes, and the degree to which they influenced policy debates (Hohenstatt, 2013). Berlin, while also suffering from pronounced gentrification (Holm, 2011), usually followed Hamburg's lead in organizing.

In particular, St. Pauli stands out for its historical legacy of urban protest. During the 1980s, an urban movement had obtained permanent squatting rights and cooperative ownership of several buildings and open areas on Hafenstrasse, a street along the Elbe adjacent the future site of Park Fiction. They defended their militant occupation with prolonged violent struggles and barricades. In 1992, twelve buildings had been transferred to cooperatives administered by residents. They now sit amid luxury residential high-rises and house some of the activists interviewed for this book. Nearby, in 2002, Bambule, a long-term trailer-park squat, had been evicted when the conservative government sought to expand the fair facilities. The eviction was resisted with violent struggle, and, in response, squatters were temporarily granted relocation on a different site.[2]

Twenty years later, this important legacy of resistance was relatively weak, as neighbors sought to block construction along the Elbe and build a public park instead. Interviews revealed that organizers did not see the legacy as special in terms of its networks or strategy. Instead, the legacy equipped participants with a form of "hope," of "knowing that it is possible to undo developers' plans," thereby displaying what McAdam (1999) called "cognitive liberation."

The most dramatic element in this campaign is how methods of protest shifted, from militancy to experiential tools. This is in part due to the prominence of cultural producers not only as participants in but also as

[2] Another important antecedent was the occupied center Rote Flora in nearby Schanzenviertel. In 1986, a German investor decided to open a second musical theater. He selected the Flora, a theater that had hosted workers' performances in the 1920 but was then used as a department store. Despite police repression to secure construction, massive local opposition led to sustained violent clashes, and both the investor and the city abandoned the plan and found a different building for the new musical theater (Friedrichs & Dangschat, 1994). Rote Flora then turned into one of the city's most enduring and influential squats. When it was threatened by eviction in 2013, it issued a nationwide protest call that led to 7,000 demonstrators and an urban uprising that lasted for weeks. While not developed in detail here, the 2013 defense of Rote Flora supports the trends observed in Hamburg, with success associated with the deployment of anarchist networks and experiential tools, leading to broad mobilization in the context of a leftist local council.

leaders of protest. In the new millennium, cultural producers in Hamburg played a pivotal role in both designing and conducting resistance, and they also typically benefited from positive outcomes, securing access to inexpensive living, working, or performance quarters in prime locations through arrangements negotiated with government support. Slogans such as "The city is our factory" (Schäfer 2010) indicate how cultural producers see themselves as inheritors of the industrial economy and the resistance of the industrial working class. A vast literature examines these cases and explores the role of cultural producers in resistance over redevelopment, as well as the contradictions that emerge when neoliberal governments focus on creative industries for growth purposes (most recently see, for example, Gängeviertel e.V., 2012; Hohenstatt, 2013; Holm, 2010; Kirchberg & Kagan, 2013; Mayer, 2009; Novy & Colomb, 2012; Twickel, 2011).

Park Fiction is the first instance in Hamburg of resistance led by cultural producers that deployed experiential instead of militant tools. Its success became a template for local activists in subsequent struggles, which can largely be understood as strategic and tactical re-elaborations of this first methodologically "revolutionary" case of resistance.

In 1995, Christoph Schäfer and Cathy Skene began mobilizing to stop redevelopment and build instead a community park, named Park Fiction. They formed a core group of about twelve activists that met weekly and networked with the local schools, churches, neighborhood associations, and participants in the music scene. Their message emphasized that the project was an opportunity for residents to reappropriate their neighborhood and to create a space for multigenerational, multiracial, and multi-class exchanges of prospects, ideas, everyday practices, and family values. As in the Santiago case, the success of the movement relied on its broad appeal, based on a carefully balanced definition of "neighbor" that enabled participation through self-expression.

A busy calendar of well-attended events celebrated the distinctiveness of the neighborhood. In these contexts, residents also interacted with artistic performances, from music to sculpture to handicrafts. They participated in games and activities such as face-painting, gymnastics, puppets, and stilts-walkers, all of which produced a carnivalesque, light-hearted, hopeful – but also politically conscious – festival of space appropriation. Events often included home-cooked food – the ultimate community glue.

At the same time, the group devised a participatory planning process to collect ideas for the park. They informed neighborhood residents about the proceedings through an accessible learning process, in the form of a garden library (with documents, maps, questionnaires and even modeling kits for children) and an enclosed infotainment space. This communication was factual and not politically partisan. Game boards made the process more interactive and entertaining: an ironic version of Monopoly, called Gentropoly, vilified gentrification. Organizers wore yellow jackets with the organization's logo and became visible points of reference, as residents would approach them on the street to ask for updates and information.

Organizers cultivated the grassroots character of the campaign, which is essential to successful experiential tool deployment. For example, archives recorded residents' desires, stories, and aspirations for the neighborhood. Tours through St. Pauli showed the physical reality of gentrification, and Park Fiction's website posted regular updates, often in the form of self-made YouTube videos and protest testimonies. All aspects of the campaign were documented in a variety of online venues as well as in a book about the protest. The city was presented as the primary stage of citizenship – the space for its quintessential experience and performance. None of these interventions was an explicit protest, but they certainly constituted implicit protest, because they represented a conscious opposition to city plans. Their peaceful and family-friendly attributes, combined with a creativity that attracts media attention, hid a subversive strategy that effectively led to the realization of Park Fiction in 2005.

Activists saw the struggle over Park Fiction as fundamentally new and different from earlier conflicts, such as Hafenstrasse. Protest participants were different, as the chronically unemployed and marginalized population behind the Hafenstrasse barricades was replaced by low- and middle-class cultural producers and families. According to interviews with activists who witnessed both waves of protest, Hafenstrasse protesters were ideologically more likely to engage in open and violent confrontation and came from the 1970s tradition, when militant action was a common protest tactic, but the Park Fiction protest emphasized instead inviting and ironic messaging – partly, perhaps, to involve families and immigrants, but also to elicit the support of the local church and its congregation, a very important node in the network of organizations that fought for the park. The Park Fiction goal was also different. As organizers stated, they wanted "to go well beyond" repair-squatting (*Instandbesetzung*) to become instead "a resource for the city," through the production of knowledge and social integration as well as the introduction of a new participatory approach to planning. Experiential tools were the most dramatic innovation: "reaching a goal through a party was huge and new" (interview with Christoph Schäfer, artist, activist, social entrepreneur, and Park Fiction organizer, Hamburg, July 27, 2011).

While prior protest was only mildly related to the successful mobilization for Park Fiction, dense networks were indeed indispensable. As in Santiago, the organization was quick to network at the international level. For example, in 2002 Park Fiction shared its method at Documenta XI, a leading international exhibition of contemporary art. It also connected with similar endeavors in Europe, Argentina, and India, convening them at the Unlikely Encounters in Urban Space Congress in 2003. Only after did the network develop a national dimension.

The Park Fiction campaign became critical to subsequent struggles largely because in the later 2000s it promoted a network of anti-gentrification groups in other Hamburg neighborhoods, in collaboration with the sister organization Es Regnet Kaviar (It Rains Caviar). They coordinated and organized demonstrations, parades, music festivals, flash mobs, and artistic happenings – for example, with the 2008 slogan "participate, let yourself be surprised, have fun," which pointed to the strategy of combining protest and entertainment. Park Fiction was often the setting of these events.

Park Fiction's success can be explained by the broad network of social institutions, artists, residents, and community workers, as well as by the fact that the resistance offered a mixture of art and activism (Höpner, 2010), in the form of experiential tools. However, the networks suffered from the lack of representation by some groups particularly affected by displacement and exclusion, such as migrant residents and welfare recipients (Füllner & Templin, 2011; Hohenstatt & Rinn, 2013). In several interviews for this book, Park Fiction organizers explained how they tried to reach out to these populations, but with limited success.

As the 2000s progressed, there was more pressure to gentrify St. Pauli, and contention likewise spread to several sites. Police reacted to protest rallies with increasingly harsh measures. They took a more militarized approach, injuring and arresting peaceful protesters. The government, whose emphasis on growth dictated risk reduction for investors, intended to depoliticize the struggle, estrange dissent from its political context, and frame it as simple disorder and noncompliance.

Developers also learned to appropriate experiential tools from activists. The development of the Bernhard-Noch-Quartier, which entailed the demolition of three residential buildings and the upgrading of a further seven, glaringly illustrates this. The location was directly adjacent to the iconic squat-turned-cooperative blocks of Hafenstrasse, which did not bode well for unopposed construction. Yet, as part of an eventually successful effort, the developer plastered walls with posters that in aesthetics and language emulated the protesters' image-making. Passersby had to focus closely to recognize that the funky graphics and hip slogans in *support* of the project were sponsored by the developer's marketing campaign, and not by opposition activists.

The Office of Urban Development (Behörde für Stadtentwicklung und Umwelt) pursued a similar strategy. Overlooking the decade-long struggle for its creation, the Office quickly incorporated Park Fiction into its leaflets as "a new park for a variegated society … in this place the ethno-pop impression is not a cliché but symbolizes a cosmopolitan, future-oriented Hamburg."

Sensitive to, and wary of, their place as gentrification catalysts, cultural activists devised a variety of responses, including a satirical YouTube video depicting a "de-gentrification kit,'" an ironic toolbox of recommendations on how to devalue buildings, turning them into sites of "broken windows" able to scare gentrifiers away and keep rents low. The tools included hanging "wife-beater" shirts and satellite antennas on the balcony, breaking and taping windows, setting hanging wire to suggest shoddy repairs, adding foreign names to the doorbell, and displaying shopping bags from a 99-cents store.[3] The group organized a permanent picnic in the park, opened the squat Centro Sociale (a self-managed community center modeled in the Italian tradition); and hosted performance tours through St. Pauli to observe the physical reality of gentrification.

In Hamburg, creative producers thus developed a repertoire of contention that exploited their comparative advantage in creativity, local knowledge, and networking. Gaining emotional commitment among broad sectors of the population was essential to the success of experiential tools and was nowhere more clearly displayed than in the Gängeviertel occupation, to which I now turn.

* * *

Hamburg has a spatially concentrated and important squatter tradition (Leach & Haunss, 2009). Yet, in the 2000s, the media, including the largest dailies, reinterpreted squatting as "innovation" and distinguished between "'good' (innovative) squats and 'bad' (destructive) squatters" (Birke, 2016, p. 217). Specifically, "all squats that were, at least in the

[3] See www.youtube.com/watch?v=A1L3iFwJ7yk.

definition of the government, not in line with the promotion of the creative class were evicted, most of them after only a few hours, and accompanied by constantly escalating violence conducted both by the police and participants in the scene" (Birke, 2016, p. 224). In other words, cultural producers had gained distinct prominence within the protest and anarchic community, thanks to the government emphasis on cultural industries. Several squats illustrated this dynamic over the first decade of the 2000s.

For example, Skam was a coalition founded in 1992 by a handful of artists that grew to 120 members. It occupied the abandoned Schauburg St. Pauli. This landmark on the iconic vice street Reeperbahn was one of the most distinct cinemas in the country from 1926 to 1945 and was later converted into a bowling alley. Skam did not have strong institutional skills and failed to obtain heritage status, so the lot was purchased by Strabag Gmbh, the largest real-estate developer in Europe. Strabag planned two iconic towers, the "Dancing Towers," which emulated sister projects in Dubai by Zaha Hadid. Skam petitioned to keep the bowling alley as a place for alternative culture. Even Richard Florida encouraged the city council to give the building to the artists to maintain the neighborhood's cachet and redistribute proceeds to the indie culture and artists at the core of the city's brand.[4] Instead, in 2009, Skam was forced to move, and the bowling hall was razed to make space for the towers.

In this case, protesters initially failed because they could not sway the district council in Hamburg-Mitte, and specifically the district mayor who favored the towers. Supporting networks were limited to the artist and squatter community, and less integrated with neighborhood residents than in the Park Fiction case, and this partly explains the failure.

However, Skam did profit from the prominence of cultural producers and was able to find political support by moving their struggle for a home to another historically leftist district in nearby Altona. The collective thus joined an Altona artist community called Frappant, which was squatting in an abandoned shopping center. When IKEA wanted to purchase the building, the squatters organized opposition, joined in that campaign by massive popular support. That struggle extended the group's political clout, so that when IKEA purchased the building in 2009, after much negotiation with the city government, both networks of artists were moved to Viktoriakaserne, an abandoned barracks building (the building

[4] See the interview at www.youtube.com/watch?v=nXwXNtfiG7A.

lay 3 kilometers northwest from the Dancing Towers toward the outskirts of the city). Viktoriakaserne became primarily a live-work space for artists, and, given the rampant redevelopment and gentrification in Hamburg, it was a significant victory.

The case of Gängeviertel, however, overshadows Skam's success. Gängeviertel is a complex of over two dozen buildings, occupying nearly a block in the heart of Hamburg. Until the middle of the twentieth century, Gängeviertel (which translates as "Alleys' District") referred to the entire neighborhood, characterized by neglected tenements with passageways. Due to unsustainable hygienic conditions, after the cholera epidemic of 1892, the city of Hamburg began a rehabilitation process. Most buildings were razed, the last between 1958 and 1964 to make way for a Unilever headquarter. By 2000, only a couple of dozen decayed buildings remained – as if forgotten – surrounded by residential and office glass and steel towers. Rather than rehabilitating the buildings, the city government sold them to the highest bidder. After a failed redevelopment attempt in the early 2000s, in 2008, the Dutch investor Hanzevast received from the city a purchase offer for the Gängeviertel complex, which cancelled all remaining tenants' agreements.

A large group of cultural producers related to the Park Fiction group had just circulated an influential pamphlet, "Not in Our Name, Brand Hamburg!" which called for cultural producers to sharply critique the city's use of artists for marketing purposes. On the wake of that exhortation, on August 22, 2009, with the support of leading artist Daniel Richter, about 200 artists occupied Gängeviertel and demanded space for creatives as well as the complete preservation of the historic complex. On that day, 3,000 residents visited the squat and enjoyed exhibitions, film screenings, readings, concerts, and several workshops. Visitors to the dilapidated buildings-turned-art squat reached 30,000 within the first six months. Gängeviertel quickly became more than "a building ensemble in which artists exhibit and work, but a space for all citizens of the whole city" (Gängeviertel e.V., 2013).

Even though Gängeviertel was primarily devoted to cultural production, activists carefully communicated broader social relevance, from their slogan "Komm in die Gänge" (a smart play on words that means "Come to the alleys" but also "Get moving") to website photos of a mother and child, for example, walking through a dark passage out into the radiant alleys of Gängeviertel (Gängeviertel e.V., 2013).

The Komm in die Gänge initiative promoted creative and artistic free spaces. Typical of successful experiential tools, organizers emphasized grassroots control and activities with broad appeal. In twelve buildings, with a total usable area of about 8,700 square meters (60 percent of which housed about 125 residents), squatters provided workshops, laboratories, and open spaces with low rents. Amateurs and professional artists were invited to utilize space next to each other, to produce an interesting, animated, and functional cultural center. This inclusivity extended to children, youth, seniors, people with disabilities, students, and freelancers interested in the arts. Network activation went well beyond the anarchist artist scene, as the group began to collaborate with art institutions in Hamburg, such as the Thalia Theater, the Deutsche Schauspielhaus, the Kunsthalle, universities, the museum for Hamburg's history, and the music hall. The goal was a mixing of high, popular, and sub culture for mutual enrichment.

The occupation was tolerated because it was perceived as an "artistic" occupation and fit perfectly with the city's emphasis on creative industries. It also confirmed the abandonment of militant protest (Hohenstatt, 2013). The innovative strategy undertaken in Park Fiction was thus perfected in Gängeviertel, as well summarized by a leading activist: "We are less militant. We occupy with paintings. We protect ourselves with art. We try to get through differently, without black masks, by gaining sympathy instead" (interview with Nicole Vrenegor, journalist and activist, Hamburg, July 29, 2011).

What was advertised as a party-cum-art exhibition was unveiled at the end of the evening to be a squat not by artists but by artworks. This move caught the authorities off guard, because removing artworks was more awkward than removing squatters (interview with Heiko Donsbach, architect and Gängeviertel activist, Hamburg, July 27, 2011). Cultural producers persuaded the mass media and public opinion that withholding redevelopment would benefit art for all citizens. Given its own emphasis on Hamburg as a "creative city," the government was pressured to give in or lose face, and brand credibility.

The creatives' discursive advantage was compounded by their stated motivation for the occupation. "Hamburg is a beautiful city," the group argued,

> but this has rarely been enough for the rulers: she shall be the most beautiful and brightest in international global city comparisons, a magnet for corporations and tourists. This has been the premise for decades of urban development. Hamburg was transformed into a company and advertised as "talent city," then became the "growth city" – with the result that more and more space is devoured by trade and expensive housing. The city puts millions in large-scale projects instead of

buildings that benefit the citizens of Hamburg. Land is given to investors, who are only interested in profit – and not in the welfare of those who have to live with their projects. Hospitals, public buildings, green spaces and open spaces are sold at the highest prices to meet growing budgets. The living community is suffocated. Meanwhile, even the last niches and free spaces are endangered, forever to be lost. The inner city of Hamburg has become a place unworthy of humans, where nothing other than consumption and events is possible. All over the city, public spaces and old buildings disappear, and in their place grows smooth investor architecture. Glass, steel and concrete buildings displace typical ones – and worse still, people. Increasingly, financially weak inhabitants are pushed to the outskirts of the city. Because rental housing is converted into for-sale property, social housing is falling and rents are rising. Hamburg is being redeveloped for a deluxe market [*Luxussaniert*], densified and segregated by income. This development also affects artists.

(Gängeviertel e.V., 2013)

The statement next delved into the political economy of the creative city and its adverse effects on local artists, starved not only of space but also of funding, which was geared toward projects that enhanced the city's image:

Artists are to be instrumentalized by politics and city planning; to be used as a tool for "revaluation" of city districts, laying the ground for gentrification. They are used to develop districts and settle there, but only until the neighborhood is designated as investor-friendly. We're not going to do that. We do not want to contribute to displacing settled neighborhoods and move on after the "work" is done.

(Gängeviertel e.V., 2013)

On the back of these statements, in November 2009, the pamphlet manifesto "Not in Our Name, Brand Hamburg" was republished to reach a broader audience. It appeared as an ironically glossy magazine, filled with satirical commentaries on Hamburg's branding and redevelopment campaign. In the statement, the artistic community distanced itself from the government's focus on creative industries as complementary to neoliberal growth and marketing strategies (NION, 2010). The message was powerful:

A specter is haunting Europe, since the American economist Richard Florida predicted that only the cities where the "creative class" feels well will prosper. "Cities without gays and rock bands are losing the economic development race," writes Florida. Many European cities now compete to become the settlement area for this "creative class." For Hamburg the competition has led to urban politics becoming more and more dependent on the "Image City." It is about presenting the world with a specific image of city, image of the "pulsating metropolis," which offers "a stimulating environment and the best opportunities for cultural creators of all kinds." A city-sponsored marketing agency ensures that this image is fed to the media as the "Hamburg brand." It overflows the country with brochures, in which Hamburg emerges as a Fantasialand free of contradictions and with no social tensions, with [attractions and hip neighborhoods hosting] the artists' scene. Harley-Days on the Kiez, gay parades in St. Georg, off-art spectacle in the Hafencity, Reeperbahn-Festival, Fanmeilen [sport fan esplanades], and Cruising Days. Barely a week passes without a tourist mega-event to enhance the "brand-enhancing function."

Dear location politicians: We refuse to talk about this city in marketing categories. We say: Ouch, it hurts. Stop with this shit. Don't take us for stupid. We neither want to help to "position" the neighborhood as a "colorful, naughty, diverse district," nor do we think of Hamburg as "water, worldliness, internationality" or whatever else you come up with as "building blocks of a successful brand Hamburg." We think of other things. For example, about the over million square meters of empty office space and the fact that you nevertheless continue to build up the River Elbe with premium glass teeth. [...] We say: A city is not a brand. A city is also not a firm. A city is a community. We ask the social question, which in cities today is also a question of territorial conflict. It is about conquering and defending places in this city that make it worth living in also for those who are not the target group of the "Growth City." We claim the right to city – together with all the inhabitants of Hamburg, who refuse to stand in as a location factor. We stand in solidarity with the occupiers [in other initiatives and] with the action network against gentrification [...], which opposes the city of investors.

(Excerpts from the manifesto by NION, 2010)

The manifesto reverberated throughout Germany and internationally, and was reprinted by the national newspapers *Die Zeit* and *Hamburger Morgenpost*. It expanded the debate over urban redevelopment to a much wider audience, and highlighted the role of cultural producers as objects and subjects in this dynamic. The public response meant that local politicians could not ignore it. On December 15, 2009, the Hamburg senate announced that the sale of Gängeviertel to Hanzevast had been withdrawn by mutual agreement, the €2.8 million down payment was returned, and that the city would instead pursue a project with wider public consensus. Squatters were keenly aware that without Florida's concept of the creative class, the success of the protest would not have been possible, as the city would probably not have responded to cultural producers' demands. They recognized that their status as "artists" and "creatives" – labels whose use they did not control – was a key reason for their success (activist Hannah Kowalski interviewed in Höpner, 2010, p. 52).

Yet squatters could not rest on their laurels or successes, and their behavior reveals the underlying politics of experiential mobilization. Gängeviertel members remained under clear pressure to pursue social relevance, in order to keep the public sympathy on which their autonomy depended. Programming emphasized deliverables that spoke to social contributions at large. To maintain a catchall appeal, they depoliticized both social outputs and the overall communication (Kirchberg & Kagan, 2013; Mayer, 2009; Uitermark, 2004). Punctually advertised on the groups' websites with catchy slogans and hip imagery, these products and messages were embedded in and attuned to the broader market logic, with its constant competition for resources. All aspects of the organization were sensitive to this logic. For example, a 2010 assembly meeting that I attended focused on rent levels for spaces in the buildings, as well as the maintenance of a positive relationship with the police. Even as Gängeviertel strived to offer the experience of an alternative living and social arrangement, it found itself inevitably dependent on the surrounding social, institutional, and economic system.

Gängeviertel was highly impactful. The squat led to a comprehensive urban movement in Hamburg, which convened citywide oppositional initiatives (Buchholz, 2016). In 2009, Hamburg hosted the first Right to the City network in Germany, with fifty-four local organizations, each with its own brand and a packed calendar of initiatives. Similar to the Santiago coalition, the network formalized its message and in March 2011 organized its first nationwide conference with the theme: "To Whom Does the City Belong?" Between 2009 and 2012, the network brought together a coalition with urban poor, refugees, and middle-class activists, squatters, and artists.

As the network formalized, attention shifted from isolated site-specific campaigns to policy-making. Thus, as in Santiago, Right to the City in Hamburg combined street protest with legislative initiatives, with goals such as setting a ceiling of €4 per square meter in rent, even for new leases, decriminalizing squatting, and eliminating discrimination against foreign-born applicants in public housing assignments. The campaigns also influenced city electoral outcomes. Soon after the Gängeviertel sale was reversed and the buildings assigned to the squatters, the social-democratic party regained control of the city senate by prioritizing the housing crisis in its platform. Olaf Scholz, the SPD citywide mayor elected in 2011, was reelected in 2015.

Three policy outcomes speak to the sweeping institutional changes that followed. When the long-marginalized Elbe Islands and working-class neighborhood of Wilhelmsburg were revitalized, for example, the approach was quite different from prior practice, as a special program was launched called the International Building Exhibition (IBA) that focused on redevelopment without population displacement. Activists also identified a legal tool to stop property-owners from upgrading units in order to raise rents – a common gentrification strategy. Specifically, they rediscovered the Social Preservation Statute (Soziale Erhaltungssatzung), an old regulation that blocked any physical upgrades and use changes of residential dwellings that could lead to displacement. They then invoked this statute in several areas of the city. Finally, political and economic actors formed the Alliance for Housing in Hamburg (Bündnis für das Wohnen in Hamburg) as a platform to address the housing crisis and improve social housing by accelerating construction, including that of affordable housing (Vogelpohl & Buchholz, 2017).

SQUAT PROTEST IN A LIBERAL MARKET ECONOMY: TORONTO

The squatting experience in Hamburg unfolded in a coordinated market economy. Toronto, in contrast, is set in a liberal market economy, with correspondingly less tolerance for squatting as an infringement on property rights. There is no legal protection for squatting in Canada, and, despite a dire shortage of affordable housing, the province of Ontario lifted rent control in 1998. By 2010, the waiting lists for social housing in the city had 87,715 people, even as federal spending on social housing was cut from 43 percent to 29 percent between 1989 and 2009 (Sweetman, 2011). In the early 2010s, the Toronto Community Housing Corporation came under pressure to cut costs and sell public housing units.

A number of organizations tried to raise awareness of the housing crisis in the city. The Ontario Coalition against Poverty (OCAP), a prominent and long-standing organization, advised and supported public-housing residents. Among other strategies to increase the stock of affordable housing, OCAP also supported the occupation of vacant buildings. In this respect, squatters in Toronto were inspired by the success of their counterparts in New York City. In August 2002, after years of negotiations, New York protesters had succeeded in transferring 11 Manhattan vacant buildings to the Urban Homesteading Assistance Board, a nonprofit organization focused on self-managed rental housing that turned the buildings into limited-equity co-ops (meaning the units could never be sold for profit) with 167 apartments.

In the summer of 2002, OCAP occupied a vacant building at 1510 King West in the lower-income but central neighborhood of South Parkdale. Ninety-two percent of South Parkdale residents were renters (the city average was 37 percent), and the average annual income per resident in the area was $34,491 – well below the metropolitan average of $59,502. South Parkdale was home to important psychiatric institutions such as the Queen Street Center for Addiction and Mental Health and the erstwhile Lakeshore Psychiatric Hospital. After deinstitutionalization in the early 1980s, over 1,000 patients settled in the area (Porter & Shaw, 2013). Social agencies such as Houselink and First Step Home raised hopes in the late 1980s and early 1990s that ex-psychiatric patients might get housing, but funding was cut after the 2003 conservative victories in provincial elections. This vulnerable resident population was meaningfully supported by Parkdale's long history of activism, led by groups such as the Parkdale Tenants Association, and community-based service providers such as the Parkdale Activity-Recreation Centre. Stigmatization and unfavorable media reports kept property prices low but recently gentrification had crept in, with trendy bars, galleries, and boutiques. Tensions emerged between low-income tenants (and their advocates) and gentrifying forces (Gallant, 2014; Krishnan, 2015; Slater, 2004; Whitzman, 2010).

The squat of the twenty-four-unit, four-floor King West building began in late July 2002, during the visit of Pope John Paul II (hence, the name Pope Squat), and ended in November 2002. During the squat, residents cleaned and repaired the building, with labor and donations from residents and volunteers. Even mail was delivered to the thirty to fifty residents, all of whom were previously homeless (Landsberg, 2002).

OCAP selected the building from among thirty-five that it had identified as vacant, because both provincial and municipal government had grounds for ownership, which made eviction more complex. Indirectly, this also illustrates the key role of property rights in inhibiting squats in liberal market economies. The selection was intended as a call to turn publicly owned vacant buildings into affordable housing. The squat was supported by famous activists such as Tooker Gomberg, and politicians such as Jack Layton, a councillor from Ward 28, who a year later became leader of the New Democratic Party, and his wife, councillor Olivia Chow, from adjacent Ward 20 (Lehrer & Winkler, 2006). Such support, driven by the ideological alignment of these councillors with protesters' goals, might have helped – if the council was at large. However, the support of these councillors from other wards did not have a significant effect: With single-member district council elections, the critical support is that of the councillor for the actual ward. And it was his specific support that protesters lacked.

In its short life, the squat enjoyed the support of mass media, iconic figures such as Naomi Klein, academics, and native groups such as the Mohawks of the Bay of Quinte First Nation. The squat also received statements of support from unions close to OCAP, such as the Canadian Auto Workers union and the Elementary Teachers of Toronto. All called for the building to become tenant-managed housing. Squatters also tried to engage their new neighbors. They produced and distributed door-to-door 10,000 copies of a newspaper featuring articles on the housing crisis and calling for the legalization of squatting (Harding, 2003; Sweetman, 2011).

The squat used experiential tools. The squat itself was an experience that fostered mobilization, with a festive and hopeful atmosphere, and music. Squatters regularly held events; for example, they celebrated Labor Day on September 2 with a march and an evening event. Community barbeques celebrated anniversaries of the squat.

However, the local councillor for the Parkdale-High Park ward was a renowned conservative, Chris Korwin-Kuczynski, who did not support the squatters. He refused to meet with them and threatened to cancel the request for the unit to be turned into affordable housing unless the site was vacated immediately. On August 1, 2002, he initiated a council motion to turn the building into affordable housing, which included a request for immediate evacuation by the squatters and the property's transfer from the province to the city. The squatters considered the move disingenuous. The province was reluctant to recognize its ownership of the building, and protesters also argued that the move was unnecessary since the city had already declared its intention to seize the building in 2000. Squatters questioned what was meant by affordability, recognizing that it most likely would not be aimed to the population's poorest and most needy segments. They interpreted the motion as an evasive stalling tactic.[5] Instead, Pope squatters sought permanent housing in exchange for vacating the premises. They also wanted ownership to be determined before vacating, in order to avoid legal wrangling between the city and province for years, while the building sat empty and fell into greater disrepair.

[5] See the entry of August 27, 2002, "NEW: Pope Squat Update & Events" in the blog Squat! Net (https://en.squat.net/2002/08/27/new-pope-squat-update-events/) as well as the entry of August 1, 2002, "Pope Squat: City Council Moves for Control" (http://frightlibrary.org/citizen/squat.htm#5).

For a time, it was unclear whether the police could evict squatters on behalf of the city, given that the building seemed to be owned by the province. Toward the end of August, city inspectors began regularly visiting the squat, in what residents construed as politically motivated harassment. Undeterred, squatters planned and mobilized for council meetings after the summer break. On September 13, OCAP went before the Community Services Committee of the Toronto City Council to call for action in response to the Pope Squat initiative. Trade unions, faith groups, community organizations, social activists, and neighbors testified that day. All were encouraged to lobby their councillors.

On November 4, the eve of the first snowfall of the year, twenty-five squatters were suddenly evicted, and three arrested, when officials argued that the brick building constituted a fire hazard. The following morning, a few hundred protesters retook the building for a few hours, but massive police and media presence provoked a promise of negotiations with the city and persuaded the squatters to leave. OCAP conducted further protests, such as a march with over 500 people on November 8. However, the city did not respond. Instead, the property was boarded up and twenty-four-hour security was hired to prevent a new squat. The building was sold in September 2003 to a private developer. After remaining vacant for several years, Korwin-Kuczynski petitioned the province for the building to be converted into affordable housing. It was eventually turned into a rooming house, though not affordable housing.

The impact of the Pope Squat was indirect, and complex. On the one hand, it brought attention to the paradox of homelessness amid vacant public buildings. With initiatives such as Pope Squat, direct-action organizations such as OCAP raised awareness of the housing crisis and contributed to initiatives and policies intended to address homelessness, such as the Affordable Housing Program approved in 2004, and the municipal-level Streets to Homes program approved in February 2005 (Lehrer & Winkler, 2006). On the other hand, the squat was followed by a government initiative to create a master list of vacant and abandoned properties from various databases, not with the goal of turning them into affordable housing but rather to secure them against any future squats. The vacancy register was thus used to safeguard property in Toronto, as can be expected in such a political economic context.

The case of Pope Squat illustrates how we can observe squats in liberal market economies – even waves of squats, in exceptional periods. For example, following the 2008 housing crash, several groups in the United States, such as the Chicago Anti-Eviction Campaign, squatted vacant properties for evictees and foreclosure victims. However, these waves rarely result in sustained or institutionalized occupations like those observed in coordinated market economies.

PRIOR EXPERIENCE AND SQUAT ENDURANCE: MADRID

In Madrid, the case of Lavapiés resembles St. Pauli in that both fit the category of "resilient neighborhoods" – places particularly vulnerable to dispossession where stigmatizing traits are turned into proud elements of collective identity. Both are sites where cultural production was the driving force behind gentrification; and in both of these coordinated market economies anarchist groups – thanks to extensive prior experience in squatting – were able to successfully occupy, and also secure their tenure through negotiations with government. With a protest strategy that questioned the very notion of housing commodification, both squats took over iconic buildings, became beacons of cultural life in their respective cities, and based their legitimacy on the provision of cultural content to the public. However, the experiences diverged. Gängeviertel solidified its prominence in the city, while the squat in Lavapiés soon lost credibility as cultural producers without prior squatting experience upset its organization and daily management.

Lavapiés has an exceptional number of cultural institutions: Janoschka and Sequera point out that the past twenty-five years have witnessed the opening of over a dozen public museums, universities, film and arts centers, theaters, and more, followed by a multitude of private enterprises and countercultural initiatives that range from art galleries to performance spaces. The area is thus distinguished by "state-led tourism gentrification," and here more than anywhere else in Spain, "public policies have applied Richard Florida's creative paradigm" (Sequera & Janoschka, 2015, p. 378).

Lavapiés, originally a walled Jewish ghetto, is one of the oldest neighborhoods in Madrid. In 1492, the expulsion of the Jews reduced the population of Lavapiés, which remained a slum for centuries as it took in successive waves of immigrants from the countryside. In recent decades, it became the barrio of first destination for immigrants from North and Central Africa, Ecuador, Bangladesh, India, Pakistan, and China. The neighborhood became known for its bohemian atmosphere and diverse population, and turned into a destination because of its fringe theatres, dive bars, ethnic restaurants, and important cultural institutions. The vibrant commercial street life was augmented on Sundays, when

Lavapiés filled with visitors headed to the El Rastro, the largest flea market in Madrid.

No official data is collected for Lavapiés alone, but the area nearly overlaps with the administrative barrio of Embajadores-Lavapiés, which is one of six administrative barrios in the central district of Madrid, Distrito Centro. (There are twenty-one districts in the municipality of Madrid.) In 2010, Embajadores-Lavapiés had about 50,000 residents and the highest population density of the six barrios, with 443 habitants/hectare, against a district average of 257. It also had the highest concentration of foreigners: 33 percent of residents were foreign citizens against an average of 27 percent in the district (and 17 percent in the city). According to city statistics (and bearing in mind that a significant number of residents were undocumented), foreigners were split as follows: 24 percent were citizens of the European Union, 32 percent came from the Asia Pacific (at 19 percent, Bangladeshi were the largest single immigrant group in the neighborhood); 23 percent from Latin America and the Caribbean (with a significant presence from Ecuador); and 14 percent from Africa (above all Maghreb and Senegal). According to city statistics, in 2011, 32 percent of residents had a university degree, in comparison with 39 percent for the district and 29 percent for the city. The neighborhood was historically more leftist than both the district and the city overall. For example, in the 2011 elections, the conservative Partido Popular received only 35 percent of valid votes (against 40 percent in the district and 50 percent in the city); the socialist PSOE (Partido Socialista Obrero Español) received 27 percent of votes (against 24 percent in both the district and the city); and the further-on-the-left Izquierda Unida received 23 percent of votes (against 18 percent in the district and 11 percent in the city).

The neighborhood was known for its specific architectonic form, the *corrala*. *Corralas* are tenement buildings developed in the sixteenth century to accommodate waves of poor immigrants. They typically have three or four stories, with a common courtyard in the center and outside corridors along which are the entrances to dwellings of 20 to 40 square meters. They were contemptuously referred to as "vertical shantytowns" but more recently preserved *corralas* have attracted hipsters with their charm. However, the neighborhood had a large amount of substandard housing, and it was not uncommon for buildings to have shared restrooms.

Resistance against displacement became a political priority in Madrid and other sites in Spain, especially when renters and owners struggled to pay for housing during the bubble and after the 2009 crisis (Abellán, 2014). Purchase prices for apartments had increased dramatically during the bubble from 2001 to 2008 (according to the city's Índice Inmobiliario Annual, 80 percent in Lavapiés, 90 percent in the district, and 73 percent in the city overall), and in the midst of the crisis they remained highest in the city center. (Between 2008 and 2015, apartment prices fell 30 percent in the city, but only 18 percent in the district and 20 percent in Lavapiés.)

Despite this hardship before and after the bubble, Lavapiés had an extraordinary legacy of activism that had pushed back against redevelopment and displacement for decades. A useful starting point is 1997, when, embracing neoliberal redevelopment, the Madrid city council declared the neighborhood an area of preferred rehabilitation and launched the Revitalization Plan for Lavapiés (Plan de Rehabilitación de Lavapiés, PRL). The plan provided funds for the rehabilitation of buildings, but it strongly privileged the middle classes: Squatters and renters could not access financing because they lacked the necessary matching funds. With the PRL, 4,000 shanties were identified. Thousands were demolished and their slots sold to investors, letting in speculators. Residents received incentive payments in exchange for vacating units.[6] In cases of refusal, investors turned to mobbing, making buildings uninhabitable, or initiating official evictions. During the PRL four-year period, public work investment was undertaken to attract middle classes through new cultural institutions (for example, the Valle-Inclan Theater and the library for the open university UNED), the renovation of public spaces, and the creation of several underground parking facilities. Although chain restaurants and fast food were absent, the first twenty-four-hour supermarket opened in the heart of the neighborhood, to the disadvantage of local mom-and-pop stores.

Local activists were ready to resist the PRL. Since 1985, Lavapiés had been emerging as the center of squatting and anarchist organizing in Madrid, and the neighborhood had an extensive network of objectors, activists facing judiciary charges, undocumented migrants, Sandinistas, and communists of the far left. Before the PRL, their radical politics lacked a local territorial dimension. They were looking for a place to be, and Lavapiés was chaotic, conflictual, illegible to authorities, central, cheap, and off the investor's radar. The 1997 rehabilitation plan was

[6] In Madrid, there is no rent control. Contracts are usually five years, renewable automatically every year in between, and renegotiated every five years. Within a given contract, rents can only increase a small percentage each year.

perceived as a direct threat of displacement, and a yuppie invasion. Groups affected by the plan converged with migrant groups, feminist groups, and others facing displacement. The result was Red de Lavapiés, a network of collectives that linked social centers, squats, neighbors, affected artists, and immigrants with the more leftist components of the local middle class and the neighborhood association La Corrala (Asociación Vecinal La Corrala), which was under the influence of the PSOE (Díaz Orueta, 2007; Walliser, 2013).

The squatter community engaged the conservative city council and institutions to help poor residents gain exceptions or facilitations for building rehabilitation, subsidies, and protection from demolition. They also helped residents displaced by renovation obtain alternative public housing. Since residents with a mortgage could not be rehoused, activists lobbied the city to cancel small mortgages. Renters were harder to defend because they had no rights to rehousing. Academics and professionals were widely involved: Activists benefited from their expertise in filing claims, and the expertise of architects, historians, and urbanists to document the events. They held workshops and weekly meetings where neighbors could obtain information or petition protest actions in their support.

Two elements in this early resistance were critical to subsequent protest waves. First, there was little connection to parties or unions. Instead, Red de Lavapiés relied on experiential tools, such as tours (*paseos*), and an ironic competition – the 1998 "Dereliction Contest" for the worst ruin that was not included in the rehabilitation plan. The organization invited other social organizations from outside the barrio to promote its initiatives. Activists organized protest events in conjunction with social practice artists, things such as exhibitions, videos, and murals (Díaz Orueta, 2007). Conventional protest tools such as demonstrations, assemblies, and workshops were complemented by open-air parties, debates, art exhibitions, and guided tenement tours to sites of derelict buildings, empty dwellings, and appalling living conditions. An early and powerful form of experiential tools, these interventions provided visibility to the resistance because they were newsworthy and innovative. Moreover, activists relied on self-managed community centers for their own media outlets and distribution networks. It helped that most protesters, local and largely unemployed, were available to contribute to events.

The resistance also integrated into the protest immigrant networks. The main organizations in the struggle against the PRL were: the Association of Senegal Immigrants (Asociación de Inmigrante de Senegal, founded in 1991 and still strong); the Spanish Association of Moroccan Workers and Immigrants (Asociación de Trabajadores e Inmigrantes Marroquíes en España); and the Association of Moroccan Emigrants to Spain (Asociación de Emigrantes Marroquíes en España) (Merino Hernando, 2002). Migrant associations primarily wanted to secure papers for their members, but they shared with other protesters the need for housing, work, subsistence, and protection from police raids. Squatting for these groups also became a form of political incorporation and empowerment (Martínez López, 2017). Migrants slowed the plan-initiated displacement, although they paid a price. Many of the buildings where migrants lived were not absorbed into the rehabilitation process because owners earned more from slumlording than rehabilitating (interview with Mohammad Fazle Elahi, president of the Asociación Valiente Bangla, Madrid, July 18, 2016).

With its colorful actions and lively scene, Lavapiés gained a reputation as a barrio "guay" (cool), alternative, and interesting – characteristics that attracted even more activists. Living in Lavapiés in and of itself was experiential protest: "to live in Lavapiés does not mean anything for some people, but for others it means a lot, and that's why they come, because you live next to Blacks facing raids, although material living conditions can be poor" (interview with Carlos Vidania, anarchist organizer, Madrid, July 15, 2016; see also Díaz Orueta, 2007; Gómez, 2006).

A final and critical element of legacy of resistance in Lavapiés was its social squats, or Centros Sociales Okupados Autogestionados (CSOAs). The history of CSOAs is long and complex, and beyond the scope of this book (see Martínez López, 2014; Romanos, 2014). CSOAs were deeply embedded in civic, artistic, academic, and anarchist networks. They were also anchored in their neighborhoods, where they often emerged as key political and social actors because they offered a variety of services to neighbors and acted as the organizational node for protest actions in Madrid, including protests against military service, anti-war campaigns, "hacklabs" (working groups around free software and technologies), anti-summit movements, as well as anti-discrimination and anti-gentrification movements. CSOA networks played a fundamental role in protests that turned mainstream, such as the Indignados in 2011, and the assembly movement that it generated (Flesher Fominaya, 2015).

Although several CSOAs opened in the center of the city over the years, the point of reference for the squatter movement (also referred to as Okupa) from 1998 to 2003 was the CSOA Laboratorio. Early on, Laboratorio embraced experiential tools. In 1998, Laboratorio started the

Social Conflict Week/Let's Break the Silence (Semana de Lucha Social/ Rompamos el Silencio), an influential week that combined protest, workshops, and concerts. Most of the organizers interviewed for this book started their activism in a CSOA in Lavapiés or in nearby Malasaña, and participated in these events. There they learned the power of experiential tools. Even in this early use, experiential tools did not mobilize participants on the basis of political targets; in fact, the success of Laboratorio was based on "the massive attendance of people at its events" whereby "most of these users did not care about the internal political issues of the social center such as the process of negotiation with the City and the eviction threats" (Martínez López, 2014, p. 17).

When Laboratorio was evicted in 2003, its role was largely taken over by Solar. Solar was a squat on an empty lot, and squatters experimented until their 2010 eviction with the idea of a squat that lacked a building. It continued to attract participants with experiential tools, hosting many broadly appealing neighborhood activities, from theater to book presentations, discussion days, project finance activities, music, urban agriculture, workshops to create materials for protests and other social and political events. For six years it hosted the Film Festival Lavapiés. It became a fundamental public space to criticize urban aspects of neoliberalism. In addition, Lavapiés hosted other CSOAs; communities of neighbors resisting speculation; associations of parents, consumer groups, sports, artistic and cultural associations; as well as several initiatives against government attempts to install CCTV, and against raids that targeted migrants and street vendors.

The extensive history of prior occupations and anarchic circles summarized thus far, together with experiential tools and partisan dealignment, cumulatively explain the success of the Tabacalera squat. When squatters were evicted from the CSOA Laboratorio in 2003, they were left without a physical home. Within months, members of the Laboratory in Exile (Laboratorio en Exilio) proposed to the conservative municipal administration led by Alberto Ruiz-Gallardón (2003–2011) a new use for Tabacalera, an abandoned eighteenth-century tobacco factory in the heart of Lavapiés. The last of large industrial facilities in the center of the city, the tobacco factory closed in 2000, leaving vacant a building that covered an entire city block with over 32,000 square meters.

Activists did not at first claim Tabacalera as a new home for Laboratorio. While squatters from Laboratorio were looking for a new large space, some thought Tabacalera was too large and hard to manage because of its many entrances. Instead, they proposed to open Tabacalera to a public participatory process, to decide the final destination of the building. They argued that the debate itself was a way to consolidate the social fabric in Lavapiés because it encouraged active citizenship against the usual separation between, on the one hand, professional politics and "technical" activity, and, on the other hand, everyday life practices and urban transformations. But the municipal authorities did not respond to the activists.

This was unsurprising. During the conservative Aznar government (1996–2004), the ministry of culture had proposed two new museums in Tabacalera, one of decorative arts and one of fine-art reproductions, thereby adding to the extensive museumification of the city center. The conservative municipal government strongly supported the plan and drew up the Special Plan of Urban Center Revitalization (PERCU; Plan Estratégico de Revitalización del Centro Urbano) of 2004. The surprise victory of the socialists in the March 2004 parliamentary elections and the change of government to José Zapatero (2004–2011) did not initially seem to signal any change of course.

However, activists took advantage of the change in government to increase their lobbying at the national level. They argued that the neighborhood did not need more museums, as called for by the PERCU – instead, Lavapiés needed public infrastructure such as social centers, spaces for seniors, a health center, or a retirement community. In 2004, fourteen local organizations launched a participatory process with activities, workshops, and the website "La Tabacalera a Debate" (Tabacalera under Debate). To attract participants, activists deployed a resonant and media-worthy set of experiential tools, which included dressing up as *cigarreras* – the traditional female employees rolling cigarettes in Tabacalera, known for their feisty organizing and determination. With big red flowers in the hair, and tight dresses, organizers led weekly events and marches around Lavapiés.

The stunt attracted attention, and the ministry contacted Jordi Claramonte, a philosophy professor involved in the squatters movement and political art groups such as Fiambrera Obrera (founded during the resistance against the 1997 revitalization plan for Lavapiés). Early hopes faded, however, in 2007, when the National Center for Visual Arts was approved for development, and a design competition was awarded in 2008 to the architects Nieto and Sobejano, with a €30 million project. Yet the sudden economic crisis and a reshuffling of the Zapatero government offered a new path for the building. Like in Gängeviertel, squatter groups emphasized the cultural and artistic nature of their projects for

Tabacalera, capitalizing on the government's much heralded culture-led growth strategy (Walliser, 2013). It was an effective strategy: "this creative image and the interest of the central government ... in opening up a wedge in a very conservative political area (both the city and the regional governments were controlled by the conservatives), helped the Tabacalera to start on a legal basis from the beginning" (Martínez López, 2014, p. 20).

Tabacalera had reopened for Photo España, an annual multi-site exhibition, in the summers of 2008 and 2009. After the government reshuffling, Ángeles Albert was appointed as new general director of fine arts. A geographer and historian coming from the Spanish Agency for International Cooperation, Albert was not an expert in art but was sensitive to social organizing. She called Claramonte to organize a photographic exhibition for the upcoming 2010 Photo España that involved the Red de Lavapiés network and the related art collective Fiambrera Obrera. These "creactivists" took the opening to instead launch "art as direct action." Claremonte again proposed a participatory process to decide the future use for the building, and when the ministry did not follow up Tabacalera was squatted.

The ministry did not threaten eviction, and subsequent negotiations granted squatters the lease of 5,000 square meters for a social center for one year, followed by a renewable two-year contract (interview with Carlos Vidania, July 15, 2016).[7] Like Gängeviertel, Tabacalera was thus a squat with permission, and thousands of artists, some with backgrounds in squatting or activism, but many with no political background at all, joined to shape what was widely viewed as a new form of social organization. The building became an experiment in what Spanish intellectuals called new institutionality: a more democratic and open civic and political participation and governance that would be an alternative to traditional party politics. The leadership of some of Spain's leading museums, as well as the parts of the ministry of culture, strongly supported the artists' role in articulating and shaping the new institutionality. Tabacalera became a point of reference for political organization in the city partly through its interaction with these cultural and political institutions around the country. It supplied material and human resources to the encampments of Puerta del Sol in spring 2011 and played a key role in the seismic shift that led to the 2015 elections of progressive civic platforms around Spain.

[7] See also the YouTube interview with Jordi Claramonte "Jordí Claramonte habla de la Tabacalera.mp4" available at www.youtube.com/watch?v=c7ifANioHjk.

However, the political impact of Tabacalera was fleeting, due to two related factors: lack of integration in the surrounding market context and organizational weakness. As in Hamburg, market logic determined whether the Tabacalera squatters would be able to stay. They had to demonstrate repeatedly the "social profitability" of the enterprise, as measured through the activities offered for the neighborhood and the city.

The first contract specifically highlighted "the social profitability of the building." In it, the association SCCPP (an acronym with multiple meanings that activists officially translated as Sociedad para la Cooperación y Convivencia de Pueblos y Personas [Society for the Cooperation and Coexistence of Peoples and People]), which was the legal representative for the Centro Sociale Auto-Gestionado (self-organized social center) La Tabacalera de Lavapiés, was primarily tasked with "the organization and diffusion of cultural and artistic events dealing with social problems." The contract further elaborated that "to achieve these aims, the association SCCPP organizes exhibitions, conferences, workshops, performances, and other activities that might achieve those objectives of social awareness" (cited in Durán & Moore, 2015, p. 63).

While Gängeviertel succeeded in becoming permanent through continuously offering social and political activities and events, Tabacalera struggled. Tabacalera's physical size and structure, and the much higher number of artists involved, made management that much harder. Further, Gängeviertel enjoyed the stability in planning of a long-term control over the space, while contracts in Tabacalera were short term.

As in Gängeviertel, decision-making was horizontal and based on regular plenaries. Management was organized around committees and solidarity work, in which participants took turns maintaining the space. Yet, after the first two years, Tabacalera became consumed by internal conflict. In the words of a participant,

> While the experience of Laboratorio served as a model for many, Tabacalera was not a political project with a cohesive, struggle-tested collective of committed activists running things. Fault lines appeared continuously in the process of decision-making by assembly, and in the participatory democratic structures we designed for this kind of volunteer development of cultural resources.
>
> (Durán & Moore, 2015, p. 66)

Conflict grew especially tense between immigrant groups within Tabacalera and the rest of the squatters. The free internal internet access was shut down after it was used to search jihadist sites, and the popular and profitable café was also closed. Immigrant groups' activities were suspended. Many activists abandoned the project. A common critique was that Tabacalera lacked the political and organizational commitment and discipline that was critical to the success of a squat. There were too few people with previous experience in managing a squat relative to the size of the population and the building. Chaos, rather than programming, was celebrated. The space fragmented and was privatized by each subgroup of artists, and the project collapsed as a social center: "there was prostitution, there was drug sale, and there were fights. Lots of different people tried to manage the space that were not involved with the movement and had no political conscience" (interview with Carlos Vidania, July 15, 2016). Marred by conflicts and lack of security, the center progressively cut back on activities, and at the time of fieldwork in 2016 it opened only on weekend evenings (then closing indefinitely in 2019 to "reorganize"). What was supposed to turn into the cultural and political engine for the city instead became insignificant, "and insignificance is the worst outcome" (interview with Carlos Vidania, July 15, 2016).[8]

* * *

In the squats reviewed in this chapter, experiential tools combined with prior protest to facilitate broad mobilization citywide in support of large squats perceived to be serving cultural and social purposes. In Yongsan, reliance on prior protest experience proved a fatal choice for squatters, who also faced remarkable isolation. Both factors combined to push them to a militant protest strategy that had a tragic ending. In Pope Squat, prior protest and the deployment of experiential tools allowed for significant mobilization, yet ultimately protesters were unable to sustain the squat or achieve their relocation goals because of an adverse political context. Despite a dealignment with a right-wing mayor and a leftist provincial government, protesters lacked the support of their councillor and were

[8] Tabacalera can be compared with La Quimera de Lavapiés, a popular squat and social center, which continued instead the Laboratorio tradition of a squat that is primarily a political site rather than an artist venue. La Quimera grew as a political and social actor and became relevant in the neighborhood. It offered workshops on activities as diverse as sign language and screen-printing courses, as well as free stores, free libraries and potlucks. It hosted theater productions, film screenings, and concerts as well as political forums. Several other squats existed in Madrid at the time of writing and are not being discussed for reasons of space, but parallels could be drawn for example between La Quimera and the enduring Patio Maravillas in nearby Malasaña. (For excellent reviews of these new urban activists see, Martínez López, 2014; Walliser, 2013).

therefore bereft of the necessary local ally. Further, they were resisting in a liberal market economy, which is especially intolerant of the challenge to private property entailed by squatting.

In Hamburg, Gängeviertel and associated protests countered institutional branding within the very same discursive logic of culture-led development. In places where redevelopment was deeply enmeshed with culture-led growth, cultural producers did not question the governments' turn to cultural industries per se but rather the ways in which governments understood and implemented such strategies. Their approach to protest, subverting from within the government's mantra of cultural-led growth, elicited spectacular public support and mobilization, and protesters achieved their goals.

Tabacalera in Madrid was also built on a legacy of prior resistance against displacement as well as dense and broad networks. It heavily relied on experiential tools and a high level of mobilization. Thanks to some support in city council, but above all to the leftward shift at the national government, activists were successful in securing authorization for their squat with remarkable institutional support, especially among cultural elites. However, Tabacalera displayed low endurance because its version of artistic production undermined discipline and political organizing.

The comparison with Gängeviertel is telling: Artists led both squats and depended on experiential tools, prior protest, and networks. However, after the first mobilization phase, Gängeviertel embraced institutionalization as the ownership was settled in the form of a cooperative. Its marketization was sophisticated and included a busy calendar of events, but also merchandise sales and donation platforms. Tabacalera tried to position itself outside of the market: It did not set up a donation system or develop merchandise for sale, and residents did not pay any rent. Yet both social centers were institutionally embedded in a logic of exchange, in which their right to existence depended on their effectiveness as producers of social services in their respective communities. While the provision of services to neighbors was embraced by Gängeviertel, Tabacalera turned into an attraction for outsiders and tourists and lost relevance and legitimacy in the neighborhood.

Together, these cases show the fundamental role of prior experience and experiential tools in squatting. Beyond the experiential tactics described in the chapter, squatting itself exemplifies protest that is based on the performance of identity with enduring norms and expectations.

The cases also unveil the paradox of groups that seek alternative lifestyle and the decommodification of housing yet are trapped in market logics. In liberal market economies, that market logic (expressed with the absolute primacy of private property) actually prevents the institutionalization of squats. But even in the more favorable context of coordinated market economies, these initiatives cannot escape commodification and require careful management because experiential mobilization depends on the support of participants who are largely driven by hedonistic and consumerist goals. Moreover, institutionalization limits repression but also depoliticizes squats: it makes participants vulnerable to co-optation through state resources and constraints and thereby undermines the commitment to radical politics. Instantiated as spaces for the "ungovernables" (Scott, 2010), squats are sustained but also domesticated by both experiential mobilization and institutionalization.

7

Judicial Resistance, Experiential Tools, and Protest Legacies

Even when the strategy moves from squatting to judicial action, experiential tools remain important. This might seem counterintuitive because judicial struggles require above all expertise and benefit tremendously from a legacy in kindred prior protest to understand and manipulate the legal framework. But to exert pressure and persuasion on institutions such as a municipal bureaucracy or city-council allies, organizers need to demonstrate a significant and cohesive mobilization. And they need to create spaces and opportunities to inform and forge networks among residents and even to showcase their visions of problems and alternative solutions. Experiential tools, as discussed in this chapter, are important to both of these goals and vital parts of the political dimension of judicial action. By judicial strategy, I mean direct or threatened judicial action, and complex legal negotiations with authorities. As these cases from Madrid and Los Angeles show, these strategies cannot be undertaken without a great degree of expertise, but the political and economic context influence the legal strategy and the type of government involvement.

LEGAL STRATEGIES IN A COORDINATED MARKET ECONOMY: MADRID

This chapter begins by returning to Lavapiés to examine the role of judicial resistance in this neighborhood. The analysis focuses on the largely collaborative relation of two closely connected organizations: the neighborhood assembly, Asamblea Lavapiés, and a local chapter of People Affected by Mortgages (Plataforma de Afectados por la Hipoteca, PAH). PAH was founded in 2009 as a self-help organization to prevent evictions of those unable to pay their mortgages and debts associated with evictions. It became an influential actor that was even able to win several mayoralties, including Madrid and Barcelona in the 2015 elections. Yet the Lavapiés chapter of PAH experienced only limited success due to partisan alignment with both national government and the municipality supporting neoliberal policies for the period of my observation.

PAH did promote street protest and public house squatting, and after the 2008 crisis, especially in cases of bank-owned properties, this strategy enjoyed public and media support that facilitated negotiations with authorities and increased tolerance toward squatting for housing purposes (Martínez López, 2016). However, PAH's main strategy was *legal* negotiation and extensive lobbying. Overall, PAH was distinguished by its high level of organization, its horizontal and vertical scaling (with over 200 chapters throughout Spain), and its broad networks that brought together migrant associations, neighborhood groups, squatters, and professionals. PAH predated the 2011 Indignados uprising, but the two converged, and PAH was widely considered the most prominent and effective organization within that movement.

In the spring of 2011, activists from the main squats in the city center, including Tabacalera, coordinated the Indignados encampment (*acampada*) in nearby Plaza del Sol. Before the *acampada* was removed during the summer of 2011, residents had started meeting in neighborhood assemblies (*asambleas*), first outside and then, as autumn approached, in spaces offered by nearby CSOAs.

There were 120 barrio assemblies in Madrid, one in practically every barrio. The assemblies coordinated through a single webpage (Madrid. tomalosbarrios), which reflected the idea that the *acampadas* were scaling up and aimed to take national political control, starting at the unit of the barrio. They each subdivided according to themes developed during the *acampada*, such as migration, housing, and employment. Red de Lavapiés was an important model and precedent because it had coordinated similar thematic working groups.

The *acampada* facilitated mobilization because neighbors met in Plaza del Sol and then saw each other again back in the barrio (interview with PAH organizer Mai Gredilla, Madrid, July 5, 2016). The first weekly meetings of Asamblea Lavapiés had nearly 1,000 participants. Within Asamblea Lavapiés, the thematic assemblies were open and fluid but relied on organizers. Nearly all activists interviewed from Asamblea Lavapiés and PAH Centro had been connected to the squatters' movement for several years before 2011. Therefore, what appeared spontaneous was actually the result of mobilization techniques by "people who had been activists all their lives" (interview with Asamblea and PAH organizer Gonzalo Maestro, Madrid, July 6, 2016).

In 2014, the housing committee of the Asamblea Lavapiés turned into a chapter of PAH's national network, with the name PAH Centro. As an activist explained, "When we went to the banks with our green PAH shirts and we told the director we were the PAH, we were more legitimate. PAH was stronger, PAH was on TV. All bankers knew it" (interview with Mai Gredilla, July 5, 2016). The shift from a housing committee of the barrio assembly to a PAH chapter implied a broader scope: Although it focused on Lavapiés, PAH Centro covered four barrios in the district Centro: Lavapiés, Malasaña, Austrias, and Letras. Gentripiés was a group explicitly focused on gentrification issues, which remained within the Asamblea Lavapiés but collaborated with PAH Centro on several campaigns.

In Spain, when residents default on their mortgage payment they lose the asset (the dwelling) but also still owe significant debt because the property is valued at the time of repossession: If the property has suffered from depreciation due to market conditions, as happened in the foreclosures of over 500,000 properties and the eviction of at least 250,000 families immediately following the 2008 crisis, the evictee owes the difference between the original purchase price and the value at time of repossession (García-Lamarca & Kaika, 2016). With protest at eviction sites, occupations, and legal challenges, PAH was able to turn this private tragedy into everybody's business. Through social pressure, PAH often successfully negotiated with banks on behalf of evictees to annul the mortgage debt upon relinquishment of the dwelling. (This operation was a key goal and was referred to *dación en pago*, which translates as "transfer in payment of debts.") PAH also negotiated with banks to allow residents to remain in the dwellings, paying social rents capped at 30 percent of stated income instead of a mortgage (including no rent for residents without income).

PAH Centro mobilized through social and institutional networks, including a continued reliance on CSOAs. They kept residents informed through traditional approaches, such as leafleting in core sites – the market, the health clinic, main streets, and so on. In addition, migrant networks played a key role. Migrants (especially undocumented sub-Saharan Africans and Bangladeshi at the time of research) depended on their barrio networks for work and support more than other groups, and historically had collaborated with squatters (Martínez López, 2017).

Migrapiés, as the assembly's migration committee was also known, integrated a variety of migrant groups.[1] The Asociación Valiente Bangla, which served the Bangladeshi population and worked closely with PAH Centro, connected it with people at risk of eviction and was arguably the most politically active immigrant association in Lavapiés. Founded in 2007, by 2015 the association had sixty active members and a dense support network. It focused on immigration, employment, and housing, but also provided translation in cases of conflict with the police, and helped fight domestic violence.

Residents with displacement grievances accessed PAH support through weekly meetings in Lavapiés that included an open group for mutual advice and the coordination of awareness-raising events. The meetings also organized actions against threatened evictions. For example, a 2016 PAH meeting that I attended exhibited the process specifically developed to integrate new members facing evictions as well as brainstorming for a protest. In these *stopdesahucio* ("stop-the-eviction") actions, supporters physically prevented police access to the property. On occasion, PAH also organized squatting in vacant buildings owned by banks as a solution for evictees lacking shelter, targeting banks that held mortgaged dwellings facing evictions.

Since leadership was largely found among CSOA activists, the artists' main role was to perform at fund-raising events. This was an important role because, without dues, PAH Centro organized fiestas whenever members faced fines (e.g., for performing a bank sit-in, or a protest without permit, or a squat on behalf of an evictee). Unions played a more prominent role than observed in cases thus far. While the Indignados were initially declared nonpartisan and not linked to unions, within a few months minority unions connected with Asamblea Lavapiés, and especially with its working group focused on employment. PAH Centro maintained informal relationships with the unions Confederación General del Trabajo, Confederación Nacional del Trabajo, and Solidaridad Obrera, participating in union rallies and hosting meetings. However, the

[1] Some examples are the Asamblea Sin Papeles de Madrid, formed in Lavapiés but active citywide, which organized undocumented migrants; the network Red Interlavapiés, which came from the historical Red de Lavapiés and was formed by nuns, neighbors, and migrants; the Brigadas Vecinales, a neighborhood group that documented and informed on discrimination and xenophobia by police and others; the Cooperativa Mbolo Moy Dole, which supported undocumented migrant entrepreneurs; and the Traficante de Sueños, a bookstore that served as cultural hub for progressives in Lavapiés but also doubled as work cooperative.

collaboration was based on social affinity among activists rather than official linkages.[2]

The relationship was weaker with leftist parties, including with Izquierda Unida: Both the assembly and PAH Centro upheld a staunch nonpartisan position, and PAH's statute explicitly stated that PAH representatives could not represent a political party. Around 2013, tensions escalated when part of the membership considered a transition from movement to electoral competition to achieve a more systemic impact. While a few activists continued to participate in both the resulting electoral effort of Podemos and in the assembly, most participants aligned with one camp or the other, and many who remained in the assembly were radically anti-party – including anti-Podemos. Instead of formal relationships with parties, in 2015, PAH developed a five-point program with these demands:

1. relinquishing the house retroactively eliminates the mortgage debt;
2. affordable rents;
3. end of evictions;
4. public housing;
5. guaranteed utility delivery.

Only the Izquierda Unida and Podemos parties agreed to include these points in their platforms. The tense relation with the socialist party PSOE is especially interesting. My analysis of campaign calendars for both organizations reveals that even during electoral campaigns, the PSOE in Lavapiés did not visit or refer to the assembly or PAH Centro. The party's main connection in the neighborhood was the Asociación Vecinal La Corrala, an association formed with state support soon after the fall of Franco. Despite their official non-partisanship, such associations developed strong vertical affiliation with either PSOE or Izquierda Unida. The Asociación Vecinal La Corrala affiliated with PSOE and did not develop a close collaboration with far-left and anarchist groups. Before the Zapatero government (2004–2011), conflicts between PSOE and groups further to the left were contained by the awareness of a common enemy in the conservative Partido Popular. Once the socialists won national elections, however, the collaboration was undermined because La Corrala did not support anti-government actions. Moreover, La

[2] On the other hand, PAH members displayed a clear hostility toward the unions Comisiones Obreras and Unión General de Trabajadores, which were considered members of the establishment and supporters of labor reforms that PAH Centro opposed.

Corrala focused on middle-class issues, such as noise, pest infestations, and garbage collection, and usually opposed squatters.

Experiential events – especially two annual neighborhood events, the Fiesta de la Ballesta and the Fiesta de Cayetano – were the main point of contact between far-left activists, and the Asociación Vecinal La Corrala. La Corrala was the lead organizer. PAH Centro and Asamblea Lavapiés did not want to alienate it because food stands at the festivals earned much more than at PAH-organized events, which only militant members attended. However, neighborhood groups (including Asamblea Lavapiés and PAH Centro) *also* organized "counter-festivals" through the alternative collective Plataforma de Fiestas de Lavapiés. Overall, the result was a high degree of mobilization in the neighborhood.

PAH Centro and Asamblea Lavapiés had a complicated impact. On the one hand, a significant number of evictees were assisted by PAH, and the 2015 election of Podemos allies to the mayoralty in Madrid and elsewhere was a remarkable outcome. On the other hand, while PAH was able to gain the mayoralty and introduce radical reforms in its founding city, Barcelona, in the historically conservative Madrid, the organization only entered municipal government as one partner in a centrist coalition. The shift to electoral politics split the group into reformists and radicals and demobilized its previous following. Once in government, PAH in Madrid no longer pursued debt forgiveness and social rents but rather facilitated full mortgage repayment by lengthening the terms of contract, an outcome far more auspicious for banks than evictees. The new municipal procedures delegitimized previous direct actions strategies, which had included challenging evictions in court but also occupying on behalf of evictees vacant buildings owned by the mortgage-holding banks responsible for their foreclosures. No surprise then that, overall, many PAH activists in Madrid regarded the change in political landscape as counterproductive. Further, from 2012 to 2015, several campaigns failed. PAH Centro and the assembly collaborated in three campaigns against displacement and gentrification. Despite a high mobilization in these cases, resistance in Lavapiés faced setbacks during periods of partisan alignment between municipal and national governments.

The first case is the 2012 Lavapiés Security Plan (Plan de Seguridad de Lavapiés), which built on the 1997 designation of Lavapiés as an area of preferred rehabilitation (see Chapter 6). "Harsh policing is the first sign that gentrification is under way" is a slogan I heard in many cities. Here too, the plan to improve security was interpreted as a way to stigmatize the neighborhood in preparation for subsequent redevelopment with residential and commercial upgrading through decreasing preexisting wholesale trade and increasing franchises and entertainment establishments.

Stigmatization of the barrio had accelerated during the 2000s. The government tolerated drug-dealing in broad daylight because awareness of criminality in the area would validate government intervention in redevelopment. To counter this portrayal of Lavapiés as dangerous, social centers and art collectives such as Yomango, Lavapiés Barrio Feliz, and Fiambrera Obrera digitally hacked security cameras throughout the neighborhood, showing how the collaboration between activists and social-practice artists started with Red de Lavapiés continued in current protest against displacement.

Yet the Plan de Seguridad was the most important intervention to portray the barrio as dangerous. The plan called for heightened militarization and the deployment of municipal riot police. In the plan, Lavapiés was called a "priority security zone" in relation to specific types of crime, by which it meant members of the squatter movement. The plan used discriminatory and racist language; for example, relating drug-trafficking only to Black citizens (Bonfigli, 2015). Even beyond drug-dealing, the discourse strongly portrayed immigrants as a threat:

> The plan linked the plagues of bedbugs, rats, lack of sanitation, dirt-bringing migrants, and squatters. There was a banner in the square of Lavapiés put by a neighbor that said: "Squatters, drugs, bedbugs." In other words, he believed in that story. They interviewed that guy ad nauseam. He was on TV all the time.
> (interview with Gonzalo Maestro, July 6, 2016)

However, many residents were against the plan, and occasionally threw pots at the police from balconies and protested in front of police stations. The Federation of Neighborhood Associations and its Lavapiés chapter, the Asociación Vecinal, initially signed the plan. Yet the language was so inappropriate and discriminatory that they withdrew support after they saw the protests. Despite opposition, the plan passed in 2012, and in 2012 and 2013 Lavapiés was militarized. (As a further sign of the effect of partisan change, the center–left municipal government elected in 2015 interrupted the plan and instead introduced community policing to Lavapiés.)

A second illustration of failed resistance is the deployment of local heritage to fight displacement, an approach successful in Gängeviertel and Yungay but not in Lavapiés. The typical architectural form of the *corrala* was inhabited mostly by indigent renters and therefore neglected: By 2004, Distrito Centro had 152 buildings officially declared ruins (Aller, 2004). In 2004, the city introduced a major plan to restore the city center, the Revitalization of Madrid's Urban Center (Revitalización del Centro Urbano de Madrid). However, it envisioned only renovation by owners or expropriation by the municipality. This left the *corralas* of Lavapiés as prime targets for expropriation and displacement; only El Corralon, a two-story *corrala* that was inhabited from 1860 to the 1990s, was restored by the state, which then ironically turned the building into a museum and center for "creativity and innovation" (Fidel, 2013).

To attract attention to the problem of displacement in Lavapiés, assembly activists organized a campaign largely based on experiential tools, which they called Corralas Despiertas (Awoken Corralas). It was a symbolic initiative because not all buildings involved were *corralas*. Gentripiés and PAH Centro collaborated with academics to prepare maps and several walking tours to inform, alert, and mobilize residents and the public about sites of conflict. They also organized themed festivals. *Corralas* have courtyards, which traditionally were open to the public during fiestas so that neighbors strolled from one *corrala* to the next while residents offered lemonade and hosted music and dances. PAH Centro and Gentripiés organized a reenactment of this ritual in 2014 and 2015 in Corrala Kambalache. However, the campaign did not lead to significant results, and expropriation continued. Because these were often blighted buildings, due to the especially punitive legislation in Spain, owners, deprived of their housing, continued to face mortgage payments and also had to cover demolition costs.

Solarpiés, a third case of failed resistance, is a lot adjacent Plaza Lavapiés on Calle Valencia, occupied by a dilapidated two-story building with residential and commercial renters. The owner transferred the building to the regional government (Comunidad Madrid), which planned to raze it and build social housing. In exchange, Comunidad Madrid promised the owner the entire ground floor of the future building. The historically conservative regional government declared the building a ruin in 2009 and proceeded with evictions, but after demolition, lacking funds, it built nothing. In 2012, the lot was squatted by neighbors who belonged to the assembly of Lavapiés. They used the space, called Solarpiés, for alternative barrio festivals, such as the "contrafiesta," to critique the Asociación Vecinal La Corrala's centralized and exclusionary programming. Solarpiés was ideally located because it sat right on the square where the official festival took place.

After the festival, squatters stayed on for other activities and continued the occupation with film festivals, book fairs, workshops, theater productions, activities for children, and a community garden. So Solarpiés took on many of the functions the same group had exercised in the squat Solar on Calle Olivar before their eviction in 2010. In the meantime, however, the original owner, tired of waiting for his promised ground floor, sold his property rights to a second investor. In 2013, courts ruled the Comunidad Madrid should complete social-housing construction within a year or return the lot to the private sector. Authorities moved quickly, threatening activists with €10,000 in fines for the occupation. Despite their eviction, in 2014, the building returned to private hands, due to the Comunidad's inactivity. In 2015, the new owner received investment from an international hotel chain to build a low-cost hotel, which activists from Gentripiés, the assembly, and PAH Centro interpreted as a major sign of accelerating gentrification. In the summer of 2015, the assembly started the campaign StopHotel, with leafleting and online mobilization.

Further attempts at resquatting failed, and, by 2016, the StopHotel campaign had dwindled and the building permit for the hotel was issued. As a result, following years of peak activism, many participants were discouraged by these failures, and the assembly fell into abeyance (Sawyers & Meyer, 1999; Taylor, 1989), sustained only by a small and dedicated group conscious of the cyclical nature of social movements and awaiting future waves of mobilization and better political conditions.

Although partisan alignments ultimately undermined protest impact, the case of PAH Centro and the Asamblea Lavapiés illustrates a period of broad mobilization, facilitated by the presence of all-enabling factors: experiential tools, protest legacy, dense networks, and even union support. The analysis provides further evidence for the positive interaction of experiential tools and legacy in prior protest wherever resistance centers in legal strategies, such as the debt renegotiations with banks and municipalities that PAH undertook.

LEGAL STRATEGIES IN A LIBERAL MARKET ECONOMY: LOS ANGELES

The last two cases are set in Los Angeles and typify the liberal market economy approach to protest, which is especially likely to rely on judicial avenues and litigation to deal with conflicts against private actors rather than the regulatory and intermediary role of governments. Among other key elements, these campaigns illustrate how the mere presence of a mayor affiliated with a leftist party by no means guarantees a progressive regime and often in fact contributes to development regimes with strong pro-growth coalitions.

Recent scholarship on the resistance against redevelopment in Los Angeles has focused on community benefit agreements (CBAs), which are private contracts between developers and community coalitions with the goal of moving a project through an administrative approvals process in exchange for negotiated benefits, such as living wages, local hiring and training programs, affordable housing, environmental remediation, and funds for community programs (Gross, 2007; Parks & Warren, 2009; Salkin & Lavine, 2008; Wolf-Powers, 2010). In contrast to these agreements, the cases below rely on protest, litigation, market transactions, and lobbying of government institutions.

Among *federal* statutes, judicial and legal avenues of protest most often invoke the Housing and Urban Development (HUD) statute known as HUD Section 3, which requires local developers or authorities that receive HUD funds to fulfill employment and affordability obligations; or, second, civil-rights and environmental-justice laws, and especially Title VI of the 1964 Civil Rights Act and the 1994 Executive Order on Environmental Justice, which oblige governments to consider the interests of low-income individuals and people of color.

The key *state* statutes are the 1982 Mello Act, which regulates coastal development, requires full replacement of affordable units, and mandates a share of affordable units in new construction; the 1970 California Environmental Quality Act, which requires local agencies to adopt all feasible measures to mitigate environmental impacts (typically, affordable housing is required as a traffic mitigation measure because it allows poor individuals to live where they work); and, third, the 1969 California Housing Element Law, which requires that all local governments adequately plan to meet the housing needs of "all economic segments of the community."[3]

At the *local* level, in addition to CBAs, local groups can invoke city ordinances that govern land-use approvals. However, local ordinances are more often designed to benefit developers, who can also obtain waivers from requirements through city council (for an excellent overview of legal strategies in Los Angeles struggles against displacement, see Beach, 2007).

* * *

[3] Until recently, local groups could also invoke the California Redevelopment Law. However, its use was hindered by the lack of accurate counts of affordable units in project areas. Moreover, in 2011, community redevelopment agencies were dissolved, hindering subsequent use of this tool.

TRUST South LA is an organization founded in 2005 by Strategic Actions for a Just Economy (SAJE), Esperanza Community Housing Corporation, and Abode Communities. SAJE is a leading research and advocacy organization, which protects vulnerable sectors from displacement throughout Los Angeles (for example, by initiating CBAs). Esperanza and Abode focus on the provision of affordable housing and services (their facilities include childcare centers, community centers, and computer labs).

TRUST is an acronym for Tenemos Que Reclamar Y Unidos Salvar La Tierra (We Need to Protest and Together Save the Land). Its goal was to stabilize neighborhoods in downtown Los Angeles, where residents faced significant displacement pressures and disinvestment, by developing a land trust under the control of the affected population. Lower-income residents were affected both by rent burden and the erosion of designated affordable housing. According to the rent burden standard, which defines affordable housing as housing with rent or mortgage that costs less than 30 percent of a household's income, 90 percent of all low-income renters in Los Angeles are rent-burdened. Forty percent of working households are extremely rent-burdened, meaning that they spend over 50 percent on housing. The problem is not limited to renters, as three-quarters of low-income homeowners are burdened as well (California Budget Project, 2008; Wardrip, 2012).

TRUST's founders saw the cultivation of a sense of collective and grassroots ownership as essential in political mobilization. The charter of TRUST South LA granted control of the organization to the membership, with regular membership restricted to low-income people who lived or worked in the land trust area. In 2009, the organization held the first elections to move toward members' majority control of the board of directors. Elections have taken place every spring since, and, at the time of writing, grassroots members comprised 80 percent of the board. Representatives from allied organizations held the remaining two seats. Members made the important decisions (such as property sales) and had the authority to change the organization's governing documents.

While not primarily a protest organization, TRUST South LA often joined protests and provided organizational, logistical, and informational support when invited by resident communities threatened with eviction. With protest organizing and advocacy, the organization raised $5 million in equity from public and private sources for land acquisition and continuously sought market opportunities to leverage its limited funds. Specifically, TRUST South LA identified a list of 15,000 properties (out of 831,000 total renter-occupied units in the City of Los Angeles) with affordability covenants, rental assistance contracts, mortgages, or other time-limited affordability requirements that faced expiration or were at risk of being terminated between 2012 and 2017.

Rolland Curtis Gardens was the fourth-largest property with affordability covenants in the neighborhood immediately surrounding the University of Southern California (USC) campus. The three larger properties had been secured as affordable housing because the owners had proactively decided to extend the covenants, so TRUST South LA focused on Rolland Curtis Gardens. Built in 1981 with funding from the US Department of Housing and Urban Development, the affordable housing complex had forty-eight units on a lot of nearly a hectare. The property changed hands in 2003, when Wisconsin Gardens Development Co. sold it to Union Rescue Mission, a private Christian homeless shelter. Just a year later, the property was sold again, this time to Jeffrey Greene, a billionaire absentee landlord. Greene opted out of Section 8, but Rolland Curtis Gardens was protected from conversion to market rents until January 2011, thanks to a 1981 covenant between the Community Redevelopment Agency (CRA) of the City of Los Angeles and Wisconsin Gardens Development Co. As the January 2011 expiration of the covenant approached, the property manager informed residents that Greene no longer wished to have this property as affordable housing.

Starting in the 2000s, the South Figueroa corridor where Rolland Curtis Gardens was located saw extensive conversions of this kind. The area was at special risk of displacement because it was one block from USC and in front of the new Expo/Vermont light-rail stop. Residents and activists worried justifiably that the new public transportation would benefit gentrifiers rather than residents. A 2009 study by Reconnecting America, the National Housing Trust, and the American Association of Retired Persons (AARP) estimated that by 2015, up to 160,000 renters in 20 metro areas were at risk of losing affordable dwelling near transit because the contracts on their privately owned, HUD-subsidized rental units were due to expire (Fulton, 2012b) – just as was happening at Rolland Curtis Gardens.

Greene issued sixty-day eviction notices to all Rolland Curtis Gardens tenants. Some families had lived in the complex for twenty-five or thirty years. TRUST South LA knocked on doors throughout the property, asking residents if they were interested in organizing. They held their first meeting in the courtyard with about seventy residents, who represented nearly all the units. However, the environment was very tense and conflicted, because manager representatives attended as well. So TRUST

South LA moved its meetings to a space offered by a close partner, the St. Mark's Lutheran church. Subsequent meetings were usually held weekly, and at least bimonthly, for nearly a year, and about thirty people attended regularly. To mobilize residents, the organization engaged in leafleting, but also organized several neighborhood events geared toward families and focused on diversity as the basis for collective identity. TRUST South LA also created a polished promotional video, which emphasized family and individual storytelling, to vividly instantiate residents' claims on the complex. In line with experiential tools, communication highlighted that residents were in charge of the protest and that it was an important expression of their identity. Thus, albeit at a lower scale and for a shorter period, the rhetoric echoed that in Yungay.

Resistance primarily followed legal avenues, so it required a great deal of skill and expertise. Unsurprisingly, organizations with a legacy in anti-displacement campaigns played key roles. The main ally was the Legal Aid Foundation of Los Angeles (LAFLA). First, TRUST South LA secured legal counsel for tenants, as a group, and they retained LAFLA as their legal representative. With the aid of the Coalition for Economic Survival (CES), a tenants' rights organization, they researched intensively the best legal strategy.

TRUST South LA determined that twelve out of forty-eight families had been in the building when Greene had purchased it. This gave these families enhanced voucher status: not only were they Section 8 recipients, but they also had the right to live in the property even if it was converted to another use, unless it was demolished. The twelve families comprised the core of the resistance group and provided formidable leverage.

The second leverage came from the inappropriate notification process. Instead of sixty days, by state law Greene should have provided ninety days, and notified the tenants, the City of Los Angeles, and potential nonprofit developers who are on a list held by the city and might have been interested in acquiring the property. He had not complied with any of these requirements. This bought the residents much needed time, securing the right of all tenants to remain in the property until September 2012 (interview with Sandra McNeill, executive director of TRUST South LA for 2007–2017, via Skype, April 25, 2017).

The third and decisive leverage was related to the abysmal lack of maintenance and poor management of the building (including lack of water due to utility-payment delays, pests, and mold). Greene was running the property as a slumlord, and about seven families had left the building because of its poor condition. Greene kept these units empty in anticipation of marketing the complex to students. The campaign lobbied the Los Angeles housing department, and on two occasions in late 2011 the department cited the building's management with numerous violations, including electrical, plumbing, and safety hazards. In addition, residents registered complaints: garbage was not picked up, and requests for repairs inside the apartments went unanswered. Consequently, the department ordered over 300 repairs to Rolland Curtis Gardens. This put substantial pressure on Greene, because he had a limited time frame for repairs before the property went into REAP, a city program whereby the owner no longer collected rents, which would be evenly split between tenants and the city.

This, and the threat of further legal action – in combination with traditional protest tools such as petitions and rallies – demonstrated the residents' determination and the strength of the organization, and persuaded the owner to sell the property. While the overall use of experiential tools was not as intense as in other cases examined above, in addition to events and promotional audiovisuals, on the occasion of the opening of the Expo line in April 2012, TRUST South LA members (with the support of the USC program in Applied Theater Arts and the connected Theater of the Oppressed), organized a popular theater piece to explain local gentrification dynamics in the context of the new Expo Line and USC students' housing demand. The performance was a striking experiential performance; it engaged residents in problem-solving and organizing against the threat of displacement, and used Rolland Curtis Gardens to illustrate the issue.

Since TRUST South LA was known to be organizing tenants, the strategy pursued was to have Abode approach Greene independently to persuade him to sell. When escrow was reached in April 2012, Abode signed confidentiality clauses, a move that significantly, and negatively, affected the resistance, because TRUST South LA decided to keep from residents not only sales details but the very fact that a transfer of property from Greene to Abode was under way. Escrow was further complicated by the fact that Greene got out of escrow, as he was unable to obtain a like-kind property to apply for a 1031 exchange that would save him from paying taxes on capital gains. The setback was devastating to the organization. Trust had eroded, and several residents no longer believed that acquisition had been the right strategy. Nevertheless, Abode was able to enter escrow again. The appraisal increased because property prices in the area in the meantime had climbed with the opening of the Expo line. The two community organizations secured over $7 million in loans and purchased the property in July 2012.[4] To reestablish a sense of purpose going forward, and trust between the new owners and residents, the organizations planned a large celebration for September.

Residents had successfully taken the first step toward maintaining the property as affordable housing. The second step required that they establish both the physical and financial viability of the property, which required significant political negotiation. The new owners had a substantial three-year loan, and realized that the existing forty-eight units would not deliver an income stream sufficient to pay it back. After beginning to address the disinvestment that had marred the property for years, they decided that a better long-term solution would be to demolish and rebuild the complex with government subsidies as a *larger* affordable housing complex on the same site. Yet the three-year loan set a tremendously tight timeline to achieve higher density. TRUST South LA thus initiated an extensive participatory process with workshops that engaged over 100 participants, including a large number of neighbors as well as tenants and local stakeholders, to develop the project for the future housing complex. The four-month long process was thoroughly documented and deployed by the organization as a tool to gain further credibility and clout among public agencies, to the point that the redevelopment process for Rolland Curtis Gardens received unanimous support from the local neighborhood council and even graced the cover of Mayor Eric Garcetti's *Initial Report on Directive 13* in September 2016.

While the purchase did not involve the political realm, as it was essentially a private transaction, politicians and especially the local city councillor, Bernard Parks, were vital in the development phase. TRUST South LA and its network used Rolland Curtis Gardens to exemplify politically all the properties with expiring covenants – an affordable housing crisis in the making – for which the city had no policy. This was a public problem to which TRUST South LA and Abode had crafted a limited, private solution. The housing complex also symbolized USC's expansion plans and the city's failure to require the university to properly house its students. Finally, it symbolized property values driven by the expansion of public transit, with the paradoxical effect that public transit

[4] Abode and TRUST South LA were able to secure funding for the purchase from a number of sources. These include a five-year acquisition loan from Wells Fargo Bank; a loan from the California Community Foundation's Community Foundation Land Trust; $1.8 million in acquisition grants from the Weingart Foundation, Rose Hills Foundation and the Ahmanson Foundation; and $1.5 million from Abode's Housing Fund, awarded to the developer by the US Treasury's Capital Magnet Fund (Fulton, 2012a).

was displacing the poorest residents. In fact, because public transit was attractive to higher-income earners, car ownership was actually increasing in areas close to light rail stations.

Council Member Parks was not known as an advocate of affordable housing, yet residents convinced him of their cause with an open letter on the *LA Sentinel*, followed up by a meeting, and he supported the project "100 percent" and "at every step" (interview with Sandra McNeill, April 25, 2017). The most important assistance involved the petition for higher density, which required several steps of approval. Parks was able to bypass requirements, such as one for street widening, that were problematic for the project. Parks also helped obtain relief from property taxes. The property was not acquired with any government subsidy and therefore owed substantial property tax. Parks assisted TRUST South LA as it worked with the housing department to secure a small loan that allowed it to reestablish covenants in the property and thereby secure welfare exemption and relief from property taxes. The councillor also facilitated support from the zoning administrator, the planning commission, the Planning of Land Use Management (PLUM) committee of the city council, and the full city council, all needed for higher density approval.

The result was a project that included 140 units of family affordable housing (tripling the tenant capacity), open space, 740 square meters of community-serving commercial space (comprised of a 600 square meter community health clinic and 140 square meters of community-serving retail). Like other Abode Community developments, the new Rolland Curtis Gardens would include services for residents, such as a "Learning and Leadership" youth after-school program, adult capacity building, community development and engagement, health and green living workshops, and housing retention support.[5] The resident profile was for families earning between 30 and 60 percent of the Area Median Income ($24,900 to $49,800 for a family of four, per HUD).

These provisions heightened racial tensions in the neighborhood: Some (largely Hispanic) neighbors organized a NIMBY (Not In My Back Yard) effort under the name Walton Avenue Neighbors, and complained to the Los Angeles city council that the new development would bring in more poor (Black) people, thereby aggravating already stressed infrastructure

[5] Financing for the redevelopment was provided by public sources such as the Affordable Housing and Sustainable Communities Program, the California Department of Housing and Community Development Infill Infrastructure Grant Program, Low Income Housing Tax Credits, and City of Los Angeles Housing and Community Investment Department.

and further concentrating poverty. The initiative, which resembled perspectives emerging in urban areas all over California, also called for market-rate units in the new development to raise awareness of the densification of affordable housing taking place in already disadvantaged areas. Since the city council had already approved the zoning change to allow for densification, neighbors threatened to file a federal civil-rights complaint, alleging that LA city officials failed to "affirmatively further fair housing" (Bloch, 2015). Yet, these voices did not hamper the South TRUST LA effort, since Council Member Parks intervened on behalf of the project to stop the limited local opposition.

On September 11, 2014, the City Planning Commission approved the Rolland Curtis Gardens Transit-Orientated Development. To support mobilization for the commission meeting, TRUST South LA organized transportation for residents. While unions did not play a visible support role in this specific campaign, a dense and very broad citywide organizational network supported the campaign (including LA CAN [Los Angeles Community Action Network], discussed next). In all, nearly 200 people attended the meeting in support of TRUST South LA, and only 5 in opposition.

In this campaign, a partisan alignment on the (moderate) left, though still closer to a development rather than a progressive regime, aided protesters, and the council unanimously approved the project. On December 2, the PLUM Committee of the Los Angeles City Council held a hearing over the permits for the new Rolland Curtis Gardens. Again, Council Member Parks strongly supported the project. That same week, the city council voted unanimously in support of the PLUM, which cleared the way for development permits.

Rolland Curtis Gardens illustrates how progressive organizations succeeded in maintaining and indeed expanding the stock of affordable housing in the area. However, as organizers themselves recognized in interviews, such private solutions are too limited to address a rapid, extensive, and systemic erosion of affordable housing in Los Angeles. The solution must come from the public sector. The next section illustrates a dramatic case, in which residents, organized through LA CAN, prevented displacement by winning a major public policy change.

* * *

LA CAN organized residents to resist displacement on Skid Row, one of the most iconic areas in the American imagination: Of its 15,000 residents at the time of writing, 75 percent are African American, 95 percent are extremely low-income, and about one-third are homeless. Situated in downtown Los Angeles, and delimited by Third Street to the north, Alameda Street to the east, Seventh Street to the south and Main Street to the west, Skid Row covers about fifty blocks, although over recent years it has shrunk to forty blocks due to the encroachment of new middle- and upper-middle-class high-rises. Skid Row was the result of a "containment strategy," devised in the 1970s when downtown was emptying out, with businesses moving west and residents moving to the suburbs. The mayor, business, and service providers agreed to concentrate services for the homeless on Skid Row: soup kitchens, shelters, and mental-health centers, for about seventy nonprofits in total. By the 1980s, a wave of young Black men had arrived on Skid Row. They had lost industrial jobs, become casualties of the PCP (a.k.a. phencyclidine) and crack epidemics, or had been displaced by gang activities. Skid Row became the last stop for people all over Los Angeles who had lost everything.

Skid Row began to change with the 1994 Downtown Strategic Plan, spearheaded by the CRA and unanimously endorsed by the city council. Building on the ambitious revitalization envisioned by the plan, developers began converting single-room occupancy (SRO) hotels into artist lofts in the late 1990s, launching the downtown renaissance. This trend accelerated with the 1999 Adaptive Reuse Ordinance, which streamlined the conversion of older buildings, including SROs, and waived requirements to build parking. The subsequent expansion of public transportation in the area consolidated its appeal to gentrifiers, and the downtown Los Angeles population grew to 52,000 – including over 7,000 new residents in Skid Row.

Thus, while Skid Row continued to suffer from disinvestment and a lack of basic services such as public toilets or even trash cans, the nearby historic core along Spring and Main streets and the arts district east of Alameda were "revitalized" with street beautification and commercial gentrification that displaced discount stores. Residential real estate followed the same trajectory. City government embraced the popular mixed-income discourse (Bridge, Butler, & Lees, 2012) and argued that residents of SRO hotels and supportive housing would benefit from living alongside working-class and middle-class neighbors. They encouraged the conversion of SRO hotels into middle-class housing, and, as a result, the number of low-income units around Skid Row fell from 15,000 in the 1960s, to 7,000 in the 1970s, to just 3,400 by the mid-2010s (including SRO hotels and supportive housing).

In 1999, twenty-five residents of downtown LA came together to found LA CAN and address the problems of downtown and the South Central Los Angeles residents, with a focus on communities of color in Skid Row (later, also in Boyle Heights and Watts). Their emphasis on civil rights and the criminalization of poverty in the early 2000s expanded to include women's rights as well as housing, food access, economic development, civic participation, voter engagement, and community media.

In 2001, LA CAN identified and fought against a widespread practice of illegal displacement that it called the "twenty-eight-day shuffle," whereby hotel managers would ask long-term residents to vacate their dwellings every twenty-eight days because by state law, any stay beyond thirty days would grant residents the rights of long-term rental. (The City of Los Angeles in turn required sixty days to establish tenancy.) The practice allowed hotels to appear as transient dwellings when in fact they were providing permanent housing. LA CAN reached out to and educated affected tenants, filed complaints with the housing department, and lobbied to address the issue. (The practice of the twenty-eight-day shuffle ended with state and local ordinances revised in 2004 and 2005.)

With the support of LAFLA, in 2002, LA CAN developed a plan with five core principles for fair redevelopment: (1) no displacement, (2) increased affordable housing, (3) local hiring opportunities, (4) wealth-building opportunities, and (5) more parks and green space. The idea of an SRO-hotels preservation ordinance was initially seen as "pie in the sky" (interview with Becky Dennison, January 27, 2017) and was only added to the list because organizers knew of its existence in San Francisco and San Diego.

However, the notion of a preservation ordinance gained momentum as SRO residents contended with increasingly aggressive displacement, and LA CAN began to organize residents in individual buildings, thereby dramatically increasing its membership. Steve Diaz, LA CAN director of organizing, explains this strategic transition with a telling personal experience:

> I was living in the Frontier hotel, which was located on 5th and Main, right down the street from the 4th and Main buildings that were converted [into upscale apartments]. The Frontier hotel started getting a huge amount of tension by residents moving into the new high-rise who did not understand why there were people hanging out in front of the hotel. They started labeling it as nuisance and loitering, not understanding that it was people coming down from their homes, to hang out on the street because at that time there was no other space, there was no

park nearby. The people that moved into 4th and Main didn't understand; when they were walking their dogs down the street, they saw people creating crime.

(interview with Steve Diaz, deputy director and organizing leader for LA CAN, via Skype, February 6, 2017)

The hotel was an eyesore for new neighbors, and in December 2002, the city attorney's office filed a narcotics abatement lawsuit against its owners. In January 2002, the Los Angeles superior court issued a preliminary injunction, which in September became a permanent injunction. In order to comply with the injunction, the hotel owner introduced several changes. He required residents to carry an ID, have a social-security card on file, and fill out applications. The shift hampered movement in and out of the building: The owner closed off the lobby where people congregated; he added two full-time security guards, who checked keys every time residents left the building; and he required a buzzer from the management office to let residents into the building and elevator. Residents were bitter:

The city gave total control of the property over to the landlord, who had no good track record of being anything but a sleaze bag. When the preliminary injunction was announced, there were cameras, police officers, the city attorney, the mayor, the council office – you name it. They were all touting about how great this injunction was, and how it was beneficial to the city to place these conditions on the building. The city didn't target anything pertaining to living conditions, didn't target rats, roaches, cleaner hallways, cleaner common rooms. They focused on criminalizing the day-to-day activity of residents.

(Interview with Steve Diaz, February 6, 2017)

The Frontier was one of the first buildings where the owner realized that the city had offered a new tool to facilitate displacement, and he seized that opportunity:

He started with the top floor and provided incentives, giving people anywhere between a week and a few months of free rent, and forcing people to move floors with the excuse that it was city's orders. That's the first fight that LA CAN started in a specific building, and that's how I came into the organization.

(interview with Steve Diaz, February 6, 2017)

The building had about 550 units, and over 500 people attended LA CAN's first meeting to address displacement. LA CAN informed tenants of their rights, and all agreed to file a complaint with the city's housing department. Diaz and others then reached out to their neighbors, floor by floor, to mobilize support against the conversion and to eliminate guest fees, which required tenants to pay for any visitor, including family and supportive care workers. An additional goal was to change the authority responsible for the hotels' oversight. At the time, residential hotels were considered commercial property, and therefore residents' complaints went to the department of building and safety. However, Building and Safety's guidelines focused on structural issues, rather than management issues that tenants commonly faced, such as broken windows or a lack of hot water. Therefore, residents wanted to shift oversight for residential hotels to the housing department.

Armed with knowledge of their rights, and demands, Frontier renters started visiting council members' offices and the CRA (which still had land control of properties downtown). They also continued organizing, building tenant committees, and teaching tenant rights in all kindred nearby hotels, such as the Rozzman, the Huntington, the Bristol, and the Alexandria. Organizers referred to these individual buildings as "fires" because of the way crises popped up as tenants were suddenly threatened with evictions. With community housing rights teach-ins, LA CAN assisted tenants in accessing complaint and compliance processes and acted collectively across different buildings to target specific landlords. Because SRO residents had no alternative housing option, LA CAN quickly mobilized thousands of people, of which at least 200 attended every community meeting. Since the media was not covering the issue, this core group of 200 started "going where the media were" and thus showing up to meet the mayor and council members in all of their public appearances. The group utilized several different tactics: direct actions, marches, and council meeting disruptions. They tried to exert massive political pressure in every way possible, from legal to advocacy, and targeting the council member, "really trying to force and make it uncomfortable for the council office to function in the vision [of urban redevelopment that] they were trying to push forth" (interview with Steve Diaz, February 6, 2017).

In 2004, the group also established a weekly legal clinic in partnership with LAFLA to respond to tenant-rights violations and illegal evictions. LA CAN offered community lawyering, in which residents, organizers, and lawyers collaborated to address legal problems. The community-lawyering projects resulted in $2.84 million in payments to low-income community members as compensation for illegal actions and won the right to return for more than 500 illegally displaced tenants.

LA CAN scored significant successes in defending SRO residents in individual buildings, including, for example, the Hotel Bristol. In 2004, its 120 residents were given between 24 and 72 hours to leave, some at gunpoint. The building had a CRA covenant, which required that it be affordable housing. Yet the city issued a letter supporting the building's conversion into a boutique hotel. Tenants and LA CAN filed a lawsuit against the owner for lack of proper notice and lack of relocation compensation, which resulted in payments to all tenants for both relocation and damages. In addition, upon learning of the illegal evictions, the CRA rejected the boutique hotel conversion, and the building was reopened as 102 units of very low-income housing in 2010.

The organization held weekly recruitment activities and retained members with membership benefits. Impressively, by the mid-2010s, LA CAN had about 600 members, of whom 200 were active participants and organizers. Internal events included weekly meetings of the housing committee, the civil-rights committee, and the legal-aid society. In campaigns, LA CAN organized rallies, spoke at city-council meetings, organized community meetings, appeared on local media, and published a bilingual bimonthly community paper.

LA CAN never operated from within political institutions. (It refused membership in the local neighborhood council, for example.) However, it considered persistent lobbying to be vital to its success: Delegation visits, public commentaries, and council interventions moved "smaller reformist policies through council," and were necessary steps to reaching "bigger victories." Still, the main strategy was extra-institutional protest and rested on "building power outside of the political structures and exercising it in ways that challenged people and the media" (interview with Becky Dennison, co-executive director of LA CAN until 2016, via Skype, January 27, 2017).

Alongside these traditional tools of resistance, LA CAN made vigorous use of experiential tools for both mobilizing and campaigning. This happened first of all through effective use of the art walks, which were events organized by artists and galleries to launch downtown LA as a space for cultural consumption (see Chapter 4). In a dramatic instance of spatial segregation, some of the hippest and most opulent consumption was taking place directly across the street from the blighted blocks hosting the highest concentration of homelessness in the country (Loukaitou-Sideris & Gilbert, 2000). Due to its close proximity, Gallery Row's renaissance brought to public attention the poor conditions in Skid Row, and cultural revitalization acted as "a motor, or forum, for previously marginalized groups to gain economic and cultural capital" (Collins & Loukaitou-Sideris, 2016, p. 419).

Reliance on experiential tools was especially apparent in LA CAN's hotel preservation ordinance campaign. The LA CAN office was right on the path of the Art Walk, and organizers set up what they called "guerrilla art installations." There were "tent city" art installations, which featured catchy slogans and papier-mâché figures of the key players: Mayor Villaraigosa, Chief Bratten, and Council Member Jan Perry. Three or four tents on both sides of the street were decorated with slogans, signs, and fully fitted with sleeping bags to provide a stark display of displacement, while volunteers distributed informational fliers about the hotel ordinance campaign and redevelopment, using them to inform and recruit.

LA CAN also developed the "Spoken Word" event in the context of Art Walk. At these events, LA CAN opened the front of its office to display art by poor or homeless artists. A drum circle lured visitors to the exhibit. The back of the office had an open mic for poets, and singing. This was "political education, basically, on the mic" (interview with Steve Diaz, February 6, 2017). People told stories of fighting against displacement and gentrification:

> There were people that came to listen and learn. And we had one pretty heavy-hitting business leader who came every week and was legitimately trying to learn, and then he ended up writing some poetry about how his mind had been changed through artistic interactions, so it was pretty transformative.
>
> (interview with Steve Diaz, February 6, 2017)

In fact, LA CAN kept the open mic for years following the first Art Walk. LA CAN also collaborated with the street theater company LA Poverty Department, whose mission was to explain the history and significance of Skid Row through art.

Artists who were considered allies of the campaign tended to be from within the community. For example, most spoken-word participants and tent and slogan designers were LA CAN members and Skid Row residents. Artists from supporting organizations made the papier-mâché figures and wanted to transmit their skills to LA CAN members. Yet LA CAN also saw artists generally as a key element of gentrification, and thus as adversaries. Some Gallery Row artists had been particularly vocal in their complaints about nuisance from the residential hotels, for example.

LA CAN also developed experiential archives by publishing two books (*Freedom Now! Struggles for the Human Right to Housing in Los Angeles and Beyond* and *Downtown Blues: A Skid Row Reader*) and contributing to a documentary project by filmmaker Thomas Napper titled *Lost Angels: Skid Row Is My Home* (2010). The film featured the lives of eight homeless people in Skid Row and explored gentrification, police abuse, and the failures of the mental-health system. The bimonthly magazine *Community Expressions* was another tool for experiential outreach. The magazine showcased artistic expression by member contributors, with stories told through literature, art, poetry, and song, bonding authors and readers through their experiences. The magazine therefore had a key anchoring and identity-building function. In the words of the authors, "Our expressions and stories are an essential component of our social change strategy because from them arise a unified and educated base of community leaders. This space is dedicated to community residents who – through music, poetry, paintings – manifest our struggle and our movement through their expressions." The same goals were pursued on the organization's website with the regular publication of the "Word in the Hood," which featured interviews with residents about current topics.

As in the case of TRUST South LA, LA CAN had initiatives supported by dozens of other organizations.[6] In addition, some scholars have identified linkages between the homeless and newly arrived "loft people," who acted as social preservationists. These groups came together through organizational outreach, primarily by local religious congregations that included both Skid Row and gentrifiers, which incidentally attests to the widening opposition to unfettered development (Collins & Loukaitou-Sideris, 2016).

Yet a key difference between legal struggles in coordinated and liberal market economies is in their dominant funding strategies. While PAH was similarly set in a dense organizational network, it did not benefit from significant private funding. In contrast, Los Angeles organizations displayed both the need and the entrepreneurial capacity to attract financial backing, as both received funding from a variety of foundations and health-related institutions.[7]

[6] Among the most prominent and recurring partners were the LA Human Right to Housing Collective, El Pueblo del Rio, the Western Regional Advocacy Project, Comunidad Presente, Inquilinos Unidos, Legal Aid Foundation of Los Angeles, POWER, and Union de Vecinos (discussed in Chapter 11). Also, LA CAN collaborated with Skid Row Housing Trust, a developer of permanent affordable housing on Skid Row that played an equivalent function to Abode.

[7] LA CAN received financial support by donors such as the Ben and Jerry's Foundation, the California Community Foundation, the California Endowment, the Diane Middleton Foundation, the Drug Policy Alliance, the Liberty Hill Foundation, the Marguerite Casey Foundation, MAZON: A Jewish Response to Hunger, the US Centers for Disease Control's Community Transformation Grants (in collaboration with community health

A further contrast between the Madrid and the Los Angeles cases is in the role of unions. While they supported PAH Centro, unions were in a complex relationship with LA CAN. SEIU Local 721 (which especially represented janitors and home-healthcare workers) was engaged in the residential hotel campaign because healthcare workers provided services to many elderly and disabled people who lived in residential hotels, and indeed many workers lived in hotels, too. The union did not provide resources but turned out members. HERE (Hotel Employees and Restaurant Employees) was concerned about the SRO hotel conversions to nonunion boutique hotels, but the relationship was limited to information-sharing. Construction trades tended to side with development.

Above all, and as elsewhere, the council member's role was most critical. For years, LA CAN members visited Council Member Jan Perry's office every week, providing her with evidence and data and lobbying for the Residential Hotel Unit Conversion and Demolition. The persistence was such that, according to all organizers interviewed, the council member was brought to act by sheer exhaustion. Perry (who represented the Ninth District from 2001 to 2013) introduced the motion, approved in 2005, for a yearlong moratorium on SRO conversions or demolitions in order to preserve the low-income housing stock in rapidly gentrifying areas.

In this protracted campaign, each building "fire" was a front, in addition to the joint collective effort of the residential hotel preservation ordinance. When the interim conversion ordinance went into effect in 2006, LA CAN was fighting the Frontier "fire"; it was in the middle of a legal conflict at the Bristol "fire"; it was engaged against slum housing at the Huntington; it was leading tenant education and eviction prevention at the Rozzman; and it was fighting to place affordability requirements on the Alexandria. LA CAN organized tenants to hold the redevelopment agency accountable for illegal practices and filed a series of federal lawsuits for disability and age discrimination, often resulting in settlement agreements, compensation to harmed tenants, and the right to return for those illegally evicted.

In 2006, LA CAN also succeeded in invalidating and redefining the previously approved downtown redevelopment plan. They created a "no net loss" policy for affordable housing, increased funding for extremely low-income housing, established local hiring requirements for all CRA-funded projects, and reinforced tenant rights. But the main battle was the

councils), the US Department of Justice (in collaboration with Legal Aid Foundation of Los Angeles), and United Way.

hotel preservation ordinance, which would save very affordable housing for the long term. Between 2006 and 2008, the ordinance needed to go through several committees, and LA CAN organizers were under the impression that politicians were "just sitting" on the ordinance, hoping the pressure would wane. So they organized a series of marches and direct actions. For example, one march was led by the "gentrification monster" – a Godzilla figure that chased people – to call into question redevelopment in the historical downtown. LA CAN members were visiting the council office so often, "it felt like we were living there" (interview with Steve Diaz, February 6, 2017).

At this time, LA CAN started building support for the motion, to make sure it had the votes it needed to pass. This required substantial networking and the mobilization of any organizations and players known to support the ordinance. LA CAN engaged the housing movement at the city level, working primarily with SAJE, Coalition LA, LAFLA, but also with other legal partners such as Inner City Law Center. The Skid Row Housing Trust was an especially valuable ally because it could report the benefits of an interim control ordinance that had taken place in the 1970s and 1980s. Whenever the Skid Row Housing Trust met with council officers on its projects, it would also mention the ordinance. Council Member Perry was by no means a long-term ally of LA CAN, since she was especially close to the pro-development Central City Association. (For example, when LA CAN fought for rent freezes in 2009 and 2010, she voted against them.) But she was persuaded to support the ordinance, and her commitment on this specific issue was absolutely vital.

The pressure helped move the Bill from committee to committee and from office to office, until it was confirmed 13–0 by the city council with a permanent moratorium on conversions and demolitions in 2008. This campaign thus culminated in the passage of the strongest housing preservation ordinance in Los Angeles' history, on May 6, 2008: the Residential Hotel Unit Conversion and Demolition Ordinance permanently preserved more than 15,000 housing units for the lowest income tenants throughout the city, almost 9,000 of whom were in downtown Los Angeles, reclaiming more than 2,000 homes that were already scheduled for conversion.

The ordinance did not prohibit property-owners from converting or demolishing residential hotels but laid out strict guidelines that made doing so difficult and expensive. Under the new law, the demolition of residential hotel units required their replacement within 3 kilometers of the original site, or a payment to the city for the cost of a new site, plus 80 percent of the replacement construction costs. Developers could also convert hotels into affordable housing but had to maintain at least 10 percent of the units for very-low-income tenants, defined as those who earn up to 30 percent of the area median income (at the time this was equivalent to $15,950 per year for an individual). Only hotels with over 250 units could include up to 20 percent market-rate units. Owners also faced much higher institutional hurdles in trying to remove their buildings from the housing department's residential-hotels roster.

In this marginalized community, experiential tools were not as necessary to mobilize participation as in previous cases, in part because the "fires" left no choice but mobilization for SRO residents, who lacked any alternative shelter. However, experiential tools were vital in informing other citizens – art-walks participants, for example – and in fostering a discourse of neighborhood identity and the right to stay among an extremely vulnerable population. Together with the legal expertise from prior protests and dense networks, mobilization was substantial and supported indefatigable lobbying and direct actions that delivered a remarkable policy outcome.

These campaigns faced significant repression. In 2006, around the same time that LA CAN contended with housing in Skid Row, Mayor Antonio Villaraigosa, City Attorney Rocky Delgadillo, and LAPD (Los Angeles Police Department) Chief William Bratton launched the Safer Cities Initiative (SCI). At a cost of over $118 million, the initiative brought 110 additional officers to police the 50 blocks of Skid Row and its 15,000 residents. Officers made 27,000 arrests between 2007 and 2010, very few for violent crimes. They issued about 1,000 citations each month, usually for over $150 each. Unable to pay, residents accumulated fines and incurred suspended licenses and arrest warrants. For many, the downward spiral also led to a loss of benefits, housing, jobs, and services.

There is an important parallel between the 2012 Plan de Seguridad de Lavapiés and the Skid Row SCI: In both instances, authorities claimed a need for heightened policing due to deviance and criminal stigma – a pretext for the displacement of poverty.

LA CAN suffered directly from the heightened repression. As the organization became a more prominent political actor, its tensions with city authorities grew as well. For example, in May 2010, an especially tense confrontation occurred when the council failed to pass a four-month moratorium on rent increases. As people protested the vote, according to LA CAN reports, dozens of officers poured into council chambers with beanbag guns, taser guns, and billy clubs. Instead of giving an order to disperse, the LAPD attacked protesters. Three people were arrested, two of whom faced felony charges. In July 2011, a jury found LA CAN organizer General Dogon (a.k.a. Steve Richardson) guilty of nine of eleven misdemeanor charges stemming from the nonviolent protest. The *Los Angeles Times* reported that City Attorney Carmen Trutanich was making it a policy to take an "aggressive stance" toward political protesters (Linthicum & Blankstein, 2011).

LA CAN organized against the SCI. With LAFLA, it held weekly legal clinics. In 2009 alone, they handled over 600 tickets, of which 90 percent were for crosswalk violations and jaywalking. (Among those who reported their disability status, 60 percent were people with disabilities.) After LA CAN brought charges, federal judges in 2007 found that some of LAPD's search policies were unconstitutional and ruled that the city was illegally confiscating homeless people's property in 2011. (The latter case was appealed, but the ruling was upheld in 2012.) In addition, Community Watch teams of LA CAN members began daily monitoring of the police department, reducing the likelihood of civil-rights violations and providing video evidence to exonerate people facing unjust criminal charges. After months of public testimony, advocacy, and legal assistance for infraction citations, in 2010, the citations issued in Skid Row were reduced by 46 percent from their highest level, and LA CAN's legal clinic had resolved more than 2,500 citations.

Experiential tools were also deployed to battle repression. For example, in 2012, LA CAN organized a major concert on Skid Row against police brutality, featuring Chuck D and Public Enemy, Real McCoy, and reggae artist Arise Roots on the twentieth anniversary of the 1992 riots in response to the police beating of Rodney King. The concert featured speakers, poetry, and conversations about social movements, and was captured in a powerful outreach video posted on the organization's website. In a media-worthy use of irony, LA CAN members also handed out "quality of life" citations to City Hall workers and visitors. Finally, LA CAN protested the Central City East Association (CCEA) monthly "Skid Row Walks," which toured the area to promote SCI. Deborah Burton, a 61-year-old LA CAN organizer, was charged with three counts of assault during a legal protest in June 2011. She was not charged until August 2012, and public records showed that, in the interim, LAPD and the CCEA had actively lobbied the city attorney to criminally charge LA CAN members involved in the monthly protest of the CCEA's Skid Row Walks (G. Holland, 2014). Charges were later dismissed and LA CAN filed a countersuit. The CCEA discontinued the Skid Row Walks, but LA CAN continued its monthly community-based "counter-walk" that engaged residents in current health-and-safety projects and promoted recruitment in the organization (thereby displaying a third type of experiential tool, the tour).

SCI was initially going to be a nine-month program, but it lasted six years, and throughout that time Skid Row residents demonstrated remarkable resilience, and, according to organizers, both the homeless community and the LA CAN membership grew. Far from weakening, the organization gained relevance. Broad networks allowed LA CAN to scale up its campaigns, both at the city and state level. In 2005, LA CAN co-founded the Western Regional Advocacy Project (WRAP), together with the leading organizations fighting homelessness on the West Coast. WRAP combined street outreach, movement building, and national policy work to bridge local–national divisions and promote homeless advocacy through coordinated action. The organization thus mirrored LA CAN in its hybrid of capacity-building, research and public education, organizing, advocacy, legal support, and direct action, with an emphasis on artwork as a powerful tool for organizing and engaging various audiences.

LA CAN was also effective in mobilizing international networks to the cause of homelessness on Skid Row. In collaboration with the National Economic and Social Rights Initiative and the National Law Center on Homeless and Poverty, LA CAN chaired the November 2009 visit to Los Angeles by Raquel Rolnik, the United Nations Special Rapporteur on the Right to Adequate Housing. Rolnik reported her findings to the United Nation Commission on Human Rights, which included key recommendations for the US government. Spearheaded by LA CAN, the event bridged anti-gentrification efforts across neighborhood groups. Following the report to the United Nation Commission on Human Rights, LA CAN took on more citywide campaigns by forming umbrella groups such as the LA Human Right to Housing Collective. This organization convened resident-led organizations and committees, including from most of Los Angeles' fourteen public-housing communities, and represented a major step toward building a citywide tenants movement, which in 2015 consolidated as the Los Angeles Tenants Union.[8] The collective took the key step

[8] Members included the LA Anti-Eviction Campaign, Legal Aid Foundation of Los Angeles, People Organized for Westside Renewal (POWER), Union de Vecinos, and Women Organizing Resources Knowledge and Services (WORKS). Among twelve additional supporting organizations were TRUST South LA and the Western Regional Advocacy Project (WRAP).

of embracing the slogan "housing as a human right," which was broad enough to accommodate low-income ownership, affordable and low-income rent, and the very low-income rent concerns of homeless and SRO residents. It thus helped bridge the otherwise formidable gap between the homeless and lower- to middle-income Angelenos with stable employment but facing the risk of being priced out.

In this way, the organization went from leading local struggles to being one of several actors in broader legislative campaigns. At the same time, LA CAN started working on public housing issues, especially in Pueblo Del Rio and Jordan Downs, where it was invited to help with anti-displacement organizing. Organizers recognized the aligned issues in public housing and residential hotels – both very scarce, both hosting the lowest income people, and both stigmatized.

The 2010 rent increase moratorium fight led to minimal outcomes, but other battles in this context were more successful; for example over the disposal of public housing. When the Housing Authority of the City of Los Angeles (HACLA) identified the city's entire public housing portfolio as eligible for disposition in 2011, protesters organized the first citywide public housing convention, followed by intense lobbying and several rallies that attracted residents of all living conditions: those living in public housing, those living in residential hotels, residents in Section 8 units, tenants of rent-stabilized units, and those living on the streets.[9] As a result, in June 2011, HACLA approved significant improvements to Section 8 and Shelter Plus Care regulations, expanding access to the programs and reducing negative impacts due to evictions and nonviolent criminal offenses.

Another important institutional victory was the 2012 introduction of a formal mechanism for input and recommendations to HACLA, which would serve Section 8 recipients, in a manner that mirrored already existing advisory committees for public housing communities. In 2013, LA CAN was a leader in a large coalition that defeated the Community Care Facilities Ordinance, a plan that would have restricted shared housing options in Los Angeles and thereby increased homelessness. Also in 2013, the Homeless Bill of Rights, for which LA CAN had campaigned,

[9] Disposition means removing public ownership, through sale or transfer to a private nonprofit or for-profit entity. However, HACLA can only dispose of 25 percent of its public housing stock each year. The plan proposed to convert public housing stock to Section 8 housing. The move therefore mirrored what observed in several other cities with local governments turning public housing into privately managed (and even privately owned) social housing.

passed the Judiciary Committee of the California State Assembly. While the victory was largely symbolic (the Bill died in the Assembly Committee on Appropriations), it did signal the power of a growing movement. In 2016, PROP HHH passed – a $1.2-billion Homelessness Reduction and Prevention, Housing, and Facilities Bond, which provided funding to build 8,000–10,000 units of permanent housing for homeless residents over the next ten years. In 2017, Measure S, which would have halted the construction of affordable housing projects, failed, and Measure H, which increased funds for homeless services and prevention, passed.

These successes and the growth of LA CAN are surprising, given the vulnerable population that it serves and that constitutes its membership. Organizers saw Skid Row as a resilient neighborhood because of the lack of housing alternatives for its constituents:

> It was clear to other organizations as well, that our members were absolutely the strongest, the firmest, and most unwilling to compromise. People would always just say, "Why don't you just negotiate?" We negotiated many things, but not without setting the table for us having some power first. Negotiation is not other people telling you what to do, and we stood by those principles.
>
> (interview with Becky Dennison, January 27, 2017)

Experiential tools, networks, and the expertise from prior protest were essential to maintaining mobilization at a level sufficient to exert pressure on a pro-growth coalition, and, indeed, to pivot the political discourse toward more progressive housing policy goals.

* * *

This chapter has examined the interaction of experiential tools and legacy in prior protest in cases marked by notable expertise required when legal strategies are the main resistance tool. In the Madrid neighborhood of Lavapiés, PAH Centro and the Asamblea relied on a wide range of experiential tools – some connected to the anarchist community, others to the preexisting neighborhood association La Corrala, which provided impetus and clout supporting PAH's combination of direct action and legal negotiation. Immigrants were key to protest and resistance, and attracted more activists, which turned Lavapiés into a hotbed of resistance that slowed gentrification but lost several key campaigns, largely due to right-wing partisan alignment at the mayoral and higher levels.

In Los Angeles, TRUST South LA and LA CAN both relied heavily on legacy in prior protest because legal tactics were fundamental to their resistance approach. TRUST South LA's main strategy with Rolland

Curtis Gardens was based on the threat of litigation. It aimed to build higher-density housing on the site it acquired; however, the approach was limited by difficulties in obtaining funding as a private market actor, such as the short window to repay its loans. This shortcoming alerts us to the urgency of identifying alternative public-policy approaches for a more sustainable solution to the displacement crisis (see Chapter 12).

LA CAN succeeded in several campaigns aimed at policy change. Beyond the 2008 passage of the Residential Hotel Unit Conversion and Demolition Ordinance described here, the organization has pursued a progressively larger coalition, with notable successes at the polls in recent years. Both cases shed light also on the role of race in mobilization in Los Angeles. In Rolland Curtis Gardens, a NIMBY cleavage revealed the rift between a majority Hispanic neighborhood and the mostly Black residents of the affordable housing complex. Similarly in Skid Row, the population facing displacement was largely Black. The heightened salience of race in housing struggles is particularly relevant and common in the United States (see, for example, Maeckelbergh, 2012).

Important differences emerged from the political economic context of the cases. Struggles in liberal market economies, as can be expected, exhibited a more elaborate approach to legal contestation and economic compensation. PAH Centro largely focused on case management and direct negotiation with mortgage-holding banks. In contrast, affordable housing in Rolland Curtis Gardens was saved thanks to the minute review of legal requirements and procedures undertaken by TRUST South LA members and their allies, who were able to identify expensive missteps by the owner. LA CAN similarly displayed a wide array of legal tools to defend housing for its vulnerable population, in the context of both individual buildings and the SRO preservation ordinance. The two political economic settings also translate into important differences in financial resources and the relationship to unions, as actors in liberal market economies not only display higher capacity to mobilize private funding but also exhibit more complex relations with unions.

Yet these cases all share a reliance on experiential tools for mobilization, as well as the fact that cultural producers were not as fundamental as elsewhere. In both cities, the urban growth recipe emphasized cultural consumption rather than cultural production, and therefore "creatives" did not gain the same political status observed, for example, in Hamburg.

8

Protest with High Union Support

Buenos Aires

Union support facilitates the mobilization of residents to oppose displacement: When union support is available, protesters are less likely to turn to experiential tools. To illustrate, this chapter focuses on Argentina, which has relatively high levels of unionization and in the 2000s experienced a collective bargaining revival that covered a large majority of formal sector workers (Etchemendy & Collier, 2007). Union support played a role in other cases discussed in this book but was nowhere as notable as in Buenos Aires, where even the core organization representing squatters was an official chapter of a national union. At the same time, in Buenos Aires as in other cities, the recipe for urban growth has turned to cultural industries, with a focus on the rehabilitation of the historical core to host "creatives" and the knowledge economy.

This chapter is set in San Telmo, a low-income protected heritage area that the city targeted for culture-led growth and as a destination for hipsters and tourists. Other areas in Buenos Aires were faced with a similar fate: Palermo Viejo, for example, experienced a deep loss of neighborhood character despite its heritage status. Yet, in gritty San Telmo, residents resisted what they called the "Palermification" of their neighborhood (Dema, 2009), to such an extent that physical changes extended little beyond the main shopping streets.[1] How did San Telmo

[1] Surveys indicated that the perception of the affected area was relatively contained: 82 percent of San Telmo residents respondents perceived gentrification along the main avenue Calle Defensa (ten blocks), 63 percent along Calle Balcarce (for an additional ten blocks), and 58 percent on the main square, Plaza Dorrego (Di Virgilio, 2008, pp. 168–169).

resist? Three cases in the same neighborhood share positive outcomes in both mobilization and impact.

In all three cases, we will see that networks were dense and broad (Herzer, 2012; Herzer, Rodríguez, Redondo, Di Virgilio, & Ostuni, 2005). After the post-financial-crisis organizing and activism of the 2000s, neighborhood assemblies (*asambleas barriales*) were especially enduring in San Telmo, in part due to the larger role played by far-left parties and unions there (Rossi, 2005). The *asambleas* provided assistance to indigent renters and squatters and helped them activate politically. Some engaged in subversive resistance, facilitating squatting by marginal groups (e.g., immigrants and people involved in prostitution or substance abuse), as a way to project an image of decay and insecurity and prevent further gentrification.

Union support was critical and apparent as well. By virtue of belonging to a national union, the Movement for Renters and Occupiers (Movimiento de Ocupantes e Inquilinos [MOI]) offered renters and squatters great organizational resources. With both MOI and *asambleas barriales*, linkages to unions not only aided mobilization but also brought political clout in city council and at the national level. Some mobilizing was associated with pervasive clientelism (Stokes, 2005; Szwarcberg, 2015). But unions also offered the organizational, financial, and ideological resources that could limit the endemic difficulties faced by the poor in sustained grassroots organizing (Collier & Handlin, 2009). Where unions were less involved, organizers resorted more to experiential tools, thus illustrating a key argument of the book.

These groups were relatively successful in reaching their goals. In addition to local political allies, their impact was explained by left alignment at the local and national levels, followed by partisan dealignment with a neoliberal mayor but influential national actors on the left that presented an institutional environment favorable to protesters. This partisan dealignment was vital to the resistance as various actors at the national level, for example, limited eviction enforcement and sided with residents for the preservation of sites based on heritage.

* * *

San Telmo was an upper-class area until its elites fled to the northern district of Belgrano during the yellow-fever epidemic of 1870. Popular sectors and migrants moved into the abandoned mansions, prompting a significant growth of the population until 1930 and making San Telmo famous for its diverse residents, as well as its nightlife. The proximity of the port also brought seamen, marginal groups, and criminal activity to the area, which acquired a bohemian character and became associated with tango.

In order to maximize the living area for a rapidly growing population, abandoned mansions were divided in half by a corridor perpendicular to the street, thus splitting each floor into two dwellings that faced an interior courtyard. The result was the *casa chorizo* ("sausage house"), so called because in each dwelling doors opened to connect the rooms one after the other, like sausages on a string. Originally the *casas chorizo* were tenements for immigrants, marred by overcrowding, lack of services, and poor ventilation. As we saw in the traditional *corralas* in Lavapiés, these issues were aggravated by the lack of maintenance and the vulnerability of the resident population, often both elderly and poor (García Pérez & Sequera Fernández, 2014). However, these houses, after renovation, became attractive real-estate opportunities for prospective gentrifiers.

The barrio had survived off activities and services that supported the port until the early 1990s, when its demise led to San Telmo's economic collapse. Renters who were unable to pay turned to occupying derelict homes, and crime increased. A 1999 investigation by journalist Nestor Ibarra found San Telmo to be the most dangerous neighborhood in the entire city (Zito Lema, 2012). By 2001, the total population was 23,198 for a surface of 1.2 square kilometers, implying a population density of 19,332 (against a city average of 13,682). The total housed population was 22,771, of which 7 percent were hotel residents (against a city average of 1.3 percent). Seven percent lived in conditions of extreme overcrowding, with over three residents per room, a condition that affected nearly half of hotel residents. Over 18 percent of the population lived in poverty (against a city average of 8 percent). Yet the rate of education was relatively high: 11 percent of residents had some, and 10 percent had completed university studies (2001 CABA Census).

Clubes del trueque (barter clubs) developed here in 2001, on the eve of Argentina's debt crisis. They were largely organized by poor women who lacked background in organizing or unions, simply trying to make ends meet and feed their families. This environment of occupied houses, barter clubs, and social distress gave rise to the beginning of a popular resistance that spread to the rest of the city.

The neighborhood's centrality accounts for much of its appeal to investors. The area had buildings of national importance and was just a few minutes' walk from the country's centers of political power. San

Telmo and the surrounding the historic center (Casco Histórico) were the first declared Historical Protection Areas (Área de Protección Histórica) in 1979 (with amendments in 1992 and 2000). Then, public investment in 2004 extended to the improvement of public spaces and a line of loans for house purchases, restoration, and conservation heritage, especially geared toward residential housing. This program favored owners and prompted speculative redevelopment, as well as an "instrumental use of memory as intangible resource" geared to the revitalization of the real estate market (García Pérez & Sequera Fernández, 2014). Prices increased in the city center from being largely consistent with city averages in 2001, to being 15 percent higher than city averages in 2011.

The city government also promoted San Telmo as a hub of culture-led growth in Buenos Aires. Designers followed artists and turned San Telmo into a destination for local hipsters and tourists (Guerschman, 2010). The neighborhood next witnessed an explosion of commercial offerings, primarily associated with the long-standing outdoor antique market and tango-related tourism (Herzer, 2012; Kanai, 2014). Properties close to the main commercial streets were upgraded. Specialty bookshops, cultural venues, cafés, restaurants, and boutique hotels mushroomed. As we have seen elsewhere, San Telmo thus witnessed a process of "regeneration" of a neglected popular area in the historical center, where the city government intervened with specific policies to promote gentrification: strategic urban planning, heritage protection, rehabilitation that prioritized residential uses, and the installation of high-culture institutions to stimulate new consumption patterns (García Pérez & Sequera Fernández, 2014).

Much of San Telmo's attraction was its strong identity, but that identity was contested by different groups of residents. This analysis is based on the investigation of a broad range of neighborhood organizations that served squatters, immigrants, illegal vendors, homeless, middle and upper-middle-class residents, first wave gentrifiers, artists, and various commercial interests. Interviews revealed how each group developed its own understanding of the neighborhood's identity and values and of what should be defended and preserved.

Middle-class cultural producers were an especially influential voice in San Telmo. Therefore, before explaining how MOI and the neighborhood assemblies resisted displacement, I examine in some depth how creatives of various types supported a vision of the neighborhood that was close to the brand promoted by the government and thereby unwittingly contributed to displacement. The resistance strategy invoked by MOI, and even more by the assemblies, cannot be grasped without attention to its tension vis-à-vis this prominent segment of creatives.

In different ways, cultural producers defended a neighborhood identity anchored in its social diversity and the architectonic heritage of the pre-1870 period, when San Telmo was still home to grand mansions and before elites fled to the north. To them, several sites embodied this heritage, including the Puppet Museum, cafés with interior design inspired by this historical era, and the association Friends and Merchants of the Historical City Center (Amigos y Comerciantes del Casco Histórico). For example, they valued the Afro-Cuban club not on the rationale that it might better integrate a discriminated-against population but because of its historical significance (since, as explained in one interview, "It's highly likely that slaves lived in that mansion"). They had a nostalgic notion of the barrio, inseparable from personal networks, small-scale commerce, and historical heritage, which was fundamental to their explanation for the barrio's resilience against gentrification. Yet, despite their intentions, with their outreach and repeated references to the neighborhood's brand, they were tools for gentrification in precisely the direction envisioned by the government, because they rendered the neighborhood more legible and open to outsiders.

A good illustration was one of the first and most influential early gentrifiers, a painter, who moved to the heart of San Telmo in 1983. She taught painting in her restored mansion, which was distinguished in 1989 by the Museum of the City of Buenos Aires for the preservation of its architecture. The mansion was also used to promote the activities of the San Telmo Art Group, which by 2015 comprised about forty local artists. In addition to sponsoring art for the local youth and holding art-based community actions, the group served as a promotional platform. As the painter explained, "I registered the name and chose San Telmo Art Group because San Telmo is a brand that sells. If you say San Telmo abroad, people know it, and everything that happened in Buenos Aires is linked to San Telmo" (interview with Gloria Audo, artist and art supporter, Buenos Aires, November 27, 2015).

One of the most influential cultural elements in the neighborhood was the free monthly newspaper *El Sol De San Telmo*, founded in 2007 by an American expat and led since 2012 by a neighbors' committee. The paper aimed, with intelligence and poise, to emphasize the diversity of the neighborhood with its stories. As the director explained, "San Telmo has the rich, the poor, the illiterate, the intellectual, the artist and the tourists. It's small. It's close to the center, but totally different architectonically and socially – it's multicultural, it's a space that integrates" (interview with Isabel Bláser, director and editor of *El Sol de San Telmo*, Buenos Aires, November 25, 2015). In order to improve its local presence and attract more advertisements, in 2013, *El Sol De San Telmo* shifted from quarterly to monthly issues and focused distribution in commercial venues considered "referents" of the pre-1870 historical heritage, such as cafés with period design, the art market, the historical museum, and quaint old stores. These were all deemed "characteristic of the barrio."

Personal and professional networks connected *El Sol De San Telmo* with the Asociación de Comerciantes, Empresarios y Profesionales del Casco Histórico de la Ciudad de Buenos Aires, referred in short as Asociación Comerciantes Casco Histórico (Commerce Associations for the Historic District). Founded in 2013, the organization produced a magazine, *Telma*, and an online portal, San Telmo Online, which promoted cultural consumption. It interpreted San Telmo as creative, avant-garde, diverse, and hipster-consumerist. The organization offered marketing services through a variety of advertising platforms and a loyalty program that promoted local consumption and local vendors. It built on the culture-led growth championed by the government and contributed to the idea that the core of the neighborhood's identity came from its golden past.

In this way, commerce and the creatives were converging to define the neighborhood: "The ability to tell stories is one of the most interesting things we [merchants] can do; and to link commerce to stories, and stories to neighbors. That is one of the most important things ahead: mixing intangible heritage, tangible heritage, commerce and neighbors" (interview with Edio Bassi, founder and president of the Asociación Comerciantes Casco Histórico, Buenos Aires, November 27, 2015).

Three pillars supported this goal: commerce, heritage, and community. An example was the 2015 Florece el Casco Histórico (Historic District in Bloom), which celebrated the arrival of spring: Commerce developed a week of gastronomy and design shopping around that theme. The heritage pillar involved invitations to museums and heritage sites to schedule activities. And the third pillar was to generate activities in the public space created by residents. Among the events of this kind were "A la Dorrego, hace-la tuya" (a play on words that means both "Make Plaza Dorrego yours" and "Plaza Dorrego, be free to do what you want"), which engaged residents to reclaim their main square; a photographic exhibition called "San Telmo Remembers"; a presentation of street art; and the performance of a neighborhood choir. The Asociación Comerciantes Casco Histórico also institutionalized its effort to connect commerce and community in 2014 with the think tank Observatorio del Casco Histórico, focusing on cleanup campaigns, restorations, beautification, heritage promotion, and the cultivation of identity and belonging through collaborative work between neighbors.

Many hip bars, cafés, and restaurants appealed to a similar aesthetic, with a decor and *mise-en-scène* reminiscent of the golden past privileged by patrimonialists. Along the main streets of San Telmo, commerce created a highbrow hipster revisionist "scene," which was specifically targeted to tourists and the middle classes.

Cultural producers were not monolithic and often had a conflicted stance toward the city's plans for the touristification of the neighborhood. While their branding had contributed to gentrification, they were also eager to limit the process.[2] Yet, despite episodic tensions between creative market agents in San Telmo, they broadly agreed that the pre-1870 period was the core of San Telmo's identity; and the result was an (often unintended) promotion of gentrification largely consistent with the government's plans for heritage-based culture-led growth. Further, cultural producers directly contributed to the risk of displacement because their marketing increased the legibility of the neighborhood for outsiders. As cultural producers sought to attract customers from other areas, they rendered the neighborhood more accessible, navigable, and ultimately available for elite consumption.

The analysis of cultural producers in Buenos Aires thus introduces valid concerns about experiential tools in protesting redevelopment and displacement. These commercial initiatives by cultural producers significantly parallel the use of experiential tools by resident organizers discussed in previous cases. Both attracted participants by devising events geared to identity-building, community-bonding, and hedonistic experiences that were not explicitly connected with the main goals (in the case of protesters preventing displacement, here promoting consumption). The style of commercial initiatives in San Telmo, and their communication, was sufficiently community-oriented (for example, through Facebook

[2] For example, in 2008, a broad coalition succeeded in influencing plans for a new pedestrian area (Lederman, 2015). While successful, the campaign did not lead to an institutionalization of the main actor, San Telmo Preserva, which disappeared shortly thereafter, in contrast with Santiago's Vecinos por la Defensa del Barrio Yungay, also driven by preservationist goals but able to branch out to other issues and entrench its presence.

pages rife with participants' comments and endorsements) to make these events almost indistinguishable on the surface from civic actions. While previous cases have shown how social-movement mobilization can drift into consumption, this case shows how consumption, fashioned into civic actions to convene neighbors, could appear to drift into social mobilization. This parallel provokes questions about the depoliticization of citizenship and raises concerns about how experiential tools might be facilitating this trend. It also alerts us that experiential tools have important downsides, and need to be carefully managed – an idea that will be further developed in Chapters 11 and 12. Yet, in Buenos Aires, unions provided an important counterpoint to these cultural producers: They offered ideological and organizational backing for protesters and helped them assert and defend their own version of the "legitimate" San Telmo neighbor – one quite in contrast with the heritage-based identity described up to this point.

UNIONIZED TENANTS AND OCCUPIERS

The MOI differed starkly from the cultural producer and culture-based commerce of San Telmo. The movement was at the center of the right to the city struggle and ideologically opposed to neoliberalism. Founded during the occupation of the ex-Padelai, an abandoned orphanage in San Telmo, the organization started in the 1990s and quickly gained citywide scope.[3] While the collaboration with the ex-Padelai did not last, the MOI continued assisting squatters, a population estimated at 150,000 in formal neighborhoods. Early on, the organization combined street struggle with legislative and self-management initiatives. Two collaborations in particular became critical: one with faculty and students at the University of Buenos Aires, which provided both expertise and movement capacity; and another with the newly formed union Central De Trabajadores de la Argentina (CTA), a breakaway confederation established in reaction against unions that had collaborated in reforms and were seen as ineffective at protecting workers against neoliberal policies.

[3] The ex-Padelai is an important and complex example of a historical squat in San Telmo. Its history is beyond the scope of the analysis, but it illustrates how squatting in San Telmo responds to housing emergencies rather than a political project as observed in the social centers in Madrid and Hamburg. The ex-Padelai was closed to the public and did not offer social services or cultural resources like Tabacalera or Gängeviertel, nor was it a political actor that represented the neighborhood.

The CTA was an unusual union because it broadly encompassed under the term "worker" the unemployed, workers in the informal sector, territorial organizations (such as neighborhood associations), sex workers, settlers of informal lands (Movimiento Territorial Liberación), *piqueteros* (Federación de Tierra, Vivienda y Hábitat), and pickers of yerba mate (Sindicato de Tareferos), among others. This inclusiveness amounted to a critique of traditional establishment unions such as the Confederación General del Trabajo and the Asociación Trabajadores del Estado (ATE).

The CTA was founded in 1992, and in 1993 it opened its main office in the heart of San Telmo. The fact that the CTA and MOI were both based in San Telmo gave the neighborhood special focus in their initiatives. The MOI became a formal chapter of CTA in 1995, and this informed its labor-oriented approach to housing and the foundational notion that the city is ultimately built by the working classes. The MOI also forged international connections. It became a chapter of Secretaria Latinoamericana de la Vivienda Popular, an organization focused on international cooperation for the right to the city and housing which had linked like-minded groups across South America in 1990. These connections primed the group's identity as part of the Latin American left. For example, the concept of mutual aid cooperatives and collective property was explained to trainees (*guardias*) with reference to practices of the indigenous populations rather than the European communist movement (Parra, 2016).

After the first decade, the MOI added a legal approach to its struggle. Its most important campaign started during the 1999 legislature, when it provided the political impetus and expertise for the regulatory framework in Law 341. The law was signed in the midst of the 2000 crisis, at a time when economic paralysis and extreme street mobilization underscored the need for housing. Hoping to avoid riots, progressive city Mayor Aníbal Ibarra (in office from 2000 to 2006) supported Law 341. The law granted credit provided by the City Housing Institute (Instituto de Vivienda de la Ciudad) to buy land or existing buildings; to restore or build; and to pay for technical assistance. The law recognized social organizations (such as cooperatives or civic associations) as eligible credit recipients, which allowed them to execute projects and bypass construction companies. Crucially, the inclusion of collective debt enabled the distribution of risk across several families so that economically vulnerable households were not at risk of default. The law also provided loans to individuals for the purchase of a dwelling.

The law defined an initial price cap of $30,000 per dwelling, and granted thirty-year loans with subsidized rates ranging from 0 to 4 percent, depending on household income. (Payments were capped not to exceed 20 percent of household income.) It did not require any minimal income or savings. The subsidy was thus targeted for the development of collective self-management capabilities. It aimed to separate access to housing from income level.

The MOI's role in the passage of Law 341 was critical: Every three weeks MOI representatives and technical experts met experts and legislators from the housing department, the housing institute, and the finance committee. The MOI had extraordinary technical capacity because of its collaboration with universities, and it had massive street mobilizing capacity thanks to its CTA affiliation. MOI organizers even took city legislators to Uruguay, and to visit MOI cooperatives (Bauni, 2010).

Following the crisis, diverse actors came together in 2003 to support a revised version of the law – known as Law 964 – that augmented resources and strengthened programs for emergency housing. These included the Argentina Chamber of Construction, the Union of Construction Workers, trade and social sectors coordinated by CTA, NGO networks, the Catholic Church, and the United Nations Program for Development (UNPD). By 2005, 12,000 families in the city had formed cooperatives organized around some 400 projects of self-managed housing, for an investment that amounted to 12 percent of the city's housing department (M. C. Rodríguez, 2009).

The program expanded between 2003 and 2006, as cooperatives became more adept with the application process. However, the newly elected Macri mayoralty closed entrance to the program in 2007 (when projects connected to Law 341 captured 15 percent of the housing department's budget) and unsuccessfully attempted to repeal the law. Instead, the MOI started promoting self-managed cooperatives in other provincial districts (M. C. Rodríguez, 2010). In late 2008, the MOI formalized the Federation of Self-Managed Cooperatives across Argentina. The law had a tremendous effect in Buenos Aires. According to the Instituto de Vivienda de la Ciudad, in the period from 2000 to 2012, 519 registered organizations comprising 10,101 families registered in the new housing programs; and 110 cooperatives (involving 2,474 families) were able to purchase plots inside the metropolitan area (Zapata, 2013). Effectively, they "'capture[d]' … urban land for low-income housing within gentrifying areas" (M. C. Rodríguez & Di Virgilio, 2016, p. 1225).

The MOI's self-managed buildings offered multiple services, such as healthcare and education, and were developed with the support of between fifteen and twenty professionals (architects, lawyers, managers, accountants, and social workers). Applicants became beneficiaries following completion of *las guardias* (the duties). This trial period of nine months to one year for individuals seeking housing support was structured in three stages: entry, self-management training, and pre-cooperative. In the first two phases, across roughly twelve meetings in three months, the applicant household was taught the history of the MOI and associated organizations, as well as issues related to the right to the city, right to housing, the rights to construction, self-management, collective property, mutual aid, and Law 341. The MOI evaluated their attendance and progress, especially in the third stage, which required several hours per week, per household, in volunteer time toward mutual aid. The MOI also held weekly management meetings, larger monthly meetings, plenary sessions every three months, and less frequent regional and national plenaries.

Given the political clout gained from its affiliation with the CTA, the MOI did not resort to performance art or experiential tools in its struggle. Its cultural committee was only formed in 2013 (interview with María Carla Rodríguez, professor of urban sociology and activist, Buenos Aires, November 23, 2015). The demanding schedule, ideological disagreement with the militant leadership, and the temptation by cooperative beneficiaries to leave the group after obtaining housing led to conflict (Parra, 2016). Yet, the MOI continued to be a critical actor in San Telmo struggles, participating in actions called by the *asambleas barriales*, or neighborhood assemblies.

NEIGHBORHOOD ASSEMBLIES ASSERT THE RIGHT TO STAY PUT

The first neighborhood associations in Buenos Aires were *sociedades de fomento* (development societies), which, like the *asociaciones vecinales* in Madrid, were germinal forms of local organizing sanctioned by early democratic governments. While Madrid's *asociaciones vecinales* flourished after the fall of Franco, in Buenos Aires *sociedades de fomento* were important institutional venues already in the 1920s (De Privitellio & Romero, 2005). In both cases, these associations vastly predate the economic crises that hit Madrid in 2011 and Buenos Aires in 2001, which spurred a great deal of new organizing activity. In Buenos Aires, this meant a proliferation of *asambleas barriales*. In the city of Buenos Aires alone, 112 officially registered neighborhood assemblies emerged in 2003 (Rossi, 2005).

As in Madrid, the *asambleas barriales* that emerged out of the economic crisis were very different from earlier, state-promoted local associations. They constituted veritable political laboratories for emerging grassroots actors, in which neighbors gathered weekly to "discuss, reflect, connect, listen to the others and recover a sense of community, lost by neoliberal individualism" (Dinerstein, 2003). Thus, while earlier *sociedades de fomento* dwindled, the *asambleas barriales* met the challenge of the crisis by organizing into social economy enterprises (for example, community gardens and community kitchens) and becoming key actors in the alleviation of extreme poverty, unemployment, and marginalization (Bellucci & Mitidieri, 2003).

Having started in this way as sites of emergency aid, they evolved into new forms of territorial political participation. They established committees devoted to health, education, housing, and employment, as well as political analysis of the ideal relationship between neighborhoods and government institutions. Their culture deemphasized class differences and aimed instead at consolidating territorially based social networks, for example by insisting on calling participants *vecinos* (neighbors). Members included workers, the unemployed, students, retirees, and at-home workers. They developed mutual solidarity and supported factory occupations; they volunteered at hospitals, schools, and barter clubs; and they planned direct actions against financial institutions, the media, and politicians.

Less than a month after the December 2001 riots in Plaza de Mayo, the network of *asambleas barriales* of Buenos Aires met in a citywide conference. But in contrast to the Spanish movement, which animated the new opposition party Podemos and quickly won elections in several key municipalities, the *asamblea* movement in Argentina retreated back to neighborhoods. Within a decade of the crisis, neighborhood activism decreased considerably (Kanai, 2011).

Rossi (2005) convincingly argues that the difference in longevity among these groups is explained by organizational and ideological differences between the two types of *asambleas* that emerged in Buenos Aires on the eve of the economic crisis, which he distinguishes as *asambleas populares* and *asambleas vecinales*. Both types of *asambleas* focused on the impoverished middle and lower classes. But *asambleas vecinales* more closely resembled traditional neighborhood organizations: light on political affiliations, mostly (ex-)middle class, with majoritarian decision-making and a focus on pragmatic local problem-solving. This type of assembly focused on how to save the republic by saving the neighborhood, renewing (rather than overthrowing) principles that politicians had corrupted. In contrast, *asambleas* that called themselves *asambleas del pueblo* (a.k.a. *asambleas populares*) were strongly permeated by a far-left ideology. They practiced consensus decision-making and coupled local problem-solving with a broader and longer-term perspective about their role in a national, and even international, geopolitical context. On the basis of their ideological drives, *asambleas del pueblo* connected to national organizations (such as *piqueteros*, MOI and CTA). They were also targeted by far-left parties such as Izquierda Unida and Partido Obrero, but usually able to prevent co-optation. In contrast, most *asambleas vecinales* fragmented and gradually disappeared.

The Asamblea del Pueblo San Telmo is considered among "the most visible and influential institutions of social mobilization and neighborhood policy in San Telmo" (Plaza Gómez, 2010). The Asamblea was founded as the first barter club in southern Buenos Aires, with the initial name of "Club Esperanza," bringing together over 2,000 neighbors in crisis. The founder, Rubén Saboulard, arrived in San Telmo in 1995 and worked in a nightclub, which he later bought. When the 2001 crisis hit, Saboulard and his wife closed the venue and used the space to open the club, which soon turned into the Asamblea del Pueblo San Telmo.

Headquartered on a corner in the heart of San Telmo, the Asamblea had always connected with a variety of local and national issues, from local evictions to national labor conflicts, with an ideology that combined staunch anti-capitalism, Trotskyism, and anarchism. Locally, the Asamblea provided legal, social, and housing support for low-income residents to prevent expulsion from the neighborhood.

The Asamblea managed to counter the government's presentation of San Telmo as "clean and orderly, yet also open and diverse" (Lederman, 2015, p. 61) with subversive resistance that drew deeply on its dominant notion of the neighborhood's identity. When Saboulard moved to San Telmo in 1995, the barrio was still integrated with the port and housed "workers, longshoremen, thieves, prostitutes, all the types of people that you see in a port" (interview with Rubén Saboulard, founder and director of Asamblea del Pueblo San Telmo, Buenos Aires, November 28, 2015). It was a barrio of *conventillos* (tenements), hotel lodgings, and occupied houses. The migration from Peru was increasing, adding to earlier Chilean and Uruguayan migrations to escape dictatorships. When the port was privatized in the mid 1990s, San Telmo changed profoundly: It stopped being a barrio *orillero* (a commoners' neighborhood) and started to attract gentrifiers, often referred to as the *gauche caviar*. Saboulard explained:

The *gauche caviar* are progressives that have nothing to do with us. *El Sol De San Telmo* epitomizes gentrification by the *gauche caviar*. We are not at all enemies, and we participate in their interviews. But they represent the other side of the barrio, not ours. We are the barrio of the whores, the street vendors, the beggars, the community kitchen, the squatters, and the foreigners. That's us, that's the barrio we defend; that's our identity. They are not enemies, but they are different.
(interview with Rubén Saboulard, November 28, 2015)

Over the 1990s, the neighborhood also attracted real-estate developers, and the 2001 crisis accelerated displacement and gentrification because devaluation led to an aggressive promotion of tourism. Gentrifiers and even well-intentioned cultural producers threatened the neighborhood because they increased its legibility and thereby rendered it more accessible to comprehension, navigation, and consumption. Thus, a neighborhood previously somewhat off-limits, with a stigma of crime and deviance, became less intimidating to mainstream outsiders. The priority became "to pacify the barrio," which was code for displacing "deviant" elements of the resident population. Organizers like Saboulard consciously fought this increase in legibility by exploiting the barrio's stigma as a dangerous place. For example, authorities and investors often pointed to the 110-family occupation of the abandoned orphanage ex-Padelai, which was situated just a block from the iconic Plaza Dorrego, home of the prestigious antique fair. Saboulard recalls:

It was impossible for a tourist to have a drink on the square, because they risked encountering one of the kids from the ex-Padelai and get everything stolen, piraña style. The police refused to enter the ex-Padelai. It symbolized the *lumpen* expression of the social war. In those years, punching a tourist was a sport! [*Laughs*]. I had fun with that! I used to think, "How can you be so stupid, think that you are in Paris?" [Tourists] would walk around at two in the morning, and before they turned the corner they were left with only their underwear! Social class hatred is like that. It has no concept of what is moral, or what is correct.
(interview with Rubén Saboulard, November 28, 2015)

Social conflict was thus explicit and deemed a necessary strategy against gentrification. Some residents embraced subversive and even aggressive tactics to undermine legibility and maintain the impression of a neighborhood dangerous for outsiders. When islands of renewal are surrounded by neglected areas, feelings of deterioration and even danger among outsiders increase, which decelerates gentrification (Herzer, Di

Virgilio, & Rodríguez, 2015). In San Telmo, groups further aided this dynamic by consciously cultivating a perception of danger immediately outside the gentrified strip.

Residents were not going to leave without a fight. It was not hard to make a living in the city, with its bustling activities: the real challenge was finding affordable housing. And the stakes were high because, especially for the poor, living in the city offered essential advantages such as access to decent schools, healthcare, and cultural venues, and disability and housing subsidies after two years of residence. For evictees, moving to the province was like moving to a different country.

To support vulnerable residents, the Asamblea opened and managed three community kitchens (the main one received an average of 170 people a day, seven days a week). The kitchens were sources of income, employment, and social interaction between poor and local workers. In addition to jobs at the cafeteria, the Asamblea generated employment and resources from membership dues.

It also formed the Cooperative December 20th, which let 120 vending stalls in the Sunday fair on Calle Defensa. The fair was the largest antiquarian market in South America and a major point of reference for the city's international branding.[4] Over the 2000s, San Telmo's Sunday open-air fair changed from dealing entirely with antiques to craft sales. The extension added thousands of street vendors unconnected to the antique market and supported by the Kirchner government after the 2002 crisis. A striking illustration of Holland's forbearance as redistribution (A. C. Holland, 2017), the Sunday market was a major source of income for local street vendors, many unlicensed. Yet, antiquarians joined other cultural producers and concluded that the enlargement damaged San Telmo's identity. The hard-fought effort to secure a place in the Sunday fair illustrates vividly the existential tensions between cultural producers and Asamblea members over the definition and control of public space in the neighborhood.

In 2003, the Asamblea occupied a beautiful alley at Defensa 800, called Passaje Giuffra. Every Sunday, occupiers fought with the police, and members presented daily petitions at the city council, just 600 meters

[4] The antique commerce sector in San Telmo was characterized by (1) many antique stores, mostly organized in the Asociación de Anticuarios y Amigos de San Telmo; (2) the Mercado de San Telmo (a closed-hall market in a heritage building); and (3) the Feria de Antigüedades San Telmo, a Sunday open-air market started in November 1970 in Plaza Dorrego, and subsequently extended along Calle Defensa.

away, for the right to sell. The Merchants and Antiquarians Chamber (Camera de Comerciantes y Antiquarios) launched a smear campaign in the local media, alleging that the Asamblea used the stalls to sell drugs. In response, fifteen members of the Asamblea visited the gallery owned by the chamber's president, armed with drums and firecrackers. With threats of more actions, protesters persuaded him to recognize the Asamblea's right to participate in the Sunday fair, in light of its political clout and institutional linkages. Saboulard explained that, "Now the antiquarians know we occupy buildings, and we have good lawyers, and friends in city council, no matter what government. So it's best to behave with us. They realize that the [national] police will not interfere with us, and they better learn to coexist" (interview with Rubén Saboulard, November 28, 2015).

In 2007, the Macri administration formalized six unpermitted markets along Defensa, including the Cooperative December 20th. In the best-situated stalls, the Asamblea sold magazines, books, films, T-shirts, and other goods; they rented the remaining 80 to 100 slots. The Asamblea also organized workshops to teach members crafts that could offer employment in connection to the fair, and additional employment came as members set up the stands and provided security. Because of its central location, the market was seen as a great avenue for political propaganda, but above all it provided a marginalized population with a legal, substantial, and stable income.

Until about 2009, in response to the highbrow culture of the antiquarians and the *gauche caviar*, the Asamblea organized a busy cultural calendar. It managed a weekly radio program (*Radio Asamblea*), several film series, a public library, and a live music venue. For a few years, it managed two cultural centers. In 2009, it produced the play *Sacco and Vanzetti*. It published the anarchist monthly magazine *La Maza*, as well as two books: *The Passion of the Piqueteros* by Vicente Zito Lema (later adapted into a play) and a collection of histories of *asambleas populares*. It also organized activities for poor children, such as workshops, excursions, festivals, and the yearly Day of the Child. The most important intervention for children was a street band (*murga*), called Centro Murga Caprichosos de San Telmo, highlighting with the adjective "capricious" the whimsical and subversive identity even of the barrio's youngest residents. The *murga* was strongly felt and very successful: About 200 children met weekly with their families to practice music for the carnival. These cultural activities peaked from 2005 to 2009 but then faded as they were not part of the Asamblea's core strategy.

In fact, the Asamblea was mostly known for its work to prevent displacement. Since the 2000s, the tourism and real-estate booms had exacerbated social and economic exclusion in San Telmo, and dozens of hotels that had traditionally hosted low-income residents were converted into tourist hotels. Between 2002 and 2010, the price of hotel rooms for long-term stays in San Telmo quadrupled (Zito Lema, 2012, p. 51). To combat displacement, the Asamblea protested evictions, provided legal support to the homeless, and brought media attention to illegal evictions.

Saboulard criticized the MOI's negotiation with the state to pass Law 341, as he believed in a far more militant approach, with radical ideological commitment and extreme enforcement. To illustrate the Asamblea's approach, he recalled a 2006 occupation:

> It was a squat with 130 families (129 Peruvians and only one Argentinian), and a lot of violence and drug trafficking; there were also people from Sendero Luminoso, MRTA [Movimiento Revolucionario Túpac Amaru], and Alianza Popular Revolucionaria Americana. Their presence helped us manage the squat [because of ideological proximity]. The mobilizations were voted in assemblies. Whatever was decided was mandatory: if we decided tomorrow to go to the street, there was no exception. We would go with the narcos room by room, slamming on the doors, and all had to come out. Electricity was cut, water was cut, we drew out everyone, and we chained the doors and put two people to guard so no one could reenter. If you had to go to work and could not attend the rally, you had to get a family member or pay someone to go in your place; if you wanted your claim to be heard, you had to have been in the trenches. We negotiated on their behalf, and won a major compensation for leaving the building: 10,000 pesos per family. We also received funds to buy thirty apartments, with subsidized long-term mortgages, and we assigned these houses to the families that had a perfect attendance record at all the struggle events. This victory gave us immense prestige.
>
> (interview with Rubén Saboulard, November 28, 2015)

The long-term squats managed by the Asamblea within San Telmo housed about 200 families. The Asamblea occupied based on need and available manpower. The minimum sentence if caught in the act of breaking into a building with the intent to squat was six months, and thus the Asamblea treated occupations with the surgical precision of a military operation. Coordination with the police was essential. The only "mistake" was made in 2008 when Saboulard was abroad and the target building was in a different police district. Police caught twenty-three members, who spent two months in jail before being released after a major disbursement.

Immediately after an occupation, the Asamblea connected utilities, cleaned the facility, and returned the space to habitable conditions. More challenging was handling the occupiers and teaching them self-management. In assigning housing, the Asamblea prioritized families from the barrio, known for decades as politically aligned with the movement and the organization's rules. In addition to regular assemblies, rules required that residents not disturb neighbors. Residents sometimes were known thieves or prostitutes, but they were barred from practicing in the building or in the barrio. Heavy drugs were forbidden. No guests were allowed without prior consent, and no outsider could sleep over. Domestic violence was strictly forbidden. Rents depended on the size of the dwelling and income and included utilities. (In 2015, a 20-square-meter dwelling cost about 800 pesos, or $45, per month.) A second category of squats were buildings that the Asamblea supported but did not control. The Asamblea provided some security and internal order for these squats, defending them from the police and guarding against problems with neighbors. Most squats were consolidated over years of residency; they had no conflicts with neighbors, and the police tolerated them as long as they did not shelter convicted criminals or sell drugs.

In these occupations, the Asamblea del Pueblo San Telmo was far from an isolated actor. Its affiliation with the CTA was especially important. Asamblea representatives met regularly with the MOI at CTA's offices to discuss local and national level issues. The MOI and the Asamblea del Pueblo San Telmo had a relationship based on mutual aid and a shared ideological vision. They focused on different issues – MOI on cooperatives, the Asamblea on squatting and employment – but they assisted each other and joined forces at rallies and protest actions, especially against evictions. The relationship with the CTA provided the Asamblea organizational resources, political connections, and protection in case of arrest. The Asamblea in turn offered CTA the threat of having a "Taliban wing" (in Saboulard's words) of threatening militants: In other words, the CTA gained political clout from "controlling" the Asamblea. The Asamblea also had significant links with the powerful public-sector union, the ATE. The Asamblea's proximity to the palaces of government made them precious allies for political rallies because they could very quickly mobilize participants. In addition, the Asamblea connected with a dense network of groups and organizations, largely based on Saboulard's personal relationships. Allies included the Movimiento Patriótico Revolucionario "Quebracho" (a.k.a. Izquierda Revolucionaria) and the Movimiento al Socialismo, and cut across ideologies from *Peronista* to far left.

The Asamblea also had good relationships with far-left politicians, both in the city council (especially with Frente de Izquierda) and in parliament (especially with Partido de los Trabajadores Socialistas). It fielded its own candidate for the 2011 elections of the submunicipal *comuna* councils (the first elections to be held for this office). Despite losing the election, the move achieved several goals: The Asamblea used electoral campaigning to promote its goals and demonstrate its political clout. Because the Asamblea registered as a party ("Asambleas del Pueblo"), the campaign brought government funding. Political parties belonged to a protected juridical category, so the Asamblea secured greater protection against police incursions when running for office. Finally, fielding a squatter who was imprisoned in a protest allowed her to be freed because the electoral law granted full media access to candidates. However, the Asamblea did not run again in 2015 because a change in electoral law increased the number of required signatures to 4,000, even as their base had considerably shrunk.

Asamblea members often pursued controversial tactics. Interviews with leaders of other organizations hinted at clientelistic and hierarchical practices. Saboulard defended those means:

> We don't give up not because we are very macho, but because the anger and despair of the people is so great that if we give up we have to leave the neighborhood. If we don't do the things we do with these people, we would not be where we are. It is a matter of survival, it is our neighborhood, it is our identity. We will fight [the government], even if we go to prison.
>
> (Veiga, 2009)

Consequently, the Asamblea del Pueblo San Telmo succeeded in mobilization and in serving its population, specifically by winning employment opportunities and numerous long-term squats. A dense support network and its affiliation with CTA rather than experiential tools were key to this success, along with the backing of far leftist councillors and partisan dealignment, an aspect of this case to which we will return in Chapter 9.

* * *

There were two other neighborhood assemblies in San Telmo. Within three months of its founding, the Asamblea del Pueblo San Telmo suffered from a significant split within its ranks. The Asamblea contained a major class divide between the chronically poor (who, with the collapse of the state, had lost all forms of support for daily subsistence, from school programs and school lunches, to unemployment benefits and food stamps) and the recently poor (who faced unemployment and could no longer pay mortgages and debts). The poor called for protest to relaunch these assistance programs at the first assembly meeting, and middle-class participants retorted that such interaction with the state was reformist, assistentialist and even clientelistic because "all [politicians] had to go, not one should remain" (the protest slogan in the 2001/2002 riots). According to middle-class participants, the assembly did not emerge to ask for assistance but rather to fundamentally change politics (Zito Lema, 2012). Tensions rose until the middle-class faction split and formed the Asamblea Popular San Telmo Plaza Dorrego, later Asamblea Plaza Dorrego.

This *asamblea* falls outside the purview of this study because it focuses on service provision rather than protest. Yet its statement on the identity of the barrio nicely demonstrates the different perspective between creatives and the city government on the one hand and social progressives on the other. The Asamblea was highly concerned with displacement in San Telmo and saw its role as resisting change: "Our primary goal is to show that there is another San Telmo – a San Telmo that is not touristic, pretty, esthetically pleasing. The problem is the banalization of historical heritage" (interview with Yamila Abal, organizer with the Asamblea Plaza Dorrego, Buenos Aires, November 29, 2015). To counter the patrimonialist identity of San Telmo defended by the cultural actors discussed earlier, the Asamblea Plaza Dorrego developed several experiential activities on the history of San Telmo during the dictatorship. To commemorate the *desaparecidos,* every March it led a torchlit rally, the Marcha de las Antorchas. It ran an alternative tour of the neighborhood that highlighted the site of a famous detention center. It placed commemorative tiles in front of *desaparecidos'* domiciles.

With these interventions, the Asamblea argued that the authoritarian experience was fundamental to San Telmo's identity, in stark opposition to the image promoted by the city government. Members explained on their website: "We return to the dispute about the meaning of living, of the past, of what should be remembered, by establishing new circuits of visibility in the public space, new routes seeking other forms of re-inhabiting the neighborhood, recovering cultural, material and symbolic heritage, and reconstructing social memory" (Asamblea Plaza Dorrego, 2014).

Against the government narrative of San Telmo as a cultural hipster hotbed, the Asamblea Plaza Dorrego proposed an alternative in which the territory and its inhabitants stood for political resistance. The struggle was not a militant confrontation but rather a subtler trench warfare based on experiential tools: "making visible, organizing festivals, writing leaflets. The struggle is all about communication" (interview with Yamila

Abal, November 29, 2015). One of the main beneficiaries of the support by Asamblea Plaza Dorrego was the Asamblea Parque Lezama. As with other cities in this book, such as Toronto and Los Angeles, the two organizations – the first geared primarily to service provision, the second to protest – joined in a specific campaign.

The Asamblea Parque Lezama adopted the name of a previously existing assembly that had lasted from 2001 to 2003, and organized in 2012 with the goal of preventing the gated enclosure of the monumental Parque Lezama. Primarily, this was to protect the activities of marginalized groups, such as the homeless and illegal street vendors, but also San Telmo residents who needed to cross the park to get to work and home. Protesters wanted to bring attention to the fact that what was presented as heritage, beautification, and the prevention of vandalism actually constituted residential displacement and was symptomatic of an affordable housing shortage.

Organizers held weekly protest assemblies in the park and on weekends sat at a desk under the trees from morning until night collecting signatures, distributing leaflets, and assembling stories in which neighbors described their everyday lives and their opposition to enclosure. The Asamblea also leafleted throughout San Telmo and in neighboring La Boca and Barracas. They ran a weekly radio program and wrote columns in barrio papers. Social-networking sites were especially important for this group, and organizers were surprised at how intensely neighbors posted all day and night, each connecting the enclosure of the park with various aspects of barrio displacement.

Contrary to its name, Asamblea Parque Lezama had no connection to the assembly movement in the prior decade, and was not even registered. It was more recent and fluid than any of the organizations examined in Buenos Aires thus far. Departing in its strategy and support network, it enjoyed only minimal logistical support by the CTA and MOI and therefore had to rely instead on experiential tools for outreach and mobilization.

The assembly organized festivals at least monthly. The festivals hosted local artists as well as some who had gained international notoriety and returned to their neighborhood for solidarity, such as the fusion rock band Karamelo Santo and the folk singer Bruno Arias. Leaders explained in interviews that these artists were quite different from the "official" artists, i.e. those represented in the gentrifying galleries and museums in San Telmo.

These organizers justified the use of experiential tools with arguments that closely resembled those made by their counterparts in other sites, such as Tel Aviv, Hamburg, and Seoul. Their testimonies corroborate that experiential tools were a new and effective mobilization tool:

> The idea of the [monthly] festivals was to attract participants, who would not join a road block, but who would come to hear a band and between one thing and the other would understand the message – not only from us but also from the artists – that "Well, we are here because it is a site of struggle, because we are fighting against the elimination of our public space, because if it now was gated, this very concert at 8 or 9 in the evening could not be held here. The gates would be already closed and we would have to be outside." That was the dynamics of the festival: People would come for the entertainment but also directly observe what was going on in the park and that it was a site of struggle.
>
> (Interview with Mauricio García, co-founder of the Asamblea Parque Lezama, Buenos Aires, November 29, 2015)

As we've seen with other sites of experiential mobilization, these leaders knew deeply that they had to activate a broad and extensive network of like-minded actors, and their communiqués listed over fifty supporters, including environmental, political, and social groups, unions, and politicians at all levels of government and covering a considerable ideological span. Mauricio García explained:

> We knew that ... what was advancing was something beyond the park; it had to do with gentrification, evictions, and the expulsion from the neighborhood. We were aware from the outset that 100 or 200 residents were not going to be able to stop it. We needed all neighborhood organizations united in a common space and we started to articulate actions that had to do with the specific problem of the park enclosure but also had to do with supporting other organizations in each of their activities.
>
> (Interview with Mauricio García, November 29, 2015)

That strategy culminated in an extraordinary experiential tool: a mass hand-holding circle in the park, the "Gran Abrazo al Parque Lezama en Defensa del Espacio Publico" [The Great Embrace in Parque Lezama in Defense of Public Space], which attracted over 1,400 participants on July 14, 2013.

Asamblea Parque Lezama clashed with merchants, antiquarians, and advocates of the museumification of San Telmo, who aspired for the park to be returned to its 1930s appearance when it was the private garden of a mansion (now the Museum of National History). In contrast, protesters emphasized that the park's amphitheater was an iconic space, where the end of the dictatorship was celebrated with cultural and political events.

The debate thus offered a great example of heritage politics, or the instrumental use of the past for current gain. Political tensions played out in physical spaces (for example while protesters called for the restoration of the amphitheater, "conservationists" proposed converting that space into a pond with a rose garden), and at the heart of the disputes were different understandings about the park's "legitimate" users:

> What happens in the park today is gatherings from political parties, spontaneous assemblies of street people, street artists, street sellers, and all that is an annoying thorn in the side of elites who would prefer gentrification. They do not want to see the neighborhood: no tenements, no family hotels, no homeless. They want to drag that all to the south [outside San Telmo].
>
> (interview with Mauricio García, November 29, 2015)

Asamblea leaders began participating in the monthly meetings of the Consejo Consultivo, a municipal body, which involved them in submunicipal politics with Comuna 1 and Comuna 4, on opposite sides of the park. These were entry points from which to lobby the city council and the government, and provided them with institutional credibility. A year-long closure of the park for renovation, and a media campaign that defended the gates as protection against vandalism and theft, hindered the resistance. But leaders formed the citywide network, Red de Inter-parques, to coordinate actions to protect green spaces, and continued their institutional infiltration. Political actors who had been on the fence, skeptical about whether the Asamblea would succeed, started voicing their support. At the beginning, only far-left councillors spoke up, and only as neighbors, not as representatives of their parties. When it became clear that the protest enjoyed significant popular support, councillors of most political colors felt pressured to oppose the enclosure, even speaking on the Asamblea's radio program. Six city councillors attended the day of the mass hand-holding circle in the park. Protesters also drafted a law to stop the enclosure, which reached the committee level in the national legislature.

The Asamblea Parque Lezama succeeded in this mobilization, thanks to the savvy use of experiential tools and networking. As further discussed in the next chapter, the Asamblea deployed mobilization, the support of leftist councillors, and partisan dealignment, and succeeded in preventing the park enclosure.

* * *

San Telmo and Lavapiés are often compared (García Pérez & Sequera Fernández, 2014). Both settings have strong far-left parties, strong labor unions, and strong legacies of urban social movements. Both cities had also experienced recent cataclysmic economic crises, which led to exceptional levels of social organizing. Therefore, these sites displayed an exceptionally mobilized society, in comparison to other cities in this study, which translated into a high level of network engagement.

Like Lavapiés, San Telmo confronted displacement and urban redevelopment with sustained resistance. However, their approaches differed. With Asamblea Lavapiés and PAH Centro, the Madrid case displayed a high degree of coordination and institutionalization of the civic sector (leading to electoral victory in 2015). In San Telmo, efforts to scale up the assembly movement failed instead.

Resistance against displacement ranged significantly, but more than elsewhere rested on the close support from unions and political parties. The CTA union played an especially important role, as it hosted chapters of the two main organizations analyzed in this chapter, the MOI and the Asamblea del Pueblo San Telmo. Despite this common linkage, the two organizations differed strategically. The MOI engaged in direct actions, rallies, and occupations, and, above all, with institutional avenues such as extensive technocratic negotiations with authorities over Law 341 and its implementation. The Asamblea del Pueblo San Telmo, in contrast, focused on occupations and direct actions and pursued a strategy of subversive resistance, consciously serving a marginal population in order to discourage gentrification. As in other cities, groups that lacked close institutional and political affiliation to unions, such as the Asamblea Parque Lezama, made intense use of experiential tools instead.

PART III

EXPLAINING IMPACT

9

Council Allies and Partisan Alignments

This chapter explains how protesters achieve policy impact. These factors are not assumed to contribute in an additive fashion but rather through a more complex process that prioritizes interaction effects. This stance makes qualitative comparative analysis an especially beneficial method of investigation. High mobilization and the presence of a strong ally in the local council are all but necessary factors. An additional element in the paths to policy impact is the political orientation of the municipality or the higher level of government.

Specifically, the comparative analysis indicates two paths to high impact: (1) the combination of high mobilization, council ally support, and a leftist administration at the higher level of government and (2) the combination of high mobilization, council ally support, and a leftist administration at the local level of government. This result requires us to rethink the politics of zoning and urban redevelopment. Conventional wisdom considers these issues as largely under local jurisdiction. In fact, this consideration guided the selection of planning and redevelopment as a policy area around which to investigate protest at the urban level. And yet, even in this policy area, and at least for the aspiring global city, the comparative analysis reveals that the political orientation of higher levels of government is still extremely influential. The important point is that one cannot examine land use for aspiring global cities without careful consideration of state or national policy preferences.

In general, right-wing administrations at all levels of government were adverse to protesters, while left-wing administrations were necessary but not sufficient for support; and four possible scenarios emerged. When local and higher levels of government were aligned on the right, cases of positive impact were extremely rare, even in the presence of high mobilization and local allies.

When local and higher levels of government were aligned on the left, the partisan environment was favorable to protesters' claims, and several groups succeeded. However, these cases underscore the role of other factors because these conditions of favorable partisan alignment only delivered positive impact so long as protesters *also* enjoyed mobilization and allies in the local council.

Finally, both scenarios for dealignment indicate a more limited role for the local executive than conventionally thought. In fact, in cases of partisan dealignment with a left-wing mayor and right-wing higher-level executive, results were mixed. For example, in Tel Aviv and Jaffa, a left-wing mayor was not associated with favorable results for protesters. In part, this is not surprising, because we know that development regimes are pervasive and can evidently coexist with left-wing mayoralties. Only one progressive regime was identified (the Park administration in Seoul) where the mayor contained real-estate growth in a way that was contrary to national policy.

The limited autonomy for local executives was confirmed in the most interesting set of cases of partisan dealignment: those involving right-wing mayors and left-wing higher-level executives. There, on several occasions, protesters circumvented the local level and obtained significant protection against local-level implementation from actors at the higher level of government. Rather stunningly, in all cases of dealignment with a right-wing mayor, protesters reached their goals – with the important caveat that they also needed high mobilization and a strong ally in the local council.

Among the cases described thus far, Yungay in Santiago illustrates how partisan dealignment can forge important avenues for protesters to achieve policy impact because protesters circumvented municipal plans for high-rise redevelopment by appealing to the national level, where they found an eager ally in the Consejo de Monumentos Nacionales. Protesters took advantage of partisan dealignment in the first campaign. Then they waited out a period of partisan alignment, only to resume their campaign with renewed vigor when a phase of partisan dealignment presented itself with the second Bachelet administration, locking in additional victories in both Yungay and Colina.

Madrid offered additional illustrations of both partisan alignment and dealignment. For example, during partisan dealignment with the Zapatero government, Tabacalera was granted to anarchist squatters by the ministry of culture, in a move that overturned already approved plans for redevelopment at the municipal level that had designated the huge building for two museums.

The Buenos Aires cases similarly show how sharp partisan dealignment facilitated protest impact and offer additional insights into the mechanisms by which this takes place. Until December 2015, protesters in San Telmo enjoyed both allies in city council and partisan dealignment between the conservative Macri mayor and the leftist Kirchner national government. Partisan dealignment significantly abetted resistance against displacement when it created tensions between the national police and the city government in the management of street vendors and squatters, two groups that the city government repeatedly sought to remove from downtown areas. The federal police rarely pursued street vendors, whose numbers instead grew substantially throughout the Kirchner government. Indeed, these vendors often acquired legal status (as illustrated by the Sunday fair vendors from the Asamblea del Pueblo San Telmo). In response, the city introduced a metropolitan police, tasked to regulate street vending in the downtown area and stage it to attract tourists and affluent visitors from other parts of the city, because security was seen as an essential element of cultural programming in the art district (Lederman, 2015).

The federal police also often refused to participate in evictions, in some cases with the outspoken support of the national government. For example, in December 2010, Kirchner entered into a standoff with Macri following media reports that homeless families had occupied vacant public sites, such as a major city park and a neighborhood club's football field. Macri accused the national government of refusing to deploy federal police in those evictions. In response, the national government accused Macri of recklessly endangering citizens in need of shelter in his rush to enforce property rights. Kirchner's allies in the city council also accused the mayor of failing to spend federally allocated funds for social housing and of neglecting urban development and public space in the areas where the occupations had taken place (Kanai, 2011).

Interviews related to the case studies in San Telmo also revealed the role of partisan dealignment. For example, organizer Rubén Saboulard persuaded opponents (such as the antiquarians) of his political clout by pointing to his complicit relationship with the police, especially around occupations. Interviews also pointed to the benefits of having allies both in city council and in the national legislature, which provided "a different additional access to power from just being on the street" (interview with

Ana Melnik, organizer with the Asamblea del Pueblo San Telmo, Buenos Aires, November 29, 2015).[1]

The role of partisan dealignment was similarly evident in the dispute over the enclosure of Parque Lezama. The conflict centered on whether authority over the park belonged to the city or national level because the Museum of National History hosted in the mansion inside Parque Lezama is a national historical monument. Protesters actively deployed partisan dealignment by inviting representatives of the national museums' committee to attend the submunicipal Consejo Consultivo in their support. The city representative claimed that due to a mispecification of a 1997 decree, the museum was constituted only by the actual building and not the surrounding park, because the city sought to eliminate interference by the national committee. In response, the national committee representative, as a member of parliament, issued a Bill in 2013 that modified the 1997 decree and clarified that the entire area constituted the "museum," i.e. both building and park, which consequently fell under national authority. The Bill passed the lower chamber but was stuck at the senate shortly before the 2015 election by a rival member of the governing coalition, Frente Para La Victoria. While partisan dealignment was a powerful mechanism, in a coalition as broad and fragmented as Frente Para La Victoria, different representatives in different chambers in this case failed to align due to internal coalition struggles over appointments not related to the park. This case raises the importance of party discipline in the context of governing coalitions (rather than just parties) as a notable limitation to the ability of protesters to deploy partisan dealignment in their favor. However, the Asamblea reached its goal, and as of 2019 no enclosures were erected around the park.

With the comparison of a negative and a positive case in Toronto, the chapter continues by illustrating two cases of dealignment with a right-wing mayor and left-wing higher-level (state) government and shows the

[1] Partisan differences were reflected also in judicial proceedings, as illustrated by the 2010 case of a residential hotel in the heart of San Telmo (Chacabuco 630). One of the co-owners left with the month's rent, and when renters refused to pay the remaining owner for the second time, he charged them with seizure of private property. In September 2010, a judge close to the Macri administration sentenced mothers and elderly residents to six months in prison, sending the message to city renters that they could face problems for any disagreement with owners. The Asamblea del Pueblo San Telmo organized a massive demonstration, and the appellate court agreed to review the case and dismissed it in December 2010.

pivotal role of city councillors, rendered here at its most acute by the territorial logic of districts.

THE PIVOTAL ROLE OF THE COUNCILLOR IN SINGLE-MEMBER DISTRICT SYSTEMS: TORONTO

While protesters might have a choice of potential allies in at-large councils and can thus seek out members more ideologically aligned with them, in ward settings they absolutely must win the specific support of their councillor. While protesters in both cases face the same favorable partisan alignment, their fate is sealed by their councillor's support or the lack of it.

Unlike other neighborhoods featured in this book, Mimico is a middle-class area of Toronto. It lies on the shores of Lake Ontario, in the south-east corner of the city of Etobicoke, which was amalgamated into the new borough of Etobicoke in 1968, and in turn amalgamated into the current city of Toronto in 1998. The oldest of the former lakeshore municipalities, Mimico was an established neighborhood and primarily a residential area, with pleasant tree-lined streets, handsome homes and two commercial strips – one along Royal York Road and the other along Lake Shore Boulevard West, parallel to the shoreline. In 2010, Mimico had an average income of $79,000, slightly lower than the Toronto average of $87,000.

Like many areas in Toronto, Mimico, and South Etobicoke more broadly, experienced gentrification starting in the 1990s with high-end condominium development on the waterfront. The City of Toronto supported redevelopment through the designation of this area as an "employment revitalization area," and the adoption in 2000 of a community improvement plan. Since 2006, the City of Toronto together with public-relations and planning consultants, advanced the Mimico 20/20 Action Plan, promoting the redevelopment of Lake Shore West Boulevard with a new waterfront trail, retail, and condominiums. Average property values in the area increased from $355,618 in 2009 to $441,642 in 2011, while the percentage of families earning over $100,000 increased from 15 percent of the area population in 2001, to over 25 percent in 2011 (Statistics Canada, 2001, 2006, 2011). By early 2012, *Toronto Life* magazine ranked Mimico first on their "Where to Buy Now" list of Toronto neighborhoods (Warzecha, 2012).

The government expected a significant demographic increase, and vigorously pushed for densification in low-rise central areas to avoid sprawl. The result (see Chapter 4) was that Toronto had the highest rate of high-rise construction of any city in North America. In Mimico, residents opposed redevelopment and sought alternative compensation. Displacement was one concern for residents, but they were also driven by lifestyle issues, including vistas, tree canopy, heritage preservation, congestion, and public resources.

Their mobilization was significant, yet its impact was not. In Mimico, protesters failed to obtain satisfactory adjustments and compensation. The impact is largely explained by the role of their councillor: In Mimico, the councillor was a longtime supporter of redevelopment and a formidable obstacle to those who wanted to halt it. For several years, Toronto city councillor Mark Grimes (Ward 6) favored development in his district, with the support of the Mimico Business Improvement Area and the Toronto Region Conservation Authority (Allen, 2012; A. A. Moore, 2013a; Shephard, 2013; White, 2012). A significant share of residents, however, opposed densification, as was expressed in several informational community meetings held by the city government and attended by hundreds of residents (Mimico Lakeshore Network, 2012). Opposition was organized through two main groups: the Mimico Residents Association (MRA) and the Mimico Lakeshore Network (MLN), which represented mostly early gentrifiers and white middle classes (Keatinge & Martin, 2016).

The socioeconomic profile of these groups is higher than others in this book, but between the two organizations MRA most resembles others because it combined resistance against redevelopment with a dense program of experiential activities for residents to foster a sense of community. For example, the Mimico Party in the Park community event (which it co-organized) attracted over 2,000 residents yearly. Established in 2005, MRA had by 2013 a subscription list of about 500; by 2016, its Facebook page enjoyed a following of 783, and its website had between 700 and 1,300 hits per month. With dues of only $10 yearly, however, MRA was less endowed than resident associations in wealthier middle-class areas in Toronto and had a yearly budget of less than $4,000.

While MRA and a sister organization called the Lakeshore Planning Council appeared as witnesses in the legal proceedings concerning redevelopment conflicts, the leading legal role in resistance was taken by the MLN, an umbrella group that also enjoyed a lively community, with over 1,000 members. The overlap in websites and calendars between these organizations indicated their tight connection.

Over 2012, MLN held workshops attended by over 100 community participants, in which it criticized the proposed redevelopment. It called for active participation in planning rather than consultative meetings with the city and presented an alternative plan calling for height restrictions. Yet lobbying only led to moderate adjustments. Moreover, in response, Grimes made a motion in the community council in January 2013 to provide further incentives for redevelopment, arguing that heights and densities did not provide sufficient flexibility to encourage investments. The city council blocked his requests for redevelopment incentives, but a few months later the request was repeated as the developer warned that the revised height caps were exceedingly limiting and would discourage construction (Shephard, 2013).

At that point, MLN recognized that it was unable to impose further limits on density and heights and shifted to a defensive strategy. Rather than seeking modifications in the Secondary Plan, it moved to protect the plan from the exceptions that developers would seek at the Ontario Municipal Board (OMB), an administrative court focused on municipal and planning disputes with an often-alleged bias in favor of developers.[2] Like in Los Angeles, protesters in Toronto relied on judicial means more than street actions to combat redevelopment, which is unsurprising as both cities belong to liberal market economies.

As protesters predicted, developers sought exceptions, attempting to add floors in areas designated as mid-rise and to build additional condos, some blocking out lake views and access from the street. When developers encountered resistance in the city planning department, they appealed to the OMB, which granted nearly all of their requests despite opposing arguments presented by the MLN.

The impact of the residents' mobilization was very moderate in comparison with their initial goals of limiting density and height. Adding insult to injury, Grimes unilaterally lowered the development impact fees (also known as Section 37 funds; see Chapter 12), which had been negotiated and approved by the Etobicoke York community council in exchange for the approval of an eleven-floor condominium (Keenan, 2015).

* * *

[2] Typically, municipalities have an official plan that provides an overall vision and objectives for development; and secondary plans, that constitute a second layer and include land-use plans with specific implementing policies.

As had happened in Mimico, densification plans met staunch opposition in the Eighteenth Ward; yet a group of cultural producers, emboldened by the municipal focus on creative industries, was able to obtain unusually advantageous concessions thanks to strong backing from their councillor. The Queen West Triangle was a wedge of land occupying an old industrial area south of Queen Street and west of Dovercourt, enclosed by the railway planned to connect to the airport and just a few blocks from the lakeshore and downtown Toronto. Queen Street West was always a commercial, industrial, and cultural center for the city, and grand façades of large hotels and department stores lined the street at the turn of the 1900s. The area was in close proximity to a mental hospital and the bohemian area of Parkdale, a resilient neighborhood that by some accounts was blighted but that was also the thriving center of an alternative cultural scene. As industrial employers left in the 1960s, warehouses filled with unsanctioned artist and craftsmen studios. In the most prominent example, at 48 Abell Street, estimates for the number of live-work units ranged between sixty and 100. This was well representative of the neighborhood, which had approximately 4 hectares of studio, light industrial and retail space, and 31 percent of the area's employment in 2005 associated with creative industries.[3]

In the late 1990s, eager to revitalize and densify, the city listed the area as a "regeneration zone" in its official plan. The zoning change allowed for intensification of development precisely on sites where industrial warehouses were converted into illegal artist live-work units (McLean, 2001). In the early 2000s, developers started buying land and buildings and embarked on one of the most intense densifications and gentrification processes in the entire city.

The artist community organized, and a group called Active 18 was formed by local bohemian business owners, a journalist, writers, artists, students, landscapers, architects, and planners. It held its first meeting at the historical Gladstone Hotel (which was also due for conversion to a hipster venue) in November 2005, with about sixty-five participants. The group's primary goal was preventing the demolition of 48 Abell, but they also sought landmark preservation of buildings and employment spaces. The City of Toronto feared losing excessive employment land due to the exorbitant number of applications for condo constructions and agreed to

[3] See Artscape's website at www.artscapediy.org/Case-Studies/Artscape-Triangle-Lofts.aspx.

designate the Queen West Triangle as an "employment district," thereby restricting residential development.

The growing group attended community meetings where participants displayed frustration about their lack of input in planning. In March 2006, Margie Zeidler, a founder of Active 18, sponsored a charrette (a meeting where architects draw and formalize planning ideas of lay participants). The event produced a booklet summarizing the group's position, which was presented to the public and the press, giving Active 18 a voice in the public debate (C. Campbell, n.d.). When the demolition of 48 Abell was approved in 2006, its prior artist residents staged a "Funeral for a Building" protest, showing that experiential tools were part of the toolkit of these activists. In the same period, Active 18 also retained a lawyer and began preparing for the OMB hearing scheduled for fall 2006. Excluded from discussions between developers and the city, Active 18 was provided in May with a copy of the city's position on the West Queen West redevelopment, in which the City proposed a "no-net-loss" of non-residential space, with a focus on creative employment. It thereby required developers to replace any displaced employment space as a compromise in exchange for zoning alterations.

In response, Active 18 prepared and circulated a list of amendments to several councillors, although it recognized the pivotal role of their ward representative: "We knew the 'rule' was that the local councillor had *the only vote that counted* but we made the rounds anyway [because] we felt we were unsuccessful in getting Adam [Giambrone, the councillor]'s serious attention" (C. Campbell, n.d., emphasis added).

Toronto's embrace of culture-led growth provided cultural producers not only with heightened status but also with financial and exclusionary pressures. Starting in 2000, several new iconic cultural buildings fulfilled "the dual tasks of promoting economic competitiveness and establishing a national reputation for knowledge-intensive creativity" (Jenkins, 2005, p. 174). Festivals further fed cultural consumption, although programming privileged high-profile artists to the outrage of grassroots organizations and artists whose funding was decimated under austerity (McLean, 2014). In 2003, the city council adopted a ten-year Culture Plan for the Creative City. Like in Buenos Aires, Madrid, and Seoul, the policy included an incubation program, which subsidized studio spaces to promote creative clusters, albeit requiring that artists justify their work by assessing its economic impact (Boudreau, Keil, & Young, 2009).

The emphasis on creative industries at the municipal level, and the preservation of employment land in the OMB hearing against the developers put both the city and Active 18 at odds with those whose priority focused on affordable housing. Their proposals included little subsidized housing and focused on preserving industrial buildings for creative live-work spaces. The lawyer who represented Active 18 explained how the interests of Active 18 and the city converged around the discourse of creative industries as economic engine:

> The first take on the "employment" issue by Active 18 was, it must be admitted, rather self-interested and reflected our arts-oriented membership. … We weren't opposed to new construction at 1171 Queen and 150 Sudbury [two condos]. But we wanted it to contain substantial light industrial space, which would be suitable for arts studios. And we wanted to save 48 Abell, which had the best studio space going. We put forward a target of eighty artist live-work spaces … While arts uses were the immediate focus of our efforts given the nature of the neighborhood, not to mention our membership, the broader question was space for the employment generally, light industry, creative industry, of which artists were/are a mere but important vibrant subset. Perhaps for some members this was purely tactical, but I believe most saw the big picture. The city needs jobs – and we are the local stalking horse, in this particular area. And as the city caught fire on the employment issue it was a good strategy to ride with them … [In the OMB hearings] the city's lawyer … added strong evidence from the city's economic development and cultural departments and then from noted urban sociologist, Meric Gertler, on the theory of the "creative city" and the importance of employment in the "creative sector," the importance of the arts to this sector and then, last but not least, the importance of the West Queen West Triangle as a hub of artistic activity. In this part of the OMB evidence we were happy observers of the city's excellent efforts.
>
> (C. Campbell, n.d.)

After the OMB granted developers demolition of 48 Abell and approval for the Triangle Lofts development, while requiring only a half-hectare park in development compensation, the City of Toronto took the unusual step of appealing the OMB ruling to the divisional court. The city subsequently settled with two of the three developers, but the divisional court agreed to hear the third case, which was against Urbancorp's 150 Sudbury site.

The prospect of a long legal battle provided incentives for compromise. A key actor in the negotiations between Active 18 and the developer was Artscape, a nonprofit urban development organization funded in 1986 with the goal of creating artists' hubs. Landscape had promoted similar projects in Queen Street West, opening the first legally zoned artist live-work project there in 1995 and was a critical player in culture-led gentrification. Its website described the chain-reaction effect on the neighborhood of the first Artscape project:

The project served as a significant catalyst in the revitalization of Queen Street, west of Trinity Bellwoods Park. Soon after, the Candy Factory Lofts project was launched across the street. Jamie Angel and other creative entrepreneurs began setting up shop, triggering an influx of galleries, cafés and specialty retail. The Drake and Gladstone Hotels opened in 2004 and 2006 respectively, providing a significant boost to the neighborhood's creative cachet. By 2005, when the Museum of Contemporary Canadian Art moved in, West Queen West had become the heart of Canada's cultural scene.[4]

As soon as Active 18, thanks to Artscape's intercession, formed a relationship with the developers, the local councillor turned very supportive and helped forge a Section 37 agreement. Initially, Active 18 leaders were offered street resurfacing by the developers – clearly something that they were not interested in. With the support of the local councillor, Active 18 was able to extract an agreement including three floors of the new eighteen-floor structure for permanent artist live-work spaces, of which forty-eight were destined for ownership and twenty for rental. The lofts were seen as a victory yet they excluded poor artists because rents were set at 80 percent of the average market rent for Toronto, and owners paid hefty condo fees.

In addition to the live-work spaces (known as the Artscape Triangle Lofts), the floors included an art gallery (Propeller), for a total of 5,200 square meters at 38 Abell Street. The deal also included the repurposing of a 100-year-old library as a state-of-the-art theater. The group influenced planning in several ways, for example by shaping the small public park required by the OMB hearing, which was designed to suit cultural producers, with café-style seating and lighting mounted on poles and timber columns to serve as a venue for arts events and performances.

Since then, Active 18 has been at the table for almost every Section 37 negotiation in their neighborhood. The group also organized candidate debates for the 2010 Ward 18 elections. It supported Ana Bailao, who, elected, in turn became a staunch ally.

With projects such as the Triangle Lofts, Artscape grew into a major force in the city's redevelopment, and its art-led gentrification process, building and managing several multi-tenant facilities focused on sustaining artistic hubs through the provision of below market live-work facilities. Thus, despite gentrification, some Toronto artists were able to ride the wave of creative industry. The beneficiaries were mostly established

[4] See Artscape's website at www.artscapediy.org/Case-Studies/Artscape-Triangle-Lofts.aspx.

institutions and artists (who are able to pay the "affordable" rates of units gained), rather than alternative or marginal artists and organizations. This kind of approach repeated throughout the city and became a model.

Several cases illustrate a pattern of Section 37 funding used to finance spaces for cultural producers. In 2010, the city allowed Daniels Corporation to raise the height restriction from 30 to 143 meters and thereby build on the lower portion of the condominium the Bell Lightbox, home of the Toronto International Film Festival, as well as galleries and classrooms. Daniels Corporation also proposed the City of Arts, in a 900-unit condo on the lakeshore, which hosts the Artscape headquarters, Manifesto (a nonprofit that runs a hip-hop festival), and the Remix Project (which assists marginalized youth). In 2012, the city granted Urbancorp a density bonus in exchange for the Toronto Media Arts Centre, which gave a nonprofit group of media-art organizations 3,500 square meters in the bottom floors of a condo development. (Active 18 later led protests for the implementation.) Urbancorp developed a similar arrangement with the Museum of Contemporary Canadian Art. In 2013, the Toronto Arts Council launched a pilot project called Space for Art aimed at offering affordable gallery and workshop spaces in Toronto condominiums; four such galleries opened in the first year alone.

In negotiating density bonuses, developers focused on cultural amenities (rather than social uses, such as childcare, employment centers, and affordable housing) because they offered a win-win. In addition to granting additional floors, the inclusion of artist spaces greatly enhanced condo branding. As the Urbancorp vice president explained, "Cultural impact to the area certainly affects our ability to sell and develop in a 'hip, cool' place, and additional density yields additional profits" (cited in Sandals, 2013).

This use of the funds created mutually beneficial connections between some groups of cultural producers and developers. As a result, some cultural producers were involved in boosterish plans and cultural events, which put a shiny veneer on the ongoing gentrification and undermined the voicing of concerns over displacement by vulnerable populations, as will be discussed in Chapter 10.

In Mimico, Active 18 and the cases discussed in the opening of the chapter, two dominant paths emerge in association with high impact: (1) the combination of resident mobilization, support by allies in the city council, and a left-wing higher executive; and (2) the combination of resident mobilization, support by allies in the city council, and a left-wing mayor. The analysis next illustrates paths to impact in the more adverse setting of right-wing alignment.

POLITICAL ALLIES LIMIT THE EFFECTS OF RIGHT-WING PARTISAN ALIGNMENT: ISTANBUL AND SEOUL

If groups have local politicians ready to defend them and mediate on their behalf with developers, then protesters can make modest gains and have an impact even in the most adverse judicial environment and political setting, where we observe partisan alignment on the right.

The cases in Istanbul, with its overlapping national, metropolitan, and district partisanship under the conservative AKP starkly illustrate the power of both partisan alignment and council allies. In Sulukule and Gezi Park, protesters faced a set of executives strongly determined to pursue redevelopment, regardless of resistance. Sulukule was razed. In the wake of the protests, Turkey's top administrative court blocked the Gezi redevelopment; yet the success was short-lived: In 2015, the court reversed its decision following an appeal by the municipality of Istanbul.

A different outcome was observed in Fener and Balat, due to high support in the local council as well as the lower symbolic profile of the redevelopment. There, the same partisan divisions that created dissent within FEBAYDER also allowed individual organization members to lobby with their respective political parties and gain the support of a large number of opposition parties, among them the Nationalist Movement Party (Milliyetçi Hareket Partisi [MHP]), the Great Unity Party (Büyük Birlik Partisi [BBP]), the Felicity Party (Saadet), and the Republican People's Party (Cumhuriyet Halk Partisi [CHP]). This broad lobbying was very impactful: When the Fener and Balat redevelopment project came to the Fatih council, the vote was partisan, with twenty-four councillors from the AKP in favor, and *all* thirteen opposition councillors against (interview with Çiğdem Şahin, by email, December 18, 2018).

At the same time, the partisan alignment between local and national executives was extremely strong. With adroit multilevel engagement, protesters sought to enlist *national* institutions *outside of the executive* in their struggle against the municipality, invoking the support of the National Committee of the International Council on Monuments and Sites (Turkmen, 2014). However, this body lacked the political clout to oppose policies supported by the government. In 2012, protesters, represented in court by the Chamber of Architects, managed to halt the redevelopment on the basis of heritage conservation, but the national government circumvented the court's decision by issuing an "urgent expropriation" procedure. Since that approach is reserved to emergencies of national interest, the courts blocked the expropriations in 2013. Following this ruling (and possibly concerned to lose support in an AKP stronghold), the government sidelined the redevelopment project and moved on to other areas in a significant and highly unusual success for these Fatih residents.

* * *

In Seoul, national and metropolitan governments aligned for nearly the entire period under review. Two mayors from the conservative Grand National Party succeeded each other in the 2000s. Mayor Lee Myung-bak served from 2002 to 2006, and became national president from 2008 to 2013. Oh Se-hoon succeeded Lee at the mayoralty in 2006 and served until 2011.

Although during the period 2007–2011 both presidency and mayoralty were focused on raising Seoul's global status through redevelopment and branding, district conditions varied, and affected the impact of protest. The cases below, Duriban and Myeong-dong, illustrate how similar strategies and levels of mobilization in two related and nearly simultaneous campaigns nonetheless might produce different outcomes – largely due to local political variations and contexts. The Hongdae district, home of the Duriban restaurant case, leaned more progressive, which meant that protesters had better access to institutional allies. Duriban restaurant owners were successful in mobilizing youth to defend their protest squat for over a year and, with the mediation of leftist politicians from the local district, were able to corner the developer into acquiescing to their compensation requests. Upon victory, protesters immediately moved to Myeong-dong, a commercial district facing a similar case of eviction. They initiated the same mobilization strategy. However, protesters lacked a local political actor willing to mediate on their behalf, and this was revealed to be vital: With no such constraint, developers violently crushed the squat.

In a third case in Seoul, the artist community Mullae Art Village, succeeded in mobilizing popular support through experiential tools and obtaining political support by entering friendly political institutions and lobbying from within. Momentously, they persuaded both audiences – the general public and politicians – that the neighborhood encapsulated the essence of the cultural industry growth recipe, thus turning a discourse that usually promotes displacement into one that legitimized the status quo. The result was the surprising survival of two vulnerable communities in the neighborhood: a metal workshop district and the hippest avant-garde artist community in the metropolis.

* * *

The repertoire of protest has changed radically over the past two decades in Korea. Evictee protests from the 1980s deployed risky militant demonstrations, picketing, and violent confrontations, thus attracting only the most determined participants. The Yongsan case showed how reliance on the militant legacy proved counterproductive (see Chapter 6). In contrast, recent social movements have taken the character of mass rallies, with civic experiences such as candlelight vigils or festive congregations (M.-R. Cho, 2008; Kang, 2012). The shift conferred political influence on those best suited to devise powerful social experiences – above all, artists.

The case of the Duriban restaurant presents one of the few instances of recent urban redevelopment in South Korea that was peacefully resolved with the protection of tenants' rights (Kee, Kim, & Lee, 2014). It is important that the restaurant was located in Hongdae. This iconic neighborhood in Korean popular culture is known as a district of artists, designers, musicians, street art, and club culture. It lies east of Hongik University, one of the city's hotbeds of progressive politics, in the district of Mapo-gu. Within the district, the area of Hongdae discussed here largely overlaps with the official neighborhood of Seogyo-dong, with a surface of 1.6 square kilometers, a population of 29,098 (resulting in a density of 17,852, slightly above Seoul's average) and a renters' rate of 55 percent (against a city average of 51 percent). In the 1980s and 1990s, graduates began settling in this area, inexpensive at the time, and turned garages and basements into art studios (Y.-J. Lee, 2011). Single-story tile-roof houses from the 1950s dominated the area, and intimate courtyards and narrow alleys encouraged deep bonds between artists, students, and musicians.

In the 1990s, the emphasis moved from art to music as club-owners became the trendsetters of the underground culture. Hongdae became famous nationally as a center of indie rock when it hosted Korea's first Street Punk Festival in 1996. Hongdae also hosts some of the leading street events in Seoul, such as the Free Market (a weekend arts-and-crafts market), the annual Street Art Festival of Public Art, and the theater

Fringe Festival. Around 2000, the electronic music scene grew and young people began leaving the center to attend rave parties in the city's outskirts. So, in 2001, a Hongdae entrepreneur created Club Day – a monthly event in which participants could gain entrance to several participating Hongdae bars for the price of a single ticket under $10. This event succeeded wildly and initially helped the unique, small bars that it was intended to support. Yet it also revealed the commercial potential of the area, at a time when corporate control of the nightlife economy was gentrifying markets and marginalizing alternative local development (Hollands & Chatterton, 2003). Over time, the monthly hordes of rowdy clubbers undermined the cultural character of the neighborhood and accelerated large-scale commercial redevelopment, especially of multistory mega-clubs and chain stores (Youn, 2007).

Despite higher rents and commercial redevelopment, the area remained a cultural point of reference in Korea for several reasons. Hongik University, with its emphasis on the arts, continued to draw students eager to settle in the area and supported significant infrastructure for cultural entrepreneurs, such as publishing houses, architecture and design offices, and exhibition spaces. Moreover, in contrast to other universities in downtown Seoul, Hongik was surrounded by relatively inexpensive areas beyond Hongdae, so higher rents pushed artists to the fringes of that neighborhood – but not so far that their networks were broken. The strong and numerous ties between artists, small-scale entrepreneurs, and students in the community produced a distinct awareness about the neighborhood, exemplified by the local magazine, *Street H*, one of the only independent, free monthlies in Korea. This awareness created fertile territory for resistance.

Also in Hongdae, on the opposite side of Hongik University, is Seongmisan (also known as Sungmisan). Seongmisan was an innovative "village community," renowned for having developed a system of citizen mobilization, participation, and cooperation, which led to significant achievements, such as communal childcare, neighborhood schools, elderly-care facilities, and several cooperatives (O. Kim, 2013; K.-O. Park & Ryu, 2012). Seongmisan promoted a new approach to sustainable, local economic development (H. T. Lee & Jung, 2012). With an emphasis on "folk knowledge" (Križnik, 2013) and on the need to harmonize "social and economic processes for vulnerable populations" (TaeJeong Park, 2013), the community fought back against global-city aspirations (Min et al., 2011) and called for development that was participatory and firmly rooted in preexisting local economic realities. Seongmisan would prove an important precedent to subsequent resistance against redevelopment, as we will see.

Hongdae dramatically differed from Yongsan because it enjoyed a place-based identity that spanned across many groups in the community and thus provided a solid basis for resistance. Hongdae was "a place of art, youth, and vitality" (Kee et al., 2014), which imbued sites of contention with a narrative and meaning that went well beyond physical buildings.

Duriban's small victory would be heralded by many as "miraculous" (*H-Street*, 2014), and pointed to a distinctly new approach to protest against redevelopment in Seoul. In 2007, the city block where Duriban was located was designated as a development zone and sold to GS Engineering and Construction, which planned to build a new station for the airport subway line. Duriban's owner Ahn Jong-yuh and her husband, novelist Yoo Chae-rim (both in their early fifties), had a past as activists in the democratization movement, and he had been in prison during the dictatorship. They acquired the restaurant in 2005 and invested in it their savings and a loan, for a total of over $100,000. In 2008, the couple was offered about $2,700 for relocation costs and ordered to vacate the building immediately. They fought back in the most inauspicious of circumstances: Contrary to Yongsan, the planned development of Duriban was entirely private, with no public-interest component, and this setting protected tenants the least.

Local, leftist political allies played a role right at the start. Together with eleven other commercial tenants, the couple obtained support from the Democratic Labor Party and formed a committee to pursue adequate compensation through litigation (interview with Yoon Sun-gil, district representative from the Democratic Labor Party, Seoul, September 18, 2012). However, compensation for commercial renters was inadequately protected in Korea (see Chapter 6), and the legal strategy proved grueling. The lawsuit lasted two years, during which time most tenants gave up their claims, until only Duriban was left. Apart from the three-story building that hosted the restaurant, the only other standing buildings on the block were a traditional house (*hanok*), which protesters wanted to preserve, and a police station.

GS hired a "phantom" company called Namjeon DNC for demolition and evictions, a customary move to avoid bad publicity. This company in turn subcontracted eviction to one of the most infamous eviction companies, known for its violence and brutality, called Samojin. On Christmas Eve 2009, a team of thirty hired thugs attacked the restaurant, dragging out customers, Yoo Chae-rim, a part-time worker, and the cook. Eviction attacks were common during the holidays, when supporters were usually with their families and less available to help. The thugs destroyed the interior of the restaurant and other floors and removed all furniture and appliances. Then they installed metal fences around the building, blocking the entrance. Desperate, Ahn returned the following night, and began a sit-in that would last 531 days. The initial four occupiers were convinced they would be the victims of another Yongsan tragedy. Yoo, who worked in a publishing company, gave up his job so they could survive the sit-in on his retirement pension. News about their situation spread by word of mouth and through social-networking sites, where Duriban was dubbed "Little Yongsan" (A. Lee, 2011) and came to symbolize a campaign to strengthen tenants' rights in the aftermath of the Yongsan tragedy.

Publicizing the event was key because the couple could only keep thugs away by constantly having a large number of people on the premises. Squatters occupied the ground floor of the three-story building to safeguard access and ensure their gas and oil heaters were visible through the windows, to discourage attacks. They draped a banner on the building reading: "People live here. So, don't kill this place" (S. Park, 2011). More banners decried GS Construction, with the idea that if anything happened observers would point their fingers at the construction company, tarnishing its brand (Karl, 2011). Thugs occupied a high floor on a nearby building, to keep an eye on the site, and infiltrated events to gather information that might facilitate an attack (interview with Az, Duriban and Myeong-dong organizer, Seoul, September 15, 2012).

To attract large crowds, protesters organized a wide range of arts and cultural activities. First, Yoo's fellow writers came to offer their support. Indie musicians Hahn Vad and Dan Pyun-sun held a solidarity concert and were soon joined by other local bands. What started as a single event mushroomed into nearly 200 concerts over the course of a year. Participating in the protest was significantly risky as artists lacked protest experience and feared losing expensive musical instruments in case of an attack. Squatters largely relied on an anti-violence manual, recognizing that thugs were clearly superior in violent struggle.

Starting in February 2010, a schedule began taking shape, with music shows on Fridays and Saturdays, and documentary screenings on Tuesdays. Then, Hahn Vad and Dan Pyun-sun suggested a large concert to celebrate May 1st, with fifty-one bands and the catchy title "51+." Over three weeks, volunteers cleaned up and remodeled the building to stage the festival. Early sales tickets were modestly priced at 5,100 Won (about $5). Musicians issued press releases and attracted mass media to the festival. The festival had sixty-two bands and lasted for two days. It was a huge success: Over 2,500 people attended (A. Lee, 2011), and it became a yearly event in different locations (including in Mullae Art Village in 2013).

The festival's success was a turning point: It consolidated the cultural strategy as a completely new approach to protest:

> At first, the Duriban people tried to fight with [support of] the Federation against Housing Demolition but as time went on they collided over the strategy. The Federation wanted to stage militant and formal demonstrations; their attitude was "We lead the fight, and you follow; you don't know anything about eviction struggles so you can learn from us." That attitude created conflicts. The concerts were something totally new for them. In the preceding struggles, concerts and such activities were supportive, they backed the struggle, they were not the core of the struggle. Here, music was the core of the struggle. The Federation did not feel comfortable with that and was awkward towards the musicians. The activists from the Federation did not fit well with the Duriban activists, so they parted ways ... When the Federation left, a unique form of struggle started. We were all by ourselves, no organization to direct us. It was a constant PR battle; keeping attention and attracting people. We constantly PRed on Twitter, on Facebook, in progressive newspapers and magazines.
>
> (interview with Az, September 15, 2012)

Several interviews with key participants corroborated this version of events. The schedule became much more crowded, with concerts on Mondays and Fridays, movie screening on Tuesdays, candlelight services on Thursdays, and poetry and language courses on Sundays. Additional events were scheduled irregularly (Kee et al., 2014). A committee for daily activities met in plenary sessions on Sundays twice monthly to discuss programming, but the emphasis was on openness: "As long as people were not against Duriban, they were not turned away. There was something for everybody, whether you liked music or wanted to listen to a seminar or were religious. We simply provided space. It was a platform for self-expression" (interview with Pyun-sun Dan, September 15, 2012). As a result, Duriban became a cultural hot spot, much like other sites where experiential tools were deployed. Above all, witnesses' statements paralleled those from the Tel Aviv encampments, pointing to a transformative experience of freedom and self-expression:

> People became used to thinking [that in Duriban] there is a distinct air and a special atmosphere of freedom because there you could do almost anything. It became a cultural hot spot. People were attracted to go and hang out because it

gave them confidence that they could do something special, have an impact. They all knew that what they were doing would not scare the construction companies away in the long term. They were realistic. But they also knew that what they were doing was right in their conscience and it was fun to do so at the same time. I felt freedom there. There was this atmosphere ... when I went there I could feel something special.

(Interview with Az, September 15, 2012)

The struggle was governed by the Duriban Committee, which – contrary to the free spirit of the occupation – was small, hierarchical, and institutional. It was comprised of the couple-owners; the secretary of the writers committee (who mostly lent his prestige); and a handful of individuals with networks and experience with eviction struggles. Clerics played a key role, with both the minister from Yoo's church and the minister leading "Christians Lighting Candles," a religious group particularly active against evictions, which participated also in Yongsan and Myeong-dong (Ok & Kim, 2013). They were joined by a leading organizer from the Seongmisan community and the anarchist Jo-yak Gol (who advised the couple on resistance and legal strategy because the couple faced criminal charges and a trial for destruction of property, obstruction of business, and illegal trespass). The final two members of the committee were from political parties: Yoon Sun-gil from the Democratic Labor Party and Jeong Kyong-sup from the New Progressive Party (a splinter of the Democratic Labor Party founded in 2008). The Democratic Labor Party had seats in the national legislature, and the New Progressive Party, further to the left, had one seat in the Mapo-gu council. These politicians acted as private citizens rather than official party representatives, yet they used their networks and influence to mediate between the district government and protesters as well as to communicate with developers (interview with Jo-yak Gol, September 17, 2012).

The backroom work of the committee contrasted starkly with the celebratory atmosphere of the occupation. While event programming was relatively free, all aspects of communication and archiving were monitored. Media outlets were tightly controlled. Only committee members could post on the website, and Yoo wrote daily updates and journal entries on the community page, which archived the struggle. (Yoo later also published a book.) Duriban hosted tours from nearby elementary and high schools, as classes would visit to learn about displacement and gentrification. Funding for the occupation came mostly from donations and fund-raising through concerts and events. The couple also issued bonds, promising participants that once they reopened the restaurant in a new location they could redeem the bonds for the same amount in noodles.

After Namjeon DNC cut electricity to the building on December 24, 2009, Duriban reconnected it through a neighboring construction site, operated by workers who sympathized with the protest (A. Lee, 2011). In July 2010, Namjeon DNC again cut electricity, and the national human-rights council ignored multiple complaints from protesters. So the Duriban committee next turned to the district government and held a two-week sit-in in the Mapo-gu offices, which prompted the district to supply an electric generator. Protesters deemed this contribution insufficient and remained critical of the district government, which they believed did "not see Duriban's success as positive because they feared this kind of activism would discourage investment in the area" (interview with Pyun-sun Dan, September 15, 2012). However small, the gesture by the district office pointed to a far more cooperative stance than usual in this kind of struggle and indicated that even a minor opening can help protesters, if local allies can be identified.

In fall 2010, the eviction company realized that the sit-in would continue indefinitely and recommended that GS switch from intimidation to negotiation. In another move that indicated the tacit support of local authorities, negotiations were held in the Mapo-gu office, which amounted to a significant commitment given that negotiations continued from October 2010 to June 2011. Committee members obtained what they wanted, which was enough funding to open a similar restaurant in a nearby location and cover legal fees associated with the negotiation.

Duriban's triumph might seem small and isolated. Yet a peaceful resolution in favor of evicted commercial tenants was unprecedented and received considerable media attention. The story was captured in a feature-length documentary released in 2014. Coverage on the front page of the leading national daily *The Kyunghyang Shinmun* on June 9, 2011, stated that

> the resolution of this incident has been accompanied by predictions that Duriban will become a milestone in the quest to secure rights for tenants in commercial properties ... This will remain as a precedent that shows that development must take place in a way that guarantees residential and survival rights within communities.
>
> (*The Kyunghyang Shinmun*, 2011)

Several factors contributed to Duriban's success. The sustained and extensive mobilization was critical because over time it signaled that a forced eviction was impossible without major collateral damage, thereby inducing the developer to negotiate. The exceptional mobilization was reached not because participants wanted to aid two restaurant owners but rather because the struggle was construed as one in which all artists and youth were targeted, due to gentrification in Hongdae. Mobilization even reached participants who were not aware of the conflict because Duriban had turned into the "cool" place to be in Seoul. The strategy of mobilization avoided evoking pity; an organizer commented that,

> the strategy with a cultural core, with music and culture and constant PR, was unprecedented because it erased pity out of the struggle ... Most of the people who visited, did so not *for* Duriban: they did their own stuff there. I assure you we did not do it out of sympathy.
>
> (interview with Az, September 15, 2012)

So joyful and exciting was Duriban that even the owners met victory and the end of the squat with a little sadness (A. Lee, 2011).

Existing research corroborates the role of culture in Duriban's protest mobilization, arguing that this case presents a fundamentally new approach to protest in Korea (Kee et al., 2014; Ok & Kim, 2013). However, scholarly analysis underestimates the role of leadership in Duriban's success. For example, Kee et al. argue that, contrary to Korean culture, "the Duriban community structure was decentralized, non-hierarchical or horizontal, and informal" (Kee et al., 2014). My interviews caution against this interpretation. True, a feeling of extreme freedom at the site was critical to youth mobilization; cultural programming was relatively spontaneous; and everybody could participate in the plenary sessions. Yet the Duriban committee took all key legal and strategic decisions behind closed doors, with a leadership that was emphatically not horizontal or freewheeling. The setup allowed a specific group of institutional players – including leftist politicians – to play a key mediating role with authorities and the developer. The absence of these pivotal political allies in the subsequent struggle of Myeong-dong, as we will next see, contributed to its quick demise.

* * *

Within days of the Duriban victory, protesters transferred its networks and strategies to Café Mari in Myeong-dong. It is hard to overstate the difference between Hongdae and Myeong-dong as neighborhoods. The Seoul official tourist site describes Myeong-dong as Seoul's "shopping mecca" and "a must-see for tourists." From early morning until late night, the area teems with visitors and locals, drawn especially by its famous fashion and cosmetics stores. Walking through the neighborhood is a sensory experience, as merchants compete for customers by blaring dance music, and a wealth of stalls sell everything from street food to souvenirs. Myeong-dong is among the priciest real estate in Seoul. The neighborhood is part of the district of Jung-gu, which in 2011 contributed 15 percent to Seoul's regional economic product – vastly more than the 4 percent contribution of Duriban's district Mapo-gu. A center of commerce, banking and culture in an area of just under one square kilometer, it had an official population of only 4,099 (of which 58 percent were renters) but a daytime population of 1.5 to 2 million. Dominated by glass-and-steel high-rises, the area still had pockets of tiny back alleys with low-rise buildings that housed basic industrial production and services as well as eateries serving the local population. Café Mari was noteworthy for its very close proximity to the Catholic Myeong-dong Cathedral, long considered a center of political and labor protest as well as a sanctuary for protesters.

Café Mari's block was designated for a twenty-six-story financial center building, and on April 2, 2011, fourteen commercial tenants (bars, restaurants, and various shops) were handed eviction notices by Daewoo Construction and Industrial Bank of Korea, with the customary compensation of about $2,700, and told to evacuate by May. The district government refused to intervene. Developers undermined protest by offering advantageous conditions to a single household within a group of dissenting evictees, thereby turning them against each other (Jeon, 2011).

On June 15, tenants began a sit-in. The demolition company cut water and electricity services, but courts refused to intervene. On June 19, armed thugs attacked the sit-in. They wrapped participants in blankets and threw them on the street, injuring four people. The news hit social media and went viral, attracting sympathizers from Duriban and beyond. Organizers developed a full program of activities, and some interviews refer to individual events that were even more successful than in Duriban, such as a music festival that attracted 3,000 people. One estimate puts the total number of concerts organized in the brief period of this struggle at nearly 150. In order to enlarge the space and make space for activities, protesters tore down the walls of two neighboring evicted establishments (a space used as a dormitory and a second space used for seminars), and Café Mari hosted concerts.

The protest surpassed Duriban in its spirit of egalitarianism and collective participation. Plenary sessions were held weekly and covered all aspects of the protest. At the same time, due to the threat of violence, protesters also embraced defensive militancy, and at the end of June founded the Myeong-dong Liberation Front (MDLF).

The dense calendar of activities was unable to prevent attacks. After an assault on July 18, between 100 and 200 thugs (depending on the reports) congregated at the site in the early morning hours of August 3 and brutally charged protesters. At the time, few people were at the sit-in because protesters had received an emergency call and had raced to assist an eviction-related attack in a shantytown at 266 PoiDong, in the southern district of Gangnam. (It is likely that the eviction companies coordinated the attacks on Myeong-dong and 266 PoiDong.) Just a handful of protesters were left at Café Mari, aside from tenants. Once thugs stormed the place, squatters called for reinforcements, and about 100 people came back from PoiDong to defend the sit-in, to no avail. Footage and photos reveal extreme violence, yet the police failed to respond to emergency calls from protesters. Protesters again resorted to music, staging a concert during the day to state their resistance and coordinate a counterattack. Fighting continued until the morning of August 4, and involved about 100 protesters and 200 eviction personnel.

In the negotiations that followed, protesters agreed to give the construction company access to the redevelopment area so long as they could remain in Café Mari, which was deemed a safer protest site than the small back alleys because it faced a street with a lot of foot traffic. For some weeks, experiential tools continued to be deployed with the connected goals of maximizing participation and preventing attacks. Despite exhaustion from the fighting, the café continued to be the site of literary seminars, photographic exhibitions, solidarity concerts, a flea market, and artistic events such as costume parades around the neighborhood to denounce the redevelopment project. The sit-in was intensely documented on Facebook and Korean social media, with daily footage and photos. On any given day, about thirty protesters mingled inside and outside the café, and sympathizers offered services such as hairdressing on the busy sidewalk.

Yet, despite appeals to normalcy, young protesters were constantly on edge for a new attack. In early September, taking advantage of a sparse number of protesters onsite, construction workers managed to secure in place a demolition crane, undermining further resistance. Protesters abandoned Café Mari on September 8. Witnesses indicate that the tenants received a slightly improved compensation but not sufficient to relocate in the same area (MDLF & Karl, 2011).

Comparing Duriban and Myeong-dong highlights the important interaction of place, organizational approach, and leftist allies. Due to the character and legacy of participation in Hongdae, Duriban was able to elicit broad support, mobilizing networks of artists who were also threatened by redevelopment. While Hongdae hosted both artists and youth, Myeong-dong is a densely commercial and transit area that did not generate a deep sense of belonging. Neighbors did not support the struggle as they did in Duriban. Instead, in Myeong-dong, evictees were seen as isolated victims. However, interviews indicate that the deployment of experiential tools and mobilization levels were not appreciably below those in Duriban. What made the biggest difference in impact was the lack of formal organizational and institutional allies.

In Myeong-dong, tenants had neither protest experience nor a systemic understanding of their struggle, and this hampered their ability to mobilize institutional allies (interview with Eun-jung Lee, September 15, 2012). The organization lacked a steering committee. Instead, a general assembly made all decisions. This meant that newcomers overwhelmed the debate with issues not directly related to the sit-in:

> Issues like ageism, feminism, hierarchy in Duriban were not problematized. But in Myeong-dong these became key issues that were much discussed. It was a distraction from the focus of the protest. Communication with the evictees got harder by the minute. [In Duriban] there was a hierarchy. Sometimes requests to avoid those topics would come directly from above. The struggle lasted a long time, and agreements were in place about what not to discuss to avoid conflict.
>
> (interview with Pyun-sun Dan, September 15, 2012)

Leftist parties were also absent from the district government and thus not influential in the area. Thus, party representatives, who played a key role in Duriban, were absent in Myeong-dong, and there were no institutional allies available for support or mediation.

* * *

In the final case in Seoul, commercial tenants (artists and, to a lesser degree, metalworkers) resisted redevelopment and displacement by lobbying and networking with authorities. They promoted the neighborhood in its current form as a vital asset to the city and an outstanding expression of "cultureconomics," the development strategy envisioned by the Seoul metropolitan government (as well as the national government, presided over by ex-Seoul mayor Lee).

Mullae-dong is an official neighborhood covering about 1.5 square kilometers in Youngdeungpo-gu district, in the west of Seoul. The area did not face the same real-estate price escalation as other cases yet had many pockets considered ripe for redevelopment due to their excellent access to the city. A bird's-eye view of the neighborhood would reveal blocks of residential high-rises dominating the landscape, with large commercial developments and glass office towers lining the main avenues, and a park for middle-class residents framing the subway station. According to the 2011 Census, density was 22,043 residents per square kilometer (against the city average of 17,397), with a renters' rate of 53 percent (against a city average of 51 percent). The largely residential area contributed 8 percent to Seoul's regional economic product.

Yet interspersed between these blocks were several pockets of low-rise and low-income commercial and residential areas. The two areas contrasted dramatically, one exemplifying modern Seoul, the second conjuring a bygone era with increasingly rare, socially dense communities in alleys lined with one-story brick buildings, small and rundown wholesale stores, and occasional manufacturing shops. A clear example of this typology was the concentration of metal workshops spanning north of Dorim-ro, over about 4.5 hectares, which hosts the case described here.

Despite its unassuming presence, the area had a rich past. Along the first railroad in Korea, connecting Seoul and Incheon in 1899, Mullae-dong was first a textile center (the term Mullae refers to its spinning wheels) and then became the main site for heavy industrial war supplies during the Japanese occupation (Jang, 2011). Before the 1970s, it hosted the South Korean film industry. In the late 1970s, it became a core steel-production center of more than eighty independent factories that served the industrial giants behind the Korean miracle growth. In the mid 1980s, steel demand surged, fed by construction and manufacturing in preparation for the 1988 Olympics Games. Since then, the area had declined. With the 1997 Asian financial crisis, many smaller workshops closed, while larger factories moved to better facilities on the periphery (Hong, 2012). A barren and desolate atmosphere beset the neighborhood, now dwarfed by surrounding high-rise buildings and apartment complexes. This left a reservoir of centrally located workspace – in poor condition but with very low rents. Around 2005, artists began flowing into the area, displaced by increasing rents in Hongdae and lured by the new theater district of Daehagno, just ten minutes away by subway. The artist community grew dramatically over the course of a couple of years and within a decade gained recognition, legitimacy, and, with that, surprising tenacity.

By 2010, this area of Mullae-dong had over 175 ironworks workshops, over 60 of which were occupied by over 170 artists (Reigh & Choi, 2012). The artists, mostly in their twenties and thirties, used the space as a combination of living, creative work, and community space (H.-J. Kim, 2013). Artworks spanned from paintings and photographs to installation art, sculpture, design, illustration, video art, calligraphy, film animation, and other genres of visual art, including dance, theater, street performances, and traditional arts. Some of the most visible and symbolically poignant artworks involved ironwork.

Over time, artists developed a rich array of activities with an increasing focus on public art, performance, and exhibition. At any corner, desolate elements of the industrial past were rejuvenated with original interventions, such as a seemingly impromptu photographic exhibition in an old set of mailboxes or stacked steel bars colorfully painted. Most artists started working after sundown, and to the visitor wandering through the alleys that had been empty during daytime hours these interventions appeared like anonymous place-appropriations. The result was an unexpected combination of post-industrial desolation and playful charm.

Most spaces were multifunctional and operated out of the second floors of buildings, above closed foundries. A leading example was Lab39, a key organizing force in Mullae. The director, Kang Kim, explained they opened the center "to show the power of art in the gentrification phenomenon" and to maintain a production core in this "consumption city" (interview with Kim Kang, activist, artist, and Lab39 founder and director, Seoul, September 21, 2012). Venues often combined exhibition space with outreach programs. For example, the art venue Jaemi Gongjakso had moved from Hongdae and offered exhibition space, small indie rock concerts, cultural workshops, poetry readings, and a coffee bar. The Gallery Jungdabang Project served as a café and hosted events such as pottery for children, wall painting, and wine tasting. Other spaces, in addition to artistic events, specialized in hosting indie musicians, such as the Alternative Space "Moon" (Hyesun, 2015).

In 2007, art studios opened to the public through a program of exhibitions and public art. The main outreach event was the Mullae Art Festival, held annually for two weeks in August since 2007, with attractions ranging from video-art installations to performances such as street dancing and musical concerts as well as audience participation activities. In 2008, the number of participating studios increased, together with the influx of visitors. Collaboration with the local community grew deeper through the introduction of programs linking artists and local residents, such as the Mullae Public Art Project and the Gaenaribozzim (backpack) Art Education Program aimed at students.

In 2009, programs were expanded and diversified. Initiatives to attract foreign artists turned Mullae-dong into a key node in the artist network of Seoul. Outreach was extended with a second edition of the Mullae Public Art Project, but also the creation of the public Rooftop Art Gallery "The City Belongs to Us"; programs titled Boundless Art Project and Art Play; and a further program intended for students called BanzzakBanzzak (Sparkling) Art School Program (Jang, 2011). In 2010, new nonprofit entertainment spaces opened, including art cafés. Artists also created the agricultural group "Mullae City Farmer," the cinema "Cine Moon," the "Mullae Arts Day," in addition to regularly held "Arts Market." The urban agriculture initiative "Mullae Gardens" promoted the combination of ecology and art, the autonomous creation of alternative energy, and the promotion of fair trade (Reigh & Choi, 2012). The outreach program offered a space to spread shared values and participate. It provided innovative economic experiments and led to broad discussion of social issues. All initiatives were characterized by horizontal organization, with a flexible leadership that rotated depending on the project.

The Mullae Art Village also had an active online and web presence, as well as info-points where visitors could collect printed materials to guide them through the industrial maze in search of art studios and event locations. The evening calendar was packed with exhibitions, vernissages, installations, and street performances. Documentation was key, and not only online. Writers composed the periodic *Mullae Culture Magazine*, featuring news of art events and distributed freely in the neighborhood and online. A Mullae Arts Archive was established in 2011 to document the community, under threat of displacement due to redevelopment.

Artists connected through active, robust networks both inside and outside Mullae (Hong, 2012; Jang, 2011). Through surveys and comparative analysis, H.-J. Kim (2013) finds that Mullae hosted exceptionally dense networks, both within and across specialty clusters, as well as with artists outside of Mullae. However, at the time of fieldwork in 2012, Mullae still lacked an organized connection between artists and residents. Both groups were almost exclusively renters, yet ironworkers were not interested in the artists' arrival initially. Over time, relations developed based on everyday interaction, including sports. Contact took place also at work, because artists working with metal sought specialized workers' machinery and technical support. As a result, ties deepened – and, in fact, exhibitions were often hosted in the factories (interview with Beomchul Kwon, researcher, Institute of Arts and Urbanism, Seoul, September 20, 2012). Driven by a concern about redevelopment, in 2012 activist artists (in particular those based at Lab39) tried to form a neighborhood committee composed of both artists and commercial tenants. However, few commercial tenants were interested in a formal organization.

During this grassroots experiment, the Seoul metropolitan government threatened displacement in several ways. Yet, with experiential tools, resistance turned from confrontational to preemptive and was fought through discourse rather than protest. In so doing, Mullae artists took experiential tools – and their ability to define meaning, authenticity, and thereby legitimacy – to their logical extreme.

The most direct threat was a revision to the urban planning ordinance, passed by the city council in 2008, which softened semi-industrial zoning and thus quickened fears of high-rise residential redevelopment. The mayoral administration favored maintaining semi-industrial zoning and even introducing high-tech to the area, but the city council was instead eager to bring in more profitable residential developments.

Between 2008 and 2010, through public art, symposia, and scholarly reports, artists mobilized mass media and public support to oppose redevelopment, aiming their outreach efforts specifically at government representatives. Their research effort intended to build arguments to protect the area from redevelopment, and one member of the standing research group was exclusively dedicated to the development of political relationships and personal connections (interview with Beomchul Kwon, September 20, 2012).

At the same time, an initiative came about that at first seemed ideal to promote the Mullae Art Village but in fact profoundly undermined its delicate ecology. The Seoul metropolitan government, to recall, had identified several cultural hot spots and opened ten new Seoul Art Space facilities throughout the city to nurture creative industries. Significantly called the Mullae Art Factory, the Seoul Art Space facility in Mullae aimed to intervene in the vivacious artistic milieu of Mullae Art Village, to support artistic production, and to facilitate exchange and interaction with both government and market, with repeated emphasis on the "creative cultural city," and the "creative industry." The four-story building, located about 500 meters from the village core, housed various facilities for creating and presenting artistic output, such as a common workshop, a multipurpose theater space, a recording studio, a video-editing studio, a large gallery space, dance studios, and a seminar room. The top floor had hostel rooms and lounges.

The facility was intended as a stronghold of cultural production in south and west Seoul. It developed several programs, such as the Incubator Program for artists, international exchanges, and hip-sounding initiatives such as Project MAP (Mullae Art Plus) and Project MEET (Mullae! Emerging & EnergeTic).

The Mullae Art Factory further legitimized Mullae as an art area and brought additional visitors by commodifying not only art but the community itself, in the name of "cultureconomics." It was developed with very limited involvement by the preexisting artists' community, and relations with Mullae artists were tense because they saw the Art Factory as exceedingly bureaucratic and a direct product of city government. (An attempt to form a unifying steering committee failed in 2013.) Its explicit market orientation undermined the deeply alternative, progressive, and anarchic community of artists.

In the face of these threats, artists began to resist redevelopment by infiltrating the bureaucracy. They influenced policy-making from within institutions rather than opposed adverse outcomes from outside the halls of power. The co-director of Lab39, Kim Youn Hoan, was a clear example:

> The city accepted some members [of Mullae Art Village] to assist in the design of the Art Factory. For example, Kim Youn Hoan was invited on the taskforce for the entire city for Seoul Art Space program and Culture and Art Department. In return, he got more information about what the city is really trying to do with this area. The urban planning department seeks to develop and the cultural department seeks to protect. Kim is now an insider, and meets all these people including in city council. ... This networking put us in a good position to resist redevelopment ... Our strategy was to become an insider. By becoming insiders, the entire area of Mullae [not just the area surrounding the Art Factory building] was then recognized as art district. Now we can protect the entire community. This is a very different approach from NYC or Beijing, where artists were pushed out. We want to control the system we live in, and we realized we needed to infiltrate. The difference between here and Duriban is that we had time. In Duriban, evictions were already taking place, but we could negotiate during the project.
>
> (interview with Kim Kang, September 21, 2012)

The turn to the progressive left in the municipal government with Mayor Park Won-soon, who assumed office at the end of 2011, supported this strategy. Mayor Park, a lawyer and social-justice activist, campaigned on issues of displacement, poverty, and gentrification. When elected, he halted several important development proposals across the entire city and introduced progressive land-use preferences, such as urban farming. These values created a propitious climate for the Mullae artist community, which in 2012 succeeded in excluding Mullae Art Village from the redevelopment area, due to its high concentration of cultural production.

However, significant challenges remained. Commercialization intensified, and real-estate pressure increased (J.-H. Lee, 2015). Some artists began guided tours to the neighborhood, rooftop dinners, and music parties for tourists and advertised online to attract nearby office workers. The constant stream of camera-armed visitors fundamentally changed the atmosphere from a place of industrial work to a tourist attraction. The flow of outsiders disrupted social relations among artists and between artists and ironworkers, who saw tourists largely as a nuisance (Hyesun, 2015). Finally, the process of appropriation by the government of Mullae Art Village culminated when the Seoul Art Space started calling the Art Factory "Mullae Art Village," which created a superficial overlap between the artists' community and the government-sponsored facility (Kimura, 2013).

Despite these qualifications, artists from the Mullae Art Village did achieve their main goal of protecting the area from redevelopment. In their analysis, Reigh and Choi (2012) argue that the Mullae Art Village succeeded because of five main elements. Artists capitalized on the old factory area and converted it into an unfamiliar landscape; they were then able to shape active collaborations and relationships of mutual respect with ironworkers; the performing arts festival stimulated a variety of cultural and artistic exchanges and broadened organizational networks, legitimacy and support for the enterprise; artists actively encouraged residents and visitors to explore the exotic landscape of the foundries, allowing outsiders to reconsider Mullae not as space of blight but rather as an avant-garde of the creative city; finally, the artists' outreach created a performance space that was easily accessible but also subversive and surprising.

These tools and strategies legitimized artists in the neighborhood. Their discourse was powerful partly because it overlaid, or paralleled, the city's own growth discourse. The narrative of revitalization through the convergence of industry and culture fit with an official position shared across the political spectrum. In fact, both the leftist mayor Park Won-soon and the conservative president Park Chung-hee visited the Art Village in 2013, meeting with artists and ironworkers and praising the neighborhood as a model of an artist's haven and artist-led regeneration.

Just as the city branded Seoul as a hybrid of tradition and modernity, the artists' narrative highlighted the ironworkers' endangered historical legacy and revived it through their innovation. Uniquely among cases of gentrification, Mullae artists did not replace but rather coexisted with industry – and, in fact, the discourse of grassroots creative production that artists developed to resist redevelopment made artists and metalworkers mutually dependent.

Academics played a central role in validating the artists' discourse, based as it was on historicity, place-appropriation, and place-reinterpretation. They produced a large body of work in the humanities, sociology, urban studies, architecture, urban planning, and beyond. Some scholars interpreted Mullae Art Village as a close and regenerative fit with the city's "cultureconomics" imperative (Jang, 2011; H.-J. Kim, 2011, 2013; Kim, Kim, Seo, & Choi, 2010). Yet most scholars emphasized the discrepancy between Mullae Art Village and the city's notion of "cultureconomics" and aggressive urban redevelopment (Jung & Kang, 2014; Ra, 2008; Reigh & Choi, 2012; Yoon, 2011).

Academic interventions had ambiguous effects. They equipped the artist community with the status and legitimacy they needed to fend off redevelopment. At the same time, the large body of academic analysis, including a census and several surveys, turned the previously underground space into a legible enterprise and made production and diffusion of Mullae's artists quantifiable, predictable, and hence readily primed for commodification by the government. While artists had successfully appropriated the old industrial area, the academic intervention, together with the extensive public-outreach program, contributed to the government's takeover of the artist community. In the end, although artists met their goal of preventing displacement, it was hard to distinguish whether artists had co-opted institutions, or the other way around.

* * *

Taken together, the four cases in Seoul confirm that militancy has been an attenuated resistance tactic in aspiring global cities and show the knowledge gap that militant protesters contend with when they turn to festivalization. The analysis also highlights the importance of place in shaping a successful deployment of experiential tools, with the comparison of Duriban and Myeong-dong. In these cases, experiential tools were used not only to muster mobilization but also to thereby guarantee the safety of protesting residents in the face of significant physical threat.

Finally, artists in Mullae took the phenomenon to its extreme: with experiential tools, resistance shed earlier confrontational meanings and turned preemptive, implicit, and something fought at the levels of discourse and diplomacy. The case of Mullae also provides a cautionary tale of how their use increases the visibility, legibility, and attractiveness of areas that were previously "under the radar," and in so doing contributes to the very consumption and gentrification dynamics that these tools are intended to impede. This conundrum, which is shared by all the cases in this book where experiential tools are successfully deployed (especially Hamburg and Santiago) is addressed directly by protesters in Boyle Heights (Chapter 11).

All cases indicate that experiential tools and the associated festivalization of protest were most successful when the victims of displacement prominently included artists, owing to their ability to engage audiences, which positioned them especially well to create effective ludic experiences.

Together, the cases of Toronto and Seoul discussed in the chapter illustrate the important role of local political allies in affecting protest impact. While the Toronto cases pinpointed the effect of councillor support (or lack thereof) in district environments, Seoul illustrated the effect of political allies in multiple multimember districts, where their ideological orientation is pivotal. Local political allies limited the effects of strong partisan alignment in Duriban, while the lack of such allies lead to the brutal defeat of protesters in Myeong-dong. Mullae offers instead the most likely case of resistance under a progressive regime – which explains why residents were able to expand the scope of their claims and accomplish *legislative* protections for their neighborhood, despite powerful encroachments by the previous administration with the Mullae Art Factory.

10

Shaping Redevelopment in Public Housing Estates

Successful resistance can occur in the most unlikely contexts – in these cases, public housing redevelopment at two sites each in Melbourne and Toronto. In theory, these are settings where we are unlikely to observe either mobilization or impact because these populations are not only at the bottom of the socioeconomic ladder, they also include large percentages of recent immigrants from extremely heterogeneous backgrounds, which further inhibits collective action. Further, public housing experiences high turnover. However, exceptional cases defy trends observed in earlier cases and open up new possibilities for protest.

In the first case in Toronto, cultural producers supported boosterish approaches to redevelopment that silenced displaced residents, while, in the second, civic networks played a pivotal role, together with experiential tools, in helping vulnerable groups construct collective identities and influence redevelopment. The cases in Melbourne confirm two critical factors in the context of public housing. First, they underscore the dramatic effect of an ally in city council in a heretofore-unexamined institutional context. The same stark variation in impact seen in Toronto is clear in the case of multiple multimember districts in Melbourne. In contrast to single-member districts, where protesters have to gain the support of their ward representative regardless of ideological concerns, territoriality combines with ideological orientation in these cases to explain why a specific councillor becomes a staunch ally of residents fearing displacement. When protesters have options, the ideological orientation of representatives unsurprisingly plays a more significant role in their choice of allies. Second, the Melbourne cases confirm the importance (see Chapter 8) of high union support.

CONTRASTING CASES OF MOBILIZATION AND IMPACT IN DISADVANTAGED SETTINGS: TORONTO

The Toronto cases unfolded in the context of the city's retrenchment from public housing. The conservative provincial government transferred responsibility for public-housing administration to municipal control in December 2000 with the Social Housing Reform Act (Boudreau, Keil, & Young, 2009). In 2002, the City of Toronto created the Toronto Community Housing Corporation (TCHC) for the management of public housing, with the City of Toronto as sole shareholder. The TCHC is run by a thirteen-member board of directors appointed by the City of Toronto and composed of up to three city councillors, the mayor or mayoral representative, and nine citizens, including two TCHC tenants. Like other cities discussed in Chapter 4, the TCHC contended with chronic obstacles in maintaining an aging public housing stock, accumulating by 2011 a $650-million repair backlog. They responded to the crisis as other cities had: They sold public housing, shrunk housing subsidies, and devised increasingly stringent eligibility criteria for rent-geared-to-income (RGI) units.[1] Attempts at sale of public housing were hindered by public outcry, so the TCHC embarked on an expansive program that dealt with the fiscal shortage through mixed-income redevelopment, i.e. redevelopment of public-housing complexes that included intense densification, combining public housing with market units.

Provincial and federal governments – the historical providers of public housing – continued to play an essential role, but local councillors were also critical because they could voice residents' concerns over planning and displacement. Such institutional support for residents was not evident in Regent Park, though it was in Lawrence Heights.

Approved by city council in 1945 and built between 1947 and 1959, Toronto's Regent Park was the oldest social-housing development in Canada (Lehrer, Keil, & Kipfer, 2010). It was also the largest, with a complex that covered 28 hectares and included 2,087 residential units bounded by Gerrard, Dundas, Shuter and River Streets. In the early 2000s, 80 percent of Regent Park residents were people of color, most of

[1] Rent-Geared-to-Income (RGI) housing is subsidized housing, in which the rent is based directly on the tenant's income, usually 30 per cent of the gross monthly household income. If the renter receives social assistance, the rent charges are based on the rent benefit set by the Ontario government, rather than 30 per cent of the gross monthly income.

whom were immigrants. Fifty-seven languages were spoken on the estate, and most residents were low-income, underemployed or welfare-dependent families (James, 2010). As was true in the famous case of Cabrini Green in Chicago, physical space was considered inherently responsible for the social ills that marred Regent Park, and thereby justified redevelopment.

Plans for redevelopment dated back at least to 1995 and were first initiated by residents in collaboration with city authorities (Brail & Kumar, 2017). Approved by the city council in 2003 and 2005, the project envisioned a six-phase demolition of all 2,087 units and their replacement with new ones. A public–private partnership between the TCHC and the developer Daniels Corporation allowed the TCHC to pay for the replacement of public housing with the sale of market-rate units. Some scholars and planners embraced the mixed-income redevelopment approach, as did nearby resident associations. They lobbied to have only 25 percent of RGI units in the new complex, arguing that the dilution of poverty would improve the neighborhood (Micallef, 2013). Further, in order to "normalize" the complex, and better market the redevelopment, the neighborhood undertook a massive investment in infrastructure. Daniels Corporation built commercial amenities such as a supermarket, a bank, and a coffee shop. The City of Toronto opened a new aquatic center. The Toronto District School Board completely renovated the local K–8 public school. The TCHC and Maple Leaf Sports and Entertainment built a large new sports field.

Initially, the plan was to increase the resident population from 7,500 to 12,500, with a 60:40 mix of market-rate and subsidized apartments. Over the course of the project, the total number of condo units climbed from 2,400 to 5,400, meaning that RGI units fell to less than 30 percent of total units. The original 2,087 RGI units would thus be replaced by 1,877 RGI units, 262 "affordable" rental units (public housing offered at 80 percent of average market rent), and 5,400 privately owned condo units. Moreover, while initially residents were guaranteed rights-to-return, conditions disadvantaged them during the project: Off-site rehousing was added to Phase 1 for 266 RGI units, and rehousing tenants went from a 'first-out, first-back' policy to allocation by lottery (August, 2016). As a result, the number of on-site RGI units was only 25 percent of the total (corresponding to only 77 percent of the original number of on-site RGI units). Observers worried that numbers would worsen yet further as the project continued. Therefore, despite initial guarantees by the TCHC to residents, redevelopment was going to entail substantial displacement, further exacerbated by the frictional loss due to temporary relocation, either to off-site units or to vacant units in Regent Park (McLean, 2014). Moreover, the much-touted social mixing was only pursued across buildings and not within buildings. While planners made repeated reference to diversity and social mixing, they decided against buildings with both rental and condo units, to facilitate the marketing of condos to private buyers (Kelly, 2013).

The acquisition of units was out of the question for the vast majority of Regent Park residents. Daniels Corporation presented prospective buyers with financing programs designed to help moderate-income, first-time homeowners put together a down payment. However, they only allowed buyers to borrow up to 35 per cent of the purchase price of their condo or townhome. Thus, for example, only thirteen Regent Park tenants bought condos in two of the first market buildings, and first-time homeowners using the mortgage assistance program purchased only a third of the 469 condo units in those buildings (Lorinc, 2013).

Phase 1 started in 2005. By 2009, those tenants had returned to new off-site and on-site units. The second round of relocation began in 2010, and residents returned to the completed Phase 2 homes in 2017. In 2014, relocations and demolition started Phase 3 of the project (August, 2016).

When plans for redevelopment into a mixed-income community were announced, several academics (and even some planners) argued against the intervention, stating it was "seemingly enlightened, but substantively regressive" and a blatant case of "state-managed gentrification" (Kipfer & Petrunia, 2009, p. 111; see also August, 2014; Lehrer et al., 2010; McLean, 2014).[2] Scholars criticized the plan, at times comparing it to a process of colonization because it aimed to "recommodify public housing lands, recompose the resident population by reintroducing private ownership housing, and reengineer the sociocultural dynamics on the site with physical design measures and 'place-based' social planning" (Kipfer & Petrunia, 2009, p. 121). Critics construed off-site relocation as a new form of ghettoization of poverty. They also challenged the plan's emphasis on "normalization," where normalcy was defined by an aesthetic consistent with the neighboring gentrified high-rise condominiums and the wealthier population of owners rather than renters, who were expected to settle in the new mixed-income complex and make Regent Park "unrecognizable as a housing project" (Kipfer & Petrunia, 2009, p. 94).

[2] Planners views were represented for example in Mehler Paperny (2010).

Researchers found that some residents, too, were wary of the "normalization" of the area and the corresponding dilution of poverty (Kelly, 2013). A 2014 study by anthropologists and health scientists at McMaster University found that a substantial portion of those who could be rehoused on-site were happy about the new dwellings and even appreciated the prospect of a less stigmatized neighborhood.[3] However, August found that some tenants perceived advantages to living in areas of concentrated poverty and had deep attachments to Regent Park because of "the strong sense of community" and "the dense networks of friendship and support, local amenities and convenience, and services and agencies that suit their needs" (August, 2014, p. 1317). They argued that solving physical neglect and crime did not necessarily require social mixing, and that having the poor reduced to a small minority in the new complex would adversely affect their sense of security and belonging (August, 2014; McLean, 2014). Critics thus perceived the outcome as geared mainly to wealthier residents, since inundating lower income renters with wealthier owners would dilute their voices. The concern persisted, and at the 2017 Regent Park Film Festival, a documentary *My Piece of the City* by Toronto director Moze Mossanen profiled community's response to revitalization showing how residents were experiencing new racist and classist behaviors, with looks and comments by their recent middle-class neighbors.

Despite these widely shared concerns, opposition to a project of this magnitude was hard to mount. Tenants were eager to improve the blighted housing, and revitalization and social mix were popular buzzwords in mainstream media. The vulnerable socioeconomic status of public housing tenants meant that they perceived resistance as risky. However, given the considerable size of the tenant population, and the significant displacement that took place, some organized opposition would have been conceivable, especially given documented frustration by several residents (Orr, 2012). In winter 2005, residents and social-service agencies organized a protest at City Hall to condemn the introduction of off-site rehousing and the "yuppie colony" character of the redevelopment. However, rather than organized and sustained, opposition remained subterranean and isolated (Kelly, 2013; Kipfer & Petrunia, 2009). The Ontario Coalition against Poverty, introduced in Chapter 6 with the case of the Pope Squat, also protested the Regent Park

[3] The study was only temporarily posted online and otherwise reported by Friesen (2014).

redevelopment in 2009. The group organized a poorly attended demonstration (Bonnar, 2009).

Several academics have studied the reasons for this lack of protest – most compellingly, Martine August (August, 2014, 2016; August & Walks, 2012). She identified several obstacles to tenant organizing. First, the public-housing authority built support for revitalization by branding it as tenant-driven, yet the plans were actually driven by bureaucrats, politicians, developers, and local ratepayer groups. The myth that renters initiated and shared the revitalization was reinforced by numerous media accolades for the project, praised as an exemplary model of community engagement and awarded the 2003 Canadian Institute of Planning Award of Excellence. The media diverted criticism by referring to new condo owners as "'brave' residents catalyzing the 'rebirth' of the neighborhood," while the same newspapers framed frustrated residents "as negative, unreasonable and unable to cope with progressive change" (McLean, 2014, p. 2164). The TCHC similarly discouraged criticism, for example, by threatening to evict the Regent Park Film Festival because the organization had hosted a critical panel about race, gentrification, and displacement.

August notes as a second element that the consultation process was devised to limit collective interaction among tenants. Contrary to public statements, tenant engagement was limited to four informational workshops, targeted to specific ethnic communities, and deployed to legitimize controversial aspects of the plan. In 2007, following an uproar at a community meeting when redevelopment was announced for the public housing estate of Lawrence Heights (see the next section), the TCHC changed the format of meetings in Regent Park to constrain public criticism by canceling the public Q&A and breaking up participants in small groups, and meetings with residents presented plans as already accomplished (Kipfer & Petrunia, 2009). Protesters are not the only actors who learn from past experience.

Third, August writes, critical voices were co-opted, most notably when the TCHC and Daniels Corporation hired dissenters. With acquiescence thus secured, the Social Development Plan was devised in 2007 by the TCHC, several City of Toronto departments, three nonprofit social-service agencies, and Regent Park Focus (a local youth center funded by the TCHC), intending to promote job training, community facilities, and programs on the future site. Tenants were also scared to speak out because they understandably feared retribution around their relocation or unit assignment. By invoking "social inclusion" and creating dependency, these bodies legitimated redevelopment and undermined dissent.

August's factors are valid and partly explain the absence of mobilization, but two additional factors are critical, and underexamined. First, comparison with the Lawrence Height Estate draws attention to the lack of preexisting residents' networks. The modest legacy of participation in Regent Park was discontinuous and limited. In 1969, a women-led tenants' movement had organized for better maintenance, more democratic housing management, and less restrictive RGI guidelines. However, the movement was not sustained after 1978 (Purdy, 2004). Two tenant-related bodies introduced by the TCHC (the Regent Park Resident Council in 2002 and the Revitalization Committee in 2003) lacked the autonomy, mandate, and capacity to forge an opposition network.

Second, art-led gentrification helped legitimize the redevelopment and thereby weakened opposition. This is not say that there were no instances of social praxis art that benefited residents – as illustrated by a collaboration between service providers and artist communities.[4] Yet, in Regent Park, the Daniels Spectrum arts center, completed early in the process, effectively branded the project and diverted criticism. The Daniels Spectrum was developed by Artscape (in partnership with Daniels Corporation and the TCHC). Daniels and Artscape representatives reiterated in interviews the idea that art space interventions in Regent Park resulted from the community's desires (Dixon, 2013; Lorinc, 2013). Yet one of the key advocates for the art center was the organization representing the new *condo* owners in Regent Park, the Regent Park Neighborhood Initiative, which valued art-led gentrification to "normalize" the neighborhood.

The political effects of art-led gentrification in Regent Park were also evident in a 2009 initiative called Streetscape, which took place during the Luminato festival. Hosted in Toronto since 2007, Luminato was an international festival of "creativity" intended to reinforce the branding efforts of art-led growth already evident with the city's investment in iconic performance spaces and museums. The festival aimed to place

[4] Numerous compelling campaigns that involved artists in social practices emerged, for example in Parkdale (e.g., the collaboration between the service provider PARC and the artist groups Design Hope Toronto and Public Displays of Affection; the Live without Culture campaign; and the Lord of the Slum Bus Tour organized by the Parkdale Tenant Association and the Ontario Coalition against Poverty). Yet these cases were not immune from the unease that in their critiques artists also attracted an audience of outsiders who would undermine the long-term goal of keeping the area affordable. Once again, activists faced the conundrum concerning what audience their experiential tools actually targeted and benefitted.

Toronto in the international art festival circuit and received funding of $20 million in its first three years, which generated intense criticism by grassroots arts organizations starved for funding (McLean, 2014). In response, festival organizers introduced programming with a social component, thereby cooperating with the TCHC and an urban art collective called Manifesto, which enjoyed solid connections with government, funders, and other actors involved in art-led gentrification. (It had participated in several initiatives tied to Richard Florida.) Thus, as part of the Luminato festival, Manifesto curated events under the title "Streetscape: Living Space at Regent Park" – participatory art practices that promoted civic engagement in Regent Park through creative work. Programming involved mentoring local youth in graffiti production, as well as performance and photography workshops, and included youth-led walking tours.

The initiative was controversial. Tensions between the intended social goal and the promotion of art-led gentrification highlighted the complexity of developing social practices and grassroots neighborhood-based art and raised questions about who controlled programming and funding, as well as who decided the intended audience. Critics complained that Manifesto used the event to fortify its reputation as a leader of participatory arts and that, counterproductively, its intervention erased the history of previous work by local organizations.

Streetscape contributed to gentrification by increasing outsiders' access to the neighborhood – thereby making the place more legible. This emerged in interviews where participants stated the festival allowed participants "to feel more comfortable venturing into a 'neighborhood that they were uncomfortable walking into before'" (as stated by a Streetscape participant quoted in McLean, 2014, p. 2165). This was true despite the fact that Streetscape animators, largely artists of color, were committed to critical engagement and encouraged discussion of race, displacement, and "social mix" redevelopment. Their critique was to little avail, however: their very presence – regardless of their intentions or even actions – facilitated gentrification because it was in the context of the Luminato festival, and ultimately largely aimed to an outsider audience.

* * *

Lawrence Heights is a case of public housing redeveloped into mixed housing, also undertaken by the TCHC soon after Regent Park, where yet the resident community was more successful at negotiating outcomes and preventing displacement. It deserves careful analysis not only because of its unlikely success but because, unlike Regent Park, it has not received a great deal of scholarly analysis.

Lawrence Heights is a suburb in northern Toronto, and in this respect differs from Regent Park's inner urban core location. Because of its close proximity to a small airport, the 1950s public-housing complex did not feature towers but was composed of townhouses and small low-rise apartment buildings. Middle- and upper-middle-class neighbors had opposed the settlement, so planners agreed to a layout expressly designed to keep residents separated from the rest of the area, with disconnected streets that loop around scattered cul-de-sacs. The entire complex was also fenced in, although most of this barrier was removed over time to allow for foot and bicycle crossing.

Spanning 40 hectares, the complex comprised 1,208 family units for 5,700 residents. By the 2000s, about half of residents were immigrants, and almost two-thirds were visible minorities from the Caribbean, East Africa, Latin America, and West Asia. Comprising 40 percent of the population, Blacks were the largest visible minority. More than 53 percent of families were headed by a single parent (compared to a city-wide average of 20 percent), and 52 percent of all people were living with before-tax income below Statistics Canada's Low Income Cut-off (Statistics Canada, 2006).

In 2007, then city councillor Howard Moscoe (Ward 15, Eglinton-Lawrence) launched a redevelopment plan for the public housing area. According to the plan, over the next twenty years all 1,208 units of social housing would be demolished and replaced by 9,500 units of mixed-income housing. This number was quickly reduced to 7,500 after neighbors complained. The shopping plaza would also be rebuilt.

In stark contrast to Regent Park, public housing residents were able to channel their demands through governmental institutions and obtain on-site relocation during revitalization and zero displacement following redevelopment. They also played a role in selecting a developer, as candidates presented their proposals to the entire community rather than only to the TCHC. Further, residents won consideration for building new schools and a new square (these projects referred to different planning authorities such as the school board) and secured funding from the TCHC to support their grassroots organizing in the short and medium term. Following years of negotiation with the community, North York community council and the Toronto city council approved the revitalization plan, including the secondary plan in November 2011.

In the process, residents ensured that their voice would not be silenced after they became a minority in the mixed-income redevelopment.

They formally requested resident-led discussion forums, associations, and social events "specifically tailored to assist in conflicts arising from new housing," as well as community structures "focused on building a sense of belonging to the community, regardless of whether our residents live in RGI, ownership, or other forms of housing found in the new community" (Social Development Plan Steering Committee, 2012, p. 37). The work on community identity building translated into a more powerful and inclusive approach to social development than seen in Regent Park. The main focus of the Social Development Plan in both settings was employment, but in Lawrence Heights the emphasis on communal identity and the sense of ownership of the process contrasted vividly with Regent Park.

Lawrence Heights differs from Regent Park mostly in its level of prior local organizing. In Regent Park, a tenant organization active in the 1960s and 1970s had not been sustained. In contrast, organizing in Lawrence Heights significantly predated revitalization plans. After an explosion in gang-related violence, residents in 2005 advocated to establish the Lawrence Heights Inter-organizational Network (LHION), a coalition of providers and residents' organizations that delivered programs and services in Lawrence Heights. Although key participants were the Lawrence Heights community health center (later known as Unison) and Family Service Toronto, over its first decade, more than forty community agencies and numerous community leaders participated in LHION "to strengthen the capacity and effectiveness of neighborhood governance structures and to increase resident participation and empowerment."[5]

LHION's governance was an elected steering committee with members from various focus areas, such as community safety, education, employment and training, food justice, revitalization, adult literacy, youth outreach, and worker network. LHION undertook several initiatives related to violent incidents, developing a crisis protocol and contributing to the province-level *Roots of Youth Violence Report*. It supported a grant application by the East African Community Association for a year-round community market, coordinated job fairs, and organized a weekly employment café. LHION, as well as each of the workgroups, met monthly.

[5] From the organization's website: http://unisonhcs.org/locations-maps/lawrence-heights/community-building/lhion.

Once the revitalization process had started, several LHION member organizations committed their community development workers to giving residents a voice (interview with Gillian Kranias, employee of the health center Unison, via Skype, May 11, 2017). Further, LHION had access and support through its member organizations to insiders across most city departments, which proved a significant advantage in negotiations with the city and the TCHC (interview with Denise Earle, activist, animator, and heritage-plan resident liaison, via Skype, May 30, 2017). The group thereby developed networks that were essential in the quick formation in 2008 of the LHION revitalization workgroup, which allowed residents, community groups, and local agencies to discuss the revitalization.[6]

The LHION revitalization workgroup coordinated outreach and networking among residents and initiated the Community Action Team (a space for residents to gather and discuss revitalization and other concerns, with support from community-development workers of three LHION organizations). Shortly afterwards, this group launched the community-based research project BePart (Building Equitable Partnerships), which conducted community-based research based on surveys, focus groups, and case studies of other revitalizations, including Regent Park (BePart Steering Committee, 2010). It also received a grant to develop a grassroots research project on community governance models and hosted meetings with the city for broad input into revitalization.

In addition to its networks and grassroots presence, the TCHC's investment in community relations and outreach led to an approach of negotiation rather than protest. The TCHC community revitalization manager, responsible for community relations, was deeply committed to inclusion. She was very active with LHION and was eager to work with community-based organizations to develop a cooperative approach to revitalization in which local actors would collaborate with the TCHC. In this spirit, she worked to articulate and support all of the residents' priorities, in particular the co-leadership in the design and hosting of public consultation events. She later supported the community request

[6] The revitalization workgroup had only one resident member because daytime meetings (to accomodate city planners and ther agency staff) made it difficult for most residents to attend. The full LHION meetings had stronger resident voice on revitalization concerns while the workgroup served more as a forum for nonprofits and government agencies to share information and to strategize to support the venues for resident voice, including the Community Action Team, the TCHC animators, and city planning events (interview with Gillian Kranias, May 11, 2017).

for involvement in the selection of the redeveloper, a dramatic departure from standard practice.

Early in the redevelopment planning process, residents organized the Community Action Team, a resident-run information and action-oriented group with Gillian Kranias from Unison as the only regular agency staff member. Soon thereafter the TCHC community revitalization manager hired residents to be *community animators* – individuals who were paid (typically for 10–15 hours per week) to share information and engage residents. A few Community Action Team members were hired as animators, which allowed for a natural communications link between activities residents worked on as TCHC animators, and the independent organizing of residents through the Community Action Team. In other words, these animators had a dual role, as employees of the TCHC and as community advocates.

As TCHC employees, animators could conduct research on behalf of residents and local organizations (for example, they could learn from the Regent Park experience). They learned details about the revitalization through their jobs, and, once off the TCHC payroll, they were well informed to advocate for resident interests. Animators also helped shape the Community Action Team, a group that presented residents' requests to other stakeholders – not confrontationally but rather as advocacy based on personal relationships and mutual trust. Indeed, the team did not invite media when they thought confrontation might be possible. Animators nourished the supply of local leadership because, together with leaders from community-based organizations, twenty-five to thirty animators rotated in and out of leadership positions over the years, which ensured a core of four to ten energized organizers.

These formal organizational structures, and the informal networks between them, facilitated a positive relation with authorities, encouraged negotiation, and secured support by councillor Moscoe, who was well known and respected in the public housing complex. The same held for Josh Colle, who won Moscoe's seat after his retirement in 2010. LHION facilitated relations with the TCHC, which needed resident support to get city council approval for the revitalization during the conservative mayoralty of Rob Ford (2010–2014) and wanted to avoid the costs and bad press that followed Regent Park. LHION threatened swift organization should requests not be met, but it also promised TCHC on-site resident relations help.

The TCHC saw its collaboration with LHION and its revitalization workgroup as critical for the redevelopment process. At the same time, other agencies within LHION offered residents space and facilitation for powerful organizing. For example, through the Community Action Team, residents could meet and prepare before meetings with officials:

> The week before, they talked about the issue among themselves. So then when they went to the meetings they had a stronger voice, it's not like they came up with any group demand but they just created space to actually hear what they were thinking, and to validate their thoughts before they went to the meetings so they felt more confident to speak up.
>
> (interview with Gillian Kranias, May 11, 2017)

The association with LHION also provided residents with legitimacy and credibility in their interactions with TCHC representatives. Certain LHION member agencies likewise helped build trust and communication; in particular, they were well positioned to reach out to ethno-specific resident associations because their workers were co-ethnics (interview with Gillian Kranias, May 11, 2017).[7]

In November 2008, the grassroots Community Action Team released a joint document titled "Lawrence Heights: Grassroots Community Priorities for Revitalization." The document listed for the authorities ten priorities in redevelopment that would secure resident support:

1. support a bottom-up process to create a level playing field and direct contact between residents and actors involved in revitalization planning;
2. zero displacement;
3. environmental health during construction;
4. security – during and after construction (features and maintenance);
5. better schools, community and health programs;
6. integrated mix (maximum integration as with the St. Lawrence Neighborhood model);
7. equivalent size and type in unit replacement (e.g., three-bedroom "unstacked" townhouse with yard);

[7] In addition to the high level of organizing, some interviews pointed to the ethnic composition as an advantage in mobilization in Lawrence Heights. The population in Regent Park was more diverse than in Lawrence Heights, undermining coordination efforts due to language barriers. While interviews indicate that over the years Lawrence Heights experienced different waves of refugees, during the 2000s the activists recruited in Lawrence Heights were mostly of English mother tongue, and the largest non-English speaking group was composed of Somali immigrants who were organized in the influential East African Resident Association.

8 concrete employment objectives with adequate funding to address them;
9 green spaces;
10 diverse homeownership options.

Most requests were accepted by the TCHC, with the important exception of within-building integration of different income-level households.

LHION mediated and supported not only residents but also a variety of organizations, including some of LHION's own member organizations, which were approached and lobbied by authorities to depose in favor of the revitalization when city council was discussing the secondary plan. Most local organizations lacked expertise on the revitalization and approached the larger organizations within LHION and the revitalization workgroup for support. To decide on recommendations, LHION organized four meetings and invited representatives from Regent Park to the first one so they could learn from their experiences. It ended up presenting requirements that focused on social services related to member groups' activities; for example, the needs of disabled residents or residents with special health care during relocation. The TCHC largely agreed to the requests.

* * *

Experiential tools were critical to sustain residents' involvement. The case of Lawrence Heights is remarkable because *institutions* played such a substantial role in the reinforcement of communal identity through experiential tools. With the support of the organizational infrastructure described above, Lawrence Heights residents developed a heritage plan that identified key cultural and historic references, to keep alive the memories and vitality of the community once redevelopment begun. The idea of a heritage plan did not emerge directly from residents; instead, it was introduced by the TCHC community revitalization manager based on recommendations and initiatives by committed individuals in the city planning office. This was not just serendipitous: After the failure to include residents in Regent Park, the TCHC was eager to try a more inclusive approach.

Proponents used two documents to justify the need for a heritage plan: first, the cultural turn embodied by the Ontario Heritage Act RSO 1990. The Act was introduced in 1975 but significantly amended in 2005. Its primary focus was still "to protect heritage properties and archaeological sites," and the Act conformed generally to a neoliberal vision of cultural heritage, which was ultimately seen as a tool for economic growth. But cultural heritage was defined as aspects of the *social* landscape that embodied "the expressions and aspirations of those who have gone before us as well as today's culturally diverse communities" (Ontario Ministry of Culture, 2006, p. 1). While the focus remained on conservation, this version gave new emphasis to cultural rather than architectural features. Heritage was extended to include "cultural landscapes" and to invigorate the role of citizen participation in their definition. The Ontario Heritage Act encouraged "local citizen participation" by authorizing municipal governments to create municipal heritage committees comprised of local citizens to "advise municipal councils and residents on local heritage matters and help municipalities carry out their heritage conservation programs" (Ontario Ministry of Culture, 2006, p. 1).

A second document, the 2005 Ontario Planning Act, was even more important. It enumerated a number of policies that municipalities were expected to implement, including the Provincial Policy Statement (PPS). The PPS defined "provincial interest" and required municipalities to consider provincial interest in their planning. Cultural heritage, and the conservation of cultural heritage resources, was explicitly identified at that time as a matter of provincial interest. It was a new legislative hook (interview with Mary MacDonald, heritage planner, via Skype, June 21, 2017). However, the step from physical to social heritage conservation was significant and required a new commitment in the city planning office to learn from mistakes made in the Regent Park revitalization. Heritage planner Mary MacDonald explained:

> Before I worked for the city, I worked for a heritage consulting firm that had been hired to do some work, largely archeological, for the Regent Park redevelopment. And I was struck at the time by how much erasure was happening, not just at the buildings, which everybody seemed to agree needed replacing, but also the movement of the people that was required. All of the histories of the people who lived there, but also the ideas that informed the planning of Regent Park, when it was first built: those planning ideas were intended to be very progressive ... I thought that it was a shame that some of that history would be lost, because I'm a social historian. Some people wanted it to be lost because it had ended up with a traumatic underpinning; the people who lived there experienced violence and disenfranchisement. But at the same time there was a strong social cohesion amongst the generations of people who lived there and the immigration waves over the years. I wasn't in a position where I could really have any influence on that, but it stayed with me. So when I heard that Lawrence Heights was being redeveloped, and I was actually working for the city ... I asked a very uncomfortable question in [a key meeting about Lawrence Heights] where everyone was talking about removing everything ... and I asked, "What was the heritage study that went along with this?" I knew that there wasn't one ... and they came up with some extra money to hire a heritage consultant to do that review.
>
> (Interview with Mary MacDonald, June 21, 2017)

E. R. A. Architects, hired in 2008 to conduct the heritage study, initially focused on the physical space and the historical overview of development, yet tried to shift from the physical to the social sphere. The E. R. A. *Heritage Impact Statement and Cultural Heritage Resource Assessment*, completed in April 2010, called for interpreting and celebrating the history of the community as part of the revitalization process and identified potential cultural heritage resources. The shift from physical to social preservation came as a relief to other planners, initially worried that heritage requirements would stall or inhibit smooth redevelopment of the physical space. The planning office was quickly on board once it realized that the heritage requirement was not focusing on the physical space (who all agreed was in dire need of redevelopment) but rather its sociocultural component. The focus also met MacDonald's concerns because

> When you lose the buildings often you lose the stories too. And buildings aren't just about buildings, they are also about the people that live there. Disenfranchised groups are easily erased, despite what was being promised by revitalization of public housing as being better places to live and more integration with different classes. The neighborhood mix is something that's promised as de-ghetto-izing the place, right? But there's a real judgment, I think potentially implicit in that: it's the erasure of people.
>
> (interview with Mary MacDonald, June 21, 2017)

MacDonald asked for a heritage interpretation plan, intended as a "strategy that would assist in making sure that the people who had lived there over time" would not be "lost when all the sites were lost" – and most importantly, she also hoped the plan "would be an opportunity for community members to gather, to talk about their experience of loss" (interview with Mary MacDonald, June 21, 2017). This institutional voice joined and reinforced preexisting efforts among residents. For example, already in 2007, before the redevelopment planning was publicly launched, a photographer, Rodrigo Moreno, received funding for a heritage project to document community experiences in advance of the impending revitalization. Unison framed the photos with quotes from the subjects and displayed them in the hallways of the health center, illustrating how community nonprofits facilitated resident-led initiatives and shaped the heritage construction at Lawrence Heights. In the period 2009–2012, the TCHC and local arts organizations also supported various youths to produce videos that documented their stories of growing up in "Jungle," as the neighborhood was derogatorily nicknamed. Yet the institutional intervention advocated by planners such as MacDonald widened the scope and impetus of these isolated efforts and were a formal way to gather and preserve the rich cultural heritage that residents valued.

Institutional and residents' voices came together in spring 2012, when a key document was issued, *Shaping Our Community Together: Our Social Development and Action Plan for Lawrence Heights*. In it, the TCHC, the City of Toronto, the Social Development Plan steering committee, and community groups described the community's perspective on the revitalization and called for a documentation of the history of the community and its transformation with a heritage plan to identify key cultural and historic references in the neighborhood and keep alive the community's memories and vitality (Social Development Plan Steering Committee, 2012).

In response, Heights Development Inc., the developer partner for Phase 1 of the revitalization process, brought together Gadki Planning Associates and Art Starts (a community art organization based in Lawrence Heights) as part of the Heritage Interpretation Planning team, joined by a local resident hired as a community engagement coordinator to be the primary liaison between the team and the community. The final version of the heritage plan (Gladki Planning Associates & Art Starts, 2015) specified goals and strategies for cultural valorization and preservation, with a focus on promoting a shared sense of identity and history for the community and an emphasis on artistic tools.

Remarkably, in this case, the emphasis on social planning and preservation emerged not from local grassroots but from the city planning office and the TCHC, as they "prioritized the implementation of a comprehensive community engagement strategy in partnership with local organizations and community groups" (Gladki Planning Associates & Art Starts, 2015, p. 19). The office of city planning conducted a cultural heritage resource assessment for Lawrence Heights as a part of the redevelopment plan, followed by a heritage impact assessment, which made recommendations. Then the office wrote the secondary plan policy, which required the heritage interpretation plan.

An already coalescing set of local activists and organizations took advantage of these heritage requirements to create meaningful linkages and to mobilize residents. To the actors on the ground interacting with residents over revitalization, the heritage requirement morphed into the obligation to bear witness to the community of Lawrence Heights (interview with Carmen Smith, community engagement officer for the TCHC from 2007 to 2016, via Skype, June 6, 2017). Thus, in Lawrence Heights, as in Yungay, heritage meshed with social history and invigorated the collective identity of the community, which was integral to the process of organizing, dissenting, gaining clout, and participating in protest against displacement. In a remarkable contrast to Yungay, however, authorities played a key role in introducing social archives in Lawrence Heights, because the TCHC believed that more resident buy-in would facilitate the revitalization.

The resulting social archives quickly veered from their initial technical planning goal of heritage preservation to become a political tool for resident outreach and recruitment. The TCHC and the local community arts organization Art Starts organized two community-heritage planning workshops at the Lawrence Heights Community Centre in October and December 2013, attended by approximately thirty residents, as well as a former city councillor, city planners, and TCHC staff (Gladki Planning Associates & Art Starts, 2015). From that meeting, the TCHC community revitalization manager orchestrated a two-month outreach and survey to ask community members about their preferences for a heritage plan. A consensus emerged for a fun event, and so the "Lawrence Heights and Neptune Collective Memory Bank: A Friday Night Café" was organized to create an opportunity for residents "to showcase neighborhood experiences, memories, stories and objects, while documenting and collecting these items and stories as archival pieces for future use in heritage projects" (Gladki Planning Associates & Art Starts, 2015, p. 21). Residents identified landmarks and community icons and celebrated the identity and history of the original community through oral and visual displays at community events. Other initiatives included public art projects, storytelling and pre-demolition community mapping, community walks and tours that documented the physical history of Lawrence Heights, and time capsules to preserve community history.

On November 14, 2014, the residents' collection of neighborhood stories, memories and treasures was displayed as the Collective Memory Bank project at the Lawrence Heights Community Centre. During the event (attended by over fifty-five residents and reported in local media), participants used a video booth to record two minutes of their memories, a photo booth to document archives, a 6-meter memory wall to draw or write recollections, and a children's area of art activities. Everyone shared a potluck dinner. The Lawrence Heights Archive (and YouTube) posted numerous video blogs about the community, telling stories about residents and the revitalization.

Residents were also included in the naming process for new streets, buildings, and public spaces as a way to involve them in the planning, design, and governance of new community spaces. Interviews had indicated that residents considered it essential that they have some control over street renaming. In other revitalizations – including Regent Park and Don Mount Court, an estate that was renamed Rivertowne after revitalization – residents had no input on names, and this had exacerbated and came to symbolize their sense that the neighborhood had been taken from them (personal communication with Gillian Kranias, April 19, 2019).

The final version of the heritage plan summarized all the work conducted between 2012 and 2016, and identified several themes for the social history of this community; for example, private life, neighborhood change, social life, and neighborhood culture. It then provided ideas to interpret and represent the various storylines: tools such as storytelling, visual interventions, place-naming, programming, and storage of information. The plan documented potential locations for heritage interpretation in the revitalized neighborhood, as identified by residents. It also broke down the various heritage preservation tasks in great detail based on the tasks and needs relevant to various components of the heritage plan in the different phases of redevelopment.

While work toward social heritage preservation was taking place, in 2014, the TCHC commissioned Artscape to explore the development of a community-driven vision for a new cultural hub. The engagement with the community was much more substantial than at Regent Park and entailed meetings with the residents' advisory group, the community animators group, LHION, in addition to engaging three Lawrence Heights residents as local research and community engagement coordinators. It also entailed holding five focus group sessions, two roundtable meetings, one large-scale public event, nineteen one-on-one key informant interviews, and a community survey completed by 211 residents across the study area. Moreover, Artscape also attended local community events (i.e. community design charette, talent show, library youth committee, local BBQs, Lotherton community festival and a community report-back event). The results were also very different from Regent Park. After the engagement, Artscape recommended against including the art hub in the first phase of revitalization. Community concerns about safety and exclusion prompted Artscape and the local actors to propose postponement of the cultural hub to Phase 2 (Artscape, 2015). As a further sign of local autonomy and efficacy, some residents (with the support of Heights Development Inc.) then organized a temporary art hub – a project called Houses on Pengrath (HOP) – in two houses slated for demolition. The project was inspired by Project Row Houses in Houston, Texas, which turned houses in one of the city's oldest African-American neighborhoods into art space and brought attention from international artists.

Residents gained significant victories in the 2011 secondary plan, but leadership and activism needed to be sustained far beyond that point: With implementation over two decades, a key challenge was to ensure that the secondary plan promises were fulfilled, even in the face of significant resident turnover. A perceived limitation was that LHION relied more on organizations than grassroots or individual resident input. Also, LHION was at times seen as disconnected from the community, and especially from youth, business, and faith groups. To respond to these weaknesses, LHION undertook a community consultation process from October to December 2016 based on interaction with sixty residents and forty-one agency staff who participated in seven focus groups (Bankasingh & Dyer, 2016). As a result, LHION introduced a new form of governance with two co-chairs – one elected (and salaried) resident and one community agency leader – in order to pursue equitable representation of residents and member organizations (LHION, 2016). LHION's ability to examine and address organizational weaknesses to improve inclusiveness and sustainability was a promising sign of its continued role in the revitalization. Behind this ability to self-criticize and improve was a radical commitment to residents' advocacy that deeply informed its organizational culture. To illustrate, one organizer explained the initial tensions over the term "capacity building":

> [People said] that it was all about building the capacity of residents to have a voice. But LHION did just as much capacity building with the agencies and the planners so that they would learn how to listen, how to collaborate. It's always thought that, "Oh it's the poor neighborhood that needs its capacity built," which is bullshit. It's really a two-way street. If those things are going to be solved differently, everybody has a lot of learning to do. LHION facilitated the ability to have that conversation. The approach that's coming out is a kind of "cultural humility," which is a continuous learning process.
>
> (Interview with Gillian Kranias, May 11, 2017)

The new emphasis on institutional acquisition of competencies as a necessary step in more collaborative management of resident relations, and the recognition of the previous lack of training in this regard, is a critical step forward in how we think of revitalization processes.

THE IMPACT OF AN IDEOLOGICALLY COMMITTED POLITICAL ALLY: MELBOURNE

Melbourne's government by the 2000s had branded the city as Australia's "cultural capital" based on its cultural institutions and activities in the arts, theater, film and television industries, contemporary dance, and, above all, its music scene. As with other aspiring global cities, Melbourne vigorously pursued international certification of the city's cultural cachet: it was recognized as a UNESCO City of Literature, and its Royal Exhibition Building was listed as a UNESCO World Heritage site. The city capitalized on these results by organizing an active calendar of cultural events and festivals throughout the year, the most famous being the White Night Melbourne (Mercer & Mayfield, 2015). These activities were integrated with extensive urban redevelopment, such as the redevelopment of the Docklands (Shaw, 2013a), reminiscent of Hamburg's Hafencity, and the Melbourne Convention and Exhibition Centre, completed in 2009.

The growth came at the cost of displacement. In the state of Victoria, the 2016 Homelessness Australia statistics stated that over 22,000 people (including 3,000 children) experienced homelessness, a 20 percent increase since 2006, while 35,000 people were on the social-housing waiting list. However, mobilization on public housing estates in Melbourne was especially challenging because of the resident population's ethnic fragmentation. Surveys indicated that residents formed dense support networks but also perceived significant stigma around living on the estate. They associated primarily within tight social groups based on common ethnic or familial ties and relied on these groups for advice and support. Moreover, there was a high degree of inter-group conflict, with groups competing for resources such as access to communal indoor spaces (Roberts Evaluation Pty & Victoria Department of Human Services, 2012). Such low mutual trust and high inter-group conflict on the estates was not surprising given that outreach and communication was conducted in at least six languages (Dinka, Turkish, Chinese, Vietnamese, Arabic, and Spanish). The profound heterogeneity of the resident community impeded organizing in the absence of a determined and well-connected ally in the municipal council. This is illustrated in the two contrasting sets of cases below: The Fitzroy and North Richmond estates in the leftist Yarra municipality defeated redevelopment plans with the support of an ideologically committed councillor; in contrast, the Horace Petty estate in the more conservative Stonnington municipality could not mobilize resistance because residents lacked political allies.

Atherton Gardens, part of the Fitzroy estate, was a large public-housing complex with 800 apartments in 4 20-story towers. The complex sat in the middle of lively Gertrude Street in Yarra, one of the twenty-six cities and five shires that together form Melbourne metropolitan area. Just a ten-minute drive from the core of Melbourne, Yarra was a reliably leftist district with remarkable diversity: the 2011 Australian Census found that 37 percent of Yarra residents were born outside Australia, with the largest numbers being born in England, Vietnam, New Zealand, Greece, and China. In addition to public housing, the area was endowed with a dense network of community housing programs as well as service centers (Shaw, 2009).

With a prime location and great rent gap, Yarra was a target for gentrification. A migration of artists had turned Gertrude Street into a Melbourne epicenter of alternative art. Hip bars and boutiques populated the east side of the street, nicknamed the "Paris end," along with workaday commerce, cheap eateries, and second-hand stores. The commercial sector, banded together in the Gertrude Street Traders Association, displayed tags in support of Yarra's diversity, its community cohesion, and local organizations that served vulnerable populations, but the presence of public housing and the connected infrastructure to serve the poor could not be taken for granted as a brake on gentrification (Shaw, 2013a).

What made a difference in Yarra was its enduring core of far-left voters. Marginal and early gentrifiers who moved to the area in the early 1970s joined forces with the preexisting aboriginal population and promoted services for the neglected community. They took control of the local Yarra council from entrenched conservative forces and played a pivotal role in promoting leftist causes and candidates at the city level. They founded the Victorian Tenants Union, Shelter (the national umbrella group for affordable housing advocates), the Fitzroy Community Legal Centre and the Victorian Council of Social Services, which were all important local actors. In sum, "the combination of sustained political activism with the increasingly entrenched institutional presence of social housing and services ... perpetuated a self-selecting culture of continuing egalitarianism" (Shaw, 2009, p. 12). Adjacent to the social mixing on east Gertrude Street, the west side bucked the general trend and *grew* its stock of affordable housing, with the construction of new units spearheaded by the Yarra Community Housing.

Starting in the late 1990s, the government began controversial redevelopments of public-housing estates. Redevelopments at both the Kensington and Carlton estates would critically inform subsequent struggles. In

Kensington, the government disavowed previous agreements and changed plans without public consultation when it entered into a partnership with a private developer to introduce two-thirds of new dwellings as private units (Shaw, 2009). The government justified the deal by appealing to the benefits of social mixing and poverty dilution. In fact, these "social mix" redevelopments actually reinforced spatial segregation and the marginalization of poverty because, in order to better market the private units, developers placed them closest to neighborhood amenities and as far away as possible from public housing. The true impact was a massive displacement (Hulse, Herbert, & Down, 2004).

The Kensington redevelopment also provided a consequential lesson for future interventions: Because of its structural features, the tower's demolition turned out to be extremely expensive, relative to its limited land yield. Developers therefore turned their attention to public housing walk-ups. Walk-ups were four-story buildings with larger family units (typically three and four bedrooms). In future redevelopments, towers would be upgraded but not demolished, and walk-ups would be demolished and substituted with higher buildings (typically from the original four to about eight stories) and smaller units. This meant that, on paper, subsequent redevelopment plans could more easily achieve a no-net-loss of on-site public-housing units, while in fact drastically reducing the number of beds (interview with Kate Shaw, Professor of Geography, University of Melbourne, via Skype, December 6, 2016). This happened in Carlton, the second mixed-income revitalization.

Despite widespread frustration, in neither case did residents turn to outright protest (Hulse et al., 2004). Two factors contributed to the lack of resistance. First, the population was very low-income, with many out of the labor force, and came from a wide variety of cultural backgrounds, with four in five speaking a language other than English at home. Second, the plans were changed when a substantial number of residents was already being relocated in preparation for demolition.

Meanwhile, in Yarra, walk-ups were being extended in public housing estates, in a redevelopment that set the stage for the subsequent conflict. A stimulus package launched by the Labor federal government funded the construction in the midst of the global financial crisis. The package funded the Victorian government to build *social* housing, an umbrella term that encompasses both public housing, which is managed by the state department of health and human services, and community housing. While public housing is owned and run by the state, community housing is owned and run by housing associations: i.e. nonprofit actors with a financial structure that shifts from guaranteed affordable rents to rents that are capped by income and not guaranteed over time. Reference to "social housing" signaled an intention to convert the public housing stock into community housing, thereby further diluting state responsibilities to provide shelter for the needy. It was a critical step in the privatization of public housing. Yet the term "social housing" blurred the distinction between public and community housing, causing a confusion that undermined activists' efforts (interview with Ranko Cosic, organizer in the Fitzroy and North Richmond campaign, via email, June 14, 2017).

The Liberal state government used the federal stimulus funding to build a seven-story building with 152 units, a community hub, and a childcare facility in Atherton Gardens (Fitzroy estate). On the nearby North Richmond estate, walk-ups were replaced with 207 social-housing units across four buildings. In the same program, 188 units were built on the Prahran estate in the more conservative municipality of Stonnington. Construction was complete in 2013, and, as part of the federal funding plan, the Victorian government agreed to develop a masterplan to guide future renewal on these estates. The state used the masterplan requirement to further pursue and legitimize the conversion of public-housing estates into mixed-income redevelopments, targeting the Fitzroy and North Richmond estates first.

In January 2013, the state government released the draft masterplan for Fitzroy's Atherton Gardens and North Richmond estates. North Richmond had 1,119 dwellings in a mix of high-rises and walk-ups. At the North Richmond estate, the draft allowed 913 additional private dwellings on the 10.9-hectare site, as well as 1,700 to 2,200 square meters of retail space and 10,000 to 20,000 square meters of office space, partly justified as a way to provide new business and employment opportunities for public-housing tenants. The Atherton Gardens in Fitzroy had 800 high-rise dwellings. (An additional twenty-four walk-up units were off-site and not affected by the plan.) At the Fitzroy estate, the proposal allowed for 800 private apartments, as well as 4,000–5,000 square meters of retail space and 2,000–5,000 square meters of office space.

Fitzroy and North Richmond residents had witnessed displacement in Kensington and Carlton and were anxious because as part of the agreement with the federal government, only 10 percent of homes on each site were required to be affordable private housing (H. Cook, 2013). Further, the masterplan to be developed in conjunction with the funding was expected to generate income for the state government and reduce the cost of running the estates. In endorsing the draft, Liberal housing minister

Wendy Lovell stated that while the plan would guarantee the number of public-housing units, it would not guarantee their location, size, or type.

Residents began organizing against redevelopment. They were led by the group Hands Off Melbourne's Estates (HOME) and Stephen Jolly, a Socialist member of the Yarra council with strong ties to the unions. Insiders were aware that after Kensington there was never serious consideration of demolishing the towers – and in Atherton Gardens in Fitzroy, there were only towers. Therefore, no resident was actually at risk of displacement. But Jolly mobilized residents by hinting at displacement, and it was a very effective argument, given what they had seen happen in Carlton and Kensington. The prospect of displacement was emphasized by other groups that Jolly had attracted to the protest, such as RISE (Refugees Survivors and Ex-detainees), which warned of increased homelessness and diminished social assistance. Jolly and his allies were mobilizing very effectively by connecting the issue of the erosion of public housing to the rise of homelessness – and while the link was warranted in general, it was not pertinent in specific to Fitzroy and North Richmond.

The Yarra council voted against the masterplan. Community pressure was such that not only the Socialists but also three Labor councillors opposed it. With the support of other Socialist party members, leaflets were distributed in the letterboxes of all residents with the facts about the master plan in Vietnamese, Chinese, Arabic, Dinka, and English. Within days, over 640 residents signed a petition.

After the community outrage, Victorian housing minister Wendy Lovell and the premier, Ted Baillieu, publicly dimissed tower demolition as an option, as it was considered both practically inefficient and politically infeasible. Jolly was backed by academics and unions in arguing that there should be no demolitions in Fitzroy's new building and the North Richmond walk-ups because they had just been renovated in 2013. That left only the existing playgrounds, community gardens, and parklands on the estates as sites for hundreds of new private apartments, offices, and shops. Yet that open space was precious to the local community, as one-third of Yarra's children lived on the two estates. The open area in Fitzroy, in particular, was the largest park in the district, enjoyed by neighbors as well as residents. Residents also feared that redevelopment would bring higher rents, a reduction in the amount of time residents would be able to live in public houses, and the privatization of building management services.

Other leftist politicians, well known in the community, joined Jolly in the protest. At the federal level, Adam Bandt, the Green Party MP for

Melbourne, appeared at rallies and made statements of support. Bandt's clout among green voters in Yarra and beyond lent protesters with an important additional network. His federal office brought media attention and institutional cooperation; for example from the police (interview with Ranko Cosic, June 14, 2017).

State-level support was especially important because, in comparison with other cases in this book, the state of Victoria retains the greatest influence over planning; although the Local Government Act 1989 grants local councils formal responsibility in urban planning, the state often drives and overrides local government decisions. The local Labor state MP, Richard Wynne, former housing minister, at the time shadow housing minister, and well known on the estates, attended all protest meetings. Despite some animosity because Greens and Labor were sometimes accused of being too soft on mixed-income redevelopments, the three politicians, operating at all levels of government – local, state, and federal – cooperated against the redevelopment plans.

Wynne and Jolly both had close and enduring connections to unions, which furthered their collaboration. Historically, unions had been influential players in redevelopment disputes in Melbourne (and the rest of Australia), often joining protest actions at the request of and in support of resident groups. These protest actions, called green bans and black bans, disrupted redevelopment with the involvement of unions such as the Builders Laborers Federation (BLF), the Golden Workers Industrial Union, and most recently the CFMEU (the Construction, Forestry, Mining and Energy Union, Australia's main trade union in construction, forestry and furnishing products, mining and energy production) (Burgmann & Burgmann, 1998; Haskell, 1977; Iveson, 2014). While green and black bans were most documented in New South Wales, in Melbourne bans led by the BLF saved several buildings, including the City Baths, the Regent and Princess Theatres, and the Windsor Hotel.

Union support for residents partly derived from their frustration with both Labor and Liberal governments. Labor had cut jobs, benefits, and wages in previous years, and the Liberal government at the national level had undertaken a series of measures to weaken unions, such as instituting the Australian Building and Construction Commission, which limited a union's ability to protest. However, interviews consistently pointed to personal friendships and long-standing relationships as much more important in explaining union support for the protest. Jolly was a shop steward for the CFMEU, and union leaders such as the Electrical Trades Union secretary had supported him during electoral campaigns. The importance of personal connections is also corroborated by the fact that the CFMEU was officially affiliated to Labor and not Jolly's Socialist party. Further, as neoliberal state and federal governments reduced union power, support for locally progressive issues allowed unions to rebrand themselves and display their continued relevance. In the case of Fitzroy and North Richmond, unions called specifically for the conversion of existing vacant government lots and buildings into new public housing, thereby satisfying both their interests and those of protesters.

The ministry of housing tried to undermine organizing. It banned the Socialist party from their usual community room for meetings, due to an alleged heat wave. Ministry staff was instructed to rip down posters against redevelopment and to infiltrate resident meetings. Representatives from the ministry of housing even sent police to investigate and possibly arrest leafletting protesters, although the police did not pursue any action, also because the presence of known political figures such as Adam Bandt indicated the lawful nature of activities. Officials from the ministry also started calling their own meetings at exactly the same time as the protesters' meetings.

Tensions between organized residents and housing representatives in charge of redevelopment ran high. Although the vast majority of tenants had no previous protest experience, the fact that residents had to fight to get access to the common rooms and the government's tactics to shut down debate actually strengthened opposition to the proposals (interview with Raoul Wainwright, officer of the Victorian Public Tenants Association, previously engaged with the trade union CFMEU, and as Ministerial Advisor for Transport in a Labor state government, via email, November 20, 2016). The government argued that mixed-income redevelopment could remove the stigma of poverty and open new business and job opportunities, but protesters referred to the critical report led by Kate Shaw of the University of Melbourne about the effect of mixed-income housing in Kensington, which the state had refused to release.

Frustration, trepidation, and the extensive outreach by Socialist activists resulted in packed meetings with over 150 participants and several translators. Chinese, Vietnamese, and Somali residents were especially well represented. An action committee was formed, and in late February it officially visited the construction unions to seek their support and ask that they refuse work on the redevelopment and instead impose a green ban to protect the open areas on the estates (*The Socialist*, 2013). Residents and their allies also launched a savvy media campaign, including several appearances on radio talk shows. The campaign planned a rally for March and focused on networking with neighbors and community groups to gather more clout and maintain pressure on the Yarra council.

On March 6, 2013, protesters celebrated the fall of Ted Baillieu's government, but the incoming Napthine government spoke even more decisively in favor of redevelopment. The change at the head of the Liberal Party did not improve conditions for protesters. Yet, on March 21, the government announced that it was backing away from redevelopment plans for Fitzroy and North Richmond housing estates, following community opposition (Price, 2013a).

As a result of this government reversal, the rally planned for March 24 became a victory celebration. The event was held at the playground, the focal point of the protest, with a concert and a potluck. Politicians, indigenous rights activists, representatives from various ethnic groups, as well as former and current residents, addressed participants. Residents reiterated that this was their first organizing experience and argued that the victory empowered them to deal with future government initiatives. The campaign reverberated across the city, becoming the object of study and inspiration for the 2017 play "A Social Service," by Nicola Gunn and David Woods, which featured guest performances by Fitzroy residents and organizers.

The case of Fitzroy was the first of the current wave of public housing redevelopments to be shelved by the government, and the postponement took place in March 2013, over a year before the state election of October 2014 that brought Labor to power. In an interview, Stephen Jolly explained that residents succeeded because they sprang into action as soon as government announced redevelopment plans, and the sudden success was largely due to the building industry group alliance of five unions who joined the campaign on March 21 and pushed for development on other sites (Price, 2013a). In addition to the pivotal role of unions, the case indicates that the effective organization relied on the unusual and enduring strength of the Socialist party in Yarra, where the council had consistently opposed any loss of open space on the estates, and the neighborhood's distinctively tight and embedded sense of civic community.

* * *

As had happened in Seoul after the Duriban success, activists quickly moved to the next endangered site – the Horace Petty estate in nearby Stonnington. To recall, the Australian government had funded the

Victorian government to build 188 new homes on the Horace Petty estate, and, as part of the funding agreement, the Victorian government was required to develop a masterplan to guide the estate's future renewal. The estate was located in one of the wealthiest parts of Stonnington, the neighborhood of Prahran. Unemployment in Prahran was 4.1 percent, compared to a Victoria average of 5.4 percent, and median individual income was $933 per week, compared to a Victoria average of 561. The municipality of Stonnington bordered with Yarra, but it did not share Yarra's leftist council. Instead, the Stonnington council was mostly led by independents, and leaned Liberal. The seat in the Victorian Parliament had passed from Labor to Liberal to Greens in the previous three electoral cycles, and Socialists lacked a presence in that part of town.

As soon as she announced the shelving of redevelopment in Fitzroy and North Richmond, the housing minister also stated that the shift would allow the government to focus on the new mixed-income redevelopment of Horace Petty and other Prahran estates. As in Fitzroy, the minister did not guarantee on-site replacement of the units, and residents risked losing open space.

The government proceeded steadfastly, combining tactics to undermine resistance with disingenuous arguments and false choices. First, in April 2013, the state department of human services tried to stop Jolly from organizing at Horace Petty by banning political candidates, parties, or representatives from holding public meetings at public-housing estates. This had the immediate repercussion of several canceled meetings, including one scheduled for April 24, which included as speakers Richard Wynne, shadow state minister for housing, and Daniel Andrews, leader of the opposition. (Andrews would become state prime minister in October 2014.) The new regulation, which also banned door-knocking at public-housing tenants' units and political messages on noticeboards, was criticized as a "Stalinist crackdown" (J. Campbell, 2013).

In response, HOME and other groups that had been supportive in the Fitzroy and North Richmond struggles stepped in to book rooms for the meetings. Further, the Human Rights Law Centre threatened action against the new regulations on behalf of two tenants, on the grounds that the ban unlawfully limited residents' rights to freedom of expression and peaceful assembly. As a result, the government backtracked and withdrew the regulation in May 2013 (Price, 2013b).

Second, the government tried to preempt Jolly from making the same claims here that he had in Fitzroy and North Richmond, implying a danger from displacement although none was imminent. On Horace Petty, the government presented residents with two masterplan options, which amounted to a false choice. According to the first option, both walk-ups and high-rise towers would be demolished to make way for a mixed-income redevelopment. The second option called for retrofitting the existing towers, demolishing the walk-ups, and building new private units on the estate (H. Cook, 2014). The choice shortchanged residents because they were not given the option of a renovation without mixed income: i.e. a renovation with only public housing. Unsurprisingly, residents chose the second option, though that meant accepting a mixed-income outcome. In 2015, Labor state housing minister Martin Foley reminded residents that the plan to demolish the towers had been proposed by the previous Liberal state government and presented the new version as a major concession to residents, when in fact the government had previously decided that the towers were too expensive to demolish (Preiss, 2015). In fact, Labor favored the towers as well because shifting the high-density inner-city public housing to outer suburbs was not in Labor's electoral interests. New high-income residents were considered more likely to vote conservative or green, while public housing towers hosted key, remaining pockets of reliable Labor voters.

Given the scant Socialist presence in Stonnington, resistance was limited and sporadic. Many residents felt apprehensive and apathetic about the prospect of protest given the conservative environment. As an indication of the differences between the Yarra and Stonnington political scenes, several local politicians were frustrated by the decision to keep the towers, including the local representative in the Victorian Legislative Assembly and members of the Stonnington council. Moreover, the 2013 change in government from Liberal to Labor meant that unions were much less available to oppose state redevelopment plans.

In spring 2013, HOME organized a few street stalls and put up some posters around the Horace Petty estate. However, tenant organizing in Stonnington – even more than in Fitzroy and North Richmond – clearly stemmed from Socialist party activists and not from tenants. Meetings continued to be held in community rooms in Fitzroy and were sparsely attended. Internal communications revealed challenges in outreach due to a lack of volunteers in that area (HOME, 2013). The effort was also undermined by the lack of support by the public-housing unions Tenants Victoria and Victorian Public Tenants Association. Also, the government's control of the consultation was so tight that even meeting organizers only had access to hard and not digital copies of the plans.

Finally, other struggles came to the fore in Yarra that diverted activists' attention, such as the anti-transit protests over the East–West Link, a proposed 18-kilometer tollway, and a related squat referred to as the Bendigo Street housing campaign. In both campaigns, Jolly was a key leader and achieved significant results. The squat in many respects was similar to the Toronto Pope Squat, as its intense experiential tool deployment and mobilization could not prevent eviction. This outcome was expected since Australia is a liberal market economy and therefore less tolerant toward squatters. However, the movement won significant press coverage and sounded another alarm about the issue of homelessness and high vacancy rates in Melbourne.

The Melbourne cases thus presented a deep contrast. In the municipality of Yarra, a Liberal government's plans for mixed-income redevelopment on the Fitzroy and North Richmond estates was defeated by a Socialist-led mobilization and union pressures. In the municipality of Stonnington, a Labor government and a Liberal-leaning local council succeeded in introducing mixed-income redevelopment on the Horace Petty estate.

* * *

In addition to the existing literature, I find that mobilization in Toronto's Regent Park was undermined by the lack of preexisting networks and the legitimation of the redevelopment by cultural producers and associated entrepreneurs. In Lawrence Heights, by contrast, we have seen how residents were able to obtain on-site relocation during redevelopment as well as unprecedented influence over the redevelopment process. These goals and others were achieved thanks to the commitment to inclusion by the councillor and city authorities, a dense preexisting organizational network, and outreach figures who promoted resident advocacy and deployed experiential tools to sustain resident mobilization and engagement.

Finally, the Melbourne comparison illustrates starkly the role of an ideologically close ally in multimember districts: While in Yarra the socialist councillor was critical in the decision to cancel unwanted redevelopment, in more conservative Stonnington, residents, lacking political support and organizational infrastructure, failed to significantly organize against displacement. The cases also show the key role played by union support, in the rare instances when it is available.

11

Militancy with a Twist

Fighting Art to Deter Displacement in Boyle Heights, Los Angeles

Militant struggles against displacement recently made a vigorous return in Los Angeles. Yet, whereas in Yongsan or in the 1980s in Hamburg direct action targeted developers or politicians, in Los Angeles the targets were cultural producers. The strategy inherently critiques the way in which neighborhood groups and nonprofits relied on negotiation in other cases in the book, including in Los Angeles.

This chapter considers a case in Boyle Heights, a neighborhood in Los Angeles adjacent to downtown and with an especially rich tradition of dense civic ties and grassroots organizing. By embracing militancy, the long-standing organization Union de Vecinos adopted a strategy to resist gentrification similar to that of Asamblea del Pueblo San Telmo. In both cases, activists aimed to discourage gentrification by making the neighborhood inhospitable to outsiders; but while members of the Asamblea targeted primarily tourists, Union de Vecinos and its coalition partners targeted art galleries.

* * *

Resistance against gentrification in Boyle Heights was deeply woven into its local ethnic identity. Traditionally the port of entry for immigrants, Boyle Heights was often referred to as the Ellis Island of Los Angeles. Between 1900 and World War II, the area was inhabited by Mexicans, Japanese, Jews, Russian Molokans, and African-Americans, and was sustained by a thriving industrial sector, largely related to the railroad. The Mexican presence exploded after the 1910 Mexican Revolution, growing from 5 to 20 percent of Los Angeles' population in just 20 years (Romo, 2010).

Discriminatory covenants of the time prevented Mexicans from settling in other desirable areas, so they concentrated in Boyle Heights. In the 1960s the construction of highways further isolated the area: a freeway and hilly terrain separate Boyle Heights from communities to the north, and railroad lines and large industrial sectors from communities on the west and south.

Located roughly one and half kilometers from downtown Los Angeles, Boyle Heights had about 88,000 residents living in 16 square kilometers by 2010. At about 5,500 people per square kilometer, it was among the densest communities in Los Angeles (the city has a density of about 3,100 residents per square kilometer). Seventy-three percent of residents were Latino (mostly from Mexico), 14 percent Asian (non-Latino), 3 percent Black (non-Latino), while only 8 percent of residents identified as (non-Latino) White. Fifty percent of the population was comprised of US-born citizens, while 17 percent were unauthorized immigrants. The neighborhood was largely low- and low-middle-income: The overall poverty rate in Boyle Heights was 53 percent (compared to 29 percent in Los Angeles County), and ranged from 51 percent for US-born residents to 61 percent for unauthorized immigrants. These disadvantages translated into low homeownership rates, which were 18 percent (compared to LA County's 47 percent), and ranged from 20 percent among US-born residents to 6 percent among unauthorized immigrants. Boyle Heights was thus a community primarily of renters (all data from Marcelli & Pastor, 2017).

Housing conditions were often precarious: 55 percent of renter-occupied units were overcrowded and 40 percent of renter-occupied units were severely overcrowded. (Overcrowding is defined as one person per room and severe overcrowding is more than 1.5 people per room.) Even owner-occupied units faced this issue, with 40 percent of owner-occupied units severely overcrowded (Avila-Hernandez, 2005). Despite these challenges, since the 1970s, the community had been known for its stability, with many families residing for generations.

Increasingly since the 2000s Boyle Heights had been targeted by outsiders who sought the home ownership that eluded them in the city's more expensive areas. The pressure increased after the Metropolitan Transportation Authority announced the Gold Line Eastside Light Rail Extension, with four of the new eight metro stations to be located in Boyle Heights, and operational beginning in 2008.

Consequently, Boyle Heights has faced extensive redevelopment in the last decade, for example with a new LA County/USC Medical Center; the expansion of the White Memorial Hospital; two new high schools; and the prospect of a massive redevelopment for the iconic but vacant Sears distribution center. Several policy interventions supported these changes, including the designation of a revitalization area in the Adelante Eastside, as well as an Empowerment Zone and an Enterprise Zone. In addition, Boyle Heights qualified as a difficult-to-develop area, had numerous qualified census tracts, and was eligible for a high-density bonus. All of these factors made investment here especially tempting, and increased the risk of displacement for long-term tenants of affordable housing.

Boyle Heights was also attractive because of its prospects for economic expansion. A 2012 report found that of the $74 million spent by Boyle Heights residents at general merchandise stores, only $22 million were spent in stores located in Boyle Heights. They spent $27 million within 3 kilometers of the neighborhood, but the remaining 25 million at distant stores. This suggested an opportunity for new stores to capture that spending (LISC Institute, 2012).

At the same time, Boyle Heights enjoyed one of the densest, liveliest, and most enduring networks of grassroots and civil society organizations in Los Angeles. Boyle Heights is considered the center of Chicano culture and activism in Los Angeles, and the concentration and ethnic cohesion helped mobilization (Acuña, 1984; Pardo, 1990; Sánchez, 2004; Shiau, Musso, & Sellers, 2015). A dense civic network had activated repeatedly in the 2000s; for example, over the Southeast Regional Energy Center's proposed power plant (the 2006 proposal was abandoned following resident opposition in 2009); the redevelopment of large affordable housing complexes such as Pico Gardens and Aliso Village (a.k.a. Pico-Aliso, demolished in 1996); and the 2004 redevelopment of the Sears complex, which would have been the second-largest in the city's history (in a telling parallel with Toronto, subsequent redevelopment plans for the Sears complex tried to acquiesce opposition for the industrial-chic lofts by setting aside 1,030 dwellings for artist and designers, as well as nearly 19,000 square meters for creative office space – but no affordable units. Negotiations were still ongoing at the time of this research).

Historically, much of this resistance to displacement solidified along ethnic lines, but developers in the 2000s explicitly marketed to Latino professionals, following a pattern of *gentefication* documented elsewhere in the country (see Hyra, 2008, for similar dynamics in Harlem and Bronzeville). The term refers to change driven primarily by Latinos, and often those with roots in the neighborhood.

In the midst of this redevelopment, Boyle Heights attracted the attention of cultural entrepreneurs as an area with great potential because of its large spaces, relatively cheap rents, and proximity to downtown LA

(DTLA). Thus, several galleries moved to Boyle Heights, especially from 2013 onward. Starting in the early 1990s, the LA gallery scene had begun moving out of the traditional enclaves of Beverly Hills and West Hollywood in search of larger spaces and lower rents. They started moving east to East Hollywood and continued to downtown (see Chapters 4 and 7) with the Art Walk and the vibrant gallery scene that sprouted close to Skid Row. Galleries then moved further east, toward Boyle Heights.

But cost was not the only reason for moving eastward: the arrival of GPS and Uber car services made distant neighborhoods more legible, and allowed patrons to easily locate the galleries and explore spaces "off the beaten path." Two important New York galleries, Gavin Brown's Enterprise and the Maccarone Gallery, opened LA outposts (under the names, respectively, of 356 Mission and Maccarone Gallery) next to each other between 2013 and 2015, and "pioneered" an industrial area east of downtown on South Mission Road, typifying the shift of galleries from downtown to Boyle Heights in search of the new cool. The galleries were soon joined by others, and residents and activists anticipated that more intense Boyle Heights gentrification would follow these cultural entrepreneurs. The demolition of the 6th Street Bridge was critical because the new bridge (known also as the 6th Street Viaduct Replacement Project) was intended to solidify links with the art district in DTLA. By 2015, Boyle Heights was encircled by development. On the south side about 5,000 units of market rehousing were being built; the LA River development was rebuilding the bridge and creating a new park next to the galleries (prompting a separate struggle between public housing residents and gallery owners over what the park should look like). On the north side there were vacant lots along the Gold Line, but also a University of Southern California campus expansion and a new hotel. Each of these locations was a front, with several ongoing struggles. The campaign against art galleries as catalysts of gentrification, which became the most prominent battlefront against displacement in Boyle Heights in the mid-2010s, must therefore be seen in the context of a broad resistance that encompassed several campaigns and spanned decades (Boyle Heights Alianza Anti Artwashing Y Desplazamiento, n.a.).

UNION DE VECINOS

A dozen organizations, examined for this chapter, have been active over the last decade in Boyle Heights in the struggle against displacement; the most enduring and influential have probably been the East LA

Community Corporation (ELACC) and Union de Vecinos. ELACC is a nonprofit organization formed in 1995 that focuses on the development of affordable housing, community services, and community organizing, and thus shares several features with Adobe and TRUST South LA (see Chapter 7). I focus on Union de Vecinos because of its prominent historical role in neighborhood struggles and its recent and ongoing campaign against art galleries. Union de Vecinos is a tenant-based organization that serves Boyle Heights and the Pico-Aliso neighborhood in particular. The organization formed in 1996 in response to the demolition of the Pico-Aliso public-housing complex. One of ELACC's founders, Leonardo Vilchis, co-founded Union de Vecinos with Elizabeth Blaney, and they both still lead the organization. Prior to founding Union de Vecinos, both Blaney and Vilchis worked at Proyecto Pastoral, which at the time acted like the social-service arm of Dolores Mission Church. Their work focused on Pico-Aliso. The complex had deteriorated and was marred by gang violence when in the late 1980s residents and community groups began negotiating truces and improving conditions. Deeply influenced by liberation theology, Dolores Mission was organized into small communities, based on Brazil's model of *comunidades eclesiales de base* (basic ecclesial communities) in the 1960s and 1970s. The church rooted itself in the community and developed from the grassroots. People sat together in small groups to read the Bible and connect its stories with the actual life and struggles of the community. For example, Jesus ate with sinners, and, similarly, the church would host barbeques with gang members to develop relationships and engage them. They became both the subjects and leaders of neighborhood change.

In 1996, the housing authority of the City of Los Angeles wrote off Pico-Aliso for redevelopment, which meant that 1,285 low-income families were facing displacement. When the church and Proyecto Pastoral endorsed redevelopment and stated their unwillingness to help residents in their protest, Vilchis and Blaney left and formed Union de Vecinos. The group was unable to stop the demolition, and only one-third of the residents were able to return to the site after redevelopment when it reopened as Pueblo del Sol, a complex with only 65 percent of the original units. However, Union de Vecinos was able to lessen the impact for its members. While most residents received a return contract with several limiting clauses regarding regulations and financial qualifications, members of Union de Vecinos who had resided in Pico-Aliso before demolition received a guaranteed right of return with a contract that had no clauses and allowed each household a choice from among three units. This was a significant achievement for its members. The organization created out of this initiative also connected the community of renters. It grew over time, and influenced local and city politics, challenging conventional understandings of affordable housing.

Primarily, the Pico-Aliso struggle is notable because it recognized and engaged with what Vilchis called the "aesthetics of displacement":

> basically, an aesthetic language has been used for the past twenty-five years to tell people that, "Your neighborhood is going to be better, your neighborhood is going to be nicer, your neighborhood is going to be beautiful." And if you accept the need for the neighborhood to be better, nice, and beautiful then you have to accept the displacement that comes with it.
>
> (interview with Leonardo Vilchis and Elizabeth Blaney, co-founders of Union de Vecinos, via Skype, April 21, 2017)

When Union de Vecinos in 1996 opposed the demolition of the projects, it headed a fight against the aesthetics of displacement:

> Everybody else was telling us, "Don't you want your community to improve? Don't you want your community to be better?" And we had to bite the bullet and say, "No, we want things to be the way they are if they are not going to change on our own terms."
>
> (interview with Vilchis and Blaney, April 21, 2017)

This understanding inspired different ways to resist cultural initiatives, green space, and public-transportation projects that threatened current residents yet were seen as neighborhood improvements.

In contrast to many nonprofits fighting displacement in Los Angeles, the organization's governance structure made the group accountable to community members rather than a board or funders. Union de Vecinos intentionally broke from the nonprofit model after witnessing Proyecto Pastoral's failure to respond to residents: One-third of Proyecto Pastoral's board was composed of residents of Pico-Aliso public housing, and this group was outvoted by the remaining two-thirds of the board, which supported demolition. Union de Vecinos' members were low-income, primarily Latinos, and area residents. The group's founders soon turned to foundations for their salaries, but the community committed itself to raise funds for the office rent and other staff salaries through weekly food sales.

And while ELACC and other nonprofits such as TRUST South LA focused on service provision, Union de Vecinos centered its activities on community organizing. It limited case management to emergencies and always connected it to larger campaigns. The organization followed liberation theology in identifying critical expertise within the community and developed an organizational structure intended to improve representation. All staff members, regardless of their professional background, were expected to be primarily community organizers, and the group heavily relied on its volunteer base. Specifically, Union de Vecinos was based on neighborhood committees (internally known as *comunidades*), which were grassroots units active in a limited geographic area (typically a block), formed by a minimum of three dues-paying members. Overall, Union de Vecinos organized fifty neighborhood committees, ten of which still met regularly at the time of this research. The average committee had between eight and fifteen members who attended weekly meetings and relied also on extensive residents' networks for other activities such as rallies. Committee activities shared some features of experiential tools because they emphasized coming together for pleasure, and beyond the specific goals or struggles of the day. Vilchis explained: "What we want is for people to come to the committee meeting because it's fun to hang out, talk, and have all this gossip going on. In Spanish we talk about just having *chisme* [gossip] and making jokes, and throwing all these [events]" (interview with Vilchis and Blaney, April 21, 2017). Successful committees set clear missions and pursued a full agenda. They met weekly or every other week because they believed in regular conversation, reflection, and evaluation, moving beyond short-term issues and into long-term mobilization. Along with neighborhood committees, Union de Vecinos formed resident advisory councils in public-housing estates. The councils' membership, largely composed of resident women, played a critical role in decision-making for the group. Residents identified the issues (e.g., pedestrian safety, violence reduction, air quality, housing, etc.), while members of different committees shared skills and expertise acquired on previous campaigns. The organization's politics were fundamentally concerned with managing cooperation among the different committees, and also their autonomy. For example, while committees developed somewhat autonomous relations with the councillor, different committees came together to negotiate top priorities for the neighborhood before approaching them.

From early on, Union de Vecinos was deeply engaged with a network of like-minded organizations. For example, in 2005, it formed the coalition Comunidades Unidas de Boyle Heights (United Communities of Boyle Heights), together with ELACC, Inner City Struggle, Legacy LA, and Proyecto Pastoral. The coalition brought together a large membership base for community education against gentrification. It also forged bonds among different organizations and transmitted to Union de Vecinos a culture of openness to people with different ideological backgrounds.

As in other cases in Los Angeles, unions were recognized as key political actors, yet relations were weak. Vilchis had worked for the Service Employees International Union and United Farm Workers, but relationships with unions broke down over disagreement about the "aesthetics of redevelopment" critique and decayed further after renters failed to qualify to return to their affordable housing after redevelopment. Clashes with union leaders eclipsed ongoing and substantial support by union members themselves, who often faced displacement. These tensions gave rise in 2009 to the LA Human Right to Housing Collective, which Union de Vecinos developed in partnership with LA CAN. (Other organizations also became members; see Chapter 7 for more detail.) On that basis, in 2015, Union de Vecinos co-founded the Los Angeles Tenants Union, following a model of horizontal organization with no board of directors and a strong reliance on assembly governance.

Networking with local business was also complex, with older Boyle Heights business establishments much more likely to support Union de Vecinos. To strengthen these ties, Union de Vecinos adapted a strategy used by North East Alliance against Gentrification in Highland Park, and went door to door asking businesses to support the struggle against gentrification (for example, by displaying stickers promoting boycotts). This contrasted sharply with campaigns in other aspiring global cities, where neighborhood commerce sponsored art programs that promoted gentrification (as illustrated by Asociación De Comerciantes Del Casco Histórico in San Telmo in Chapter 8).

Perhaps most surprising was the relationship between Union de Vecinos and the councillor for Boyle Heights (District 14). Union de Vecinos favored mobilization and even militancy over lobbying. When negotiations were pursued, the legacy and broad membership of the organization put it in a position of strength vis-à-vis the councillor because it could affect the councillor's votes and image. In a gesture of mutual goodwill, the councillor attended social and entertainment events organized by Union de Vecinos, even those without official permits, and regularly met with members in neighborhood committees and general *asambleas*. As a result of these positive interactions, when a hip brewery proposed to open in the neighborhood, despite the opposition by Union de Vecinos, the organization convinced the councillor to maintain a neutral stance. He also agreed to promote a citywide anti-harassment campaign and to launch a know-your-rights door-to-door campaign in the neighborhood, coordinated among several organizations. Although these actions were symbolic and did not directly tackle gentrification, they were a promising start, and somewhat surprising given the hostile and controversial tenor of protest in the neighborhood.

The organization also enjoyed excellent relations with higher levels of politics, primarily with John Pérez, speaker of the California assembly from 2010 to 2014, and member of the California state assembly from the 53rd District (which included downtown Los Angeles and Boyle Heights) from 2008 to 2014. In contrast, the relationship with the local neighborhood council was problematic, and shifted according to its composition. In early years, Union de Vecinos members perceived the council to be a site of *gentefication*, where Latino/Chicano middle-class residents expressed opposition to protest organizations, street vendors, undocumented immigrants, and even affordable housing. Union de Vecinos competed in elections gaining control of the council, except for the executive committee. Due to clashes, after about six months, representatives from the Union de Vecinos bloc left the council, and a special election was held for their six vacant spots. Although the result was a council still close to the interests of Union de Vecinos, after experimenting with a strategy based on infiltration and pressure from within institutions, the organization reinvigorated its focus on lobbying and, above all, protest.

THE RETURN TO MILITANCY AND THE EVOLUTION OF EXPERIENTIAL TOOLS

Three factors facilitated the Union de Vecinos' embrace of militancy: (1) prior mobilization experience in the neighborhood; (2) a strained relationship with the nonprofit sector; and (3) a new inundation of art galleries in the neighborhood.

Vilchis recalled in an interview the militancy of 1980s struggles in the neighborhood. According to him, as Los Angeles became more progressive over the years, "people began playing this inside game; everything became about negotiating with your friends, and politics died." In contrast, thanks to earlier experiences of militancy, Union de Vecinos organizers and members were willing to engage in confrontational tactics and could embrace both lobbying and militancy depending on the immediate goals, ready to deploy the "whole spectrum of confrontation" (interview with Vilchis and Blaney, April 21, 2017). As Union de Vecinos grew, it developed resistance strategies not only around renters' rights but also against police abuse, discrimination, and the persecution of immigrants. This background encouraged the organization to adopt more confrontational tactics in comparison to other affordable housing organizations in the city.

A crisis with nonprofit organizations was not surprising because Union de Vecinos organizers viewed both the problem of and the solution to gentrification as systemic. Hence, they did not target individual politicians or real-estate developers, although some progressive supporters exhorted them to. In a radical move, they argued that the "the worst part of the system of relationships" was constituted by the nonprofit sector. Organizers argued:

> Nonprofits are the shield, they are the buffer, they are the protection, they are the consensus builders, they are the inculturators of the neoliberal consensus. And they maintain that status through the economic dependency of contracts, projects, and foundations. So all of the nonprofits, as good as they are, will never sacrifice their economic sustenance. They will never risk their political position in maintaining, developing, and furthering the neoliberal consensus that says, "Privatization is a done deal, the reduction of the government is a done deal, and all we have to do is negotiate or reduce the harm that this is producing." What we're believing is: no, we have to confront this consensus, we need to crack at it, and make demands of the state that are transformative. While at the same time, we build the parallel structures where we can take care of our own needs.
>
> (interview with Vilchis and Blaney, April 21, 2017)

Therefore, in stark contrast with most of the organizations and groups discussed in this book, including those in Los Angeles, Union de Vecinos leaders argued that the status quo was defended by the nonprofit's emphasis on negotiation and on "changing policy, getting a law" (interview with Vilchis and Blaney, April 21, 2017). Focusing demands on the councillor was misplaced, because it reinforced a flawed system, instead of pursuing "alternative models and practices within the community that change the existing conditions of political and social oppression." The criticism of the nonprofit sector went further: "We strongly believe that all these nonprofits have more power than they see themselves having; and they're not exercising it – they're refusing to say no because they don't think they have the power … And the city is dependent on nonprofits to legitimize [its policies]" (interview with Vilchis and Blaney, April 21, 2017). The nonprofit sector thus legitimized displacement of the poorest by not taking a stronger stance against it.

According to organizers in Union de Vecinos, nonprofits were far less committed to geography – in contrast to governance based on neighborhood committees – and they were marred by hierarchical governance structures. Regardless of the membership requirements, and even when they pursued inclusive arrangements, as illustrated by TRUST South LA, residents still acquiesced to the recommendations of professional leadership, on the basis of its expertise, including in the determination of what constituted "reasonable" and "feasible" goals. In contrast, Union de Vecinos' membership determined the parameters for the struggle, and sometimes required the leadership to pursue goals that organizers deemed unrealistic. For example, in a series of meetings with the Metro Authority over the provision of affordable housing in the context of service extension in Boyle Heights, Union de Vecinos leaders planned to ask for housing affordable to households with at least $35,000 of yearly income for a family of four. However, that level would have barred the majority of Union de Vecinos members from qualifying, and members therefore insisted on pursuing an income threshold of $25,000. The leaders knew the request would be dismissed by Metro and ELACC, yet they represented their constituency and changed the discourse of affordability in Boyle Heights: "[Metro and ELACC] now are afraid of saying affordable housing – every time they say they're bringing affordable housing, they have to say affordable housing *for the people who make this much money*. If they don't say that, they know that somebody in the crowd is going to say, 'affordable to whom?'" (interview with Vilchis and Blaney, April 21, 2017).

Union de Vecinos leaders also criticized nonprofits for privileging institutional, long-term sustenance while chipping away at the resources that the community needed in the short term, with an argument that often boiled down to sacrificing the poor (in the short term) in order to serve the poor (in the distant long term). Mixed-income redevelopment was a clear example: In order to save some housing for the poor, build middle-income housing and displace some of the poorest.

Tensions with the nonprofit sector escalated in a dispute with ELACC over the renovation of the Boyle Hotel. The Boyle Hotel, on Mariachi Plaza, housed the mariachi population, an iconic and long-standing presence in the neighborhood. Union de Vecinos organized renters of the hotel against their slumlord and facilitated the transfer of the property to ELACC for renovation. The protest deployed experiential tools, so that the tactical choice was also imbued with symbolic communication: *protest was expressed through the performance of identity*. For example, mariachis held concerts in front of the owner's home, sending a message about their cultural legacy, and rooting their protest in the social history of the neighborhood.

ELACC guaranteed the mariachis a right of return and provided an excellent relocation plan. Yet, when the hotel reopened in 2012 as affordable housing for low-income tenants, with the addition of an upscale café on the ground floor in November 2014, only three of forty-two residents qualified to return. Additional tensions arose over ELACC's redevelopment of Cielito Lindo, a fifty-unit complex across from the Gold Line Station at Soto. Tenants received eviction notices in fall 2015, and struggled to relocate, despite 120-day notices and nearly $20,000 in relocation funds per family. Construction was expected to be complete in fall 2017, but ELACC and Union de Vecinos disagreed over the number of very affordable units to be built. ELACC accused Union de Vecinos of opposing anti-gentrification initiatives, while Union de Vecinos argued that the project itself was part of gentrification because very poor renters could not meet its qualification requirements. Following an intense public-shaming campaign by Union de Vecinos, previous residents received a guaranteed right of return with no income requirements and no background checks. In this campaign, Union de Vecinos was willing to risk a relationship with a sister organization to pursue its goals.

The third factor in Union de Vecinos' turn to militancy was the trend of art galleries in the neighborhood. When galleries started opening, the housing authority of the City of Los Angeles vetted the possibility of privatizing nearby public-housing complexes. This threatened the Union de Vecinos membership, but they did not have a clear response or strategy, partly because of the organization's historical relationship to artists. When the organization formed in 1996, its leaders connected with Dont Rhine, a sound artist, who in 1994 co-founded Ultra-red. Ultra-red was a collective that combined art with activism, initially focusing on the HIV/AIDS crisis in Los Angeles and then extending to North America and Europe, with issues such as immigration and community development. At the time, Rhine approached Union de Vecinos because he was interested in public-housing advocacy. Union de Vecinos thus became a member of Ultra-red and explored how to use artistic venues to support organizing. In that context, Union de Vecinos began to use some experiential tools, producing sound recordings and videos and entering exhibition spaces to access "an audience that knew nothing about public housing, that knew nothing about the struggle of the community" with the objective of "educating and getting support for our cause" (interview with Vilchis and Blaney, April 21, 2017). For example, in a public-housing complex composed of three-story buildings that formed a triangle around a courtyard, Union de Vecinos projected movies and slides onto the walls and hosted a pirate radio station in one of the homes. The event was a successful deployment of experiential tools: it gathered 300 artists and outsiders, who engaged with the community while dancing and having fun. As a result, the event was therefore judged to be a "very effective message in elevating the struggle" (interview with Vilchis and Blaney, April 21, 2017).

While Union de Vecinos was mulling its response to the arrival of the galleries, other groups in Boyle Heights were reacting vigorously to the same. In May 2014, real-estate agents were distributing leaflets in DTLA with the slogan "Why rent in DTLA when you can own in Boyle Heights?" and invited potential buyers on a bike tour of the neighborhood. When the initiative reached Boyle Heights, condemnation on social media was swift, and the agents had to cancel the event. Among the most visible resistance groups was Serve the People Los Angeles (STPLA). This grassroots organization, formed in early 2015, described itself as "a political empowerment and community service organization" on behalf of communities in Boyle Heights and Echo Park. An offshoot of the Red Guards, Los Angeles, which aimed to build a communist Maoist party and deliver "complete liberation from the capitalist state," STPLA had sister groups in Austin, Portland, and Washington, DC. In "serving the people" through weekly food and clothing distribution, the group was inspired by the Black Panther Party, the Brown Berets, the Young Lords, and other groups that had pursued this approach to community development. Especially before the involvement with Union de Vecinos, STPLA had relied on their Sunday distributions to create networks of affected tenants and connect them with the tenants and homeowner's weekly meetings at the Los Angeles Center for Community Law and Action at Saint Mary's Church.

In fall 2015, STPLA launched an attack against The Industry, an artist nonprofit and avant-garde opera company, which had organized a mobile opera called *Hopscotch*. From October 31 to November 22, the event took the audience aboard twenty-four limousines across Los Angeles parks and squares, telling the plot along the way and stopping for performances at locations such as Hollenbeck Park in Boyle Heights, but also Elysian Park and Glassell Park, all recently affected by gentrification. Tickets cost $125, so the event drew mostly affluent whites. The performance was intercepted by the STPLA, which was in Hollenbeck Park for the weekly food and clothing distribution. Opera staff claimed that residents should be grateful that the art industry was present in the neighborhood, but STPLA pointed to the fact that the mobile opera was bringing outsiders to the community and did not serve local residents. The repeated confrontations escalated on the show's final day, when performers of the Roosevelt High School Band, following STPLA's exhortations, drowned out the opera with their music. Media reports also indicated that protesters were physically intimidating and prompted opera members to flee the area (*Boyle Heights Beat*, 2015; Carroll, 2016). Similarly, in December 2015, STPLA stopped a group of university students on a walking tour in Boyle Heights and escorted them out of the neighborhood. When interviewed by the *Los Angeles Times*, Facundo Rompe (his activist nickname) argued that he believed tactics to deal with gentrification should turn "more militant" (Mejia, 2016).

These events took place just over a kilometer from the Union de Vecinos office, and members decided that STPLA had identified the right approach in fighting gentrification (interview with Vilchis and Blaney, April 21, 2017). This brought about an unusual collaboration between residents, artists, and radical groups. The connection with Dont Rhine and the Los Angeles Tenants Union (which Union de Vecinos had co-founded) allowed the organization to connect with displaced artists, who brought insider information based on their relationships and knowledge of the downtown galleries. Tensions with the nonprofit sector for its unwillingness to push harder against displacement and the example set by STPLA against The Industry then moved members of Union de Vecinos to seek a coalition with STPLA and similar local radical organizations. Meetings were initially tense, because STPLA and other radical groups were deeply committed to an anti-colonial approach and its ethnic implications for resistance, and Union de Vecinos had whites among its members and as one of its leaders. Yet trust deepened after a few meetings. On their part, Union de Vecinos found among artists and radical groups a level of personal commitment they had not witnessed in the nonprofit sector, which in turn drove ELACC and Union de Vecinos further apart. Two coalitions formed that coordinated what were previously isolated attacks into a coherent strategy shared among several organizations, with significant overlap in membership: the Boyle Heights Alliance against Artwashing and Displacement (BHAAD), which focused on galleries, and Defend Boyle Heights (DBH), which dealt with displacement issues.

The subsequent focus on galleries demanded a more cautious approach toward cultural events and experiential tools. Organizers learned to ensure events did "not look like a performance piece" because, they argued, "then the artists, or the clients of the galleries, think that they came here for a performance. And our community is not a performance, we are people who are under threat of displacement and losing our homes. So we have that consciousness about how we use [art events] as a tool" (interview with Vilchis and Blaney, April 21, 2017). Therefore, the organization carefully finessed its use of art interventions. Art-led mobilization with member-driven events was still integral (e.g., committees often organized community-art venues for murals paintings and film nights), but organizers moved away from art events geared toward outsiders, such as the ones developed with Ultra-red.

For example, to celebrate a gallery closure, some proposed a top-floor party with a swap meet, but organizers refused to create "*a very cool event* where people who are in the galleries *are not going to know that this is a protest*" (interview with Vilchis and Blaney, April 21, 2017, emphasis added). This approach is diametrically opposed to the experiential tools observed in Yungay, Duriban, Tel Aviv, or Hamburg, where participants who mobilized were not necessarily attracted to the event as a protest. Instead, Union de Vecinos events clearly conveyed the protest goals. The party had food and an artisan fair, but at the center was an art station to prepare a variety of pieces to be taped, sprayed, or hung on the closed gallery building, followed by a march to all open galleries to protest their presence in the neighborhood. The function of the artistic component – and thus the use of experiential tools – therefore shifted from party to protest.

In a unique twist, everyday activities became part of the protest as well. For example, when protest was to occur on an unpermitted block, organizers accustomed members to militant resistance by instructing them to continually cross the street because "by the time a hundred people cross the sidewalk, people start getting used to blocking the street." In another example, the closing of an alley was achieved by creating a nice space for the children to play: The initiative constituted an unsanctioned use of space, but this format made it less threatening to participants. Thus, community experiences were interwoven with resistance: "as we do activities we also build resistance … we've been able to engrain in the community an experience of resistance that starts with everyday life activities" (interview with Vilchis and Blaney, April 21, 2017). Union de Vecinos organizers refused to let experiential tools be ambiguous in their politics and protest goals; they used these tools to educate participants in resistance rather than to draw in participants who were just there for the party. This was a profound innovation in the deployment of experiential tools.

THE ANTI-GALLERY CAMPAIGN

Given the legacy of contention in the neighborhood, disappointment with nonprofit actors, and the commitment of artists and radical groups against the galleries, it is no surprise that the coalitions DBH and BHAAD based their strategy on disruption. As DBH stated on its website:

> Many will disagree that the community has a right and duty to organize autonomously and insist on working within the system via strict adherence to NGOs, union bureaucracies and neighborhood councils. Some of these organizations have done a lot of good work for community, but they also have the potential to compromise our demands because of fear of "biting the hand that feeds." Well, often the hand that feeds is also the hand that controls you.
>
> (DBH, 2016)

DBH critiqued the nonprofit sector as pivotal to the survival of the bourgeois state and argued that confrontation was a necessary response to gentrification advocates in the area. DBH and BHAAD combined their commitment to militancy with experiential tools, such as reading groups, concerts, films screenings, know-your-rights workshops with "cafecito and pan" for neighbors, and other regular events listed on their Facebook page, all strongly geared toward local Latino residents.

In 2016, the two coalitions turned to militant actions against local art galleries. The tactics included disrupting events, vernissages, and exhibitions, as well as critiques and attacks on social media. The confrontation was usually loud and discomfiting for gallery owners and clients. The vitriolic tone at public meetings left gallery representatives shaken – some would not even reveal their names to the press, for fear of retribution. Organizers justified the approach as an existential decision:

> The galleries are attacking our basic need for shelter. When your shelter is under threat, and it's about to be taken away, and your only choice is going to be living on the street, in your car, or crammed in a two-bedroom apartment with ten other people, there's a lot of visceral reaction like anger and fear about protecting a very basic need.
>
> (interview with Vilchis and Blaney, April 21, 2017)

The campaign's goals were clear. As Maga Miranda, an activist with DBH, stated:

> We have one pretty simple demand, which is for all art galleries in Boyle Heights to leave immediately and for the community to decide what takes their place … We're not against art or culture. Obviously, the Eastside has been an incredibly active place when it comes to art and culture. But the art galleries are part of a

broader effort by planners and politicians and developers who want to artwash gentrification.

(Aron, 2016)

By referring to artwashing in pamphlets and statements, protesters implied "the kinds of marketing and political strategies that make use of art and artists to raise the price of real estate" (Miranda & Lane-McKinley, 2017). Activists thus anchored their position in a critique of the cultural industry growth approach and the use of art initiatives by developers eager to prepare a neighborhood for marketing and gentrification. The critique did not imply a rejection of artistic interventions in the neighborhood but instead called for the right of preexisting residents to define and control this field. Boyle Height activists thus invoked artistic interventions as a dimension of and tool for community development and empowerment. This appropriative process illustrates once again a core point of this book: Conflict over space implied also a conflict over the definition of the legitimate urban resident. This was apparent in Boyle Heights, where the protesters' manifesto stated:

> [Local] residents use creative means to hold onto their homes and hold together the social fabric of their community. So, when urban planners and real-estate developers promote Boyle Heights as a new "arts district," they effectively privilege one manifestation of art – formally trained semi-professional Artists, Art galleries and the like – over and against the art which is already there.
>
> (Miranda & Lane-McKinley, 2017)

In response to outside art, activists called for "socially practiced artwork," which "emerged as a creative struggle to replace commodified objects with community dialogue and cults of personality with cultures of collectivity" and the "rasquache as a form-of-life" which "is synonymous with what BHAAD has called 'the art of survival,' in the sense that both phrases seek to challenge the artist/non artist distinction and valorize the barrio practices of social reproduction that have been marginalized by the aesthetic value system of neoliberalism." In this context, "creatives thus appear as the foot soldiers of displacement, rather than as the allies of diversity, as they prefer to imagine themselves" (Miranda & Lane-McKinley, 2017).

BHAAD's manifesto thus concluded that communities wanting to resist gentrification (and artists who supported this struggle) should promote a view of social reproduction as artistic practice:

> Artists who are veterans of the struggle to decommodify arts practice have important insights and abilities to bring to the movement to decommodify

housing, but this can be possible only when artists take up the social practices of the marginalized communities with which they seek to be in solidarity. It is in this sense that there is much to be salvaged from discourses that embrace the notion of "social practice" ... Put differently, this is not a debate about whether art is a good thing or a bad thing, as some critics would have you believe. This is not a struggle of "social practice vs. housing" so much as "Whose social practices count as Art?" and "Who is housed and who is displaced?" When we take seriously the discourses of social practice which claim that everyone is an artist and aim to dissolve the distinctions between art and life, we realize that the artists whose social practices are most at risk are precisely the unpaid and underpaid feminized and racialized practitioners of social reproduction.

(Miranda & Lane-McKinley, 2017)

On the basis of the manifesto, the coalition targeted several galleries. One was the PSSST Gallery, which had opened in May 2016. It was housed in a former warehouse building purchased and renovated in 2014 by an undisclosed investor, who had granted the gallery a twenty-year, rent-free lease to do artistic programming. BHAAD activists accused PSSST's co-founder of being a real-estate agent and an associate of a developer in nearby Highland Park (DBH, 2016). Similarly, 356 Mission, the outpost of a renowned New York gallery, was accused of being connected with gentrification because the owner was a real-estate investor who had evicted the BHAAD member Ovarian Psychos from one of his properties. A third focus of the protest was Self Help Graphics, a print-making studio founded in 1972 and relocated to Boyle Heights in 2010. The site was considered an important Eastside community space, and progressive artists employed there felt they had made their own contribution to the revitalization of the neighborhood, which gave them the right to stay. In a post that went viral, a leading figure in the Chicano movement and author of the first politically themed Latino daily comic strip argued:

I'm all against gentrification. (See my work if you don't believe it.) I'm with you too. Mostly. I have to say, attacking Self Help Graphics, or ANY artists that have contributed to making Boyle Heights or East Los a GLOBAL arts mecca is just plain WRONG. I don't know if this is a fight you are looking to pick, but I am telling you now, you are barking up the wrong tree. Self Help Graphics, and other self-respecting artists and orgs too, have put years and years, blood sweat and tears – OUR WHOLE LIVES – into making Chicano art, and to make art accessible into the community, and to let the planet know that we are here and are important, and not going anywhere.[1]

[1] Lalo Alcaraz's post on DBH's Facebook page, retrieved from www.facebook.com/defendboyleheights/posts/981929615257366 (accessed April 14, 2017).

In spite of this legacy, DBH criticized Self Help Graphics for facilitating gentrification because of personal connections to the Urban Strategy Group and the 15 Group, two real-estate firms that were attempting to demolish the historic, rent-controlled and affordable Wyvernwood Apartments complex. The complex had almost 1,200 units and was home to 6,000 residents, and was to be replaced by a $2-billion, mixed-use project. DBH also criticized Self Help Graphics for assisting producers of the mobile opera *Hopscotch*.

In response, on July 2, 2016, Self Help Graphics hosted a community meeting to discuss the role artists played in gentrification. Speakers stuck with the position that artists and galleries were not responsible for gentrification, when the meeting (with an audience of about forty-five attendees) was disrupted by about forty DBH members, including several residents and members of Union de Vecinos, Ovarian Psycos, STPLA, East Los Angeles Brown Berets, and the Backyard Brigade. Protesters chanted "El barrio no se vende! Boyle Heights se defiende!" ("The barrio is not for sale! The barrio is defended!") Residents took the stage to denounce the art galleries moving into the neighborhood.

On July 12, 2016, a community meeting took place on the protesters' turf – in the playground area of Pico Gardens – and residents again expressed their frustration with galleries, although they extended their critique to recently opened hipster bars and coffee shops. Critiques echoed the tensions of *gentefication*, pointing to class rifts within the Chicano community: Residents recognized the galleries were geared toward programming Chicano artists but argued that they erased the voices of community members facing mass evictions only a block away.

The coalitions crafted a careful outreach and media strategy. A variety of experiential events were connected to the protest, for example a multi-band concert organized by STPLA on July 23. They compounded their communication efforts with the sale of merchandise with anti-capitalist and anti-gentrification slogans. BHAAD also engaged in networking beyond Boyle Heights, for instance, with interventions at the Los Angeles Municipal Art Gallery that convened anti-gentrification groups from across East and South Los Angeles to share organizing work, compare how the cultural industry was promoting gentrification in each area, and move toward a citywide protest movement against displacement. The coalition also organized workshops about how to create and manage media communication, with the title, "Let's Build and Tell the Stories of Our Hood," thereby mirroring a strategy of community activating through experiential archives observed in other cases in this book.

DBH was notably coherent and insightful in how they managed information. They intensely monitored mass media and messaging through social networks. They also carefully limited legibility to the neighborhood, for example by forbidding media to attend their events, by escorting inquisitive scholars out of the neighborhood, and by refusing to be interviewed for this project (beyond the leaders of Union de Vecinos).

On September 17, 2016, and on a handful other occasions, DBH organized major marches along the newly nicknamed "Gallery Row" on Anderson Road, led by Blaney and attended by about 200 members. The Artist Space by the United Talent Agency, based in Beverly Hills, had opened that day. The former warehouse was intended to serve as a gallery that would bring together the film and the art scene in Los Angeles. Protesters hung an eviction notice, reading:

> YOU ARE HEREBY NOTIFIED BY THE PEOPLE OF BOYLE HEIGHTS, who have fought for decades to preserve affordable housing for low-income families, reduced violence in the neighborhood, and have given their own labor and resources to make Boyle Heights a culturally vibrant community, that you must REMOVE YOUR BUSINESS from the neighborhood immediately.

Protesters, holding posters and banging drums, surrounded the galleries, smashed bottles, banged on windows and threw feces at them, chanted slogans, and verbally attacked staff and clients. They chased the harassed clients back to their cars, and out of the area. At these protests, nearly all statements were made in both English and Spanish, and several Facebook and YouTube videos of the protest were then posted by DBH.

Alarmed by the negative publicity and the increasing inability to conduct normal business, gallery directors reached out to residents and activist groups. But the response was defiant. For example, the director of 356 Mission issued a message intended to pacify opposition and develop a viable relation with BHAAD and DBH, offering programs to support political and community-based engagement; signaling the gallery's opposition to increased police surveillance; and describing communication with public and private actors to support the local community. However, the replies were numerous and vitriolic, restating the argument that activists were not interested in any form of collaboration with the gallery. Instead, they were asking again that the gallery leave the neighborhood. This reply – rare in its more moderate tone – lucidly articulates the main argument:

> How can 356 possibly resist gentrification in Boyle Heights when they were one of the original initiators of the contrived "arts district" there? This post is just more

doublespeak to pretend like 356 doesn't have tight relationships with real-estate developers, politicians and all sorts of well connected, extremely wealthy art enthusiasts. Release your list of collectors and supporters and we will see which "community" you are here for. Everyone knows the types of people that show up at your openings and events. This post and this discourse is exactly why real-estate developers use art galleries as the first wave when they are redeveloping neighborhoods. The intention here is to confuse and deflect 356's role in the process with some surface level "community engagement" and "political programming" and to never actually confront the forces that are responsible for displacing Boyle Heights residents. As an art gallery that is already complicit in the real estate scheme to gentrify Boyle Heights and has been from the very start, the ONLY way 356 can actually communicate anything of substance is to relocate asap.[2]

As new galleries opened, they too became the target of angry activists who did not mince words. They did not want to negotiate. They wanted the galleries' outright and immediate removal from the neighborhood. In November 2016, "Fuck White Art" was sprayed above the entrance of the Nicodem gallery, and the LAPD opened a hate-crime investigation, later dropped. Yet DBH continued the campaign, calling for a boycott of all art galleries in the neighborhood. Anonymous death threats, harassment, and website hacking were also reported by gallery owners.

The campaign shook the art world, with prominent back-and-forths in art venues such as X-TRA and Hyperallergic. (Nizan Shaked, Travis Diehl, and Dont Rhine were some of the most influential contributors within the art world, while Tracy Jeanne Rosenthal made poignant interventions from her role in the LA Tenants Union.) On February 21, 2017, protesters scored their first significant victory when PSSST announced that it was closing, an event reported by national media (McPhate, 2017). The controversy and protest undermined PSSST's fund-raising efforts. Intent on finding new ways to harm galleries' ability to conduct business, the coalition expanded the campaign beyond Boyle Heights by using its channels through the LA Tenants Union and Ultra-red to reach cultural institutions in New York and discourage them from selecting Boyle Heights as a West Coast outpost. In January 2018, the gallery Venus Los Angeles closed. In March, after rallies and boycotts in Boyle Heights and New York (where at least sixteen organizations joined the campaign), the gallery 356 Mission also closed (Boyle Heights Alianza Anti Artwashing y Desplazamiento, 2018). In April, UTA Artist Space, the visual-arts outpost of the Hollywood talent agency, relocated to Beverly Hills. In

[2] This comment is in reply to a statement to the community posted on Facebook by 356 Mission (accessed at www.facebook.com/356SMissionRd/posts/1077388909038284).

May, Chimento Contemporary and MaRS Gallery also left the area. Anecdotal observation indicates that the campaign is discouraging some galleries and artists from settling in Boyle Heights (interview with Suzie Halajian, art curator, by email, April 17, 2019). The campaign also spread with protests against at least two galleries in South Central, while DBH led workshops on its approach with groups from other cities.

It is of critical importance that, throughout the campaign, Union de Vecinos maneuvered to create perceived distance between themselves and BHAAD and DBH, the official signatories of all actions. The carefully crafted and widespread public perception of Union de Vecinos as only indirectly supportive of the anti-gallery campaign gave the organization an advantage in negotiating with the councillor and others. Union de Vecinos could act as if the organization was an intermediary for the more belligerent DBH and BHAAD, and escape retribution for the controversy and bad press generated by their campaign. The councillor approached Union de Vecinos to seek mediation, and in the meetings that followed members discussed the negative impact of the galleries on the neighborhood and explained their displacement risk. Nonetheless, the relation was bound to become tenser over time, especially as more businesses catering to hipsters sought entrance to the area, and more buildings went into Ellis Act proceedings that removed them from the affordable housing market. The gallery campaign, however, was not the coalition's only focus. Union de Vecinos and DBH also continued to protest displacement more broadly and combined the gallery campaign with casework. And here again their tone and methods were significantly more aggressive than observed in other Los Angeles cases.

There were, however, significant drawbacks to this strategy. With its focus on galleries, the group devoted fewer resources to protest against and negotiation with real-estate interests. At a time when extensive construction was planned due to new state and federal incentives, the group did not exercise the same degree of pressure shown against the galleries on the councilman, especially as pertained zoning, densities, and community benefits. It thereby left ELACC and the neighborhood council as the (far less ambitious) civic counterparts to real-estate interests in the struggle for affordable housing.

The campaign is tentatively coded as not successful, therefore, because the goal of Vecinos was not the elimination of the galleries as an end in itself but rather in order to prevent gentrification and displacement. The current situation is uncertain, and it is too early to assert success on that score, though in coming years the strategy might prove successful.

There is no denying that this approach was an innovative, ambitious, and analytically coherent response to the threat of displacement.

* * *

Overall, Boyle Heights stands out as a resilient neighborhood in Los Angeles. The rate of demographic change was slower than in areas similarly targeted by gentrification in the past decade. The ability of residents to mobilize in Boyle Heights was based on the long political history of Chicanismo and resistance, which in recent years was augmented by struggles against police brutality that united residents across class divisions and included a notable share of businesses and homeowners. Another important factor was the geography of the river and the freeways that surround Boyle Heights, which made the community easier to define and identify.

With the recent campaign against galleries, Union de Vecinos presented an argument in which the role of artists in gentrification was taken to its logical conclusion. In Hamburg, when artists realized their own role as catalysts of gentrification, they developed ironic anti-hipster interventions but did not seriously question their permanence in St Pauli. Organizers in Boyle Heights argued that recognizing their complicity was insufficient and that artists should step up in immediate and active support of residents.

In Boyle Heights, residents and displaced artists united to forcibly remove any cultural actor identified with gentrification. The campaign called for a radical approach to artistic practice, able to counter institutional arts, especially in their ties to a capitalist market. It also contributed to the debate on resistance against gentrification because of its harsh critique of the nonprofit sector. Nonprofits, while conscious of the forces that caused dispossession, fell back on the neoliberal discourse of market-driven solutions. If they did not legitimize the status quo, as argued by Union de Vecinos, they most likely facilitated the position that budgetary requirements make some degree of displacement unavoidable.

Union de Vecinos presented a powerful alternative voice: It argued that such an approach provided insidious support for economic and colonialist dispossession and called instead for the need to vigorously denounce humanitarian discourses that depoliticized and naturalized victimhood.

Will we witness more instances of this approach? Does the case in Boyle Heights point to a return to militancy? Will residents elsewhere turn violent against cultural producers who move to their neighborhoods? The concluding chapter suggests an affirmative answer, while explaining the continuing relevance of experiential tools for mobilization.

12

Conclusion

Nearly all of the cases analyzed in this book that mobilized successfully did so peacefully. Militancy, as in Yongsan, was a strategy of last resort, when redevelopment plans were already under implementation, and was not successful. In fact, as Mullae illustrated, very early mobilization allowed residents to infiltrate institutions and offered the possibility to avoid protest altogether. However, the anti-gallery campaign discussed in Chapter 11 raises important questions on the enduring role of experiential tools and the degree to which they can coexist with a return to militancy.

The increasing political polarization in several countries, accompanied by the exacerbation of inequality and the problem of displacement, pits groups ready for radical action against organizations that are deemed too moderate to alter the injustice of the status quo. In a famous 2004 speech in San Francisco, Arundhati Roy aptly summed up the tensions between NGOs and grassroots resistance: "The NGO-ization of politics threatens to turn resistance into a well-mannered, reasonable, salaried, 9-to-5 job. With a few perks thrown in. Real resistance has real consequences. And no salary."

This statement meshes with the more militant Boyle Heights groups' critiques of their moderate and institutionally oriented counterparts. NGOs diffuse anger, and by pursuing market solutions to fight displacement, they are entangled in neoliberal solutions that cannot truly address the needs of the poorest – a task that can only be addressed outside of the market, by the state. Likewise, in Madrid, the Asociación Vecinal La Corrala was criticized for doing little to resist displacement; in Buenos

Aires, *El Sol de San Telmo* was criticized for reporting on yet not combating gentrification.

The critique has motivated a renewed embrace of militantism since 2015. For example, in the North American context, organizers are more likely to refuse negotiation, owing to inequality between the contending parties, and embrace open confrontation to support radical challenges of prior arrangements and practices. A remarkable illustration is the increased prominence of eviction blockades and rent strikes.

Actions in Boyle Heights set important examples for the return to militant protest, with Union de Vecinos and the LA Tenants Union at the forefront. Los Angeles makes a likely epicenter of the resurgent militancy, given the dramatic housing crisis faced by tenants there (Joint Center for Housing Studies of Harvard University, 2018).

In April 2017, residents of a Boyle Heights apartment complex close to Mariachi Plaza started a rent strike (following the path-breaking lead of a multi-year rent strike started in San Francisco on the eve of 2016).[1] The building had changed hands in 2016, and seven of the twenty-four units, many inhabited by mariachis, were presented with up to 80 percent rent increases. In response, the seven units were joined in a rent strike by an additional six units whose residents feared similar increases. Beyond the rent strike, the militant character of the offensive was displayed in the protests. The most impactful took place in December, when residents (joined by Democratic Socialists of America) camped overnight directly in front of the developer's home, chanting and handing out leaflets to his neighbors. That demonstration signaled a striking shift toward the personalization of militant protest, moving from institutional entities to the private spaces.

That rally (and others that followed in similar campaigns) was highly effective and resulted in the developer agreeing to negotiate. The strike concluded in February 2018 with a significant victory for residents, who agreed to retroactively pay a portion of the rent withheld during the strike, and to a 14 percent rent increase. In return, they received a new 42-month lease with yearly rent hikes capped at 5 percent. They also obtained the right to collectively bargain for new leases as a renters union. They were primarily assisted by Union de Vecinos, the LA Tenants Union,

[1] San Francisco is not part of this study but has been home also of a significant wave in militantism against gentrification, especially aimed at dot-com workers. For example, in much publicized campaigns, activists have shot at tech-workers' commuter buses with pellet guns and led similar disruptive actions.

and the Los Angeles Center for Community Law and Action (which provided legal assistance).

The mariachi strike was widely seen as the first move in a new approach and inspired further action. In March 2018, thirty-six tenants in the Westlake neighborhood went on rent strike, demanding to collectively bargain a new lease agreement with their landlord. An additional forty-eight joined them in April. Given the traditional respect for property rights, a rent strike constitutes a high-risk strategy in a liberal market economy. Indeed, tenants promptly received unlawful detainer notices. However, as can be expected in a setting with prior protest experience and legal expertise among civil actors, protesters found support by several groups and nonprofit legal organizations.

As part of this recent wave of militancy, there have been at least six rent strikes in Los Angeles between 2016 and 2018, and several included similar protests outside the homes of owners and developers, or their families. The wave gained national media attention and inspired similar initiatives also in Cleveland (Dougherty, 2018; Kuznia, 2018).

The recent return to militancy in fighting gentrification raises questions about the role of experiential tools when tactics turn confrontational. In some respects, militancy and experiential tools are opposite poles of the anti-gentrification spectrum, as the latter can appear as nothing but apolitical hedonism and festival and the former as nothing but political combat. Yet cases in this book suggest a keen awareness in all contexts of the importance of experiential tools – as well as their inherent potential to enable gentrification.

* * *

There are other ways to limit displacement and gentrification. Borrowing from Annunziata and Rivas (2018), this section considers how to limit displacement by distinguishing between strategies aimed at prevention, mitigation, building alternatives, and raising awareness. It draws on suggestions that emerge specifically out of the twenty-nine cases examined in this book and does not claim to be an exhaustive, detailed discussion of all possible ways to stop or limit displacement.

Displacement prevention is closely related to structural conditions, and specifically to housing and land policy, such as public-housing policy, tenant protection, and rent regulation (Annunziata & Rivas, 2018). These features depend on political economic structures and can be related to the local variety of capitalism. However, as observed in early chapters, neoliberal shifts can be observed across the board especially as pertains government retrenchment from earlier roles in the public provision and administration of subsidized housing, probably the most important barrier against residential displacement, but also evident in changes in tenant protection regulation, zoning laws, and taxation regimes.

Rent stabilization is an instrument of prevention that for decades played a key role in the provision of affordable housing, especially in coordinated market economies, where government historically played an important role not only in the provision of public housing but also the regulation of private contracts. In the United States, a growing tenant movement has brought several ballot initiatives for rent control and rent regulation in recent years, and tenants' movements have spread from areas of New York City and Washington, DC, to new areas such as Seattle, Denver, Minneapolis, and Nashville.

Union de Vecinos, and associated groups, led struggles for the extension of the city's Rent Stabilization Ordinance and the repeal of California's 1995 Costa-Hawkins Rental Housing Act, which in a few ways limited the ability of city and county governments to enact stronger rent control laws. After the repeal failed to advance in the state legislature, activists succeeded in collecting enough signatures to add it to the 2018 election ballot.

Despite the failure at the ballot box, these campaigns were especially interesting for their legislative ambition and their robust networks. What started as relatively local goals soon connected with campaigns regionally and nationally and notable extensions in rent stabilization since 2010.

Several cases in this book illustrated successful preventive efforts of *institutionalizing the right to stay put*. In Los Angeles (see Chapter 7), faced with massive evictions from residential hotels around 2003, LA CAN organized residents and worked for the passage of the Residential Hotel Unit Conversion and Demolition Ordinance, which permanently preserves more than 15,000 homes for Los Angeles' lowest-income tenants. Activists also won zoning protections in Mullae, Yungay, and Colina. As these cases have illustrated, this strategy depends on a successful mobilization and a relatively favorable political landscape: In most Istanbul cases, where mobilization was uneven and the political environment especially adverse to protesters, attempts to gain protection based on historical heritage failed, and the government argued instead that "regeneration" (and the associated displacement) would serve heritage protection better than repairs.

A right to stay put was also obtained in Hamburg by Gängeviertel, through the establishment of a long-term agreement with the government that assigned the use and management of the site to a cooperative. Recently, in Hamburg and elsewhere in Germany, activists have rediscovered and deployed an old and disregarded anti-speculative measure known as *Milieuschutz* (social environmental protection), which is intended to protect existing renters and maintain the social mix of a neighborhood (Vogelpohl & Buchholz, 2017). In areas protected by this social preservation statute (*Soziale Erhaltungssatzung*), owners are forbidden from changing floor plans (for example, merging or splitting up apartments), making modifications intended to raise rents, or renting apartments short term (as vacation rental). It is still too early to say whether these laws will deliver a strong tool against displacement, but the first applications seem promising.

* * *

In the absence of outright prevention mechanisms, or sometimes in combination, residents attempted to mitigate the effects of displacement. In several cases in this book, mitigation followed a *case-by-case defense and compensation approach*, which aimed first to defend the right to stay, and, when unable to do that, pursued what residents considered adequate compensation for leaving. This was the most common form of resistance among the cases I examined, in part because the approach was less complex than programmatic or legislative initiatives. PAH stands out for the organized, sustained, and impactful history of case-by-case defense of evictees, especially for the way its representatives were able to negotiate with mortgage-holding banks on behalf of residents. The reliance on case-by-case mitigation is observed in other Spanish-speaking cases. Vecinos por la Defensa del Barrio Yungay, while mostly geared toward legislative solutions, also engaged in case-by-case campaigns.

Union the Vecinos and LA CAN combined programmatic struggles with individual-level campaigns in their own neighborhoods – what one representative of LA CAN interviewed referred to as "putting out fires." The reliance on case-by-case campaigns was even more evident in Istanbul and in Seoul, both with adverse political environments. The Korean cases illustrate how case-by-case campaigns for adequate compensation constitute a strategy of last resort in adverse political contexts. In this sense, Duriban, Seoul, constitutes a remarkable success for protesters; the other cases show instead the shortcoming of this approach, as developers can pit residents against each other (for example, in Myeong-dong and Sulukule). Mullae Art Village stands out for its original and effective approach, though the characteristics of that mobilization and the presence of a progressive mayoralty limit the replicability of this strategy.

Squatting also falls under the case-by-case approach to mitigating displacement and is observed in a wide range of settings. Outside of liberal market economies, squats were sometimes institutionalized. Success by occupiers largely depended on property right regimes and on the degree and discipline of the organization of the squat. For instance, Gängeviertel flourished thanks to its effective internal organization and ability to muster government support. In low-property-rights regimes, such as Buenos Aires, squats survived for years or decades even without institutional arrangements.

A prominent example of ad-hoc mitigation are Los Angeles' community benefit agreements (CBAs). CBAs are private contracts between developers and community coalitions that typically require the coalition to support or at least not oppose the project in exchange for negotiated benefits, such as living wages, local hiring and training programs, right-to-unionize agreements, affordable housing, environmental remediation, and funds for community programs. CBAs are therefore distinct from settlements because they are negotiated well in advance of any litigation with the goal of moving a project through an administrative approvals process. They are also different from government-imposed covenants because they give negotiation and enforcement power directly to community groups (Beach, 2007). In 2004, LA CAN obtained quality job opportunities for low-income downtown residents at a proposed bar-restaurant catering to the new residents of the gentrifying community. However, CBAs can also be very complex. The city's most famous CBA covers development in the Los Angeles sports and entertainment district surrounding the Staples sports arena on the southern edge of downtown. This CBA covered inclusionary housing, funding for affordable housing, parking, living wages, park space, and local hiring (Parks & Warren, 2009; Saito, 2012).

Being project-specific, CBAs require coalitions to muster high coordination with a plethora of actors, some of whom often have interests likely to diverge from residents (such as construction unions, typically in support of any new construction) and which might therefore be subject to divide-and-conquer tactics on the part of developers (Gross, 2007; Salkin & Lavine, 2008; Wolf-Powers, 2010). Since CBAs are usually not prescribed by law, they require high setup costs at each and every instance and are thereby of little use when the project is not large enough for negotiations to yield significant rewards for residents. Further, their lack of institutionalized backing undermines implementation and enforcement, made especially thorny given the dependence of agreements on particular grassroots and institutional leaders, who might no longer be in office at the time of implementation.

We can expect these kinds of solutions – decisively non-public and relying on tort law for their enforceability – to emerge in liberal market economies, "given the herculean task of passing new regulations" in these settings (Parks & Warren, 2009, p. 96). However, the ad-hoc character of these solutions limits their effectiveness.

More promising are legislative forms of mitigation. An interesting form of mitigation is inclusionary zoning, whereby developers are required to make a certain percentage of the units within their market-rate residential developments affordable to low- or moderate-income households (Meltzer & Schuetz, 2010). Although valuable, this approach in its statutory (or legislative) form was not central to the cases in this book. However, the cases presented a form of inclusionary zoning in the context of public housing, where inclusionary zoning was integrated in redevelopment plans and amounted to a controversial form of social mixing.

The legislative compensatory mechanism that stands out in the cases is Toronto's Section 37 funding. This approach falls under the umbrella of land value capture mechanisms, which refer to the public sector's recovery of land value increments associated with new development. Recovery can be through taxes, fees, exactions, or improvements that benefit the community (Friendly, 2017).

With Section 37 funding, communities affected by redevelopment in Toronto have a more accessible instrument than CBAs, and in fact invoke it routinely. Section 37 funding is a type of development impact fee that is charged by a local governmental agency to an applicant for the purpose of defraying all or a portion of the cost of public facilities related to the development project. Impact fees have existed in North America since the 1920s, their use accelerated with the fall in municipal funding in the 1980s (Jeong, 2006). Depending on how the affected community is defined, and therefore on the recipients, development impact fees can have progressive or regressive effects (Feiock, 2004).

In Toronto, Section 37 is invoked when developers seek zoning exceptions, and specifically density bonuses, which is a common request in the case of high-rises. According to the law, developers can agree to provide community benefits in cash or amenities in exchange for approval. City planning staff and councillors from the affected ward negotiate benefits. Although the agreements require city council approval, the use of the funds is largely controlled by the local councillor (Friendly, 2017; Lehrer & Pantalone 2018; A. A. Moore, 2013b).

Therefore, while CBAs are agreements between community representatives and developers, and do not need to involve elected officials, Section 37 negotiations, in contrast, give local councillors a critical role. The effect is that communities have easier access to compensation in Toronto (the rule applies to all projects over 10,000 square meters in gross floor area), but they are more at the mercy of their councillor. The degree of compensation, the type of compensation and the beneficiaries are undefined and as witnessed in the case of Active 18, a capable group can gain great advantage in redistribution, while more needy and marginalized communities are excluded by the negotiations. The result is that "the true beneficiaries are local councillors" and their supporters (Makuch & Schuman, 2015, p. 324).

Recently, some activists have pushed to move the CBA model from ad-hoc to legislative form, through the adoption of model CBAs and community benefits ordinances (Belongie & Silverman, 2018). The effect is to bring CBAs closer to the practice of development impact fees. However, the fundamental distinction remains that development impact fees are negotiated between developers and municipalities, while CBAs are negotiated directly between coalitions of community-based groups and developers, with local government typically playing a mediating role.

More compelling are cases, such as the city of San Francisco and São Paulo, that have formulas for their land value capture programs, with greater transparency and less political discretion about the transfers, their purposes, and their beneficiaries (Friendly, 2017). In addition to common concerns regarding effects of redevelopment on existing infrastructure, green space, traffic, environment, and so on, progressive cities have begun to include direct as well as indirect effects on residents' health. For example, based on the California Environmental Quality Act (which considers any environmental change that may be adverse to humans), the city of San Francisco included in its impact studies for redevelopment proposals: "psychological stress, fear, and insecurity caused by eviction; crowding or substandard living conditions because of limited affordable replacement housing; food insecurity or hunger caused by increased rent burdens; and loss of supportive social networks owing to displacement" (Bhatia, 2007, p. 407).

Cities face both incentives and disincentives to pursue this route. On the one hand, establishing direct and even indirect health effects of redevelopment requires substantial administrative resources. On the other hand, the establishment of these additional costs of redevelopment can provide cities with legally sanctioned grounds to justify additional impact fees (Cramer, Dietz, & Johnston, 1980; Vanclay & Esteves, 2011).

The thorniest issues remain how to regulate the parties involved in the negotiation with developers and how to determine the use of funds – both with the goal of ensuring greater oversight of real-estate development by the affected community. Of course, this in turn begs the question of how community representation is regulated in a manner that is fair, inclusive, and exhaustive – when we can expect that precisely those groups most in need are least likely to organize effective representation.[2] As evident in the Lawrence Heights case in Toronto, a preexistent dense and active organizational network is essential to muster effective representation of typically marginalized communities when redevelopment is proposed. However, even agreed-upon goals may not get implemented, given staff changes, low institutional memory, and the protracted timeline of large redevelopment projects.

These land value capture policies are becoming more popular, and now exist in the UK, the United States, Brazil, and Colombia. Given the promise of development impact fees in systematically mitigating redevelopment and the extent of displacement, it is urgent to conduct more comparative work that sheds light on the politics of these arrangements, including determinants of participants, processes, and outcomes.

* * *

A third strategy is to build alternatives to displacement and gentrification like *community planning and construction*. A strong collaboration between government institutions and the affected community is critical in urban redevelopment because public involvement can shed light on problems hidden to experts, give voice to competing values and interests, identify common goals, and help achieve more effective solutions. It also

[2] A related issue is whether the target community is defined as the neighborhood where the development is being built (as is the case in Toronto where otherwise fees are considered illegal taxes) or the city as a whole – a distinction that has fundamental redistributive consequences, since developments are least likely in neighborhoods facing economic decline, though it is precisely these areas that most would benefit from the inflow of resources.

facilitates the buy-in necessary for effective policy implementation (Fung & Wright, 2001).

Community planning resulted in alternative plans to counter redevelopment initiatives in several cases in this book, including the Hamburg cases of Park Fiction and Gängeviertel, and the North American cases of Rolland Curtis Gardens and Lawrence Heights. In Rolland Curtis Gardens, the community-based organizations obtained buy-in for redevelopment and the city government gained a model that it subsequently presented to showcase its commitment to public responsiveness. In Lawrence Heights, a more inclusive approach was supported by a strong preexisting local NGO network, and augmented by the community-building effort of the Heritage Plan, which strengthened mobilization and solidarity among residents. For the first time, residents also participated in the selection of the developer and had a voice in various aspects of the planning. The effect was a far less contentious outcome than a similar redevelopment in Regent Park. However, as indicated by both Rolland Curtis Gardens and Lawrence Heights, the extension of community participation beyond the earliest planning stages is extremely challenging.

A step beyond community planning is community construction. The most successful and institutionalized instance of self-managed renovation was identified in Buenos Aires, where MOI led the city council passage (and implementation) of Law 341/2000, which provided credit for social organizations (e.g., renters' cooperatives) to buy and self-manage the restoration of dwellings, thereby removing developers from the equation. In contrast (and more typically), in Lavapiés, Madrid, a policy to facilitate self-managed renovation failed to support local residents because of red tape and limited funding. An additional instance of self-managed renovation and construction was observed in Yungay, where organizers spearheaded the foundation of a local school specifically intended to develop the technical skills needed for renovation of neighborhood housing by local residents.

Land trusts are another approach to building alternatives against displacement. They are usually developed after gentrification has started and thus tend to mitigate rather than prevent displacement. Cases in this book show that several groups, especially in liberal market economies, seek to develop and control land trusts. Scholars have identified this approach as a solution that decommodifies housing (DeFilippis, 2004). Collective ownership of housing, for example in the form of limited-equity housing cooperatives (as we observed in Buenos Aires with Law

341/2000) or land trusts (as observed in Los Angeles' Rolland Curtis Gardens) do achieve collective ownership of housing, and are one important solution against displacement.

Yet, where displacement was taking place, land trusts were impractical because land prices had already substantially increased, and local resident organizations lacked the funds to muster a significant trust. As a result, the dominant strategy, illustrated by TRUST South LA, was to seek out special opportunities, where land could be obtained below market prices through political pressure and threat of litigation, as in the case of Rolland Curtis Gardens.

Such cases are extremely rare. However, since 2017, California activists have begun to explore eminent domain and the 2014 California Surplus Land Act as tools to support publicly owned land trusts. The Act requires that cities, counties, transit agencies, and other local agencies in the process of selling or leasing their land must prioritize it for affordable housing development. As activists organize to pressure agencies to enforce it, they illustrate the role of expertise and prior protest experience in the development and deployment of judicial strategies that are typical of conflicts in liberal market economies. These efforts are among the recent flourishing of broad-based tenant mobilization that could transform how redevelopment supports disadvantaged and preexisting resident communities.

* * *

A fourth strategy, *raising awareness*, was observed in all successful cases in this book. Indeed, raising awareness of displacement was an absolutely critical component of protest.

Scholars are long familiar with the function of social and organizational networks, but this book has shown the essential role played by experiential tools to raise awareness in a variety of ways, including building collective place-based identities, fostering participants' commitment, publicizing concerns, and displaying political clout to allies and targets – all steps that are critical to a struggle's mobilization and impact.

The cases examined provide robust evidence that mobilization without the remarkable inventiveness and attractiveness of experiential tools faces obstacles that only significant institutional support can overcome. Thus, experiential tools are especially precious to groups that lack such institutional connection or that are new to protest – characteristics that are both common among vulnerable residents facing evictions.

However, the cases also recommend caution in the use of experiential tools. Because experiential tools increase the legibility, attractiveness, accessibility, and consumability of an area, they can in themselves turn into tools for displacement rather than mobilization or political resistance. The ways that artists can act as early gentrifiers and drive future demand for an area has been studied for decades. The role of cultural producers in pioneering neighborhoods previously considered marginal by mainstream citizens has been explained in terms of consumption patterns and branding. Yet this book warns us that before both of those dynamics occur, cultural producers impact the attractiveness of the neighborhood for gentrifiers, because their very presence and activities render the site more legible and accessible. This is an understudied and prior mechanism of gentrification and displacement that makes the presence of cultural producers who are connected with markets and networks outside the neighborhood into (mostly unwitting) pawns in the process of gentrification.

There is little that their ideology or intentions can do to counter this effect, exacerbated by online navigational aids. Their programmatic choice might have an effect on the speed at which legibility increases; for example, they might focus entirely on very local actions. Yet this is unlikely because it goes against the market logic of self-promotion inherent to today's artistic production. As Gängeviertel showed, state intervention can somewhat limit the inherently gentrifying effects of cultural production; for example, by taking properties off the market. However, the effect is limited, and even zoning protection such as the one gained in Mullae is not sufficient to ultimately prevent substantial rises in rental prices and the associated displacement.

So a cultural producer's role is complex and goes well beyond a simple dichotomy of helpless victims or conscious agents of gentrification. Notwithstanding this complexity, however, interviews with protest organizers indeed did reveal a dichotomous perception as organizers drew a stark contrast between artists who contributed to gentrification and those who lent their expertise and resources for resistance. Organizers primarily understood "friendly" artists as those involved in social practice art, that is artwork that brings together artists and non-artists in place-based work that inspires community involvement. These practices spark mutual learning and negotiation between artists, non-artists, and members of the public and affected communities. The Theater of the Oppressed and other initiatives described in the context of LA CAN, the community museum developed in Santiago, and participatory creative planning for Park

Fiction in Hamburg are all examples of such collaboration of residents and artists.

However, there is a fine line between social practice art forms that defend existing communities, and others that ultimately undermine that goal. The walking tours in the context of the Regent Park's Illuminati festival are an example. As McLean discusses, they offered a voice to local youth and raised awareness and the possibility of contestation. However they fed "exclusionary neoliberal policies" (McLean, 2014) because they ultimately were enacted in a context – the festival – that served the purpose of branding the city and the neighborhood for consumption and gentrification. Therefore, it is critical to examine not only participants, programming, and themes but also the context and audience of these interventions. This is especially the case when creative city strategies mobilize local artist communities to support wider redevelopment plans, as observed in Seoul's Mullae Art Factory. Similarly, in Boyle Heights, walking tours by planning students from the nearby University of Southern California (USC) were stopped and escorted out of the neighborhood. USC is one of the main gentrifying forces there, and despite the ideological commitment of the tour's participants, the walking tours themselves increased access to the neighborhood and made it more legible.

Once again, this reminds us of the key conundrum faced by organizers: experiential tools have the potential for extraordinary mobilization, which is especially tempting absent union support. Yet to sustain participant commitment, while avoiding inevitably facilitating future displacement, it seems that the production of cool must be performed behind closed doors.

Whatever the particular strategies, growing networks of mutual support are helping to spread the lessons learned in struggles against displacement. Organizers, academics, and residents increasingly come together to collect strategies and make them readily available for new struggles. A great illustration of the kind work that needs to be conducted is the 2014 booklet *Staying Put: An Anti-gentrification Handbook for Council Estates in London* (London Tenants Federation, Lees, & Just Space, 2014). More lessons need to be compiled and systematically compared in order to turn solidarity among residents into effective campaigns, wherever they seek to challenge and prevent displacement.

Appendix 1 Qualitative Comparative Analysis

Several factors make qualitative comparative analysis (QCA) a superior choice for this investigation, despite recent criticisms (Hug, 2013; Lucas & Szatrowski, 2014). First of all, this approach is better suited to the present dataset. The dataset has a small number of cases (n = 29) with ordinal discrete variables. The observations are not mutually independent for at least two reasons: They are set in within-city comparisons, and there is mutual learning between the observed campaigns. The impact of the variables is not additive, yet the small n prevents the inclusion of the necessary interaction effects. Ordered logit models are further undermined by the fact that some variables are sufficient or quasi-sufficient for the outcome.

Further, the method allows isolating cross-case patterns, while appreciating the heterogeneity of the cases with regard to their different causally relevant conditions. The most important advantage of deploying QCA is that it allows examining INUS conditions – causal conditions that are insufficient by themselves but necessary components of causal combinations that are unnecessary (because of multiple paths) but sufficient for the outcome (Mackie, 1980). In other words, as Ragin (2013) explains, solutions may be both conjunctural (i.e. grouping factors into combinations that are jointly sufficient for the outcome) and equifinal (i.e. reachable through multiple possible combinations). Thus, QCA allows causal patterns that are complex and involve different combinations of causal conditions capable of generating the outcome of interest. The emphasis on complex causality contrasts with the "net effects" approach that dominates conventional quantitative social science. QCA has a second significant advantage in that it requires explicit counterfactual analysis that is grounded in empirical and theoretical reasoning, while conventional comparative analysis usually fails to explicitly consider counterfactuals, often to the effect of reaching oversimplified solutions.

QCA is grounded in the analysis of set relations rather than correlations. The focus of the analysis is to identify approximate necessity and sufficiency conditions, given across-case patterns. Necessity is identified when the outcome is a subset of the causal condition; while sufficiency is identified when the causal condition is a subset of the outcome. With INUS conditions, cases with a specific combination of causal conditions form a subset of the cases with the outcome.

QCA does not seek to infer population properties from a sample, nor does it seek to make causal inferences based on a test of a causal model. It does not assess the separate impact of competing independent variables, nor interaction effects. Instead, the goal is to aid causal interpretation, supporting the scholar's knowledge of cases, in order to identify combinations of conditions linked to the outcome of interest. Results depend on the researcher's specification of causally relevant conditions (e.g., thresholds and the treatment of counterfactuals). The outcome depends therefore on the researcher's theoretical and empirical assessment of the cases (Rihoux & Ragin, 2008). The variable-oriented approach focuses on average effects, where underlying relationships are revealed by purging the cases of their specificity, and cases taken individually are considered deceptive. Case-oriented approaches like QCA instead emphasize the close examination of each case and embrace case heterogeneity as highly relevant to explanation. Cress and Snow (1996) and McAdam and Boudet (2012) illustrate this method in the study of local protest and mobilization.

EXPLAINING MOBILIZATION

QCA seeks to identify sets of cases that share an outcome and uses controlled case comparisons to eliminate causal conditions in an incremental, context-bound manner. The logical combinations of causal conditions – based on the cases at hand – are presented in truth tables. If cases with a given configuration of causally relevant conditions share an outcome, they constitute a subset of the cases with the outcome.

In order to pursue the analysis, the software package fsQCA provides three solutions types: complex, parsimonious, and intermediate. A complex solution reflects only the rows for which cases are available, i.e. remainders (rows for which cases are not available) are all set to false and there is no use of counterfactuals. Because social-science datasets are typically marred by lack of diversity, the available rows do not fully reflect the underlying population. Consequently, in complex solutions, results usually comprise convoluted paths because they reflect the high degree of specificity of the cases actually available in the dataset. They also often include spurious factors, called nuisance conditions, which do not make theoretical sense but are instead the result of limited variation.

To aid the analysis, the researcher assigns rules to examine counterfactuals. The rules are derived from theoretical and substantive knowledge, which allows defining "easy" counterfactuals, i.e. hypothetical cases that resemble empirical cases (actually present in the dataset) in all respects except one, with the one difference making the outcome *more* likely in the hypothetical case than in the empirical case. This strategy renders explicit the analysis of counterfactuals, thus improving on most small-n comparative research.

Parsimonious solutions suffer from the opposite problem faced by complex ones. They are compiled by setting in the truth table all remainder rows (combinations lacking cases in the dataset) to "don't care," regardless of whether they constitute "easy" or "difficult" counterfactuals. The effect is that any remainder that will help generate a logically simpler solution is used. (Note that correlational solutions are closest to parsimonious solutions in that they do not explicitly consider counterfactuals that could undermine the outcome.)

Usually the scholar has enough knowledge of the issue to know that *some* simplifying assumptions incorporated to arrive at a parsimonious solution are in fact empirically or theoretically untenable. That is why the recommended protocol is to select intermediate solutions. In this case, the program considers all the cases *plus* the remainders rows for which the scholar has reasonably accepted hypotheses. Only remainders that are "easy" counterfactual cases (in the sense that they conform to empirical and theoretical expectations) are allowed to be incorporated into the solution. The designation of "easy" versus "difficult" is based on user-supplied information regarding the connection between each causal condition and the outcome (Ragin, 2013). In intermediate solutions, the inclusion of easy counterfactuals allows the algebraic elimination (through Boolean simplification) of nuisance conditions. Intermediate solutions offer two additional important advantages: They allow scholars to deploy the theoretical knowledge that is accumulated in a given field by providing expected associations; and – contrary to common practice – they actually require the scholar to make *explicit* the theoretical assumptions about logical combinations that are not available in the dataset.

As discussed in Chapter 2, the social-movement literature supports the hypotheses that higher mobilization is likely to be positively associated with higher values for union support, network engagement, and prior protest. I therefore imposed the assumption that union support, network activation, and prior protest are present whenever mobilization is present.

TABLE A1.1 *Truth table analysis for mobilization.*

Model: Mobilization = f (Union, Experiential, Networks, PriorProtest, HighIncome)
Algorithm: Quine-McCluskey
Intermediate Solution
Frequency cutoff: 1
Consistency cutoff: 0.955789
Assumptions:
- Union (present)
- Networks (present)
- PriorProtest (present)

	Raw Coverage	Unique Coverage	Consistency
Union*Networks	0.241379	0.103448	1
Experiential*Networks	0.804598	0.195402	0.985915
Experiential*PriorProtest	0.655172	0.0459771	0.966102

solution coverage: 0.954023
solution consistency: 0.976471

As captured in Table A1.1, the intermediate solution then indicates that three paths explain cases with high mobilization:

1 The combination of union support and activated networks (24 percent of mobilization cases are explained by this combination, and 10 percent are explained *only* by this combination);
2 The combination of experiential tools and activated networks (80 percent of mobilization cases are explained by this combination, and 19 percent are explained *only* by this combination);
3 The combination of experiential tools and legacy (65 percent of mobilization cases are explained by this combination, and 5 percent are explained *only* by this combination).

In set theoretic terms, the outcome is explained by the intersection of union support and activated networks, or the intersection of experiential tools and activated networks, or the intersection of experiential tools and legacy.

The truth table analysis output includes measures of coverage and consistency for each solution term and for the solution as a whole. Consistency measures the degree to which solution terms and the solution as a whole are subsets of the outcome (and thereby it is a measure of sufficiency). Coverage measures how much of the outcome is covered (or explained) by each solution term and by the solution as a whole (and thereby it is a measure of necessity). These measures are computed by examining the original fuzzy dataset in light of the solution (composed of one or more solution terms). The degree to which cases in the dataset have membership in each solution term and in the outcome form the basis of consistency and coverage measures. The solution coverage value indicates that taken together, the three paths explain 95 percent of the cases of mobilization. It should be noted that network activation is a widely shared antecedent, which approximates a necessary condition. The solution consistency is at least 97 percent for each solution term and for the solution as a whole, indicating that each is a nearly full subset of the outcome. (In other words, nearly all cases fully conform to the recipe.)

In sum, three paths lead to mobilization, the first outcome of interest. First, successful protest groups are more likely to seek collaboration of labor unions in cities where the latter are strong. However, in the majority of aspiring global cities, unions are relatively weak and often espouse pro-growth agendas – thus, while they might support affordable housing construction, they are typically unsupportive of housing preservation campaigns.

In such negative contexts, protest groups mobilize by deploying experiential tools. The second path combines experiential tools with networks, confirming their role as indicated by the literature. In successful cases, resistance groups are supported by multiple cross-sectorial groups or organizations within the neighborhood and/or sectorial groups or organizations across the city.

The third path to mobilization requires a strong legacy in organizing and experiential tools. Despite its acknowledged role in the literature, in the present analysis there are paths to mobilization that do not require prior protest experience; in other words, in the current fluid political landscape there is significant space for newcomers to protest. Finally, the impact of city income per capita, added as an underlying factor, was not consistent enough to become a component of a specific path to mobilization.[1]

EXPLAINING IMPACT

The second outcome of interest is impact. In this case, no assumption was imposed to guide the intermediate solution. The truth table analysis is presented in Table A1.2. There, the intermediate solution then indicates that two paths explain cases with high impact:

[1] I ran the analysis with city GDP per capita coded with values of zero for incomes up to $30,000, 0.25 for incomes up to $38,000, 0.75 for incomes up to $43,000, and 1 for incomes above $43,000. I also calibrated city GDP per capita values in order to identify membership in a high-income city. The calibration is set with full membership in the set of high-income cities set at $45,000, the crossover point set at $39,000 and the full non-membership from the set of high-income cities at $25,000. The two approaches – with four interval sets and the calibration for high-income city group – produce the same result in fsQCA. Calibration is recommended for fsQCA, and therefore I present results based on the calibrated version of city GDP per capita.

TABLE A1.2 *Truth table for impact.*

TRUTH TABLE ANALYSIS

Model: Impact = f (Mobilization, CouncilAlly, HigherlevLeft, MayorLeft)
Algorithm: Quine-McCluskey

Intermediate Solution
Frequency cutoff: 1
Consistency cutoff: 0.846154
Assumptions: None

	Raw Coverage	Unique Coverage	Consistency
Mobilization*CouncilAlly *HigherlevLeft	0.446154	0.292308	0.90625
Mobilization*CouncilAlly *MayorLeft	0.492308	0.338462	0.888889

solution coverage: 0.784615
solution consistency: 0.87931

1 The combination of mobilization, council ally, and a leftist higher-level executive (45 percent of impact cases are explained by this combination, and 29 percent are explained *only* by this combination).
2 The combination of mobilization, council ally, and a leftist local-level executive (49 percent of mobilization cases are explained by this combination, and 34 percent are explained *only* by this combination).

In set theoretic terms, the outcome is explained by the intersection of mobilization, council ally, and a leftist higher-level executive, or the intersection of mobilization, council ally, and a leftist local-level executive. Consistency is 88 percent, and coverage is 78 percent, indicating that some cases displayed some success in impact outside of this path.

Appendix 2 Partisan Alignments

TABLE A2.1 *Partisan alignments.*

City-Site-Group	Main Campaign Period	City Mayor	Political Party in Government at the Higher Institutional Level during the Case Observation	Partisan Alignment	Political Ally in Local Council
Buenos Aires-San Telmo-Asamblea Lezama	2012–2013	Ibarra (left), 2000–2006; Telerman (left), 2006–2007; Macri (right), 2007–2015	Argentina President: DeLaRua, 1999–2001; Duhalde, 2002–2003; Kirchner, 2003–2007; Kirchner, 2007–2015 (All Left)	Dealigned with right-wing mayor	Yes
Buenos Aires-San Telmo-Asamblea Pueblo	2002–2013			Aligned Left (2002–2007), then dealigned with right-wing mayor	Yes
Buenos Aires-San Telmo-MOI	1999–2013			Aligned Left (2002–2007), then dealigned with right-wing mayor	Yes
Santiago-Colina-Pueblo Canteras	2010–2018	Alcaino (right), 2004–2008; Zalaquett (right), 2008–2012; Morales (left), 2012–2016; Vergara (right), 2016–Present	Chile President: Bachelet (left), 2006–2010; Pinera (right), 2010–2014; Bachelet (left), 2014–2018	Key victories during dealignment with right-wing mayor	Yes
Santiago-Yungay-Vecinos	2006–2018			Key victories during dealignment with right-wing mayor	Yes
Istanbul-Fener&Balat-Febayder	2009–2010	Topbaş (right), 2004–2017	Turkey Prime Minister (then President): Erdoğan (right), 2003–Present	Aligned right	Yes
Istanbul-GeziPark-Various	2013			Aligned right	Yes
Istanbul-Sulukule-Platform	2006–2008			Aligned right	No

Seoul-Duriban Restaurant-Owners	December 2009–June 2011	Lee (right), 2000–2006; Oh (right), 2006–2011; Park (left), 2011–Present	South Korea President: Lee (right), 2008–2013	Aligned right	Yes
Seoul-Mullae-Art Village members	2007–2012			Dealigned with left-wing mayor (progressive regime)	Yes
Seoul-Myeongdong-Duriban activists	Summer 2011			Aligned right	No
Seoul-Yongsan-commercial tenants	2008–2010			Aligned right	No
Madrid-Lavapiés-Asamblea/PAH Centro	2011–2015	Four mayors from the People's Party (right), 2003–2015; Carmena (center), 2015–Present	Spain Prime Minister: Zapatero (left), 2004–2011; Rajoy (right), 2011–2018	Aligned Right	Yes
Madrid-Lavapiés-Tabacalera	2003–2011			Dealigned with right-wing mayor	Yes
Melbourne-Fitzroy & NRichmond-HOME	2013	City of Yarra Council: Left (1996–present)	Victoria Premier: Baillieu (right), 2010- March 13; Napthine (right), 2013–2014; Andrews (left), 2014-Present	Dealigned with left mayor	Yes
Melbourne-HoracePetty-HOME	2013	City of Stonnington Council: Center (mostly Independents)		Aligned Right	No
Tel Aviv-Jaffa-Various	2011	Huldai (left), 1998–Present	Israel Prime Minister: Netanyahu (right), 2009–Present	Dealigned with left mayor	Yes
Tel Aviv-Rothschild-This-is-a-house	2011			Dealigned with left mayor	Yes

(continued)

TABLE A2.1 (*continued*)

City-Site-Group	Main Campaign Period	City Mayor	Political Party in Government at the Higher Institutional Level during the Case Observation	Partisan Alignment	Political Ally in Local Council
Toronto-Lawrence Heights-Various	2007–2014	Lastman (right), 1998–2003; Miller (left), 2003–2010; Ford (right), 2010–2014; Tory (right), 2014–Present	Ontario Premier: McGuinty (left), 2003–2013; Wynne (left), 2013–2018	Aligned Left then dealigned with right-wing mayor	Yes
Toronto-Mimico-MRA/MLN	2012–2014			Dealigned with right-wing mayor	No
Toronto-QueenStreetWest-Active 18	2005–2010			Dealigned with right-wing mayor	Yes
Toronto-Parkdale-Pope Squat	2002–2003			Dealigned with right-wing mayor	No
Toronto-Regent Park-Residents	2003–2007			Aligned Left	No
Hamburg-Gängeviertel-Komm in die Gänge	2009	Both districts of Hamburg-Mitte and Altona are historically on the Left, which led coalitions 2004–Present	First Hamburg Mayor vonBeust (right), 2001–2010; Ahlhaus (right), 2010–2011; Scholz (left), 2011–2018	Dealigned with left mayor	Yes
Hamburg-St. Pauli DancingTowers-Skam	2009			Dealigned with left mayor	Yes
Hamburg-St. Pauli ParkFiction-Es Regnet Kaviar	1995–2005			Dealigned with left mayor	Yes
Los Angeles-BoyleHeights-UnionDeVecinos	2015–2017	Villaraigosa (left), 2003–2013; Garcetti (left), 2013–Present	California Governer: Schwarzenegger (right), 2003–2011; Brown (left), 2011–2018	Aligned Left	No
Los Angeles-ROH campaign-LA CAN	2001–2008			Dealigned with left mayor	Yes
Los Angeles-Rolland Curtis-Trust South LA	2011–2014			Aligned Left	Yes

Bibliography

Abbas, T., & Yigit, I. H. (2015). Scenes from Gezi Park: Localisation, nationalism and globalisation in Turkey. *City, 19*(1), 61–76.
Abellán, J. (2014). Ciudad, crisis y desobediencia: Una aproximacion a las luchas por la vivienda en Madrid. In R. Hidalgo & M. Janoschka (Eds.), *La ciudad neoliberal* (pp. 257–274). Santiago: LOM.
Acuña, R. (1984). *A community under siege: A chronicle of Chicanos east of the Los Angeles river, 1945–1975*. Los Angeles, CA: Chicano Studies Research Center, UCLA.
Adanalı, Y., Korkmaz, T., & Yücesoy, E. Ü. (2009). *Living in voluntary and involuntary exclusion*. Istanbul: Refuge-Diwan.
Advisory Group on Forced Evictions. (2009). *Mission to Argentina*. Retrieved from https://tinyurl.com/yxmpgyu7
Ahmadi, D. (2016). Is diversity our strength? An analysis of the facts and fancies of diversity in Toronto. Paper presented at the Contested Cities Conference, July 4–7, Madrid.
Aksoy, A. (2010). *Istanbul: Dilemma of direction*. Paper presented at the Europa Nostra Annual Conference, June 8–12, Istanbul.
(2012). Riding the storm: "New Istanbul." *City, 16*(1–2), 93–111.
Alfasi, N., & Fabian, R. (2008). Ideological developers and the formation of local development policy: The case of inner-city preservation in Tel Aviv. *Journal of Urban Affairs, 30*(5), 489–505.
Alfasi, N., & Fenster, T. (2014). Between socio-spatial and urban justice: Rawls' principles of justice in the 2011 Israeli protest movement. *Planning Theory, 13*(4), 407–427.
Alimi, E. Y. (2012). "Occupy Israel": A tale of startling success and hopeful failure. *Social Movement Studies, 11*(3–4), 402–407.
Allen, K. (2012, May 10). Mimico waterfront: Another "wall of condos" disaster in the making? *Toronto Star*. Retrieved from https://tinyurl.com/y2t3dozc

Aller, S. (2004, July 9). Arranca la rehabilitación del Centro con la expropiación de dos edificios en Lavapiés. *ABC.es*. Retrieved from https://tinyurl.com/y289964v

Allweil, Y. (2013). Surprising alliances for dwelling and citizenship: Palestinian–Israeli participation in the mass housing protests of summer 2011. *International Journal of Islamic Architecture*, 2(1), 41–75.

Altshuler, A. A., & Luberoff, D. E. (2004). *Mega-projects: The changing politics of urban public investment*. Washington, DC: Brookings Institution Press.

Amenta, E. (2006). *When movements matter: The Townsend Plan and the rise of social security*. Princeton, NJ: Princeton University Press.

Amirtahmasebi, R., Orloff, M., Wahba, S., & Altman, A. (2016). *Regenerating urban land: A practitioner's guide to leveraging private investment*. Washington, DC: World Bank Publications.

Amit-Cohen, I. (2005). Synergy between urban planning, conservation of the cultural built heritage and functional changes in the old urban center: The case of Tel Aviv. *Land Use Policy*, 22(4), 291–300.

Ancelovici, M. (2002). Organizing against globalization: The case of ATTAC in France. *Politics & Society*, 30(3), 427–463.

Anderson, C. (2010). Urban scenes and urban development in Seoul: Three cases viewed from a scene perspective. PhD thesis, University of Incheon.

Anholt, S. (2007). *Competitive identity: The new brand management for nations, cities and regions*. New York: Palgrave Macmillan.

Annunziata, S., & Rivas, C. (2018). Resisting gentrification. In L. Lees & M. Phillips (Eds.), *Handbook of Gentrification Studies* (pp. 393–412). Cheltenham: Edward Elgar.

Aron, H. (2016). Boyle Heights activists demand that all art galleries get the hell out of their neighborhood. *LA Weekly*, July 14. Retrieved from https://tinyurl.com/y2n7mf7p

Aronson, E. (1999). The power of self-persuasion. *American Psychologist*, 54(11), 875–884.

Artscape. (2015). *Community visioning and feasibility study: Exploring an arts and cultural centre for the Lawrence-Allen community – Summary report*.

Asamblea Plaza Dorrego. (2014, March 18). Marcha de Antorchas en San Telmo, a 38 años de la dictadura. *Agencia Paco Urondo*. Retrieved from https://tinyurl.com/yxffg36e

Ashworth, G. J. (2017). *Senses of place: Senses of time*. London and New York: Routledge.

Ashworth, G. J., Graham, B. J., & Tunbridge, J. E. (2007). *Pluralising pasts: Heritage, identity and place in multicultural societies*. London: Pluto Press.

Asian Coalition for Housing Rights. (1988, September 6–10). *Eviction in Seoul 1988, fact finding team's report*. Bangkok: Asian Coalition for Housing Rights.

Atkinson, R. (2002). *Does gentrification help or harm urban neighbourhoods? An assessment of the evidence-base in the context of new urban agenda*. Bristol: ESRC Centre for Neighbourhood Research Bristol.

Atkinson, R., & Bridge, G. (2005). *Gentrification in a global context: The new urban colonialism*. London and New York: Routledge.

Atkinson, R., & Easthope, H. (2009). The consequences of the creative class: The pursuit of creativity strategies in Australia's cities. *International Journal of Urban and Regional Research*, *33*(1), 64–79.

Auerbach, A. M. (2016). Clients and communities: The political economy of party network organization and development in India's urban slums. *World Politics*, *68*(1), 111–148.

Auerbach, A. M., LeBas, A., Post, A., & Weitz-Shapiro, R. (2017). The politics of urban informality: Innovations in theory and research design from the city's margins. Working paper, University of California, Berkeley.

August, M. (2014). Challenging the rhetoric of stigmatization: The benefits of concentrated poverty in Toronto's Regent Park. *Environment and Planning A*, *46*(6), 1317–1333.

(2016). "It's all about power and you have none": The marginalization of tenant resistance to mixed-income social housing redevelopment in Toronto, Canada. *Cities*, *57*, 25–32.

August, M., & Walks, A. (2012). From social mix to political marginalization? The redevelopment of Toronto's public housing and the dilution of tenant organizational power. In G. Bridge, T. Butler, & L. Lees (Eds.), *Mixed communities: Gentrification by stealth* (pp. 273–297). London: Policy Press.

Auyero, J. (2003). *Contentious lives: Two Argentine women, two protests, and the quest for recognition*. Durham, NC: Duke University Press.

Avila-Hernandez, L. (2005). *The Boyle Heights landscape: The pressures of gentrification and the need for grassroots community action and accountable development*, Occidental College, Urban Environmental Policy. Retrieved from https://tinyurl.com/y6qn662w

Azaryahu, M. (2008). Tel Aviv: Center, periphery and the cultural geographies of an aspiring metropolis. *Social & Cultural Geography*, *9*(3), 303–318.

Baccaro, L., & Howell, C. (2011). A common neoliberal trajectory: The transformation of industrial relations in advanced capitalism. *Politics & Society*, *39*(4), 521–563.

Bain, A., & McLean, H. (2012). The artistic precariat. *Cambridge Journal of Regions, Economy and Society*, *6*(1), 93–111.

Bankasingh, K., & Dyer, J. (2016). *Residents at the centre, working from the inside out ... A report by Lawrence Heights Inter Organization Network (LHION) in transition*. Retrieved from https://tinyurl.com/y3zll2v5

Bauni, N. (2010). Movimiento de Ocupantes e Inquilinos (MOI): Entrevista realizada a Néstor Jeifetz. *Revista Osera*, *3*, 1–14.

Beach, B. S. (2007). Strategies and lessons from the Los Angeles community benefits experience. *Journal of Affordable Housing & Community Development Law*, *17*(1/2), 77–112.

Beacon Economics. (2015). The Downtown Los Angeles renaissance: Economic impacts and trends. Retrieved from https://tinyurl.com/y55rmvud

Been, V., Madar, J., & McDonnell, S. (2014). Urban land-use regulation: Are homevoters overtaking the growth machine? *Journal of Empirical Legal Studies*, *11*(2), 227–265.

Beissinger, M. R. (2007). Structure and example in modular political phenomena: The diffusion of bulldozer/rose/orange/tulip revolutions. *Perspectives on Politics*, 5(2), 259–276.

Belda-Miquel, S., Peris Blanes, J., & Frediani, A. (2016). Institutionalization and depoliticization of the right to the city: Changing scenarios for radical social movements. *International Journal of Urban and Regional Research*, 40(2), 321–339.

Bellucci, M., & Mitidieri, G. (2003). Estado actual de las asambleas barriales. *Revista Herramienta* (46). Retrieved from https://tinyurl.com/yykcseo2

Belongie, N., & Silverman, R. M. (2018). Model CBAs and community benefits ordinances as tools for negotiating equitable development: Three critical cases. *Journal of Community Practice*, 26(3), 308–327.

Benford, R. D., & Snow, D. A. (2000). Framing processes and social movements: An overview and assessment. *Annual Review of Sociology*, 26 (1), 611–639.

Bennett, W. L., & Segerberg, A. (2012). The logic of connective action: Digital media and the personalization of contentious politics. *Information, Communication & Society*, 15(5), 739–768.

Bennett, W. L., Della Porta, D., Diani, M., Johnson, E., Kolb, F., McAdam, D., ... Sikkink, K. (2004). *Transnational protest and global activism*. Lanham, MD: Rowman & Littlefield.

BePart Steering Committee. (2010). *Residents and agencies: Working and learning together*. Retrieved from https://tinyurl.com/y3fagk5w

Betancur, J. J. (2002). The politics of gentrification: The case of West Town in Chicago. *Urban Affairs Review*, 37(6), 780–814.

(2014). Gentrification in Latin America: Overview and critical analysis. *Urban Studies Research*, 1–14.

Bezmez, D. (2008). The politics of urban waterfront regeneration: The case of Haliç (the Golden Horn), Istanbul. *International Journal of Urban and Regional Research*, 32(4), 815–840.

Bhatia, R. (2007). Protecting health using an environmental impact assessment: A case study of San Francisco land use decisionmaking. *American Journal of Public Health*, 97(3), 406–413.

Bilgic, T. (2014, May 5). Turkey housing buffeted by rising rate turmoil: Mortgages. *Bloomberg News*. Retrieved from https://tinyurl.com/y626all3

Birke, P. (2014). Autonome Sehenswürdigkeit. Die "Rote Flora" in der Hamburger Stadtentwicklung seit den 1980er Jahren. *Sozial Geschichte Online/Social History Online*, 13, 80–104.

(2016). Right to the city – and beyond: The topographies of urban social movements in Hamburg. In M. Mayer, C. Thörn, & H. Thörn (Eds.), *Urban Uprisings: Challenging Neoliberal Urbanism in Europe* (pp. 283–308). Basingstoke: Palgrave Macmillan.

Bloch, S. (2015, January 28). Working folks, not the rich, fight density near USC's Expo Line. *LA Weekly*. Retrieved from https://tinyurl.com/y4n7ecpg

Blokland, T., Hentschel, C., Holm, A., Lebuhn, H., & Margalit, T. (2015). Urban citizenship and right to the city: The fragmentation of claims. *International Journal of Urban and Regional Research*, 39(4), 655–665.

Blyth, M. (2013). *Austerity: The history of a dangerous idea*. Oxford: Oxford University Press.

Bonfigli, F. (2015). Lavapiés: Seguridad urbana, activismo politico y inmigracion en el corazon de Madrid. *Sortuz: Oñati Journal of Emergent Socio-Legal Studies*, *6*(2), 61–77.

Bonnar, J. (2009, June 14). Poverty activists reject upscale housing developments in Regent Park. *Toronto Social Justice Magazine*. Retrieved from https://tinyurl.com/m8hyhh

Boudreau, J.-A., Keil, R., & Young, D. (2009). *Changing Toronto: Governing urban neoliberalism*. Toronto: University of Toronto Press.

Boyle Heights Alianza Anti Artwashing Y Desplazamiento. (2018). On 356 Mission closing. Retrieved from http://alianzacontraartwashing.org/

(n.d.). The short history of a long struggle. Retrieved from http://alianzacontraartwashing.org/

Boyle Heights Beat. (2015, November 24). Protesters force performers out of park amid gentrification concerns. Retrieved from https://tinyurl.com/y6xqtkmu

Brady, H. E., Verba, S., & Schlozman, K. L. (1995). Beyond SES: A resource model of political participation. *American Political Science Review*, *89*(2), 271–294.

Brail, S., & Kumar, N. (2017). Community leadership and engagement after the mix: The transformation of Toronto's Regent Park. *Urban Studies*, *54*(16), 3772–3788.

Brenner, N. (Ed.) (2014). *Implosions/explosions*. Berlin: Jovis.

Brenner, N., & Theodore, N. (2002). Cities and the geographies of "actually existing neoliberalism." *Antipode*, *34*(3), 349–379.

Brenner, N., Marcuse, P., & Mayer, M. (Eds.). (2011). *Cities for people, not for profit: Critical urban theory and the right to the city*. London and New York: Routledge.

Bridge, G., Butler, T., & Lees, L. (2012). *Mixed communities: Gentrification by stealth?* Bristol: Policy Press.

Bröer, C., & Duyvendak, J. (2009). Discursive opportunities, feeling rules, and the rise of protests against aircraft noise. *Mobilization: An International Quarterly*, *14*(3), 337–356.

Brown-Saracino, Japonica. (2010). *A neighborhood that never changes: Gentrification, social preservation, and the search for authenticity*. Chicago, IL: University of Chicago Press.

Buchholz, T. (2016). *Struggling for recognition and affordable housing in Amsterdam and Hamburg: Resignation, resistance, relocation*. Groningen: University of Groningen.

Bude, I., Sobczak, O., & Jörg, S. (2009). *Empire St. Pauli*. Documentary. Produced by S. Jörg. Germany: GWA St. Pauli.

Bulnes, R. (2012). *Un territorio que construye identidad en defensa de su patrimonio. El caso del Barrio Yungay*. Pontificia Universidad Católica de Chile, Santiago.

Burbank, M. J., Heying, C. H., & Andranovich, G. (2000). Antigrowth politics or piecemeal resistance? Citizen opposition to Olympic-related economic growth. *Urban Affairs Review*, *35*(3), 334–357.

Burgess, K. (2004). *Parties and unions in the new global economy*. Pittsburgh, PA: University of Pittsburgh Press.

Burgmann, M., & Burgmann, V. (1998). *Green bans, red union: Environmental activism and the New South Wales Builders Labourers' Federation*. Kensington: University of New South Wales Press.

Byeon, M.-R., & Park, M.-J. (2008). Research on the model of the creative municipal administration of Seoul [Korean]. *Seoul Institute*, 1–106.

CABA Observatorio de Industrias Creativas. (2012). *Anuario de Industrias Creativas Ciudad de Buenos Aires 2011*. Buenos Aires: Ministerio de Desarrollo Económico del Gobierno de la Ciudad de Buenos Aires.

Calcagni González, M., & Migone Widoycovich, P. (2013). *Cultura de barrio: Percepciones y valoraciones vecinales del Barrio Yungay de Santiago*. Pontificia Universidad Católica de Chile, Santiago.

California Budget Project. (2008). *Locked Out 2008: A Profile of California Counties*. Retrieved from https://tinyurl.com/y58afubm

Campbell, C. (n.d.). West Queen West: An urban planning story. Retrieved from https://chascamp.com/queen-street/-queen-street-at-the-omb (accessed September 10, 2015).

Campbell, J. (2013, April 3). Door-knocking and public meeting bans for politicians at public housing estates. *Herald Sun*. Retrieved from https://tinyurl.com/y4yjxdxw

Carbajal, R. (2003). Transformaciones socieconómicas y urbanas en Palermo. *Revista Argentina de Sociología*, *1*(1), 94–109.

Carman, M. (2006). *Las trampas de la cultura: Los" intrusos" y los nuevos usos del barrio de Gardel*. Buenos Aires: Ediciones Paidos Iberica.

Carmon, N., & Hill, M. M. (1988). Neighborhood rehabilitation without relocation or gentrification. *Journal of the American Planning Association*, *54*(4), 470–481.

Carroll, R. (2016, April 19). "Hope everyone pukes on your artisanal treats": Fighting gentrification, LA-style. *The Guardian*. Retrieved from https://tinyurl.com/y8go3duh

Carvajal, R., Pascual, C., Arancibia Rodríguez, M., & Osorio, J. (2007). *Estudio del Patrimonio Arquitectónico de Santiago Poniente*. Santiago: Fondart.

Castells, M. (1983). *The city and the grassroots: A cross-cultural theory of urban social movements*. Berkeley, CA: University of California Press.

(2015). *Networks of outrage and hope: Social movements in the Internet age*. Cambridge: Polity Press.

Catungal, J. P., Leslie, D., & Hii, Y. (2009). Geographies of displacement in the creative city: The case of Liberty Village, Toronto. *Urban Studies*, *46*(5–6), 1095–1114.

Çavuşoğlu, E., & Yalçintan, M. C. (2010). Planning system and recent agenda in Istanbul. Unpublished paper. Faculty of Architecture, Department of City and Regional Planning, Mimar Sinan University, Istanbul.

Chaskin, R. J., & Joseph, M. L. (2013). "Positive" gentrification, social control and the "right to the city" in mixed-income communities: Uses and expectations of space and place. *International Journal of Urban and Regional Research*, *37*(2), 480–502.

Chetty, R., & Hendren, N. (2018). The impacts of neighborhoods on intergenerational mobility I: Childhood exposure effects. *The Quarterly Journal of Economics*, 133(3), 1107–1162.

Cho, H., Kim, K.-H., & Shilling, J. D. (2012). Seemingly irrational but predictable price formation in Seoul's housing market. *The Journal of Real Estate Finance and Economics*, 44(4), 526–542.

Cho, M.-R. (2008). From street corners to plaza: The production of festive civic space in Central Seoul. In M. Douglass, K. C. Ho, & G. L. Ooi (Eds.), *Globalization, the city and civil society in Pacific Asia* (pp. 194–210). London and New York: Routledge.

Chong, D., & Druckman, J. N. (2007). A theory of framing and opinion formation in competitive elite environments. *Journal of Communication*, 57(1), 99–118.

Chosun.com. (2009, September 23). Yongsan has Seoul's most expensive commercial property. Retrieved from https://tinyurl.com/y6l6e92b

Ciccolella, P. (1999). Globalización y dualización en la Región Metropolitana de Buenos Aires: Grandes inversiones y reestructuración socioterritorial en los años noventa. *Revista EURE*, 25(76), 5–27.

Cin, M. M., & Egercioğlu, Y. (2016). A critical analysis of urban regeneration projects in Turkey: Displacement of Romani settlement case. *Procedia-Social and Behavioral Sciences*, 216, 269–278.

Clark, T. N., & Goetz, E. (1994). The antigrowth machine: Can city governments control, limit, or manage growth? In T. N. Clark (Ed.), *Urban innovations: Creative strategies for turbulent times* (pp. 105–145). Thousands Oaks, CA: Sage.

Clingermayer, J. (1993). Distributive politics, ward representation, and the spread of zoning. *Public Choice*, 77(4), 725–738.

Cohen, D. E. (2014). Seoul's Digital Media City: A history and 2012 status report on a South Korean digital arts and entertainment ICT cluster. *International Journal of Cultural Studies*, 17(6), 557–572.

Cohen, N., & Margalit, T. (2011). New citizens, old diversity: Asylum seekers and networked spaces in Tel Aviv. Paper presented at the Urban Citizenship: Revisited Rights, Recognition and Distribution in Berlin and Tel Aviv, International Symposium at Humboldt-University Berlin, September 15– 16.

Collier, R. B., & Handlin, S. (2009). *Reorganizing popular politics: Participation and the new interest regime in Latin America*. University Park, PA: Pennsylvania State University Press.

Collins, B., & Loukaitou-Sideris, A. (2016). Skid Row, Gallery Row and the space in between: Cultural revitalisation and its impacts on two Los Angeles neighbourhoods. *Town Planning Review*, 87(4), 401–427.

Colomb, C., & Novy, J. (2016). *Protest and resistance in the tourist city*. London and New York: Routledge.

Contreras, Y. (2011). La recuperación urbana y residencial del centro de Santiago: Nuevos habitantes, cambios socioespaciales significativos. *EURE (Santiago)*, 37(112), 89–113.

Cook, H. (2013, January 14). Plan to turn estates into property gold. *The Age*. Retrieved from https://tinyurl.com/y3l3ncu9

(2014, May 17). Radical plan pitched for Prahran high-rises. *The Age*. Retrieved from https://tinyurl.com/y4wxtdov

Cook, M. L. (2010). *Politics of labor reform in Latin America: Between flexibility and rights*. University Park, PA: Pennsylvania State University Press.

Cramer, J. C., Dietz, T., & Johnston, R. A. (1980). Social impact assessment of regional plans: A review of methods and issues and a recommended process. *Policy Sciences*, *12*(1), 61–82.

Cress, D. M., & Snow, D. A. (1996). Mobilization at the margins: Resources, benefactors, and the viability of homeless social movement organizations. *American Sociological Review*, *61*(6), 1089–1109.

Crot, L. (2006). "Scenographic" and "cosmetic" planning: Globalization and territorial restructuring in Buenos Aires. *Journal of Urban Affairs*, *28*(3), 227–251.

Cuenya, B. (2003). Las teorías sobre la nueva política urbana y los grandes proyectos en la era de la globalización. Reflexiones a partir de la experiencia de la Ciudad de Buenos Aires. In M. Carmona (Ed.), *Globalización forma urbana y gobernabilidad. La dimensión regional y grandes proyectos urbanos* (pp. 101–116). Valparaiso: Universidad de Valparaiso.

Davidson, M. (2008). Spoiled mixture: Where does state-led "positive" gentrification end? *Urban Studies*, *45*(12), 2385–2405.

Davidson, M., & Lees, L. (2010). New-build gentrification: Its histories, trajectories, and critical geographies. *Population, Space and Place*, *16*(5), 395–411.

Davis, L. K. (2011). International events and mass evictions: A longer view. *International Journal of Urban and Regional Research*, *35*(3), 582–599.

De Privitellio, L., & Romero, L. A. (2005). Organizaciones de la sociedad civil, tradiciones cívicas y cultura política democrática: El caso de Buenos Aires, 1912–1976. *Revista de Historia*, *1*(1), 1–34.

Defend Boyle Heights. (2016, July 6). Defend Boyle Heights statement about the self-help graphics accountability session and beyond: Bombard the artists nonprofits! Retrieved from https://tinyurl.com/y5uqhpge

DeFilippis, J. (2004). *Unmaking Goliath: Community control in the face of global capital*. London and New York: Routledge.

Della Porta, D. (2011). Eventful protest, global conflicts: Social mechanisms in the reproduction of protest. In R. E. Goodin & J. M. Jasper (Eds.), *Contention in Context* (pp. 256–276). Palo Alto, CA: Stanford University Press.

(2014). *Methodological practices in social movement research*. Oxford: Oxford University Press.

(2015). *Social movements in times of austerity: Bringing capitalism back into protest analysis*. San Francisco, CA: John Wiley & Sons.

Della Porta, D., & Tarrow, S. G. (Eds.). (2005). *Transnational processes and social activism*. Lanham, MD: Rowman & Littlefield.

Della Porta, D., Fernández, J., Kouki, H., & Mosca, L. (2017). *Movement parties against austerity*. San Francisco, CA: John Wiley & Sons.

Dema, V. (2009, May 18). Repudian la "palermización" de San Telmo: En un recorrido con lanacion.com un grupo de vecinos explicó por qué muchas obras atentan contra el espíritu del barrio. *La Nacion*. Retrieved from https://tinyurl.com/y4g57n4a

Departamento de Urbanismo de la Dirección de Obras de la Municipalidad de Santiago. (2006). *Desafectación de vías comunales en el sector Santiago*

Norponiente. Santiago: Departamento de Urbanismo de la Dirección de Obras de la Municipalidad de Santiago.

Desmond, M. (2016). *Evicted: Poverty and profit in the American city*. Portland, OR: Broadway Books.

Di Virgilio, M. (2008). La Renovación urbana a partir de las opiniones de los residentes de San Telmo y Barracas. In H. Herzer (Ed.), *Con el corazón mirando al sur: Transformaciones en el sur de la ciudad de Buenos Aires* (pp. 157–172). Buenos Aires: Espacio.

Diani, M. (2005). Cities in the world: Local civil society and global issues in Britain. In W. L. Bennett, D. Della Porta, M. Diani, E. Johnson, E., F. Kolb, D. McAdam, D. ... K. Sikkink (Eds.), *Transnational protest and global activism* (pp. 45–67). Lanham, MD: Rowman & Littlefield Publishers.

Diani, M., & McAdam, D. (Eds.). (2003). *Social movements and networks*. Oxford: Oxford University Press.

Díaz Orueta, F. (2007). Madrid: Urban regeneration projects and social mobilization. *Cities*, 24(3), 183–193.

Dinardi, C. (2015). Unsettling the role of culture as panacea: The politics of culture-led urban regeneration in Buenos Aires. *City, Culture and Society*, *6* (2), 9–18.

(2017). Cities for sale: Contesting city branding and cultural policies in Buenos Aires. *Urban Studies*, *54*(1), 85–101.

Dinçer, I. (2010). The dilemma of cultural heritage-urban renewal: İstanbul, Süleymaniye and Fener-Balat. Paper presented at the International Planning History Society (IPHS) Fourteenth Conference, July 12–15, Istanbul.

Dinçer, I., Enlil, Z., & Islam, T. (2008). Regeneration in a new context: A new act on renewal and its implications on the planning processes in İstanbul. Paper presented at the Conference: Bridging the Divide: Celebrating the City. ACSP-AESOP Fourth Joint Congress, July 6–11. Chicago.

Dinerstein, A. C. (2003). ¡Que se vayan todos! Popular insurrection and the Asambleas Barriales in Argentina. *Bulletin of Latin American Research*, 22 (2), 187–200.

Ding, L., Hwang, J., & Divringi, E. (2016). Gentrification and residential mobility in Philadelphia. *Regional Science and Urban Economics*, *61*(November), 38–51.

Dirección de Estadística y Censos. (2012). *Encuesta Anual de Hogares*. Buenos Aires: CABA.

Dixon, G. (2013, December 16). Beyond development: Regent Park builds its community with song. *The Globe and Mail*. Retrieved from https://tinyurl .com/y64wb268

Djankov, S., La Porta, R., López -de-Silanes, F., & Shleifer, A. (2003). Courts. *Quarterly Journal of Economics*, *118*(2), 453–517.

Domhoff, G. W. (2006). The limitations of regime theory. *City & Community*, *5* (1), 47–51.

Dougherty, C. (2018, April 12). Rent control campaign in California is taken to the streets. *New York Times*. Retrieved from https://tinyurl.com/y7hfheo5

Downtown Center Business Improvement District. (2015a). *Annual report. Breaking new ground*. Retrieved from https://tinyurl.com/y4vnx75v

(2015b). *Get urban*. Retrieved from https://tinyurl.com/y3z7wme5

Dreier, P. (1996). Community empowerment strategies: The limits and potential of community organizing in urban neighborhoods. *Cityscape*, 2(2), 121–159.

Dreier, P., Mollenkopf, J., & Swanstrom, T. (2001). *Place matters: Metropolitics for the twenty-first century*. Lawrence, KS: University Press of Kansas.

Duany, A. (2001). Three cheers for gentrification. *The American Enterprise*, 12 (3), 36–39.

Dubin, J. A., Kiewiet, D. R., & Noussair, C. (1992). Voting on growth control measures: Preferences and strategies. *Economics & Politics*, 4(2), 191–213.

Dufour, P., & Ancelovici, M. (2018). From citizenship regimes to protest regimes? In M. Paquet, N. Nagels, & A.-C. Fourot (Eds.), *Citizenship as a regime: Canadian and international perspectives* (pp. 165–185). Montreal: McGill-Queen's University Press.

Durán, G. G., & Moore, A. W. (2015). La Tabacalera of Lavapiés: A social experiment or a work of art? *Field*, 2(winter), 49–75.

Endres, D., & Senda-Cook, S. (2011). Location matters: The rhetoric of place in protest. *Quarterly Journal of Speech*, 97(3), 257–282.

Ercan, M. A. (2011). Challenges and conflicts in achieving sustainable communities in historic neighbourhoods of Istanbul. *Habitat International*, 35(2), 295–306.

Espinoza, V. (1998). Historia social de la acción colectiva urbana: Los pobladores de Santiago, 1957–1987. *Revista EURE*, 24(72), 71–84.

Etchemendy, S., & Collier, R. B. (2007). Down but not out: Union resurgence and segmented neocorporatism in Argentina (2003–2007). *Politics & Society*, 35 (3), 363–401.

EIU. (2012). Hot spots: Benchmarking global city competitiveness. Economist Intelligence Unit. Retrieved from https://tinyurl.com/y2w4g22b

Fainstein, S. (2002). The changing world economy and urban restructuring. In S. Fainstein & S. Campbell (Eds.), *Readings in urban theory* (pp. 110–126). Malden, MA: Wiley-Blackwell.

(2010). *The just city*. Ithaca, NY: Cornell University Press.

Fainstein, S., & Fainstein, N. (1985). Economic restructuring and the rise of urban social movements. *Urban Affairs Quarterly*, 21(2), 187–206.

Farro, A. L., & Demirhisar, D. G. (2014). The Gezi Park movement: A Turkish experience of the twenty-first-century collective movements. *International Review of Sociology*, 24(1), 176–189.

Feige, M. (2008). The city that is not white: The celestial Tel Aviv and the earthly Tel Aviv. *The Journal of Israeli History*, 27(1), 87–93.

Feiock, R. C. (2004). Politics, institutions and local land-use regulation. *Urban Studies*, 41(2), 363–375.

Felsenstein, D., Schamp, E. W., & Shachar, A. (2013). *Emerging nodes in the global economy: Frankfurt and Tel Aviv compared*. Berlin: Springer Science & Business Media.

Fenster, T., & Yacobi, H. (2005). Whose city is it? On urban planning and local knowledge in globalizing Tel Aviv-Jaffa. *Planning Theory & Practice*, 6(2), 191–211.

Fidel, E. (2013, September 26). Una "corrala" (desaparecida) en Lavapiés-Embajadores, Madrid. *Urban Idade: Memorias de las redes urbanas*. Retrieved from https://tinyurl.com/y2thuyly

Flesher Fominaya, C. (2015). Debunking spontaneity: Spain's 15-M/Indignados as autonomous movement. *Social Movement Studies*, 14(2), 142–163.

Florida, R. L. (2002). *The rise of the creative class and how it's transforming work, leisure, community and everyday life*. New York: Basic Books.

Freeman, L. (2005). Displacement or succession? Residential mobility in gentrifying neighborhoods. *Urban Affairs Review*, 40(4), 463–491.

(2011). *There goes the hood: Views of gentrification from the ground up*. Philadelphia, PA: Temple University Press.

Friedrichs, J., & Dangschat, J. S. (1994). Hamburg: Culture and urban competition. In F. Bianchini & M. Parkinson (Eds.), *Cultural policy and urban regeneration: The West European experience*. Manchester: Manchester University Press.

Friendly, A. (2017). Land value capture and social benefits: Toronto and São Paulo compared. *IMFG Papers on Municipal Finance and Governance (University of Toronto)*, 33, 1–54.

Friesen, J. (2014, February 19). Regent Park residents feel happier and safer with new homes, study says. *The Globe and the Mail*. Retrieved from https://tinyurl.com/y3ptyb6q

Füllner, J., & Templin, D. (2011). Stadtplanung von unten. Die "Recht auf Stadt"-Bewegung in Hamburg. In A. Holm & D. Gebhardt (Eds.), *Initiativen für ein Recht auf Stadt* (pp. 79–104). Hamburg: VSA.

Fulton, R. (2012a, September 11). Land trust and developer save affordable housing complex. *California Health Report*. Retrieved from https://tinyurl.com/y53un25y

(2012b, February 20). There's a train comin': Light rail changes South LA housing market. *California Health Report*. Retrieved from. https://tinyurl.com/yy4eg2t3

Fung, A., & Wright, E. O. (2001). Deepening democracy: Innovations in empowered participatory governance. *Politics & Society*, 29(1), 5–41.

Gallant, J. (2014, August 28). Tenants taking Akelius Canada to Landlord and Tenant Board. *TheStar.com*. Retrieved from https://tinyurl.com/yxbzbw2r

Gamson, W. A. (1995). Constructing social protest. In H. Johnston & B. Klandermans (Eds.), *Social movements and culture* (pp. 85–106). Minneapolis, MN: University of Minnesota Press.

Gängeviertel e.V. (Ed.) (2012). *Mehr als ein Viertel. Ansichten und Absichten aus dem Hamburger Gängeviertel*. Hamburg: Assoziation A.

(2013). *Zukunftkonzept*. Retrieved from http://das-gaengeviertel.info/

Garcés, M. (2002). *Tomando su sitio: El movimiento de pobladores de Santiago, 1957–1970*. Santiago: Lom Ediciones.

García Pérez, E., & Sequera Fernández, J. (2014). Gentrificación en centros urbanos: Aproximación comparada a las dinámicas de Madrid y Buenos Aires. *Quid 16. Revista de Área de Estudios Urbanos 3*, 49–66.

García-Lamarca, M., & Kaika, M. (2016). "Mortgaged lives": The biopolitics of debt and housing financialisation. *Transactions of the Institute of British Geographers*, 41(3), 313–327.

Gerbaudo, P. (2012). *Tweets and the streets: Social media and contemporary activism*. London: Pluto Press.

Gibson, E. L. (2005). Boundary control: Subnational authoritarianism in democratic countries. *World Politics*, *58*(1), 101–132.

Gladki Planning Associates, & Art Starts. (2015). *Lawrence Heights Heritage Interpretation Plan.*

Glaeser, E. L. (2000). The new economics of urban and regional growth. In Gordon L. Clark & Maryann P. Feldman & Meric S. Gertler (Eds.), *The Oxford handbook of economic geography* (pp. 83–98). Oxford: Oxford University Press.

Globalization and World Cities Research Network. (2012). *The world according to GaWC 2012*. Retrieved from: www.lboro.ac.uk/gawc/world2012t.html

Goldhaber, R., & Schnell, I. (2007). A model of multidimensional segregation in the Arab ghetto in Tel Aviv-Jaffa. *Tijdschrift voor Economische en Sociale Geografie*, *98* (5), 603–620.

Gómez, M. (2006). El barrio de Lavapiés, laboratorio de interculturalidad. *Dissidences: Hispanic Journal of Theory and Criticism*, 2(1), 1–42.

Goonewardena, K., & Kipfer, S. (2005). Spaces of difference: Reflections from Toronto on multiculturalism, bourgeois urbanism and the possibility of radical urban politics. *International Journal of Urban and Regional Research*, 29(3), 670–678.

Gordon, U. (2012). Israel's "tent protests": The chilling effect of nationalism. *Social Movement Studies*, *11*(3–4), 349–355.

Gotham, K. F. (2006). The secondary circuit of capital reconsidered: Globalization and the US real estate sector. *American Journal of Sociology*, *112*(1), 231–275.

Gould, R. V. (1995). *Insurgent identities: Class, community, and protest in Paris from 1848 to the Commune*. Chicago, IL: University of Chicago Press.

Graham, B. J., & Howard, P. (2008). *The Ashgate research companion to heritage and identity*. Farnham: Ashgate Publishing.

Grant, A. M., Dutton, J. E., & Rosso, B. D. (2008). Giving commitment: Employee support programs and the prosocial sensemaking process. *Academy of Management Journal*, *51*(5), 898–918.

Greenberg, M. (2008). *Branding New York: How a city in crisis was sold to the world*. London and New York: Routledge.

Greene, M., & Rojas, E. (2010). Housing for the poor in the city centre: A review of the Chilean experience and a challenge for incremental design. In F. Hernández, P. Kellett, & L. K. Allen (Eds.), *Rethinking the informal city: Critical perspectives from Latin America* (pp. 91–118). New York: Berghahn Books.

Grinberg, L. L. (2013). The J14 resistance mo(ve)ment: The Israeli mix of Tahrir Square and Puerta del Sol. *Current Sociology*, *61*(4), 491–509.

Grodach, C. (2013). Cultural economy planning in creative cities: Discourse and practice. *International Journal of Urban and Regional Research*, *37*(5), 1747–1765.

Gross, J. (2007). Community benefits agreements: Definitions, values, and legal enforceability. *Journal of Affordable Housing & Community Development Law*, 17(1/2), 35–58.

Grundy, J., & Boudreau, J.-A. (2008). "Living with culture": Creative citizenship practices in Toronto. *Citizenship Studies*, *12*(4), 347–363.

Guerschman, B. (2010). La marca comercial y el diseño: Una reflexión antropológica sobre la producción, el consumo y el espacio. *KULA: Antropólogos del Atlántico Sur*, *3*(October), 67–81.

Guevara, T. (2014). Transformaciones territoriales en la Región Metropolitana de Buenos Aires y reconfiguración del régimen de acumulación en la década neodesarrollista. *Quid 16: Revista de Área de Estudios Urbanos*, 4, 115–136.

Gül, M., Dee, J., & Nur Cünük, C. (2014). Istanbul's Taksim Square and Gezi Park: The place of protest and the ideology of place. *Journal of Architecture and Urbanism*, *38*(1), 63–72.

Gulersoy-Zeren, N., Tezer, A., Yigiter, R., Koramaz, T. K., & Gunay, Z. (2008). Istanbul Project: Istanbul Historical Peninsula Conservation Study Volume I – Conservation of Cultural Assets in Turkey: UNESCO-World Heritage Centre, Istanbul Technical University, Faculty of Architecture, ITU Environmental Planning and Research Centre.

Gunay, Z., & Dokmeci, V. (2012). Culture-led regeneration of Istanbul waterfront: Golden horn cultural valley project. *Cities*, 29(4), 213–222.

Gurr, T. R. (1970). *Why Men Rebel*. Princeton, NJ: Princeton University Press.

Ha, S.-K. (1999). Urban redevelopment and low-income housing policy in Seoul. *Korean Association for Local Government Studies*, *11*(4), 271–289.

(2010). Housing, social capital and community development in Seoul. *Cities*, 27(June), S35–S42.

(2015). The endogenous dynamics of urban renewal and gentrification in Seoul. In L. Lees, H. B. Shin, & E. López-Morales (Eds.), *Global gentrifications: Uneven development and displacement* (pp. 165–180). Bristol: Policy Press.

Hackworth, J., & Rekers, J. (2005). Ethnic packaging and gentrification: The case of four neighborhoods in Toronto. *Urban Affairs Review*, 41(2), 211–236.

Hajer, M. A. (1995). *The politics of environmental discourse: Ecological modernization and the policy process*. Oxford: Clarendon Press.

Hales, M., & Pena, A. M. (2012). Global cities index and emerging cities outlook. A. T. Kearney. Retrieved from https://tinyurl.com/yyamm2cw

Hall, P. A., & Gingerich, D. W. (2009). Varieties of capitalism and institutional complementarities in the political economy: An empirical analysis. *British Journal of Political Science*, 39(3), 449–482.

Hands Off Melbourne's Estates (HOME). (2013, May 1). HOME campaign comes to Prahran. Facebook. Retrieved from https://tinyurl.com/yxhq79es

Hankinson, M. (2018). When do renters behave like homeowners? High rent, price anxiety, and NIMBYism. *American Political Science Review*, *112*(3), 473–493.

The Hankyoreh. (2009, January 23). Residents in redevelopment zones get help from Demolition Federation. Retrieved from https://tinyurl.com/yy2qbmdq

Harding, K. (2003, September 10). Developer purchases "Pope Squat." *The Globe and Mail*. Retrieved from https://tinyurl.com/y69pz4x7

Harvey, D. (1978). The urban process under capitalism: A framework for analysis. *International Journal of Urban and Regional Research*, 2(14), 101–131.

(1989). From managerialism to entrepreneurialism: The transformation in urban governance in late capitalism. *Geografiska Annaler: Series B, Human Geography*, 71(1), 3–17.

(2008). The right to the city. *New Left Review*, 53(September–October), 23–40.
(2010). *Social justice and the city*. Athens, GA: University of Georgia Press.
(2012). *Rebel cities: From the right to the city to the urban revolution*. New York: Verso Books.
Harvey, D., & Williams, R. (1995). Militant particularism and global ambition: The conceptual politics of place, space, and environment in the work of Raymond Williams. *Social Text*, 42(spring), 69–98.
Haskell, M. A. (1977). Green bans: Worker control and the urban environment. *Industrial Relations: A Journal of Economy and Society*, 16(2), 205–214.
Hasson, S. (1993). *Urban social movements in Jerusalem: The protest of the second generation*. Albany, NY: State University of New York Press.
Hatuka, T. (2011, September 14). Designing protests in urban public space. *Metropolitics*. Retrieved from https://tinyurl.com/yy74h7p8
Hatuka, T., & Forsyth, L. (2005). Urban design in the context of glocalization and nationalism: Rothschild Boulevards, Tel Aviv. *Urban Design International*, 10(2), 69–86.
Häußermann, H., Läpple, D., & Siebel, W. (2008). *Stadtpolitik*. Frankfurt: Suhrkamp.
Henig, J. R. (1982). Neighborhood response to gentrification: Conditions of mobilization. *Urban Affairs Review*, 17(3), 343–358.
Hernández, S. (2013). ¿Un único modelo? La figura de los vecinos y las construcciones discursivas de lo urbano. *Quid 16: Revista del Área de Estudios Urbanos*, 3, 50–65.
Herrmann, M., Lenger, H.-J., Reemtsma, J. P., & Roth, K. H. (1987). *Hafenstrasse: Chronik und Analysen eines Konflikts*. Hamburg: Galgenberg.
Herzer, H. (2012). *Barrios al sur: Renovación y pobreza en la ciudad de Buenos Aires*. Buenos Aires: Café de las Ciudades.
Herzer, H., Di Virgilio, M. M., & Rodríguez, C. (2015). Gentrification in Buenos Aires: Global trends and local features. In L. Lees, H. B. Shin, & E. López-Morales (Eds.), *Global gentrifications: Uneven development and displacement* (pp. 199–222). Bristol: Policy Press.
Herzer, H., Rodríguez, C., Redondo, A., Di Virgilio, M., & Ostuni, F. (2005). Organizaciones sociales en el barrio de La Boca: Cambios y permanencias en un contexto de crisis. *Estudios demográficos y urbanos*, 20(2), 269–308.
Herzog, L. A. (2006). *Return to the center: Culture, public space, and city building in a global era*. Austin, TX: University of Texas Press.
Hirsch, E. L. (1990). Sacrifice for the cause: Group processes, recruitment, and commitment in a student social movement. *American Sociological Review*, 55(2), 243–254.
Hobsbawm, E. J., & Ranger, T. O. (1983). *The invention of tradition*. Cambridge: Cambridge University Press.
Hohenstatt, F. (2013). Recht auf Stadt: Über die Position Sozialer Arbeit im Konfliktfeld Stadtentwicklung. In M. Drilling & P. Oehler (Eds.), *Soziale Arbeit und Stadtentwicklung* (pp. 271–288). Wiesbaden: Springer VS.
Hohenstatt, F., & Rinn, M. (2013). Auseinandersetzungen um Wohnverhältnisse in Wilhelmsburg in Zeiten der IBA. In Arbeitskreis Umstrukturierung

Wilhelmsburg (Ed.), *Unternehmen Wilhelmsburg. Stadtentwicklung im Zeichen von IBA und igs* (pp. 96–104). Hamburg: Assoziation A.

Holland, A. C. (2017). *Forbearance as redistribution: The politics of informal welfare in Latin America*. Cambridge: Cambridge University Press.

Holland, G. (2014, March 10). Skid Row activists file lawsuit accusing city of stifling dissent. *Los Angeles Times*. Retrieved from https://tinyurl.com/y42rxawq

Hollands, R., & Chatterton, P. (2003). Producing nightlife in the new urban entertainment economy: Corporatization, branding and market segmentation. *International Journal of Urban and Regional Research*, 27(2), 361–385.

Holm, A. (2010). *Wir bleiben alle! Gentrifizierung-Städtische Konflikte um Aufwertung und Verdrängung*. Münster: Unrast Verlag.

(2011). Gentrification in Berlin: Neue Investitionsstrategien und lokale Konflikte. In H. Hermann, C. Keller, R. Neef, & R. Ruhne (Eds.), *Die Besonderheit des Städtischen* (pp. 213–232). Wiesbaden: Springer VS.

Hong, Y.-S. (2012). Interpretation of compound place identity in Mullae's creative village, Seoul [Korean]. *Urban Design Institute of Korea*, *13*(2), 19–34.

Hooghe, L., & Marks, G. (2003). Unraveling the central state, but how? Types of multi-level governance. *American Political Science Review*, *97*(2), 233–243.

Höpner, L. (2010). Die Protestbewegung der Kreativen und ihre Auswirkungen auf die Stadtentwicklung am Beispiel Hamburg. Dissertation, Geography Department, Kiel University.

Howkins, J. (2002). *The creative economy: How people make money from ideas*. London: Penguin.

H-Street. (2014, October). Miracle of Duriban [Korean]. Retrieved from https://street-h.com/past-issue

Huber, E., & Stephens, J. D. (2001). *Development and crisis of the welfare state: Parties and policies in global markets*. Chicago, IL: University of Chicago Press.

Hug, S. (2013). Qualitative comparative analysis: How inductive use and measurement error lead to problematic inference. *Political Analysis*, *21*(2), 252–265.

Hulchanski, J. D. (2004). How did we get here? The evolution of Canada's "exclusionary" housing system. In D. Hulchanski & M. Shapcott (Eds.), *Finding room: Policy options for a Canadian rental housing strategy* (pp. 179–194). Toronto: University of Toronto Press.

Hulse, K., Herbert, T., & Down, K. (2004). *Kensington estate redevelopment social impact study*. Institute for Social Research, Swinburne University of Technology.

Hutchins, E. (1995). *Cognition in the wild*. Cambridge, MA: MIT Press.

Hutton, T. A. (2015). *Cities and the cultural economy*. London and New York: Routledge.

Hwang, J., & Sampson, R. J. (2014). Divergent pathways of gentrification: Racial inequality and the social order of renewal in Chicago neighborhoods. *American Sociological Review*, *79*(4), 726–751.

Hyesun, J. (2015, March). Arts blossom in Mullae [Korean]. *Gaek-suk*, *373*, 188–193. Retrieved from http://auditorium.kr/2016/01/

Hyra, D. S. (2008). *The new urban renewal: The economic transformation of Harlem and Bronzeville*. Chicago, IL: University of Chicago Press.

Iveson, K. (2014). Building a city for "The People": The politics of alliance-building in the Sydney Green Ban Movement. *Antipode*, *46*(4), 992–1013.

Jacobs, J. (1961). *The death and life of great American cities*. London: Taylor Francis.

James, R. K. (2010). From "slum clearance" to "revitalisation": Planning, expertise and moral regulation in Toronto's Regent Park. *Planning Perspectives*, *25* (1), 69–86.

Jang, W. (2011). Urban "scene" and creative place: The case of Mullae-dong of Seoul. *Global Urban Studies*, 4(March), 3–15.

Janoschka, M., & Sequera, J. (2016). Gentrification in Latin America: Addressing the politics and geographies of displacement. *Urban Geography*, *37*(8), 1175–1194.

Janoschka, M., Sequera, J., & Salinas, L. (2014). Gentrification in Spain and Latin America: A critical dialogue. *International Journal of Urban and Regional Research*, *38*(4), 1234–1265.

Jasper, J. M. (2008). *The art of moral protest: Culture, biography, and creativity in social movements*. Chicago, IL: University of Chicago Press.

Jasper, J. M., & Goodwin, J. (2011). *Contention in context: Political opportunities and the emergence of protest*. Palo Alto, CA: Stanford University Press.

Jasper, J. M., & Poulsen, J. D. (1995). Recruiting strangers and friends: Moral shocks and social networks in animal rights and anti-nuclear protests. *Social Problems*, 42(4), 493–512.

Jenkins, B. L. (2005). Toronto's cultural renaissance. *Canadian Journal of Communication*, *30*(2), 169–186.

Jeon, A. (2011). We can rebuild houses, but not lives. *Nation*, *21*(August), 74–75.

Jeong, M.-G. (2006). Local choices for development impact fees. *Urban Affairs Review*, *41*(3), 338–357.

Jeong, M.-G., & Feiock, R. C. (2006). Impact fees, growth management, and development: A contractual approach to local policy and governance. *Urban Affairs Review*, *41*(6), 749–768.

Joint Center for Housing Studies of Harvard University. (2018). *America's Rental Housing 2017*. Retrieved from https://tinyurl.com/yxs8u28p

Judd, D., & Fainstein, S. (1999). *The tourist city*. New Haven, CT: Yale University Press.

Jung, N.-R., & Kang, J.-S. (2014). A study on a new genre of public art in Mullae Art Village: Focus on Adorno's mimesis and Benjamin's active companion [Korean]. *Korean Journal of Communication and Information Studies*, *66*(5), 87–109.

Kanai, M. (2011). Barrio resurgence in Buenos Aires: Local autonomy claims amid state-sponsored transnationalism. *Political Geography*, *30*(4), 225–235.

(2014). Buenos Aires, capital of tango: Tourism, redevelopment and the cultural politics of neoliberal urbanism. *Urban Geography*, *35*(8), 1111–1117.

Kanai, M., & Ortega-Alcázar, I. (2009). The prospects for progressive culture-led urban regeneration in Latin America: Cases from Mexico City and Buenos

Aires. *International Journal of Urban and Regional Research*, 33(2), 483–501.

Kang, J. (2012). Corporeal memory and the making of a post-ideological social movement: Remembering the 2002 South Korean candlelight vigils. *Journal of Korean Studies*, 17(2), 329–350.

Karaman, O. (2014). Resisting urban renewal in Istanbul. *Urban Geography*, 35 (2), 290–310.

Karaman, O., & Islam, T. (2012). On the dual nature of intra-urban borders: The case of a Romani neighborhood in Istanbul. *Cities*, 29(4), 234–243.

Karl, C. (2011, May 8). Duriban: 500 Days of Struggle against "Reconstruction." Retrieved from http://blog.jinbo.net/CINA/2488

Keatinge, B., & Martin, D. G. (2016). A "Bedford Falls" kind of place: Neighbourhood branding and commercial revitalisation in processes of gentrification in Toronto, Ontario. *Urban Studies*, 53(5), 867–883.

Kee, Y., Kim, Y., & Lee, Y. (2014). Sing, dance, and be merry: The key to successful urban development? *Asian Social Science*, 10(9), 245–261.

Keenan, E. (2015, January 16). The peculiar uses of Section 37: From public art to affordable housing. *TheStar.com*. Retrieved from https://tinyurl.com/y4apd7fr

Kelly, S. (2013). The new normal: The figure of the condo owner in Toronto's Regent Park. *City & Society*, 25(2), 173–194.

Kern, L. (2010). Gendering reurbanisation: Women and new-build gentrification in Toronto. *Population, Space and Place*, 16(5), 363–379.

Kim, C., & Kim, S. (2010). *Branding Seoul strategy*. Seoul: Seoul Institute.

Kim, H.-J. (2011). The characteristics of creation networks and placeness of Mullae Artists [Korean]. *Land Planning*, 46(3), 207–219.

(2013). A comparative study on creation network of Mullae in Seoul, Daein Art Market in Gwangjum Totatoga in Busan [Korean]. *Seoul Institute*, 14(3), 159–173.

Kim, H.-S. (2010). Research on brand management process for city brand image: The analysis brand management system of Seoul metropolitan city [Korean]. *Design Study*, 23(5), 47–58.

Kim, I., Kim, Y., Seo, J., & Choi, W. (2010). Culturenomics approach for urban regeneration focused on Mullae-Dong specialized district [Korean]. *Architectural Institute of Korea*, 26(5), 285–296.

Kim, O. (2013). *Governing with the commons: The commons system's potential as an experimental local public sphere and its implication to deliberative democracy*. Paper presented at the Fourteenth International Association of Study of the Commons Global Conference, June 3–7, Mt. Fuji, Japan.

Kim, S. (2009). Re-locating the national: Spatialization of the national past in Seoul. *Policy Futures in Education*, 7(2), 256–265.

(2010). Issues of squatters and eviction in Seoul: From the perspectives of the dual roles of the state. *City, Culture and Society*, 1(3), 135–143.

Kimura, N. (2013, April 9). Mullae Arts Village, a base for artists of Seoul's "new wave." *Performing Arts Network Japan*. Retrieved from https://tinyurl.com/y34stv6w

Kipfer, S., & Keil, R. (2002). Toronto Inc? Planning the competitive city in the new Toronto. *Antipode*, *34*(2), 227–264.

Kipfer, S., & Petrunia, J. (2009). "Recolonization" and public housing: A Toronto case study. *Studies in Political Economy*, *83*(1), 111–139.

Kirchberg, V., & Kagan, S. (2013). The roles of artists in the emergence of creative sustainable cities: Theoretical clues and empirical illustrations. *City, Culture and Society*, 4(3), 137–152.

Kitschelt, H. (1986). Political opportunity structures and political protest: Anti-nuclear movements in four democracies. *British Journal of Political Science*, *16*(1), 57–85.

Klandermans, B. (1992). The social construction of protest and multiorganizational fields. In A. D. Morris & C. McClurg (Eds.), *Frontiers in social movement theory* (pp. 77–103). New Haven, CT: Yale University Press.

Knell, M., & Srholec, M. (2007). Diverging pathways in central and eastern Europe. In D. Lane & M. Myant (Eds.), *Varieties of capitalism in post-communist countries* (pp. 40–62). Houndsmills: Palgrave.

Knudsen, B. B., & Clark, T. N. (2013). Walk and be moved: How walking builds social movements. *Urban Affairs Review*, 49(5), 627–651.

Koopmans, R. (2004). Movements and media: Selection processes and evolutionary dynamics in the public sphere. *Theory and Society*, *33*(3–4), 367–391.

Krätke, S. (2010). "Creative cities" and the rise of the dealer class: A critique of Richard Florida's approach to urban theory. *International Journal of Urban and Regional Research*, 34(4), 835–853.

Kriesi, H., Koopmans, R., Duyvendak, J. W., & Giugni, M. G. (1995). *New social movements in Western Europe: A comparative analysis*. London and New York: Routledge.

Krishnan, M. (2015, March 22). Parkdale tenants battle back-to-back rent increases. *TheStar.com*. Retrieved from https://tinyurl.com/y5wmwfsv

Križnik, B. (2011). Selling global Seoul: Competitive urban policy and symbolic reconstruction of cities. *Revija za sociologiju*, *41*(3), 291–313.

(2013). Changing approaches to urban development in South Korea: From "clean and attractive global cities" towards "hopeful communities." *International Development Planning Review*, 35(4), 395–418.

Kuran, T. (1995). *Private truths, public lies: The social consequences of preference falsification*. Cambridge, MA: Harvard University Press.

Kuznia, R. (2018, June 2). Los Angeles tenants increasingly engaging in rent strikes amid housing crisis. *Washington Post*.

Kwaak, J. S. (2015, February 12). At Seoul slum, a struggle over how to rebuild. *Korea Real Time-Wall Street Journal*. Retrieved from https://tinyurl.com/yyk6zjkh

Kyung, S., & Kim, K.-J. (2011). "State-facilitated gentrification" in Seoul, South Korea: For whom, by whom and with what result? Paper presented at the International RC21 Conference, July 7–9, Amsterdam.

The Kyunghyang Shinmun. (2011, June 9). Noodle restaurant Duriban reopens: Agreement between tenant couple and construction company ends 531-day struggle. Retrieved from https://tinyurl.com/y4k3k47b

La Porta, R., López-de-Silanes, F., Shleifer, A., & Vishny, R. W. (1998). Law and finance. *Journal of Political Economy*, *106*(6), 1113–1155.

Laclau, E., & Mouffe, C. (1985). *Hegemony and socialist strategy: Towards a radical democratic politics*. London: Verso Trade.

Lakoff, G. (2008). *The political mind: Why you can't understand 21st-century politics with an 18th-century brain*. New York: Viking.

Landry, C. (2012). *The creative city: A toolkit for urban innovators*. London: Earthscan.

Landsberg, M. (2002, September 28). Canada, Toronto, Media, Michele Landsberg on the squat. *The Toronto Star* Retrieved from https://tinyurl.com/y3de97up

Lazzarini, J. L. (2000). El juicio de amparo. *Anuario iberoamericano de justicia constitucional*, 4, 211–220.

Leach, D. K., & Haunss, S. (2009). Scenes and social movements. In H. Johnston (Ed.), *Culture, social movements, and protest* (pp. 255–276). Aldershot: Ashgate.

LeBas, A. (2013). Violence and urban order in Nairobi, Kenya and Lagos, Nigeria. *Studies in Comparative International Development*, *48*(3), 240–262.

Lederman, J. (2015). Urban fads and consensual fictions: Creative, sustainable, and competitive city policies in Buenos Aires. *City & Community*, *14*(1), 47–67.

Lee, A. (2011, June 29). Duriban did it! Now go for Myeong-dong [Korean]. *Mediatoday*. Retrieved from https://tinyurl.com/y6ghu8g8

Lee, C., Lee, J., & Yim, C. (2003). A revenue-sharing model of residential redevelopment projects: The case of the Hapdong redevelopment scheme in Seoul, Korea. *Urban Studies*, 40(11), 2223–2237.

Lee, E.-G. (2010). A study on the consolidation of the legal status of commercial tenants in the downtown remodeling area [Korean]. *Real Estate Law*, *17*, 141–165.

Lee, H. (2015). Branding the design city: Cultural policy and creative events in Seoul. *International Journal of Cultural Policy*, *21*(1), 1–19.

Lee, H. T., & Jung, S.-h. (2012). Community business and regional development: A case study of village in Mapo-Gu Sungmisan, Seoul [Korean]. *Journal of the Economic Geographical Society of Korea*, *15*(4), 706–718.

Lee, H., & Lee, J. (2013). A study on the characteristic of creative city in Seoul art space [Korean]. *Applied Geography*, *30*(12), 1–43.

Lee, J. Y. (1990). The politics of urban renewal. PhD thesis, Political Science Department, City University of New York.

Lee, J. Y., & Anderson, C. (2010). The Yongsan tragedy and the politics of scenes. *Proceedings of the Korean Society of Public Administration*, 6, 1926–1948.

(2012). Cultural policy and the state of urban development in the capital of South Korea. In C. Grodach & D. Silver (Eds.), *The politics of urban cultural policy: Global perspectives* (pp. 69–80). London and New York: Routledge.

Lee, J.-H. (2015, March 8). Mullae Dong Culture Street: A place where the iron industry and art meet [Korean]. *ChosunBiz*. Retrieved from https://tinyurl.com/y5h3pz4t

Lee, S.-H. (2013, January 16). Four years since the Yongsan disaster. *The Kyunghyang Shinmun*. Retrieved from https://tinyurl.com/y2raj2qf

Lee, S.-Y. (2014). Urban redevelopment, displacement and anti-gentrification movements. *The Korean Geographical Society*, 49(2), 299–309.

Lee, Y.-J. (2011, July 14). The rise of Hongdae as a center of culture. *The Weekly Hankook*. Retrieved from www.koreafocus.or.kr/design2/layout/content_print.asp?group_id=103646 (accessed November 10, 2013).

Lee, Y.-S., & Hwang, E.-J. (2012). Global urban frontiers through policy transfer? Unpacking Seoul's creative city programmes. *Urban Studies*, 49(13), 2817–2837.

Lees, L. (2003). *Visions of an urban renaissance: The Urban Task Force report and the Urban White Paper*. Bristol: Policy Press.

(2008). Gentrification and social mixing: Towards an inclusive urban renaissance? *Urban Studies*, 45(12), 2449–2470.

Lees, L., & Ferreri, M. (2016). Resisting gentrification on its final frontiers: Learning from the Heygate Estate in London (1974–2013). *Cities*, 57, 14–24.

Lees, L., Shin, H. B., & López-Morales, E. (Eds.). (2015). *Global gentrifications: Uneven development and displacement*. Bristol: Policy Press.

Lees, L., Shin, H. B., & López-Morales, E. (2016). *Planetary gentrification*. San Francisco, CA: John Wiley & Sons.

Lees, L., Slater, T., & Wyly, E. K. (2008). *Gentrification*. London and New York: Routledge.

Lefebvre, H. (1996). *Writings on cities*. Hoboken, NJ: Wiley-Blackwell.

(2003). *The urban revolution*. Minneapolis, MN: University of Minnesota Press.

Lehne, W. (1994). *Der Konflikt um die Hafenstraße*. Pfaffenweiler: Centaurus-Verlagsgesellschaft.

Lehrer, U. (2017). Willing the global city: Berlin's cultural strategies of interurban competition after 1989. In N. Brenner & R. Keil (Eds.), *The globalizing cities reader* (pp. 332–338). London and New York: Routledge.

Lehrer, U., & Laidley, J. (2008). Old mega-projects newly packaged? Waterfront redevelopment in Toronto. *International Journal of Urban and Regional Research*, 32(4), 786–803.

Lehrer, U., & Pantalone, P. (2018). The sky is not the limit: Negotiating height and density in Toronto's condominium boom. In K. Ward, A. E. G. Jonas, B. Miller, & D. Wilson (Eds.), *The Routledge handbook on spaces of urban politics* (pp. 127–137). London and New York: Routledge.

Lehrer, U., & Wieditz, T. (2009). Condominium development and gentrification: The relationship between policies, building activities and socio-economic development in Toronto. *Canadian Journal of Urban Research*, 18(1), 140–161.

Lehrer, U., & Winkler, A. (2006). Public or private? The Pope Squat and housing struggles in Toronto. *Social Justice*, 33(3), 142–157.

Lehrer, U., Keil, R., & Kipfer, S. (2010). Reurbanization in Toronto: Condominium boom and social housing revitalization. *disP: The Planning Review*, 46 (180), 81–90.

Leibovitz, J. (2007). Faultline citizenship: Ethnonational politics, minority mobilisation, and governance in the Israeli "mixed cities" of Haifa and Tel Aviv-Jaffa. *Ethnopolitics*, *6*(2), 235–263.

Leitner, H., Peck, J., & Sheppard, E. S. (2007). *Contesting neoliberalism: Urban frontiers*. New York: Guilford Press.

Lelandais, G. E. (2014). Space and identity in resistance against neoliberal urban planning in Turkey. *International Journal of Urban and Regional Research*, *38*(5), 1785–1806.

(2016). Gezi protests and beyond: Urban resistance under neoliberal urbanism in Turkey. In M. Mayer, C. Thörn, & H. Thörn (Eds.), *Urban uprisings* (pp. 283–308). Basingstoke: Palgrave Macmillan.

Leslie, D., & Catungal, J. P. (2012). Social justice and the creative city: Class, gender and racial inequalities. *Geography Compass*, *6*(3), 111–122.

LeVine, M. (2004). Re-imagining the "White City": The politics of World Heritage designation in Tel Aviv/Jaffa. *City*, *8*(2), 221–228.

(2007). Globalization, architecture, and town planning in a colonial city: The case of Jaffa and TelAviv. *Journal of World History*, *18*(2), 171–198.

Ley, D. (1997). *The new middle class and the remaking of the central city*. Oxford: Oxford University Press.

LHION. (2016). A road less travelled ... Paper presented at the SW Ontario Forum, November 16, Toronto. Retrieved from https://tinyurl.com/y5ygyycy

Limoncu, S., & Çelebioglu, B. (2012). *Assessment of the urban and tourism development in the Fener-Balat Districts*. Paper presented at the Sixth Conference of the International Forum on Urbanism (IFoU): Tourbanism, January 25–27, Barcelona.

Linthicum, K., & Blankstein, A. (2011, February 11). Los Angeles gets tough with political protesters. *Los Angeles Times*. Retrieved from https://tinyurl.com/y53s8z9u

LISC Institute. (2012). *Decision time in Boyle Heights: Shaping the future*. Retrieved from http://www.instituteccd.org/MetroEdge/MetroEdge-News/Decision-Time-in-Boyle-Heights-Shaping-the-Future.html (accessed July 20, 2014).

Littler, J., & Naidoo, R. (Eds.). (2005). *The politics of heritage: The legacies of race*. London and New York: Routledge.

Logan, J. R., & Crowder, K. D. (2002). Political regimes and suburban growth, 1980–1990. *City & Community*, *1*(1), 113–135.

Logan, J. R., & Molotch, H. (1987). *Urban fortunes*. Oakland, CA: University of California Press.

Logan, J. R., Whaley, R. B., & Crowder, K. (1997). The character and consequences of growth regimes: An assessment of 20 years of research. *Urban Affairs Review*, *32*(5), 603–630.

Lohmann, S. (1994). The dynamics of informational cascades: The Monday demonstrations in Leipzig, East Germany, 1989–91. *World Politics*, 47(1), 42–101.

London Tenants Federation, Lees, L., & Just Space. (2014). *Staying put. An anti-gentrification handbook for council estates in London*. London: Just Space, SNAG.

López-Morales, E. (2010). Real estate market, state-entrepreneurialism and urban policy in the "gentrification by ground rent dispossession" of Santiago de Chile. *Journal of Latin American Geography*, 9(1), 145–173.

(2016). Gentrification in Santiago, Chile: A property-led process of dispossession and exclusion. *Urban Geography*, 37(8), 1109–1131.

Lorinc, J. (2013, March 27). The new Regent Park. *University of Toronto Magazine*. Retrieved from https://tinyurl.com/yyjv5t88

Loukaitou-Sideris, A., & Gilbert, L. (2000). Shades of duality: Perceptions and images of downtown workers in Los Angeles. *Journal of Architectural and Planning Research*, 17(1), 16–33.

Lucas, S. R., & Szatrowski, A. (2014). Qualitative comparative analysis in critical perspective. *Sociological Methodology*, 44(1), 1–79.

Mackie, J. L. (1980). *The cement of the universe*. Oxford: Oxford University Press.

Maeckelbergh, M. (2012). Mobilizing to stay put: Housing struggles in New York City. *International Journal of Urban and Regional Research*, 36(4), 655–673.

Makuch, S. M., & Schuman, M. (2015). Have we legalized corruption: The impacts of expanding municipal authority without safeguards in Toronto and Ontario. *Osgoode Hall Law Journal*, 53(1), 301–333.

Maraniello, P. A. (2011). El amparo en Argentina. Evolución, rasgos y características especiales. *Revista IUS*, 5(27), 7–36.

Marcelli, E. A. & Pastor, M. (2017) Unauthorized and uninsured: Boyle Heights and Los Angeles County. Retrieved from https://tinyurl.com/y32038ef

Marcuse, P. (1985). Gentrification, abandonment, and displacement: Connections, causes, and policy responses in New York City. *Journal of Urban and Contemporary Law*, 28, 195–240.

(2009). From critical urban theory to the right to the city. *City*, 13(2–3), 185–197.

Mardones, F. (2009, August 2). Barrio Concha y Toro bajo amenaza: Municipio y empresarios quieren "subirle el pelo." *Radio Universidad de Chile*. Retrieved from https://tinyurl.com/y648a8dk

Mardones, G. (2016). Renovación y gentrificación en barrios "patrimoniales." El caso del barrio Yungay, Santiago de Chile. *Revista Eltopo*. 7(June–July), 10–37.

(2017). El proceso histórico de la gentrificación en barrios "patrimoniales." El caso del barrio Yungay, Santiago de Chile. In M. A. Guérin & F. E. Rojas (Eds.), *Historia sociocultural urbana de América Latina. Espacio, migraciones y tiempo* (pp. 54–70). Buenos Aires: Miguel Guérin.

Margalit, T. (2009). Public assets vs. public interest: Fifty years of high-rise building in Tel Aviv-Jaffa. *Geography Research Forum*, 29, 48–82.

(2013). Land, politics and high-rise planning: Ongoing development practices in Tel Aviv–Yafo. *Planning Perspectives*, 28(3), 373–397.

Margalit, T., & Alfasi, N. (2016). The undercurrents of entrepreneurial development: Impressions from a globalizing city. *Environment and Planning A*, 48 (10), 1967–1987.

Marom, N. (2011). *"Affordable housing" and the globalizing city: The case of Tel Aviv*. Paper presented at the International RC21 conference, July 7–9, Amsterdam.

(2013). Activising space: The spatial politics of the 2011 protest movement in Israel. *Urban Studies*, *50*(13), 2826–2841.

Marom, N., & Yacobi, H. (2013). "Culture capital for all"? Cultural diversity policy in Tel Aviv and its limits. *Mediterranean Politics*, *18*(1), 60–77.

Martin, D. G. (2003). "Place-framing" as place-making: Constituting a neighborhood for organizing and activism. *Annals of the Association of American Geographers*, *93*(3), 730–750.

Martínez López, M. A. (2014). How do squatters deal with the state? Legalization and anomalous institutionalization in Madrid. *International Journal of Urban and Regional Research*, *38*(2), 646–674.

(2016). Between autonomy and hybridity: Urban struggles within the 15M movement in Spain. In M. Mayer, C. Thörn, & H. Thörn (Eds.), *Urban uprisings: Challenging neoliberal urbanism in Europe* (pp. 253–281). Basingstoke: Palgrave Macmillan

(2017). Squatters and migrants in Madrid: Interactions, contexts and cycles. *Urban Studies*, *54*(11), 2472–2489.

Mayer, M. (2003). The onward sweep of social capital: Causes and consequences for understanding cities, communities and urban movements. *International Journal of Urban and Regional Research*, 27(1), 110–132.

(2009). The "Right to the City" in the context of shifting mottos of urban social movements. *City*, *13*(2–3), 362–374.

Mayer, M., Thörn, C., & Thörn, H. (Eds.). (2016). *Urban uprisings: Challenging neoliberal urbanism in Europe*. Basingstoke: Palgrave Macmillan.

McAdam, D. (1999). *Political process and the development of black insurgency, 1930–1970*. Chicago, IL: University of Chicago Press.

McAdam, D., & Boudet, H. (2012). *Putting social movements in their place: Explaining opposition to energy projects in the United States, 2000–2005*. Cambridge: Cambridge University Press.

McAdam, D., McCarthy, J. D., Zald, M. N., & Mayer, N. Z. (1996). *Comparative perspectives on social movements: Political opportunities, mobilizing structures, and cultural framings*. Cambridge: Cambridge University Press.

McCann, E. J. (2002). The urban as an object of study in global cities literatures: Representational practices and conceptions of place and scale. In A. Herod & M. W. Wright (Eds.), *Geographies of power: Placing scale* (pp. 61–84). San Francisco, CA: John Wiley & Son.

McCarthy, J. D., & Zald, M. N. (1977). Resource mobilization and social movements: A partial theory. *American Journal of Sociology*, *82*(6), 1212–1241.

McFarlane, C., & Robinson, J. (2012). Introduction: Experiments in comparative urbanism. *Urban Geography*, *33*(6), 765–773.

McLean, H. (2001). Go West, young hipster: The gentrification of Queen Street West. In A. Wilcox & J. McBride (Eds.), *uTOpia: Towards a New Toronto* (pp. 156–163). Toronto: Coach House Books.

(2014). Cracks in the creative city: The contradictions of community arts practice. *International Journal of Urban and Regional Research*, *38*(6), 2156–2173.

McPhate, M. (2017, March 15). A gallery flees and neighborhood activists cheer. *New York Times*. Retrieved from https://tinyurl.com/y2kjmm88

Mehler Paperny, A. (2010, November 16). Is Regent Park revitalization crumbling? *The Globe and Mail*. Retrieved from https://tinyurl.com/y287lv5r

Mejia, B. (2016, March 3). Gentrification pushes up against Boyle Heights – and vice versa. *Los Angeles Times*. Retrieved from https://tinyurl.com/y4sva3eb

Melanson, T. (2013, February 22). Toronto falling from grace? Yeah, right. Canada's No. 1 city is soaring. *Canadian Business*. Retrieved from https://tinyurl.com/y5xv7rdz

Meltzer, R., & Schuetz, J. (2010). What drives the diffusion of inclusionary zoning? *Journal of Policy Analysis and Management*, 29(3), 578–602.

Menahem, G. (1994). Urban regimes and neighborhood mobilization: The case of an Arab-Jewish in Israel Neighborhood. *Journal of Urban Affairs*, *16*(1), 35–50.

(2000). Jews, Arabs, Russians and foreigners in an Israeli city: Ethnic divisions and the restructuring economy of Tel Aviv, 1983–96. *International Journal of Urban and Regional Research*, 24(3), 634–652.

Méndez, A., & Tyrone, A. (2014). Marca ciudad: Buenos Aires Ciudad de Todos. Cultura ciudadana tras una estrategia de marketing polıtico en Buenos Aires. *Escritos en la Facultad (Centro de Estudios en Diseño y Comunicación, Facultad de Diseño y Comunicación)*, *96*(10), 13–14.

Mercer, D., & Mayfield, P. (2015). City of the spectacle: White Night Melbourne and the politics of public space. *Australian Geographer*, 46(4), 507–534.

Merino Hernando, M. A. (2002). *Historia de los inmigrantes peruanos en España: Dinámicas de exclusión e inclusión en una Europa globalizada*. Madrid: Editorial CSIC.

Meyer, D. S., & Staggenborg, S. (1996). Movements, countermovements, and the structure of political opportunity. *American Journal of Sociology*, *101*(6), 1628–1660.

Micallef, S. (2013). *Regent Park: A story of collective impact*. Toronto: Metcalf Foundation.

Miller, B., & Nicholls, W. (2013). Social movements in urban society: The city as a space of politicization. *Urban Geography*, 34(4), 452–473.

Mimico-Lakeshore Network. (2012, February 11). A report on revitalization in the Mimico-Lakeshore community. Retrieved from https://tinyurl.com/yy3xdkfh

Min, H., Shin, K., Song, J., Jung, Y., Lee, K., Lee, Y. . . . Jung, T. (2011). *Creation of Slow City in Seoul* [Korean]. Seoul: Seoul Institute.

Miranda, M., & Lane-McKinley, K. (2017, February 1). Artwashing, or, between social practice and social reproduction. Retrieved from https://tinyurl.com/y67rctyj

Mische, A. (2008). *Partisan publics: Communication and contention across Brazilian youth activist networks*. Princeton, NJ: Princeton University Press.

Mitchell, D. (2003). *The right to the city: Social justice and the fight for public space*. New York: Guilford Press.

Moncada, E. (2013). The politics of urban violence: Challenges for development in the Global South. *Studies in Comparative International Development*, 48 (3), 217–239.

Monterescu, D. (2009). To buy or not to be: Trespassing the gated community. *Public Culture*, 21(2), 403–430.

Montgomery, J. (2005). Beware "the creative class": Creativity and wealth creation revisited. *Local Economy*, 20(4), 337–343.

Moore, A. A. (2013a). *Planning politics in Toronto: The Ontario municipal board and urban development*. Toronto: University of Toronto Press.

(2013b). Trading density for benefits: Toronto and Vancouver compared. *IMFG Papers on Municipal Finance and Governance (University of Toronto)*, 13, 1–42.

Moore, N., & Whelan, Y. (Eds.). (2007). *Heritage, memory and the politics of identity: New perspectives on the cultural landscape*. London and New York: Routledge.

Murillo, M. V. (2001). *Labor unions, partisan coalitions, and market reforms in Latin America*. Cambridge: Cambridge University Press.

Musterd, S., De Vos, S., Das, M., & Latten, J. (2012). Neighbourhood composition and economic prospects: A longitudinal study in the Netherlands. *Tijdschrift voor Economische en Sociale Geografie*, 103(1), 85–100.

Mutman, D., & Turgut, H. (2011). *A social and spatial restructuring in inner-city residential areas: The case of Istanbul*. Paper presented at the Eurpean Network for Housing Research Conference, July 5–8, Toulouse.

(2018). Colliding urban transformation process: The case of Historical Peninsula, Istanbul. *ArchNet-IJAR*, 12(1), 164–181.

Myeongdong Liberation Front, & Karl, C. (2011, September 08). Myeong-dong "redevelopment" section (#4). Retrieved from http://blog.jinbo.net/mdlf/35

Navarro Ayala, M. (2006, June 12). Proponen polémico seccional en área de Santiago poniente. *El Mercurio*. Retrieved from https://tinyurl.com/yydvb8u7

Negri, A. (1989). *The politics of subversion: A manifesto for the twenty first century*. Cambridge: Polity.

Newman, K., & Wyly, E. K. (2006). The right to stay put, revisited: Gentrification and resistance to displacement in New York City. *Urban Studies*, 43(1), 23–57.

Nicholls, W. (2003). Forging a "new" organizational infrastructure for Los Angeles' progressive community. *International Journal of Urban and Regional Research*, 27(4), 881–896.

(2009). Place, networks, space: Theorising the geographies of social movements. *Transactions of the Institute of British Geographers*, 34(1), 78–93.

Nijman, J. (2007). Introduction: Comparative urbanism. *Urban Geography*, 28 (1), 1–6.

Nion, B. H. (2010). Not in our name! Jamming the gentrification machine: A manifesto. *City*, 14(3), 323–325.

Nitzan-Shiftan, A. (1996). Contested Zionism, alternative modernism: Erich Mendelsohn and the Tel Aviv Chug in Mandate Palestine. *Architectural History*, 39, 147–180.

(2000). Whitened houses [Hebrew]. *Theory and Criticism*, *16*, 227–232.

Norton, A. (1988). *Reflections on political identity*. Baltimore, MD: Johns Hopkins University Press.

Novy, J., & Colomb, C. (2012). Struggling for the right to the (creative) city in Berlin and Hamburg: New urban social movements, new "spaces of hope"? *International Journal of Urban and Regional Research*, 37(5), 1816–1838.

The Observatory for the Protection of Human Rights Defenders. (2010). Annual Report, Republic of Korea. Retrieved from https://tinyurl.com/y47hxscy

Oh, J.-J. (2012). A critical study on the decisions of the constitutional court about redevelopment: The assumption of public interest vs. the rights for stable residence [Korean]. *Busan University Law Review*, 53(2), 291–311.

Ok, E., & Kim, Y. (2013). New social movement in the form of cultural practices: A Case Study of the Duriban Movement [Korean]. *KACIS*, *63*(3), 53–75.

Ontario Ministry of Culture. (2006). *Heritage property evaluation*. Retrieved from https://tinyurl.com/yyokvdcw

Orr, C. (2012, April 3). Regent Park revitalization draws mixed reactions from residents. *National Post*. Retrieved from https://tinyurl.com/y6qnuep9

Overmeyer, K. (2010). *Kreative Milieus und offene Räume in Hamburg*. Hamburg: Behörde für Stadtentwicklung und Umwelt.

Pardo, M. (1990). Mexican American women grassroots community activists: "Mothers of East Los Angeles." *Frontiers: A Journal of Women Studies*, *11* (1), 1–7.

Park, B.-G. (1998). Where do tigers sleep at night? The state's role in housing policy in South Korea and Singapore. *Economic Geography*, 74(3), 272–288.

Park, K.-O., & Ryu, H.-S. (2012). Case study of opinion coordination between residents and coordinators on the planning process of community housing in Sungmisan Village [Korean]. *Journal of the Korean Housing Association*, 23(3), 1–11.

Park, S. (2011, June 12). A victory against redevelopment project. *Korea Times*. Retrieved from https://tinyurl.com/y5v6xd86

Park, T. (2012, January 17). Couple torn apart by Yongsan tragedy still hanging on. *The Hankyoreh*. Retrieved from https://tinyurl.com/y696dkql

(2013). Empirical study of sustainable community development in South Korea: A special focus on village community. *OIDA International Journal of Sustainable Development*, 6(2), 49–54.

Parker, B. (2008). Beyond the class act: Gender and race in the "creative city" discourse. In J. DeSena (Ed.), *Gender in an urban world* (pp. 201–232). Bingley: Jai Press/Emerald.

Parks, V., & Warren, D. (2009). The politics and practice of economic justice: Community benefits agreements as tactic of the new accountable development movement. *Journal of Community Practice*, 17(1–2), 88–106.

Parra, I. D. (2016). Lucha por centralidad y autogestión del espacio: El Movimiento de Ocupantes e Inquilinos en Buenos Aires. *Iconos: Revista de Ciencias Sociales*, (56), 43–61.

Pasotti, E. (2009). *Political branding in cities: The decline of machine politics in Bogotá, Naples, and Chicago*. Cambridge: Cambridge University Press.

Paulsen, A. (2014). Negocios inmobiliarios, cambio socioespacial y contestación ciudadana en Santiago Poniente. El caso del barrio Yungay: 2000–2013. In R. Hidalgo & M. Janoschka (Eds.), *La ciudad neoliberal* (pp. 75–100). Santiago: LOM.

Peck, J. (2005). Struggling with the creative class. *International Journal of Urban and Regional Research*, 29(4), 740–770.

(2011). Creative moments: Working culture, through municipal socialism and neoliberal urbanism. In E. McCann & K. Ward (Eds.), *Mobile urbanism: Cities and policymaking in the global age* (pp. 41–70). Minneapolis, MN: University of Minnesota Press.

Peterson, P. E. (1981). *City limits*. Chicago, IL: University of Chicago Press.

Pickvance, C. (2003). From urban social movements to urban movements: A review and introduction to a symposium on urban movements. *International Journal of Urban and Regional Research*, 27(1), 102–109.

Pírez, P. (2002). Buenos Aires: Fragmentation and privatization of the metropolitan city. *Environment and Urbanization*, 14(1), 145–158.

Plaza Gómez, G. (2010, February 17). El Movimiento Asambleas del Pueblo. *El Sol de San Telmo*. Retrieved from https://tinyurl.com/y5msx5ct

Polletta, F. (2006). *It was like a fever: Storytelling in protest and politics*. Chicago, IL: University of Chicago Press.

Porter, L., & Shaw, K. (Eds.). (2013). *Whose urban renaissance? An international comparison of urban regeneration strategies*. London and New York: Routledge.

Post, A. (2018). Cities and politics in the developing world. *The Annual Review of Political Science*, *21*: 115–133.

Preiss, B. (2015, August 24). High-rise towers to remain in Prahran public housing estate. *The Age*. Retrieved from https://tinyurl.com/y48kkktw

Price, N. (2013a, March 21). The state government backs away from development plans for Yarra housing estates. *Melbourne Leader*. Retrieved from https://tinyurl.com/y3s8dnus

(2013b, April 24). State government ban on pollies meeting at housing estates lifted. *Melbourne Leader*. Retrieved from https://tinyurl.com/yxhq79es

Pruijt, H. (2013). The logic of urban squatting. *International Journal of Urban and Regional Research*, 37(1), 19–45.

Purcell, M. (2008). *Recapturing democracy: Neoliberalization and the struggle for alternative urban futures*. London and New York: Routledge.

(2013). To inhabit well: Counterhegemonic movements and the right to the city. *Urban Geography*, 34(4), 560–574.

Purdy, S. (2004). By the people, for the people: Tenant organizing in Toronto's Regent Park housing project in the 1960s and 1970s. *Journal of Urban History*, 30(4), 519–548.

Quartz, S., & Asp, A. (2015). *Cool: How the brain's hidden quest for cool drives our economy and shapes our world*. New York: Farrar, Straus & Giroux.

Ra, D. (2008, July 21). *Special creative planning zones* [Korean]. Seoul Institute.

(2010). Seoul's strategy for strengthening soft power [Korean]. *Seoul Institute*, (73), 1–20.

Ra, D., Park, E., Oh, M.-G., & Woo, Y. (2008). Meaning and cases of creative city [Korean]. *City Data*, (317), 3–18.

Rae, E. (2015). Creativity and social mix: The promotion and policies of "positive gentrification" at CityPlace condominiums. Paper presented at the American Association of Geographers, April 21–25, Chicago.

Ragin, C. C. (2013). *The comparative method: Moving beyond qualitative and quantitative strategies*. Oakland, CA: University of California Press.

Raijman, R., & Semyonov, M. (2004). Perceived threat and exclusionary attitudes towards foreign workers in Israel. *Ethnic and Racial Studies*, 27(5), 780–799.

Razmilic, S. (2015) Impuesto territorial y financiamiento municipal. *Estudios Públicos*, *138*(fall), 47–91.

Reigh, Y., & Choi, S. (2012). A study on the role of art and culture programs in process of urban regeneration through the case of Monrae Steel Factory Art Village [Korean]. *Journal of Korea Culture Industry*, 12(4), 73–90.

Rihoux, B., & Ragin, C. C. (2008). *Configurational comparative methods: Qualitative comparative analysis (QCA) and related techniques*. Thousand Oaks, CA: Sage Publications.

Rim, Y., & Lee, J. (2011). A study on the analysis of the influencing factors on resettlement of commercial tenants involved in urban redevelopment [Korean]. *Korea Real Estate Society*, 29(2), 83–102.

Rithmire, M. E. (2017). Land institutions and Chinese political economy: Institutional complementarities and macroeconomic management. *Politics & Society*, *45*(1), 123–153.

Roberts Evaluation Pty, & Victoria Department of Human Services. (2012). Social impact assessment. Retrieved from www.dhs.vic.gov.au/__data/assets/pdf_file/0003/753348/Social-impact-assessment-baseline-report-Richmond-November-2012.pdf (accessed October 18, 2013).

Robinson, J. (2002). Global and world cities: A view from off the map. *International Journal of Urban and Regional Research*, 26(3), 531–554.

(2011). Cities in a world of cities: The comparative gesture. *International Journal of Urban and Regional Research*, *35*(1), 1–23.

Rodríguez, A., & Rodríguez, P. (2014). Cuando el mercado destruye la ciudad y los vecinos la conservan. *Quid 16: Revista de Área de Estudios Urbanos*, *3*, 17–48.

Rodríguez, M. C. (2009). *Autogestión, políticas del hábitat y transformación social*. Buenos Aires: Espacio.

(2010). Las políticas habitacionales argentinas post 2001: Entre la gestión de la "emergencia" y la emergencia de la producción autogestionaria. *Revista Osera*, 3, 1–23.

Rodríguez, M. C., & Di Virgilio, M. M. (2016). A city for all? Public policy and resistance to gentrification in the southern neighborhoods of Buenos Aires. *Urban Geography*, 37(8), 1215–1234.

Rodríguez, M. C., Arqueros Mejica, S., Rodríguez, M. F., Gomez Schettini, M., & Zapata, M. C. (2011). La politica urbana "PRO": Continuidades y cambios en contextos de renovacion en la Ciudad de Buenos Aires. *Cuaderno urbano*, *11*(11), 101–121.

Rojas Morales, L. R. (2014). Hacia el desarrollo sostenible de los barrios patrimoniales de Santiago: La comunidad como generadora de desarrollo en base al patrimonio cultural. *Revista Planeo*, *15*(April), 1–24.

Rojas, E., Rodríguez, E., & Wegelin, E. (2004). *Volver al Centro: La recuperación de áreas urbanas centrales*. Division of Social Programs of the Department of Sustainable Development. Inter-American Development Bank. Washington, DC.

Romanos, E. (2014). Evictions, petitions and escraches: Contentious housing in austerity Spain. *Social Movement Studies*, *13*(2), 296–302.

Romo, R. (2010). *East Los Angeles: History of a barrio*. Austin, TX: University of Texas Press.

Rosen, G., & Razin, E. (2009). The Rise of Gated Communities in Israel: Reflections on Changing Urban Governance in a Neo-liberal Era. *Urban Studies*, *46* (8), 1702–1722.

Rosen, G., & Walks, A. (2015). Castles in Toronto's sky: Condo-ism as urban transformation. *Journal of Urban Affairs*, *37*(3), 289–310.

Rosenhek, Z., & Shalev, M. (2014). The political economy of Israel's "social justice" protests: A class and generational analysis. *Contemporary Social Science*, *9*(1), 31–48.

Rossi, F. M. (2005). Las asambleas vecinales y populares en Argentina: Las particularidades organizativas de la acción colectiva contenciosa. *Sociológica*, *19*(57), 113–145.

Rotbard, S. (2015). *White city, black city: Architecture and war in Tel Aviv and Jaffa*. Cambridge, MA: MIT Press.

Routledge, P. (2003). Convergence space: Process geographies of grassroots globalization networks. *Transactions of the Institute of British Geographers*, *28* (3), 333–349.

Sabatini, F. (2000). Reforma de los mercados de suelo en Santiago, Chile: Efectos sobre los precios de la tierra y la segregación residencial. *Revista EURE*, *26*(77), 49–80.

Saito, L. T. (2012). How low-income residents can benefit from urban development: The LA Live Community Benefits Agreement. *City & Community*, *11* (2), 129–150.

Salkin, P. E., & Lavine, A. (2008). Understanding community benefits agreements: Equitable development, social justice and other considerations for developers, municipalities and community organizations. *UCLA Journal of Environmental Law & Policy*, *26*, 291–331.

Sampson, R. J. (2012). *Great American city: Chicago and the enduring neighborhood effect*. Chicago, IL: University of Chicago Press.

Sampson, R. J., McAdam, D., MacIndoe, H., & Weffer-Elizondo, S. (2005). Civil society reconsidered: The durable nature and community structure of collective civic action. *American Journal of Sociology*, *111*(3), 673–714.

Sánchez, G. J. (2004). "What's good for Boyle Heights is good for the Jews": Creating multiracialism on the Eastside during the 1950s. *American Quarterly*, *56*(3), 633–661.

Sandals, L. (2013, August 6). "The Match Game": Are condos a boon or blight for the urban art scene? *Canadian Art*. Retrieved from www.building.ca/features/the-match-game

Sassen, S. (1994). *Global city*. Princeton, NJ: Princeton University Press.

Sawyers, T. M., & Meyer, D. S. (1999). Missed opportunities: Social movement abeyance and public policy. *Social Problems*, 46(2), 187–206.

Scarpaci, J. L. (2005). *Plazas and barrios: Heritage tourism and globalization in the Latin American Centro Historico*. Tucson, AZ: University of Arizona Press.

Schäfer, C. (2010). *Die Stadt ist unsere Fabrik | The City is our Factory*. Leipzig: Spector Books.

Schipper, S. (2015). Towards a "post-neoliberal" mode of housing regulation? The Israeli social protest of summer 2011. *International Journal of Urban and Regional Research*, 39(6), 1137–1154.

Schneider, B. R. (2013). *Hierarchical capitalism in Latin America*. Cambridge: Cambridge University Press.

Schneider, M., & Teske, P. (1993). The antigrowth entrepreneur: Challenging the "equilibrium" of the growth machine. *The Journal of Politics*, 55(3), 720–736.

Schnell, I. (2007). Sheinkin as a place in the globalizing city of Tel Aviv. *GeoJournal*, 69(4), 257–269.

Schnell, I., & Graicer, I. (1993). Causes of in-migration to Tel-Aviv inner city. *Urban Studies*, 30(7), 1187–1207.

Schwegmann, M. (2013). Istanbul and the grassroots: Civil society organisations, local politics and urban transformation. PhD thesis, Technischen Universität Berlin.

Scott, A. J., & Storper, M. (2015). The nature of cities: The scope and limits of urban theory. *International Journal of Urban and Regional Research*, 39(1), 1–15.

Scott, J. C. (1985). *Weapons of the weak: Everyday forms of peasant resistance*. New Haven, CT: Yale University Press.

(2010). *The art of not being governed: An anarchist history of upland Southeast Asia*. New Haven, CT: Yale University Press.

Sequera, J., & Janoschka, M. (2015). Gentrification dispositifs in the historic centre of Madrid: A reconsideration of urban governmentality and state-led urban reconfiguration. In L. Lees, H. B. Shin, & E. López-Morales (Eds.), *Global gentrifications: Uneven development and displacement* (pp. 375–394). Bristol: Policy Press.

Shaw, K. (2009). A curiously qualified legacy of resistance ... the right to the city: The entitled and the excluded. *The Urban Reinventors Online Journal*, 3 (November), 1–15.

(2013a). Docklands dreamings: Illusions of sustainability in the Melbourne docks redevelopment. *Urban Studies*, 50(11), 2158–2177.

(2013b). Independent creative subcultures and why they matter. *International Journal of Cultural Policy*, 19(3), 333–352.

Shaw, K., & Hagemans, I. W. (2015). "Gentrification without displacement" and the consequent loss of place: The effects of class transition on low-income residents of secure housing in gentrifying areas. *International Journal of Urban and Regional Research*, 39(2), 323–341.

Shephard, T. (2013, June 24). Will secondary plan revitalize Mimico? Even local councillor "concerned" development may not happen. *Etobicoke Guardian*. Retrieved from https://tinyurl.com/y5ym93n6

Shiau, E., Musso, J., & Sellers, J. M. (2015). City fragmentation and neighborhood connections: The political dynamics of community revitalization in Los Angeles. In C. N. Stone, R. P. Stoker, J. Betancur, S. E. Clarke, M. Dantico, M. Horak, ... E. Shiau (Eds.), *Urban neighborhoods in a new era: Revitalization politics in the postindustrial city* (pp. 131–154). Chicago, IL: Chicago University Press.

Shin, H. B. (2009). Property-based redevelopment and gentrification: The case of Seoul, South Korea. *Geoforum*, 40(5), 906–917.

(2018). Urban movements and the genealogy of urban rights discourses: The case of urban protesters against redevelopment and displacement in Seoul, South Korea. *Annals of the American Association of Geographers*, *108*(2), 356–369.

Shin, K.-H., & Timberlake, M. (2006). Korea's global city: Structural and political implications of Seoul's ascendance in the global urban hierarchy. *International Journal of Comparative Sociology*, 47(2), 145–173.

Shirky, C. (2008). *Here comes everybody: The power of organizing without organizations*. London: Penguin.

Short, J. R., Breitbach, C., Buckman, S., & Essex, J. (2000). From world cities to gateway cities: Extending the boundaries of globalization theory. *City*, 4(3), 317–340.

Siavelis, P. M., Valenzuela Van Treek, E., & Martelli, G. (2002). Santiago: Municipal Decentralization in a Centralized Political System. In D. J. Myers & H. A. Dietz (Eds.), *Capital city politics in Latin America: Democratization and empowerment* (pp. 265–295). Boulder, CO: Lynne Rienner.

Silva, E. (2009). *Challenging neoliberalism in Latin America*. Cambridge: Cambridge University Press.

Silver, D., & Miller, D. (2013). Contextualizing the artistic dividend. *Journal of Urban Affairs*, *35*(5), 591–606.

Silver, D., Clark, T. N., & Navarro Yanez, C. J. (2010). Scenes: Social context in an age of contingency. *Social Forces*, *88*(5), 2293–2324.

Silvestri, G., & Gorelik, A. (2000). Ciudad y cultura urbana, 1976–1999: El fin de la expansión. In J. L. Romero & L. A. Romero (Eds.), *Buenos Aires, historia de cuatro siglos* (pp. 461–499). Buenos Aires: Altamira.

Simmons, E. S. (2016). *Meaningful resistance: Market reforms and the roots of social protest in Latin America*. Cambridge: Cambridge University Press.

Sirmans, C., & Worzala, E. (2003). International direct real estate investment: A review of the literature. *Urban Studies*, 40(5–6), 1081–1114.

Skaburskis, A. (2012). Gentrification and Toronto's changing household characteristics and income distribution. *Journal of Planning Education and Research*, 32(2), 191–203.

Slater, T. (2004). Municipally managed gentrification in south Parkdale, Toronto. *The Canadian Geographer/Le Géographe canadien*, 48(3), 303–325.

(2006). The eviction of critical perspectives from gentrification research. *International Journal of Urban and Regional Research*, 30(4), 737–757.

Small, M. L. (2009). "How many cases do I need?" On science and the logic of case selection in field-based research. *Ethnography*, *10*(1), 5–38.

Smith, J. (2001). Globalizing resistance: The battle of Seattle and the future of social movements. *Mobilization: An International Quarterly*, *6*(1), 1–19.

Smith, N. (2002). New globalism, new urbanism: Gentrification as global urban strategy. *Antipode*, *34*(3), 427–450.

Snow, D. A., & Benford, R. D. (1988). Ideology, frame resonance, and participant mobilization. *International Social Movement Research*, *1*(1), 197–217.

Snow, D. A., Rochford, E. B., Worden, S. K., & Benford, R. D. (1986). Frame alignment processes, micromobilization, and movement participation. *American Sociological Review*, *51*(4), 464–481.

Social Development Plan Steering Committee. (2012). Shaping our community together: Our social development and action plan for Lawrence Heights. Retrieved from https://tinyurl.com/y309plf4

The Socialist. (2013). Campaign to defend public housing formed in Melbourne. *91*(March), 12–13.

Soja, E. W. (2010). *Seeking spatial justice*. Minneapolis, MN: University of Minnesota Press.

Soskice, D. W., & Hall, P. A. (2001). *Varieties of capitalism: The institutional foundations of comparative advantage*. Oxford: Oxford University Press.

Statistics Canada. (2001). City of Toronto Ward Profiles: Ward 6 Etiboke-Lakeshore.

(2006). City of Toronto Ward Profiles: Ward 6 Etiboke-Lakeshore.

(2011). City of Toronto Ward Profiles: Ward 6 Etiboke-Lakeshore.

Statistisches Amt für Hamburg und Schleswig-Holstein. (2013). Sozialleistungen in den Hamburger Stadtteilen 2011. Retrieved from https://tinyurl.com/y5u5fugw

Steinberg, M. W. (1998). Tilting the frame: Considerations on collective action framing from a discursive turn. *Theory and Society*, *27*(6), 845–872.

Stokes, S. C. (2005). Perverse accountability: A formal model of machine politics with evidence from Argentina. *American Political Science Review*, *99*(3), 315–325.

Stone, C. N. (1989). *Regime politics: Governing Atlanta, 1946–1988*. Lawrence, KS: University Press of Kansas.

Stone, C. N., Stoker, R. P., Betancur, J., Clarke, S. E., Dantico, M., Horak, M., … Shiau, E. (2015). *Urban neighborhoods in a new era: Revitalization politics in the postindustrial city*. Chicago, IL: University of Chicago Press.

Sweetman, M. (2011, December 19). Occupying housing from the Pope Squat to Occupy Toronto. Rabble.ca. Retrieved from https://tinyurl.com/y2zlljjy

Szwarcberg, M. (2015). *Mobilizing poor voters: Machine politics, clientelism, and social networks in Argentina*. Cambridge: Cambridge University Press.

Tarrow, S. G. (1998). *Power in movement: Social movements, collective action and politics*. Cambridge: Cambridge University Press.

(2005). The dualities of transnational contention: "Two activist solitudes" or a new world altogether? *Mobilization: An International Quarterly*, *10*(1), 53–72.

(2013). *The language of contention: Revolutions in words, 1688–2012*. Cambridge: Cambridge University Press.

Tarrow, S. G., & McAdam, D. (2005). Scale shift in transnational contention. In W. L. Bennett, D. Della Porta, M. Diani, E. Johnson, F. Kolb, D. McAdam, … K. Sikkink (Eds.), *Transnational protest and global activism* (pp. 121–150). Lanham, MD: Rowman & Littlefield Publishers.

Tasan-Kok, T. (2004). *Budapest, Istanbul and Warsaw: Institutional and spatial change*. Delft: Eburon.

Taylor, V. (1989). Social movement continuity: The women's movement in abeyance. *American Sociological Review*, *54*(5), 761–775.
Tilly, C. (1976). Major forms of collective action in western Europe 1500–1975. *Theory and Society*, *3*(3), 365–375.
(2005). *Trust and rule*. Cambridge: Cambridge University Press.
Tilly, C., & Wood, L. J. (2015). *Social movements, 1768–2012*. London and New York: Routledge.
Todd, G. (1995). "Going global" in the semi-periphery: World cities as political projects – The case of Toronto. In P. L. Knox & P. J. Taylor (Eds.), *World cities in a world system* (pp. 192–212). Cambridge: Cambridge University Press.
Torres, H. A. (2001). Cambios socioterritoriales en Buenos Aires durante la década de 1990. *Revista EURE*, *27*(80), 33–56.
Torres, M. (2006). Recuperación de la renta urbana: Una tarea ética pendiente. *Revista Invi*, *21*(58), 42–70.
Trivelli, P. (2006). Sobre el debate acerca de la política urbana, la política de suelo y la formación de los precios de la tierra urbana en el Gran Santiago, antecedentes teóricos y empíricos. *Boletín Mercado del Suelo Urbano Área Metropolitana de Santiago*, 97, 1–30.
(2011). La propuesta de modificación del Plan Regulador Metropolitano de Santiago PRMS 100 requiere una justificación más sólida. *Revista EURE*, *37* (111), 179–184.
Trounstine, J. (2018). *Segregation by design*. Cambridge: Cambridge University Press.
Trounstine, J., & Valdini, M. E. (2008). The context matters: The effects of single-member versus at-large districts on city council diversity. *American Journal of Political Science*, *52*(3), 554–569.
TUIK (2006) www.tuik.gov.tr. Ankara: Turkish Statistical Institute.
Tunbridge, J. E. (2004). *The geography of heritage: Power, culture and economy*. London: Arnold.
Tunbridge, J. E., & Ashworth, G. J. (1996). *Dissonant heritage: The management of the past as a resource in conflict*. San Francisco, CA: John Wiley & Sons.
Turkmen, H. (2014). *Urban renewal projects and dynamics of contention in Istanbul: The cases of Fener-Balat-Ayvansaray and Suleymaniye*. PhD thesis, Cardiff University.
Twickel, C. (2011). *Gentrifidingbums oder eine Stadt für alle*. Hamburg: Edition Nautilus.
Uitermark, J. (2004). The co-optation of squatters in Amsterdam and the emergence of a movement meritocracy: a critical reply to Pruijt. *International Journal of Urban and Regional Research*, *28*(3), 687–698.
Uitermark, J., Duyvendak, J. W., & Kleinhans, R. (2007). Gentrification as a governmental strategy: Social control and social cohesion in Hoogvliet, Rotterdam. *Environment and Planning A*, *39*(1), 125–141.
Uitermark, J., Nicholls, W., & Loopmans, M. (2012). *Cities and social movements: Theorizing beyond the right to the city*. London: Sage Publications.
UNESCO. (2006, May 8). *World Heritage Report historic areas of Istanbul (Turkey) (C 356)*. Paris: UNESCO.

(2008, May 8). *Report on the Joint UNESCO World Heritage Centre/ICOMOS Mission to the historic areas of Istanbul World Heritage Site*. Paris: UNESCO.

Uysal, Ü. E. (2012). An urban social movement challenging urban regeneration: The case of Sulukule, Istanbul. *Cities*, 29(1), 12–22.

Van Biezen, I., Mair, P., & Poguntke, T. (2012). Going, going, … gone? The decline of party membership in contemporary Europe. *European Journal of Political Research*, 51(1), 24–56.

Vanclay, F., & Esteves, A. M. (2011). *New directions in social impact assessment: Conceptual and methodological advances*. Northampton: Edward Elgar Publishing.

Veiga, G. (2009, March 23). Acusados por protestar contra Macri. *El Pais*. Retrieved from https://tinyurl.com/y4nskc3b

Verón, N. (2014). Desalojos en la ciudad de Buenos Aires: La producción de las categorías y los espacios de la asistencia habitacional. *Quid 16: Revista de Área de Estudios Urbanos 3*, 170–194.

Vick, K. (2011, October 25). What Occupy Wall Street can learn from Occupy Tel Aviv? *Time*. Retrieved from https://tinyurl.com/y6okzptb

Vigdor, J. L., Massey, D. S., & Rivlin, A. M. (2002). Does gentrification harm the poor? *Brookings-Wharton Papers on Urban Affairs*, 133–182.

Vogelpohl, A., & Buchholz, T. (2017). Breaking with neoliberalization by restricting the housing market: Novel urban policies and the case of Hamburg. *International Journal of Urban and Regional Research*, 41(2), 266–281.

Wacquant, L. (2010). Crafting the neoliberal state: Workfare, prisonfare, and social insecurity. *Sociological Forum*, 25(2), 197–220.

Wallerstein, M., & Western, B. (2000). Unions in decline? What has changed and why. *Annual Review of Political Science*, 3(1), 355–377.

Wallerstein, S., & Silverman, E. (2009). *Housing distress within the Palestinian community of Jaffa: The end of protected tenancy in absentee ownership homes*. Tel Aviv: BIMKOM.

Walliser, A. (2013). New urban activisms in Spain: Reclaiming public space in the face of crises. *Policy & Politics*, 41(3), 329–350.

Wardrip, K. (2012). *An annual look at the housing affordability challenges of America's working households. Housing Landscape 2012*. Washington, DC: Center for Housing Policy.

Warzecha, M. (2012, January 4). Where to buy now: Mimico, because it's one lakefront revitalization that's on schedule. *Toronto Life*. Retrieved from https://tinyurl.com/y32lfbxh

Wetherell, M., Taylor, S., & Yates, S. J. (2001). *Discourse as data: A guide for analysis*. Thousand Oaks, CA: Sage.

White, C. (2012, October 19). Davies Smith breaks ground on Eleven Superior in Mimico. UrbanToronto.ca. Retrieved from https://tinyurl.com/yydvck3l

Whittier, N. (2010). *Feminist generations: The persistence of the radical women's movement*. Philadelphia, PA: Temple University Press.

Whitzman, C. (2010). *Suburb, slum, urban village: Transformations in Toronto's Parkdale Neighbourhood, 1875–2002*. Vancouver: UBC Press.

Wolf-Powers, L. (2010). Community benefits agreements and local government: A review of recent evidence. *Journal of the American Planning Association*, 76(2), 141–159.

Wong, C. J. (2010). *Boundaries of obligation in American politics: Geographic, national, and racial communities*. Cambridge: Cambridge University Press.

Wood, L. J. (2012). *Direct action, deliberation, and diffusion: Collective action after the WTO protests in Seattle*. Cambridge: Cambridge University Press.

Xiao, Q., & Park, D. (2010). Seoul housing prices and the role of speculation. *Empirical Economics*, 38(3), 619–644.

Yeo, K.-H., & Choi, G.-H. (2012). A study on the conflicts structure of the urban redevelopment projects through a policy network perspective focusing on the 4th Yongsan Region, Seoul [Korean]. *Urban Public Administration*, 25(1), 109–137.

Yi, H.-S. (2009). Local culture and the theory of the creative city: The cases of Seoul and Seongnam [Korean]. *Korean Culture*, 35, 315–341.

Yiftachel, O. (2006). *Ethnocracy: Land and identity politics in Israel/Palestine*. Philadelphia, PA: University of Pennsylvania Press.

Yim, S.-H., & Lee, Y.-W. (2002). Social polarization and its spatial characteristics: The case of Seoul, South Korea [Korean]. *Journal of the Korean Regional Geography*, 8(2), 270–279.

Yim, Y.-S., Lee, C., & Min, S. (2012). Relations between the right to a new lease and the revealed renewal: Judgement 2009DA64307 held by the Supreme Court on June 10, 2010 [Korean]. *Law Studies*, 48, 209–229.

Yoon, J. (2011). A study on the production of urban space and appropriation activity: The case of Mullae Art Village in Seoul [Korean]. *The Korean Geographical Society*, 46(2), 233–256.

Youn, E. S. (2007). *A comparison of cultural districts in Seoul: Recent policies and possibilities for creative industry growth*. Paper presented at the HKIP & UPSC Conference on "When Creative Industries Crossover with Cities," April 2–3, Hong Kong.

Zapata, M. C. (2013). El programa de autogestión para la vivienda: El ciclo de vida de una política habitacional habilitante a la participación social y del derecho al hábitat ya la ciudad. *Documentos de Jóvenes Investigadores*, 36 (pp. 978–950). Buenos Aires: Instituto de Investigaciones Gino Germani.

Zhang, Z., & He, S. (2018). Gentrification-induced displacement. In L. Lees & M. Phillips (Eds.), *Handbook of gentrification studies* (pp. 134–154). Northampton: Edward Elgar Publishing.

Zito Lema, V. (Ed.) (2012). *La historia de las Asambleas del Pueblo*. Buenos Aires: Ed. Estrella Libertaria.

Zuk, M., Bierbaum, A. H., Chapple, K., Gorska, K., Loukaitou-Sideris, A., Ong, P., & Thomas, T. (2015). Gentrification, displacement and the role of public investment: A literature review. Paper presented at the Federal Reserve Bank of San Francisco.

Zukin, S. (1987). Gentrification: Culture and capital in the urban core. *Annual Review of Sociology*, *13*(1), 129–147.

(1995). *The cultures of cities*. Hoboken, NJ: Wiley-Blackwell.

(2008). Consuming authenticity: From outposts of difference to means of exclusion. *Cultural Studies*, 22(5), 724–748.

(2010). *Naked city: The death and life of authentic urban places*. Oxford: Oxford University Press.

Zukin, S., Trujillo, V., Frase, P., Jackson, D., Recuber, T., & Walker, A. (2009). New retail capital and neighborhood change: Boutiques and gentrification in New York City. *City & Community*, *8*(1), 47–64.

Index

Books in the Series (continued from p.ii)

Lars-Erik Cederman, Kristian Skrede Gleditsch, and Halvard Buhaug, *Inequality, Grievances, and Civil War*
Christian Davenport, *How Social Movements Die: Repression and Demobilization of the Republic of New Africa*
Christian Davenport, *Media Bias, Perspective, and State Repression*
Gerald F. Davis, Doug McAdam, W. Richard Scott, and Mayer N. Zald, *Social Movements and Organization Theory*
Donatella della Porta, *Clandestine Political Violence*
Donatella della Porta, *Where Did the Revolution Go? Contentious Politics and the Quality of Democracy*
Mario Diani, *The Cement of Civil Society: Studying Networks in Localities*
Nicole Doerr, *Political Translation: How Social Movement Democracies Survive*
Barry Eidlin, *Labor and the Class Idea in the United States in Canada*
Todd A. Eisenstadt, *Politics, Identity, and Mexico's Indigenous Rights Movements*
Olivier Fillieule and Erik Neveu, editors, *Activists Forever? Long-Term Impacts of Political Activism*
Diana Fu, *Mobilizing Without the Masses: Control and Contention in China*
Daniel Q. Gillion, *The Political Power of Protest: Minority Activism and Shifts in Public Policy*
Marco Giugni and Maria Grasso, *Street Citizens: Protest Politics and Social Movement Activism in the Age of Globalization*
Jack A. Goldstone, editor, *States, Parties, and Social Movements*
Jennifer Hadden, *Networks in Contention: The Divisive Politics of Climate Change*
Michael T. Heaney and Fabio Rojas, *Party in the Street: The Antiwar Movement and the Democratic Party after 9/11*
Tamara Kay, *NAFTA and the Politics of Labor Transnationalism*
Neil Ketchley, *Egypt in a Time of Revolution: Contentious Politics and the Arab Spring*
Joseph Luders, *The Civil Rights Movement and the Logic of Social Change*
Doug McAdam and Hilary Boudet, *Putting Social Movements in Their Place: Explaining Opposition to Energy Projects in the United States, 2000–2005*
Doug McAdam, Sidney Tarrow, and Charles Tilly, *Dynamics of Contention*
Holly J. McCammon, *The US Women's Jury Movements and Strategic Adaptation: A More Just Verdict*
Sharon Nepstad, *Religion and War Resistance and the Plowshares Movement*
Olena Nikolayenko, *Youth Movements and Elections in Eastern Europe*
Kevin J. O'Brien and Lianjiang Li, *Rightful Resistance in Rural China*
Silvia Pedraza, *Political Disaffection in Cuba's Revolution and Exodus*
Héctor Perla Jr., *Sandinista Nicaragua's Resistance to US Coercion*
Federico M. Rossi, *The Poor's Struggle for Political Incorporation: The Piquetero Movement in Argentina*
Chandra Russo, *Solidarity in Practice: Moral Protest and the US Security State*
Eduardo Silva, *Challenging Neoliberalism in Latin America*
Erica S. Simmons, *Meaningful Resistance: Market Reforms and the Roots of Social Protest in Latin America*

Sarah Soule, *Contention and Corporate Social Responsibility*
Sherrill Stroschein, *Ethnic Struggle, Coexistence, and Democratization in Eastern Europe*
Yang Su, *Collective Killings in Rural China during the Cultural Revolution*
Sidney Tarrow, *The Language of Contention: Revolutions in Words, 1688–2012*
Sidney Tarrow, *The New Transnational Activism*
Wayne P. Te Brake, *Religious War and Religious Peace in Early Modern Europe*
Ralph A. Thaxton Jr., *Catastrophe and Contention in Rural China: Mao's Great Leap Forward Famine and the Origins of Righteous Resistance in Da Fo Village*
Ralph A. Thaxton Jr., *Force and Contention in Contemporary China: Memory and Resistance in the Long Shadow of the Catastrophic Past*
Charles Tilly, *Contention and Democracy in Europe, 1650–2000*
Charles Tilly, *Contentious Performances*
Charles Tilly, *The Politics of Collective Violence*
Marisa von Bülow, *Building Transnational Networks: Civil Society and the Politics of Trade in the Americas*
Lesley J. Wood, *Direct Action, Deliberation, and Diffusion: Collective Action after the WTO Protests in Seattle*
Stuart A. Wright, *Patriots, Politics, and the Oklahoma City Bombing*
Deborah Yashar, *Contesting Citizenship in Latin America: The Rise of Indigenous Movements and the Postliberal Challenge*
Andrew Yeo, *Activists, Alliances, and Anti-US Base Protests*

CPSIA information can be obtained
at www.ICGtesting.com
Printed in the USA
LVHW031946220520
656325LV00003B/243

9 781108 745444